PROTO OTOMANGUEAN KINSHIP

INTERNATIONAL MUSEUM OF CULTURES

PUBLICATION 11

William R. Merrifield
Museum Director

Jacqueline E. Bernhardt
Academic Publications Coordinator

PROTO OTOMANGUEAN KINSHIP

William R. Merrifield

INTERNATIONAL MUSEUM OF CULTURES
Dallas, Texas
1981

Some of the materials incorporated in this work were developed with the financial support of National Science Foundation Grant BNS 7826376. However, any opinions, findings, conclusions, or recommendations expressed are those of the author and do not necessarily reflect the views of the Foundation.

Library of Congress Catalog Number: 80-50558

ISBN: 0-88312-161-1

ISSN: 0197-3746

Cover design by Barbara Adams
Illustrations by David Beasley

This title available at:
  International Museum of Cultures
  7500 W. Camp Wisdom Road
  Dallas, Texas 75236

PREFACE

This study was begun in 1961 as a modest plan to collect and publish kinship schedules of indigenous languages of Mexico through the cooperation of my SIL colleagues in Mexico. A brief questionnaire and model write-up were accordingly designed and distributed to facilitate the collection and presentation of the data. But two things became clear very soon after the material began to come in.

In the first place, the sheer bulk of material made it expedient to postpone giving attention to all but one of the major linguistic groups of Mexico. Since my own research interests were centered more in Otomanguean than in Mayan or Utoaztecan, these latter groups were put on the shelf at least temporarily. It was possible to report on a handful of systems outside of Otomanguean (Hoogshagen and Merrifield 1961, Merrifield 1963a, Waterhouse and Merrifield 1968, and Brockway 1969), but the focus of the study was otherwise narrowed for the time being.

In the second place, the lack of attention in earlier Otomanguean kinship studies to extended ranges of reference gave special significance to the new data being collected. This was particularly true in light of the surge of interest in formal approaches to the study of kinship which were being published at the time, following the seminal articles of Goodenough (1956) and Lounsbury (1956).

The significance of the data began to be apparent, but there were important shortcomings in the theoretical materials available to describe them. The componential approach, while attracting a good deal of interest and providing many worthwhile insights into semantic systems of various sorts, including systems of kinship reference, was better suited to the analysis of individual systems as systems than to the comparison of partially different systems. Even the generative focus of Lounsbury did not seem to have direct application to the Otomanguean data since the particular rules of extension which he formulated primarily accounted for skewing of underlying bilateral systems along male or female lines to form unilateral Omaha or Crow systems. But the underlying bilateral systems were described componentially rather than being reduced to their simplest terms first.

Otomanguean systems show very little skewing of the sort to which Lounsbury applied his rules of extension (or reduction). They do, however, show primary ranges of reference which are enlarged by extension in several very interesting ways. And it frequently turns out that cognate Otomanguean systems differ precisely in the way such primary ranges are extended. The need to deal with such details gave rise to the development of the theory and notation used in this volume, stimulated at first by Goodenough and Lounsbury and later by a myriad of studies which appeared in the sixties.

Phonological studies of comparative Otomanguean were also limited in the early stages of this study in comparison to the present situation, especially with the completion of the work of Bartholomew on Proto Otopamean (1965) and Rensch on Proto Chinantecan (1968), Huave (1973), Proto Tlapanec (1977), and Proto Otomanguean itself after long publication delays (1976). The delay of this present study, forced as it was by the pressure of other duties, has thus, in the long run, permitted a more worthwhile result in being able to capitalize upon the availability of this more recent comparative phonological work.

But delays eventually reach the point of becoming intolerable. The time had come to complete this stage of POM kinship analysis. I am grateful to my SIL colleagues for permitting me to set aside other pressing responsibilities for a number of months in order to finish it. The final stages of analysis and writing were also generously supported by National Science Foundation Grant BNS-7826376. I am particularly indebted to Paul G.

Chapin, the NSF Program Officer for Linguistics, who gave sensitive consideration to the proposal which resulted in NSF support. Major credit must, of course, be given to those SIL field research teams who have learned the Otomanguean languages through months and years of living in the field among Otomanguean-speaking peoples and to those peoples themselves who have without exception welcomed us as their neighbors and shared their language and culture with us, to say nothing of their friendship which we hold as an incomparable treasure.

Going back in time, before the 1961 beginnings of this study, I need to mention five individuals whose kindness encouraged me to pursue an incipient interest in Otomanguean kinship. I had discovered a Palantla Chinantec system of kinship reference which relied upon the principle of relative age to a remarkable degree for classifying kinsmen. Rudy Troike and Herb Harvey were both in Mexico at the time and helped me with the materials through counsel and encouragement. The late Roberto J. Weitlaner, ever interested in Chinantec materials, was also a great friend and encouraged me in many ways. But most of all, the late Howard Cline gave unsparingly of his time and experience to help polish the manuscript which became Merrifield 1959 and, ultimately, the seed from which the present study has grown. Howard also put my analysis before A. Kimball Romney whose particular expertise in kinship directed us to send the manuscript to the American Anthropologist for publication. I am grateful to all of these men for nourishing my early interests in kinship studies which later matured at Cornell under the tutelage of Lauristan Sharp.

I am not sure I can even remember all of the SIL colleagues who helped in technical ways throughout the nearly two decades that this study has been periodically creeping towards completion. I do want to mention Noreen McElhanon who typed much of one of the early drafts, Phyllis Doty who helped assemble the bibliography, and Bob Chaney who helped Grace get the final draft onto the computer for editing. Rex Burgett will not soon forget the process of developing computer codes for editing and typesetting a very complex manuscript, nor will I his patient persistence and goodwill. Special thanks are due my children—Kathleen, Scott, Ruth, and Ken—who had to put up with me spending more time away from them than I would have liked, and to Grace, my wife, who typed the manuscript and retyped it and who supported me in so many ways that I can only dedicate the finished product to her.

William R. Merrifield

Duncanville, Texas
November, 1979

This book is for Grace.

CONTENTS

Abbreviations of Language Names

The following outline presents the abbreviations of language names used in this volume in the order they are cited in cognate set listings.

POM	Proto Otomanguean		At	Sierra Juárez Zapotec (Atepec)
PMn	Proto Mixtecan		Cm	Choapan Zapotec (Comaltepec)
PM	Proto Mixtec		Ct	Coatlán Zapotec
At	Atatláhuca Mixtec		Cx	Miahuatlán Zapotec (Cuixtla)
Ay	Ayutla Mixtec		I	Isthmus Zapotec (Juchitán)
Ct	Coatzospan Mixtec		L	Lachixio Zapotec
D	Diuxi Mixtec		Mt	Mitla Zapotec
M	Metlatónoc Mixtec		Mx	Mixtepec Zapotec
O	Ocotepec Mixtec		Oc	Ocotlán Zapotec
P	Peñoles Mixtec		Oz	Ozolotepec Zapotec
S	Silacayoapan Mixtec		T	Texmelucan Zapotec
SM	San Miguel Mixtec		V	Valley of Oaxaca Zapotec (1578)
SP	South Puebla Mixtec		Yg	Rincón Zapotec (Yagallo)
J	Western Jamiltepec Mixtec		Yt	Yatzachi Zapotec
Y	Yosondúa Mixtec		PCh	Proto Chatino
PT	Proto Trique		Y	Yaitepec Chatino
Ch	Chicahuaxtla Trique		T	Tataltepec Chatino
Cp	Copala Trique		PCn	Proto Chinantecan
PC	Proto Cuicatec		A	Ayotzintepec Chinantec
Tp	Tepeuxila Cuicatec		C	Comaltepec Chinantec
Tt	Teutila Cuicatec		Ch	Chiltepec Chinantec
PPn	Proto Popolocan		L	Lalana Chinantec
PMz	Proto Mazatec		M	Mayultianguis Chinantec
H	Huautla Mazatec		O	Ojitlán Chinantec
J	Jalapa de Díaz Mazatec		P	Palantla Chinantec
Q	Chiquihuitlán Mazatec		Q	Quiotepec Chinantec
PP	Proto Popoloc		S	Sochiapan Chinantec
A	Western Popoloc (Atzingo)		T	Tepetotutla Chinantec
O	Eastern Popoloc (Otlaltepec)		Tl	Tlacoatzintepec Chinantec
T	Northern Popoloc (Tlacoyalco)		U	Usila Chinantec
I	Ixcatec		VN	Valle Nacional Chinantec
C	Chocho		Y	Yolox Chinantec (1730)
POP	Proto Otopamean		A	Guerrero Amuzgo (Xochistlahuaca)
PO	Proto Otomí		H	Huave
E	1640 Otomí (Ecker)		PTl	Proto Tlapanec
H	Eastern Otomí (Huehuetla)		M	Malinaltepec Tlapanec
J	State of Mexico Otomí (Jiquipilco)		T	Tlacoapa Tlapanec
Ms	Mesquital Otomí		PCM	Proto Chiapanec-Mangue
T	Tenango Otomí		PCh	Proto Chiapanec
Mz	Mazahua		Ch	Chiapanec
CP	Central Pame		PM	Proto Mangue
Ch	Chichimeca-Jonaz		M	Mangue
PZn	Proto Zapotecan			
PZ	Proto Zapotec			
Am	Amatlán Zapotec			

List of Figures

INTRODUCTION

This study focuses upon the reconstruction of Otomanguean terminological systems of kinship reference. Phonological reconstruction is based primarily on the previously published work of others, although the primary purpose of the volume could not have been met without making many proposals which have phonological implications since cognate sets proposed by my predecessors in Otomanguean studies are inevitably revised both phonologically and semantically on the basis of the new kinship data which make up the corpus for this study.

An agressive approach to reconstruction has been taken. Every effort has been made to follow the phonological interpretations of those who have specialized in the phonological materials. At the same time, when new data point to relationships for which earlier work does not provide a clear understanding, such relationships are, nevertheless, often proposed. It has seemed best to provide a clear set of claims regarding the various Otomanguean systems of reference and the terms which define them as a foundation for future clarification and correction. It is hoped that a sufficient number of new ideas have proceeded from this study to stimulate many more future analyses—phonological, grammatical, and semantic—to clarify and correct the approximations proposed here.

The reconstruction of semantic systems is, of course, a tricky business. The margin for error must, in the nature of the case, be higher than for the reconstruction of the

1

phonological materials because of the more dependable record a sound shift is likely to provide. Semantic systems can be examined only indirectly even in contemporary language.

It would be nice to be able to enumerate a set of methodological principles which, when applied, would naturally result in sound semantic reconstructions. The scientific method urges us to do so. Dyen and Aberle (1974) have recently attempted such an approach in their analysis of Athapaskan kinship terminologies by an extensive use of statistics, as well as more timeworn methodologies which they expound at great length and in great detail.

The present analysis is not based on airtight methodology. It includes a lot of guessing, some of it fairly avant-garde. At the same time, I have tried to apply standard canons of judgment in both assembling and evaluating cognate sets. Perhaps a couple of things should be mentioned which have been done to educate the guess. First, the kinds of social organization which early Otomanguean society most likely exhibited are constantly addressed. The POM system of kinship reference cannot be considered deduceable as the common denominator from among contemporary systems since contemporary social conditions differ considerably from those of the POM horizon. Second, decisions regarding semantic change are always made in reference to systems of reference as a whole and not just by surveying the semantic reflexes of individual sets of cognates. This point is of genuine significance since few studies exist which seriously account for fully extended senses of all terms in a system. A possible shift in range of reference for siblings, for example, is not assessed apart from the effect it would have upon ranges of reference of terms for other collateral kinsmen. Finally, the elementary semantic principles upon which kinship systems appear to be based have been re-examined and a formal set of notational devices has been defined to provide an explicit means for expressing the ways in which they combine to form systems of kinship reference.

Most of the remainder of this introduction introduces the reader to the notational devices which appear throughout the study. The study then proceeds with the analysis as Part I and the individually-authored data papers upon which the analysis is based as Part II. A unified bibliography for the entire study is placed at the end of the volume.

The analysis of Proto Otomanguean kinship is presented first, beginning with a brief statement of the reconstructed system of terms and their proposed ranges of reference. Justification for the analysis is then presented in the form of a discussion and presentation of the cognate sets which have been assembled. Finally, a summary of the way POM developed in the daughter families closes the first chapter.

Successive chapters then address each of the major Otomanguean families on this same pattern: summary of the reconstructed system followed by the evidence for the analysis. In a few cases, additional reconstructions for intermediate horizons are also summarized briefly in these chapters.

Because of the relatively limited amount of data involved, several smaller language families are grouped together in a final chapter of the first part of the study. The Otomanguean families are discussed in the order presented in Rensch (1976), except that Amuzgo and Chiapanec-Mangue have been grouped with Huave and Tlapanec in this final chapter.

Reconstructed forms are marked with an asterisk (*) with the exception of POM forms which are marked with a double asterisk (**). In addition to the master reconstruction which heads each cognate set, more specific forms of the etymon which are individually supported by each of its reflexes are also proposed, following Rensch's (1976) practice.

Notational Considerations

The formal approaches to kinship analysis which were being discussed during the early years of preparation of this study did not provide the insights which bilateral systems of reference of the type most Otomanguean languages exhibit seemed to require. This lack resulted in the development of the approach reported in Merrifield 1980, developed particularly for these materials, and which is the basis for this presentation of Otomanguean data and analysis. The following brief introduction is designed to permit the reader to understand and use the notation. Further explanation should be sought in Merrifield (1980) and subsequent articles which will seek to speak more directly to the efficacy of the approach.

Otomanguean systems of kinship terminology generally reflect open systems in which filial relationships extend without limit. While a given system might include a statement of the filial distance beyond which a marriage prohibition (incest rule) might apply, filiation itself is not denied beyond that distance. Where such statements are known to exist, the filial distance in question is great enough that, in practice, consanguineal terms generally extend without limit to all kinsmen whose filial relationships are in fact known. Goodenough (1965) provides the prototype for a graphic presentation of this potentially limitless genealogical space in what I have come to refer to as a *filial tree*. The filial tree has no theoretical limit, so that only a portion of it is representable, as in Figure 1.

Each node of the tree represents a genealogical position (or kintype at one level of abstraction) labeled by a *PC string*. *P* and *C* stand for the two sides of the assymetric filial relation which exists between parent and child. (Several other notational devices have been proposed in the literature to identify the two sides of this relationship, but none is as efficient for the purposes of the present analysis as *P* and *C*.) Following the English *apostrophe s* genitive construction commonly used in English-language kinship studies, *P* and *C* combine meaningfully in a string in only one way, with all *P*s preceding all *C*s, and a string such as PPCC can be verbalized *parent's parent's child's child*.

The assymetry of the filial relation is based on *priority*. Parent precedes child. A lineal kintype is one which is defineable by a *PC* string which contains only *P*s or only *C*s, but does not combine both *P*s and *C*s. A *PC* string which identifies a lineal relationship, thus, clearly identifies a kinsman's priority relationship to ego as well as his genealogical distance. If the string consists entirely of *P*s, the kinsman is senior (= prior) to ego; if it consists entirely of *C*s, the kinsman is junior. (Genealogical distance is measured by the number of *P*s or *C*s in the string.)

In the case of a nonlineal kinsman, however, priority may be independent of the priority inherent in the filial relationship. The string *PC*, for example, designates a sibling who may be prior to ego or not. This situation is theoretically true for many nonlineal kintypes. In such cases, the symbols *e*, for elder, and *y*, for younger, are placed at the beginning of a *PC* string for which nonlineal priority is in focus. The string *ePPCC*, thus, denotes a senior cousin.

For any given system, the basis for defining nonlineal priority must be stated. In Chinantec, it is the relative age of ego and alter. In certain Utoaztecan systems (Romney 1967), seniority in the parent generation is defined by the relative age of kinsman and ego's parent. By defining such facts independently, *e* and *y* can serve any such situation: *ePPC* defines an uncle older than ego for Chinantec but an uncle older than parent for Papago.

The affinal relation is symmetrical, requiring just one symbol *S* for *spouse*. *S* may

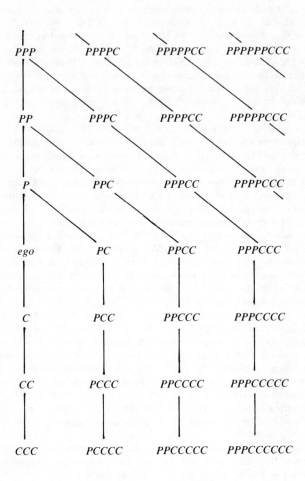

Figure 1. The Filial Tree.

initiate or end a *PC* string, as in *SPC spouse's parent's child* or *PCS parent's child's spouse*. Since a *PC* string is primarily a means for naming a filial relationship, any string with *S* not in one of these two positions is considered compound, as in *CSP child's spouse's parent*.

Finally, ego or any of his kinsmen can be male or female. It may therefore be necessary to mark any position in a *PC* string for sex of referent. This is accomplished by use of *m* or *f*, marking the sex of ego at the beginning of a string, and the sex of any kinsman immediately following the *P, C,* or *S* which names his relationship to ego, as in *mPfCmSf male ego's female parent's male child's female spouse* or, more simply, *man's mother's son's wife*.

A fully specified *PC* string marks each position for sex by *m* or *f* and specified seniority for nonlineal kinsmen by *e* or *y*. These symbols are omitted, however, to conflate a list of *PC* strings whenever details of sex or seniority are not diagnostic of the range of a given term. The English term *sibling* may be represented by the string *PC*, a conflation of the strings *mPmCm, mPmCf, mPfCm, mPfCf, fPfCf, fPfCm, fPmCf,* and *fPmCm*, each of these eight themselves being a conflation of two strings specifying priority as in *emPmCm* and *ymPmCm*. Sixteen strings are thus conflated to one for the term *sibling* which does not distinguish sex or priority in any way.

The variables *a* and *b* may be used for *m* and *f* to conflate strings for which the relative sex of ego and alter is important. Thus, *aPCb* conflates *fPCm* and *mPCf*.

Bifurcate categories which distinguish cross kinsmen from parallel may be specified by placing the symbol = (for parallel) or *x* (for cross) at the beginning of a *PC* string, thereby permitting the conflation of strings which differ only by the sex designation of particular kinsmen in the genealogical chain which the strings represent. Since there are several kinds of bifurcate categories (Merrifield 1980), the specific implications of = and *x* must be defined for each system. In the present study, Central Pame is the only system which exhibits bifurcation. Unfortunately, Gibson does not provide sufficient data to determine the type of bifurcation which exists there but it is most likely of the same type as Seneca (Lounsbury 1964). This is discussed more fully in the Proto Otopamean chapter of this study, but the range of Central Pame **rawé?** is unambiguously stateable as *=Pm(G)* which implies *Pm, PmPCm, PmPPCCm,* and so forth, while **rabbéo?** *xPm(G)* ranges over *PfPCm, PfPPCCm,* and so forth.

Kinship terminologies are often made up of subsets of terms colled *reciprocal sets* in that every member of a corresponding subset of kintypes is named by one and only one term of the subset without remainder. In English, the terms *father, mother, son,* and *daughter* constitute such a reciprocal set. Every member of the parent-child dyad is named once and only once by one or another term of the set. It is useful to recognize such sets in the analysis of a terminological system since it is quite possible that one or more of them will correspond to a significant social group of the particular society being studied.

Whenever both parties of any ego-alter dyad are named by a single term, that term is *self-reciprocal*. The English terms *sibling, cousin,* and *spouse* are of this sort. Each names a set of kintypes the members of which are named once and only once without remainder by one (the only) member of the set of terms. The English term *brother* is not self-reciprocal since, although the male kinsman who uses it is also so named by the kinsman to whom he refers, the female who uses it is not. Rather, *brother* and *sister* together constitute a reciprocal set of two terms. In this case, there are two reciprocal sets which name the same group of kinsmen. One set is generic and self-reciprocal, and does not designate the sex of kinsman; the second set is specific to the extent of designating sex of kinsman. In the parent-child dyad, the four terms mentioned above constitute a set which marks both seniority and sex of kinsman. No generic, self-reciprocal term names this set.

For self-reciprocal terms like *sibling* or *cousin* which name kinsmen of ego's generation without reference to sex or seniority, the *PC* strings which name their ranges of reference (namely, *PC* and *PPCC*, respectively) are themselves self-reciprocal in that they both consist of an equal number of *P*s and *C*s. Each *P* and *C* separately names a single assymetric relationship, but when they occur together in equal numbers within a string they balance each other out.

This is often not the case for terms which mark either seniority or sex. A term may be self-reciprocal but at the same time exhibit a range of reference which is defineable only in terms of two foci within that range. For example Central Pame **ràhę́ŋ** is used by ego of either sex to name a grandfather. This fact is expressed by the string *PPm* which designates *(male or female) ego's (male or female) parent's male parent*. But **ràhę́ŋ** is self-reciprocal in that such a male grandparent refers to grandchild of either sex, in turn, by the same term **ràhę́ŋ**. This fact may be expressed by the string *mCC* which names *male ego's (male or female) child's (male or female) child*.

In order to directly express the fact that *PPm* and *mCC* are not two distinct ranges of reference in respect to **ràhę́ŋ**, a special symbol is defined to mark its range of reference as self-reciprocal. There are at least three kinds of self-reciprocity in kinship terms for which three special symbols are defined.

In the case of **ràhę́ŋ**, the symbol *R* (for *reciprocal*) is placed in parentheses following either *PPm* or *mCC* to denote both strings. It may or may not be possible, on the basis of linguistic or nonlinguistic evidence, to determine in any given case if one of the two foci of a self-reciprocal range is in some sense more basic than the other. In the absence of such evidence, it is my practice to make no strong assumption on the subject but to choose the senior kintype as the citation form. Thus, in the case before us, the range of reference is defined as *PPm(R)* which implies both *PPm* and *mCC*.

In another case, there might in fact be evidence that the junior kintype is the more basic of the two foci in a self-reciprocal range. Huave **òkwáàc** names both *mSP male ego's (male or female) spouse's (male or female) parent* and *CSm (male or female) ego's (male or female) child's male spouse*. (In the latter case, since *CmSm* would not occur, *CSm* is invariably an abbreviation for *CfSm*.) Without developing the argument here, it will be seen later in this study that the junior focus of this self-reciprocal range appears to be in some sense more prominent and, for this reason, *CSm(R)* is chosen as the citation form to denote the range of **òkwáàc**.

Rule R implies a reciprocal range in the fullest sense, taking into account all details of the citation form. To generate the reciprocal of a citation form, read it backwards (from right to left), rewriting *m* and *f* without change, but replacing *e* for *y*, *y* for *e*, *P* for *C*, and *C* for *P*. Since *e* and *y* are always placed at the beginning of the string, by convention, these symbols are always rewritten first. Thus, the reciprocal of *emPmPCf* by Rule R is *yfPCmCm*.

A second type of reciprocal range is not self-reciprocal in the fullest sense, since it operates only on filial and affinal relationships but not on relationships of priority (for nonlineal kinsmen) or sex. The symbol *I* (for *inversion*) is placed in parentheses following a citation *PC* string to indicate this type of reciprocity. The range of Amatlán Zapotec **šey** is stated as *PPm(I)* in that it includes both *PPm* and *CCm*. The range of Western

Popoloca *číʔní* is defineable as *ePPCm(I)* in that it includes both *ePPCm* and *ePCCm*. Rule I is, thus, read in every respect like Rule R except that *e* and *y* are not exchanged for each other and *m* or *f* are not rewritten in reverse order.

Finally, a third type of reciprocal range is required for certain affinal terms. The symbol *V* (once again, for *inversion*) is placed in parentheses following a citation string to indicate a reciprocal focus of the term in which the affinal symbol *S* is moved to the opposite end of the string without altering any other relation implied by the string. Thus, the range of Lalana Chinantec ki²³ʔę·n³² is defineable as *PPCSf(V)* in that it includes both *PPCSf* and *SPPCf*.

While I have not found a contemporary kinship term which entails more than one kind of reciprocal range, I believe such a situation did in fact exist in at least one stage of the development of certain Proto Mixtecan terms. Again without arguing the point here, I suggest in the body of this study that the range of PMn *Өuʔwe is defineable as *emPPCf(I,R)* in that it includes *emPPCf*, *emPCCf*, *yfPCCm*, and *yfPPCm*.

Up to this point in the discussion of notational considerations, the focus has been only upon primary ranges of reference. Even though a range may include more than one focus, as in the case of self-reciprocal terms, it is not necessarily true that one of the foci is more basic or prominent than the other. Many terms, however, clearly do have primary as opposed to extended senses. A good notation should clearly distinguish such differences in range.

The two main kinds of extension are affinal extension and filial extension. Affinal extension is the extension of a basically consanguineal term to certain affinal kintypes by the addition of *S* at the beginning or the end of a *PC* string. A case in point is the English term *aunt* which ranges over *PPCf* in its primary sense but extends to *PPCSf* and perhaps also to *SPPCf*. Copala Trique ži⁵³ ranges over *PPm* and *PPSm*. Lalana Chinantec še·n²³ ranges over *Pf* and *SPf*. The symbol *-S* is the name given that affinal extension rule which adds *S* to the end of a *PC* string. *S-* accordingly adds *S* to the beginning of a string, and *S* (without hyphen) stands for a conflation of rules *-S* and *S-* to indicate that either of the rules (but not both) can apply to a particular *PC* string. By placing these symbols in parentheses following the string which defines a term's primary range, the extended affinal range of that term may be indicated. The ranges of *aunt* may be stated as *PPCf(S)*, those of ži⁵³ as *PPm(-S)*, and those of še·n²³ as *Pf(S-)*.

An affinal term may also extend by affinal extension to a co-affinal kintype which entails two marriages. Thus, the range of Yosondua Mixtec kàsà is defineable (in part) as *PCSm(V,S-)* to include *PCSm*, *SPCm* (by inversion), and *SPCSm* (by extension).

Of far more interest than affinal extension is filial extension, wherein consanguineal terms exhibit both a more narrow, primary range of reference as well as a wider, more extended range of reference to consanguineal kinsmen. Sociolinguistic evidence is often available to support the claim, for a particular system, that the *PC* string (or set of *PC* strings) which consists of the fewest number of *Ps* and *Cs* for a particular term defines the *primary* referential meaning of that term, and that longer *PC* strings define the referential meaning of the term in some *extended* sense (Lounsbury 1965:149). Many Otomanguean languages, for example, exhibit sibling terms which range over the kintype *PC* and longer strings like *PPCC*, *PPPCCC*, and so forth, but can specify reference to the nearest kintype or, conversely, to more distant kintypes by special modifiers. Several languages employ a phrase meaning *one father, one mother* to specify a kinsman of range *PC*. Others postpose a modifier to the sibling term to specify the range as not being *PC* but that of a more distant kinsman.

Filial extension may be viewed as the lengthening of shorter *PC* strings by the addition of *P*s or *C*s. The primary range *PC* is extended to *PPCC* by the addition of one *P* and one *C*. It is extended to *PPPCCC* by the addition of two *P*s and two *C*s, and so forth. Filial extension may, thus, be conceived in its most unrestricted form as a rule with two parts:

(A) $\emptyset \rightarrow P$
(B) $\emptyset \rightarrow C$

Part A of the rule adds *P* to the first half of a *PC* string; part B adds *C* to its second half. Certain kinship terms have unlimited extended ranges which may be characterized as unlimited application of the two parts of the rule, but it is more often the case that extended ranges are defined by particular limitations placed upon its application. Seven such limitations are characteristic of Otomanguean ranges of kinship reference. An extended discussion of each such limitation is given in Merrifield (1980), but they are briefly discussed below for the convenience of the reader.

The symbol *L* is placed in parentheses following the *PC* string which characterizes the primary range of reference of a term if that term extends lineally (vertically on a filial tree) without limit. *L* has the effect of creating new strings by the addition of *P*s to kintypes of ascending generations (by application of part A of the filial extension rule) and *C*s to kintypes of descending generations (by part B of the rule). The ranges of Mesquital Otomí **títá** are *PPm(L)* in that they include *PPm* as primary range but extend to *PPPm*, *PPPPm*, and so forth. Conversely, **ʔbǎtó** *CC(L)* ranges over *CC*, *CCC*, *CCCC*, and so forth.

The symbol *G* is similarly placed to state that a term extends throughout a generation without limit by applying the two parts of the extension rule without limit except that the two parts apply an equal number of times. Rincón Zapotec **žíila?** *fPCf(G)* ranges over *fPCf*, *fPPCCf*, *fPPPCCCf*, and so forth.

These two limitations upon the application of the filial extension rule, *L* and *G*, may be thought of as unidirectional. *L* defines vertical extension, *G* horizontal. There are, in addition, several interesting kinds of bidirectional extension which allow terms to extend both vertically and horizontally in particular ways. In the absence of a good mnemonic device for naming these limitations upon the application of the filial extension rule, they are simply numbered *1*, *2*, and *3*, with *0* standing for unlimited filial extension.

Rule 1 extends a term both lineally and throughout each generation covered by lineal extension including the primary generation. Eastern Otomí **cìhci** *PPCf(1)* extends to all of ego's nonlineal female kinsmen of ascending generations, while **ʔbǎʔwe** *PCC(1)* extends to all of his nonlineal, male and female kinsmen of descending generations.

Rule 2 extends to all the kintypes of Rule 1, but also to those of the next generation below that of a primary kintype of an ascending generation or those of the next generation above that of a primary kintype of a descending generation. Chichimeca-Jonaz **nąhę́** *PPm(2)* ranges over all lineal and collateral (nonlineal) kintypes beyond the parent generation and all collateral kintypes of the parent generation too. (It does not range over the lineal kintype *P* of parent generation because the primary *PC* string contains two *P*s. The filial extension rule only adds *P*s or *C*s but never deletes them.) Coatzospan Mixtec **ènú** *CSf(2)* ranges over all wives of ego's descending generation (male) lineal kinsmen and all wives of his (male) colateral kinsmen of his generation or below.

The symbol *3* stands for the next logical progression after Rule 2 but, in this study, designates a form of extension found only in Trique. The extension of Chicahuaxtla Trique **ži³če²¹** *SP(3)* ranges over all direct ancestors of spouse and all collaterals of spouse above the grandchild generation. Conversely, **ža⁵ko?⁵** *CSf(3)* ranges over the wife of all direct descendents of ego and the wife of all collaterals of ego below the grandparent generation.

The symbol *G2* represents extension which combines characteristics of Rule G and Rule 2 in that extension is throughout a generation adjacent to that of the primary kinsman. I consider this type of extension to represent a minor transitional phase in the development of a terminology. (It may, in some cases in this study, be the result of limited affinal data.) The extension of Peñoles Mixtec **sánu** *CSf(G2)* ranges over the wife of ego's son and of ego's male generation peers.

Interestingly enough, many Otomanguean terms exhibit unlimited filial extension. This is indicated by the symbol *ø*. The extension of Usila Chinantec **rẹu?³** *PC(0)* ranges over all nonlineal kintypes.

As a further aid to the reader, a formal statement of how each of these rules of extension applies to a primary range of reference is presented in Figure 2 and a graphic representation of their application over all primary ranges found in Otomanguean languages is presented by use of a series of filial trees in Figure 3. Ego's position in each tree is marked by *e*, while *x* marks the primary range of reference in focus.

Of the possible forty-nine combinations of seven extension rules and seven Otomanguean kintypes, only fourteen are not known to occur in Otomanguean. These nonoccurring combinations are identified in Figure 3 by asterisk (*).

Figure 2. Filial Extension Rules.

LINEAL EXTENSION *(L):* Given a primary kintype of an ascending generation, apply part A of the filial extension rule *(ø → P)* one or more times; otherwise, apply part B of the filial extension rule *(ø → C)* one or more times.

GENERATION EXTENSION *(G):* Apply parts A and B of the filial extension rule *(ø → P and ø → C)* an equal number of times.

TYPE 1 EXTENSION: Apply part A or B of the filial extension rule *(ø → P, ø → C)*, or both, without limit except that, given a primary kintype of an ascending generation, B may apply only as many times as A; otherwise, A may apply only as many times as B.

TYPE 2 EXTENSION: Apply part A or B of the filial extension rule *(ø → P, ø → C)*, or both without limit except that, given a primary kintype of an ascending generation, A may apply one once more than A; otherwise, A may apply only once more than B.

TYPE 2 GENERATION EXTENSION *(G2):* Apply parts A and B of the filial extension rule *(ø → P and ø → C)* without limit except that, given a primary kintype of an ascending generation, B must apply exactly once more than A; otherwise, A must apply exactly once more than B.

TYPE 3 EXTENSION: Apply part A or B of the filial extension rule *(ø → P, ø → C)*, or both, without limit except that, given a primary kintype of an ascending generation, B may apply one twice more than A; otherwise, A may apply only twice more than B.

UNLIMITED EXTENSION *(0):* Apply part A or B of the filial extension rule *(ø → P, ø → C)*, or both, without limit.

To this point, both primary and extended ranges of reference are defined in strictly genealogical terms which can be mapped directly onto a filial tree without ambiguity. There are some Otomanguean systems, however, where age relative to ego overrides genealogical considerations for certain terms. In Palantla Chinantec, the ranges of ŋiu[1] may be expressed as *ePCm(0)* to indicate that any elder male collateral kinsman is included. Genealogical generation is not in focus at all; *ePPCm, ePCm, ePCCm,* and even more distant kintypes all have the potential for being matched by kinsmen to whom ego should refer by this term. This in itself does not require special comment, perhaps, except that a second term **hj²giu?**[13] not only refers to *PPm*, but also to any senior male collateral kinsmen who is *two degrees older* than ego. This concept corresponds roughly to genealogical distance by generations, but the basis for reckoning is relative age and not the exact genealogical tie. If ego's elder male collateral kinsman corresponds roughly in age to himself or perhaps even his father, he tends to refer to him by ŋiu[1]; but if that kinsman is much older than ego's father, ego tends to refer to him by **hj²giu?**[13]. The symbol e_2 is coined to stand for this second degree of seniority.

The primary range of **hj²giu?**[13] is clearly *PPm,* and, as far as genealogical considerations go, there does not seem to be any theoretical limit to the applicatiion of the filial extension rule so long as the correct degree of seniority (e_2) exists. Rule 0 is thus tied to e_2 in such a way that the ranges of *hj₂giu?*₁₃ may be defined as *PPm(e₂0).* The corresponding rule *y₂0* is also required in the analysis of Otomanguean kinship (although not found in contemporary Palantla Chinantec) to designate unlimited filial extension tied closely to alter being two degrees younger than ego.

Sources

Otomanguean source materials for this study fall into two general categories: published studies dealing with the phonological history of Otomanguean languages and Otomanguean kinship studies the majority of which were prepared especially for this study and which are included herein. The first category of studies is very large. A thorough statement on the subject is given by Rensch (1976:1-8) and need not be repeated here. I have profited, however, from the following works in particular: for Proto Mixtecan, Longacre 1957 and Longacre and Millon 1961; for Proto Mixtec, Mak and Longacre 1960; for Proto Popolocan, Gudschinsky 1958; for Proto Mazatec, Kirk 1966; for Proto Otopamean, Bartholomew 1965; for Proto Otomian, Newman and Weitlaner 1950a and 1950b and Bartholomew 1960; for Proto Chatino, Upson and Longacre 1965; for Proto Chinantec, Rensch 1968; for the relationship of Huave to POM, Rensch 1973; for the relationship of Tlapanec to POM, Rensch 1977; and for Chiapanec-Mangue, Fernández de Miranda and Weitlaner 1961.

Most of the data concerning Otomanguean kinship terms were compiled especially for this study and have not appeared elsewhere, but there are a few exceptions. This study stimulated a paper on Copala Trique (Hollenbach 1973) which is summarized here. It also supplied data for Bradley's (1965) study of Proto Mixtec kinship terms which is reprinted here in only slightly edited form. Cowan 1947, on Huautla Mazatec kinship is summarized here. Kirk's (1962, 1966) earlier studies focus on the use of kinship terms in direct address, so that his contribution here in regard to referential use of the terms is new. Ixcatec terms are taken from Fernández de Miranda's dictionary (1961) and accordingly do not provide complete information on extended ranges of reference. The same limitation exists for Ixcatec terms from Hoppe and Weitlaner 1969a and for Chocho from Hoppe and Weitlaner 1969b. Data from Central Pame, formerly referred to as North

Figure 3. Filial Extension Rules Illustrated.

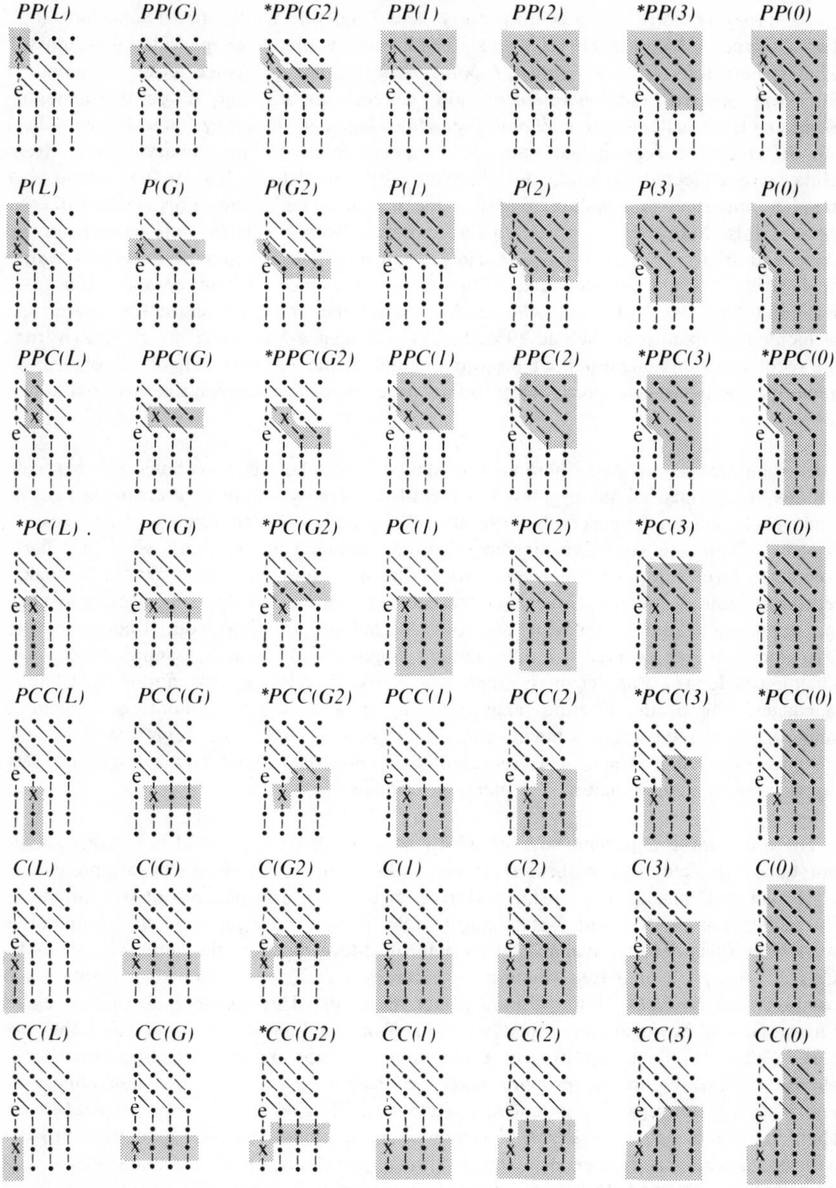

*Not found in contemporary or reconstructed Otomanguean languages.

Pame, is summarized here from Gibson 1954, and data from Chichimeca-Jonaz is taken from Driver and Romero Castillo 1963. An unpublished manuscript by Lawrence Ecker (1930) provides early seventeenth-century data from one unidentified Otomí language. For Zapotec, Córdova's (1942) late sixteenth-century dictionary provides the data for what is here referred to as Valley Zapotec. A few Coatlán Zapotec terms are found in Robinson 1963, but additional investigation by Reeck for this study fill out that material. Romney (1967) includes three Zapotec schedules supplied to him by Laura Nader Miller-on, of which the Juquila materials are of special interest. The primary material from Mitla were collected especially for this study by Stubblefield, but Parsons (1936) also supplies important information regarding the use of some of the terms. Pride gathered data for this study from Yaitepec Chatino, but data from Tataltepec were taken from the Pride and Pride (1970) dictionary. Palantla Chinantec data are summarized from Merrifield 1959. Yolox Chinantec data from the early eighteenth century are taken from Barreda (Cline 1960). Material collected for this volume by Warkentin for Huave are supplemented by data from Diebold 1966. Finally, Chiapanec-Mangue terms are drawn from the reconstructions of Fernández de Miranda and Weitlaner (1961). There are, of course, numerous reconstructed proto terms found in many of the comparative materials cited above.

It is unnecessary to name here each of the persons who has contributed primary data for this study since all such material is identified later by author as a major part of the study itself, but a summary will serve to evaluate how well Otomanguean languages are covered. There are sixty-five kinship schedules included in the study which are fairly complete. Twelve Mixtec languages, two Trique languages, and two Cuicatec languages represent Proto Mixtecan. Three Mazatec languages, three Popoloc languages, and Ixcatec represent Proto Popolocan as does limited information from Chocho. Proto Otopamean is represented by five Otomí languages, Mazahua, Central Pame, and Chichimeca-Jonaz. Zapotecan is represented by fifteen Zapotec and two Chatino languages, one of the Chatino languages only in a limited way. Fourteen Chinantec languages represent Proto Chinantecan. Amuzgo and Huave are represented by one language each while Tlapanec is represented by two. Chiapanec and Mangue are only represented by limited material, as mentioned above.

There are three important sources which have not been mentioned but which should not be overlooked. The earliest is Harvey 1963, which was the most comprehensive collection of Otomanguean kinship materials of its time. The manuscript was submitted for publication in 1957 and was unable to take into account much of the comparative work which has become available in the interim. More recently, the impressive study by Casasa García (1976), based primarily on Harvey's data, has presented generative and componential analyses of the Otomanguean materials. Through no fault of Harvey or Casasa García, however, these analyses suffer from the limited data upon which they are based. While the data do represent a wide range of Otomanguean languages, they focus almost exclusively on the primary ranges of reference of the terms with almost no information at all regarding extended ranges. They thus do not have a great deal to say about the Otomanguean systems of reference as complete systems or of their broader anthropological significance for the historical development of Otomanguean social organization. Intermediate between these two studies is Romney 1967, which does focus on the systems as systems, but only in cursory fashion.

Cognate Set Format

An attempt is made to give identity to reconstructions of kinship terms proposed in earlier works by retaining, wherever possible, the cognate set numbers assigned by original analysts. Longacre (1957), for example, proposed Proto Mixtecan cognate sets numbered from 1 to 279. Several sets from this original group are kinship terms which are referred to in this study by their original numbers. New PMn sets proposed here are numbered from 301. Since cognate sets for PC and PT were not worked out separately from the PMn sets, those proposed here are numbered from 1. Proto Mixtec sets are numbered from 101 except for set 54 of Longacre and Mak (1960).

I generally follow Rensch's (1976) rephonemicization of PMn but reverse the order of syllable final laryngeals and nasals to *CV?m rather than *CVm?. Longacre (1957:47) chose the order *CVm? on the basis of data from Amuzgo which he has subsequently decided is not a Mixtecan language (1966a). He notes, however, that the source of *m probably varies: in some instances it is best considered as an inherent part of a root, in others a grammatical element postposed to a root. In this study, where *m is not consistently supported by PM, PT, and PC, it is separated from the reconstructed PMn stem by hyphen on the assumption that it represents a separate grammatical form. Lack of hyphen in the reconstruction indicates either that the *m was an inherent part of the root or that no evidence to the contrary is available.

Gudschinsky provides 356 Popolocan sets, new ones proposed are numbered from 357. Kirk proposes 732 Proto Mazatec sets, new ones are here numbered from 733. Gudschinsky did not reconstruct terms at the Proto Popoloc horizon by looking at Popoloc languages apart from Mazatec, Ixcatec, and Chocho. Sets here proposed for this family are numbered from 1.

Otopamean has been subclassified in a variety of ways, but I here follow what appears to me to be the majority opinion in accepting the oldest grouping as between Pamean and Otomian. Pamean is further divided between Central Pame and Chichimeca-Jonaz. Central Pame has been frequently referred to in the literature as North Pame, but recent dialect studies by Gibson show it to be distinct from other North Pame groups and is being referred to by her and Bartholomew in forthcoming work as Central Pame. Bartholomew establishes Proto Otopamean sets numbering from 1 to 811. New ones proposed here number from 812. Bartholomew did not establish separate sets for the Pamean group, nor is it done here since it is represented by only two languages. Newman and Weitlaner (1950a) proposed 330 sets for Proto Otomí, excluding Mazahua. Bartholomew (1960) later suggested some revisions in the form of new sets numbered from 1 to 94. The two terms taken from Bartholomew, 31 and 55, are here recast as of a 400 series as 431 and 455, respectively. New sets proposed here for Proto Otomí are numbered from 501. Newman and Weitlaner (1950b) also proposed 202 Central Otomian sets, including Mazahua with Otomí. This horizon has not been developed in this study. Unfortunately, the southern Otomian languages, Matlatzinca and Ocuilteco, are not included in the study for lack of data.

Because of a system of stem-initial consonantal alternations found in Otopamean languages, Bartholomew considers many stems to have had four forms which she labels A, B, C, and D. She believes these alternations developed in pre-POP times from morphophonemic shifts between stems and prefixed material which has since been lost. These alternations are quite prominent in the kinship material from Central Pame and Chichimeca-Jonaz, and multiple forms are accordingly listed and identified here by labels

A through D. By a generative approach, she finds the need for only four vowel symbols in Central Pame (1965:46), for which **i, e, o,** and **a** are here used.

In the interpretation of Proto Zapotecan (PZn) kinship, we must consider an intermediate time horizon when the Zapotecan community had presumably divided into Zapotec and Chatino branches. Proto Zapotec (PZ) terms have been provided in part, by the late María Tereza Fernández de Miranda as of October, 1963, at which time she communicated them to me by letter. Since Fernández de Miranda's important general reconstruction of PZ continues unpublished, I have chosen to publish her letter as the most direct means of indicating her views regarding the forms she postulated. Swadesh (1947) had previously proposed 94 Proto Zapotec cognate sets, but since only three of these represent kinship terms—for father, mother, and child—the more recent materials from Fernández de Miranda are relied upon in this study. Proto Zapotecan sets (including Zapotec and Chatino) and Proto Zapotec sets (excluding Chatino) are here both numbered from 1. Proto Chatino sets were numbered by Upson and Longacre from 1 to 251. New sets proposed here are numbered from 301.

Rensch 1968 is a revised version of the descriptive portion of Rensch 1963, but does not include the complete set of cognates which he numbers from 1 to 773. Since those sets have never been published, the original numbers are not used in Rensch 1968 or subsequent publications by him. The original numbers are used in this volume to distinguish Rensch's sets from new ones numbered from 801. The revised phonological inventory of Rensch 1976 is used in the Proto Chinantecan reconstruction, as well as more recent phonological transcriptions of some of the modern terms than were available to Rensch prior to 1963. A single exception is the use of the raised numeral [1] to indicate low tone and [2] for high tone in PCn rather than the letters L and H in parentheses.

In addition to the larger families of Otomanguean languages, there are a few smaller families for which extensive discussion is not warranted. Projections directly to Proto Otomanguean are made from a single Amuzgo language and a single Huave language. A tentative proposal regarding Proto Tlapanec sets numbered from 1 to 25 is made on the basis of just two closely-related languages and, finally, Proto Chiapanec and Proto Chiapanec-Mangue sets are taken directly from Fernández de Miranda and Weitlaner (1961).

Until recently, there has been little serious consideration of either Huave or Tlapanec as members of the Otomanguean group of languages. Swadesh (Fernández de Miranda, Swadesh, and Weitlaner 1959; Swadesh 1960 and 1964) suggested that Huave is a member of the group. Longacre later (1968) agreed, and Rensch (1973 and 1978) supplied formal evidence. In the case of Tlapanec, Rensch (1977) claimed that it is a member of the group, in apparent contradiction to Sapir's (1925) earlier suggestion that it is Hokan.

Many Otomanguean sets which appear in the literature include kinship terms from Otomanguean languages not otherwise represented directly in this study. But such material almost never provides the information needed in this study concerning extended ranges of reference. It has therefore seemed sufficient to recognize the relevance of such material to the reconstruction of the phonological form of such terms without going to the trouble of repeating them all in cognate set listings in this study.

PART ONE

ANALYSIS

CHAPTER 1
PROTO OTOMANGUEAN KINSHIP TERMS

This chapter proposes a set of POM kinship terms with corresponding ranges of reference, presents and discusses the evidence upon which the proposal is made, and summarizes a possible sequence of development from POM to PMn, PPn, POP, PZn, PCn, A, H, PT1, and PCM horizons.

POM KINSHIP TERMS

The Proto Otomanguean system of kinship reference proposed here classifies all kinsmen into five major classes, as defined by five reciprocal sets of terms: parent and child terms, grandkinsman terms, sibling terms, affinal terms, and spouse terms.

POM Parent and Child Terms

The first class of kinsmen, which includes only parent and child in its narrowest definition, distinguishes three kinds of kinsmen: father, mother, and child—marking the sex of parent but not that of the junior member of the dyad except by inflectional materials added especially for that purpose. This three-way classification is extremely well supported by modern Otomanguean languages. The system of classification is, thus, quite straightforward.

The inventory of terms which named these kinsmen is, however, large and complex. One important factor underlying this complexity is the POM pattern of stems having more than one form, based on several patterns of consonantal variation. In addition, there is reason to believe that morphophonemic processes, not yet fully understood, complicate the picture. In particular, **i and **u are clearly distinguishable at the POM horizon, but show evidence of relating to each other morphophonemically.

These two types of variation result in the reconstruction of three forms of a term of reference for father, a term of address for father, three sets of alternating forms for making reference to mother, a set of three forms for addressing mother, and three forms for referring to child.

**kwin-yu-wa, **kin-yu-wa, **nwin-yu-wa	*Pm*	*father*
**Ytah	*Pm(vocative)*	*father*
**siHn, **niHn	*Pf*	*mother*
**suhn, **nuhn	*Pf*	*mother*
**kwin, **kin, **win	*Pf*	*mother*
**ntaHn, **naHn, **yaHn	*Pf(vocative)*	*mother*
**?ntan^3	*C*	*child*
**Yhnsan, **hyan	*C*	*child*

The penult of the term of reference for father and the ultima are to be identified with **yu *person* and **wa *male,* respectively. Their presence as a part of the father term in some Otomanguean languages is considered to be the result of the need to distinguish it from the very similar term of reference for mother. Normal sound change and regular patterns of stem alternation apparently brought about a situation wherein these father and mother terms became indistinguishable in some contexts, or nearly so, requiring the additional appositional material to make the clarification.

Another factor in the complexity of parent and child terminology is the indication that, in one form or another, they did play a role in naming certain collateral kinsmen at a very early date. But more on this later.

POM Grandkinsman Terms

The second class of kinsmen is named by just two terms and encompasses grandfather, grandmother, grandson, and granddaughter, and then any more distantly related lineal kinsman and any collateral kinsman other than sibling. The two terms are self-reciprocal, each marking the sex of the senior member of the ego-alter dyad.

**seh, **hkeh	*PPm(R,2)*	*grandfather*
**Ynsan, **Ynan	*PPf(R,2)*	*grandmother*

There is evidence that this class of kinsmen was further divided by the use of modifiers to specify particular subclasses of grandkinsmen. A diminutive was preposed to specify junior members of the dyad. A modifier was postposed to specify a distant grandkinsman of more than two generations distance from ego. Sibling terms were combined with grandkinsman terms to specify collateral grandkinsmen.

There is also evidence that lineal grandkinsmen could be classified as a subclass within an extended parent and child range by the use of parent and child terms with postposed modifier to designate lineal kinsmen beyond the first ascending and first descending generations. Such terms appear to compete with the above set of two self-reciprocal terms at a fairly early date, and may represent an old innovation in a move to a new system of classification which no longer merges junior and senior kinsmen by reciprocal terms or classes collateral kinsmen together with lineals.

POM Sibling Terms

The third class of kinsmen is the sibling class which ranges over all collateral kintypes and overlaps in part with the range of grandkinsman terms. Two sets of sibling terms existed to name these kinsmen.

One set consisted of three terms which divided elder siblings in Jivaran fashion by specifying males or females of the same sex, or siblings of the opposite sex.

**tu, **nu, **yu	*emPCm(0)*	*man's elder brother*
**kwaHn, **kaHn	*efPCf(0)*	*woman's elder sister*
**nsi-ʔya	*eaPCb(0)*	*cross-sex elder sibling*

A second set consisted of a single term to classify any sibling without regard to sex or seniority, but this term appears to have occurred quite commonly with a second element preceding or following it to specify junior sibling as the reciprocal of the Jivaran terms above.

**kuHn	*PC(0)*	*sibling*
**nsi-kihn, **kihn-si	*yPC(0)*	*younger sibling*

Another POM form, ****taʔn** *companion,* was probably not a kinship term in the strictest sense, but it pops up in various places in the development of Otomanguean kinship vocabularies, indicating that it was probably easily interchangeable with ****kuHn** and its diminutive forms in many POM social contexts.

The overlap of grandkinsman and sibling ranges is consistent with several hypotheses regarding POM society. First of all, it is quite likely that small, semi-nomadic POM bands manipulated the genealogical facts to their advantage, classifying collateral kinsmen more on the basis of social considerations than genealogical. The exigencies of a particular social situation, for instance, would dictate that in one case a mother's brother be classified as grandfather while in another he be classified as elder brother or even younger brother.

The grandkinsman range is presented above as extending to collateral kinsmen by Rule 2, a genealogically-based rule. There is evidence, however, that relative age may more accurately represent the basis for defining seniority between collateral kinsmen at the POM horizon than does strict genealogical reckoning. It may be that there were two degrees of seniority so that elder collaterals within a nearer range were classed as siblings while elder collaterals of a more distant range were classified as grandparents. The relatively small size and changing composition of a POM band probably also gave rise to considerations of *social* distance which must have also affected the classification of such collaterals.

As was indicated above, there were also occasions—or perhaps a stage in the development of POM terms—where sibling and grandkinsman terms were combined to specify particular collateral kinsmen who were not ego's closest kinsmen but not the most distant either. The details of this which are fairly complex, are discussed later in this chapter.

POM Affinal Terms

Only two terms are proposed for naming POM affinal kinsmen, both of them self-reciprocal. The first names the husband of ego's daughter and, reciprocally, the parent of male ego's wife, without regard to the sex of parent. The second names the wife of ego's son and, reciprocally, the parent of female ego's husband, also without respect to the sex of parent. These are the primary ranges of the two terms, but they appear to extend without limit (by Rule 0) to any kinsman of spouse, marking sex of ego, and to spouse of any kinsman, marking sex of spouse.

**kah	$CSm(R,0)$	*male affinal kinsman*
**nsan, **nyan	$CSf(R,0)$	*female affinal kinsman*

Further subclassification of affinals was accomplished by the use of modification of these two terms or other circumlocutions.

POM Spouse Terms

No special terms for spouse appear to have been used in POM times other than possessed forms of more general terms designating persons of *male* or *female* gender. As in the case of parent terms, numerous POM forms (as presently analyzed) are supported as having functioned in this way.

**sehn, **yehn	Sm	*husband*
**kwa, **ka, **wa	Sm	*husband*
**kwin, **kin, **nwin	Sm	*husband*
**siHn, **niHn	Sf	*wife*
**suhn, **nuhn	Sf	*wife*
**kwin, **kin, **win	Sf	*wife*
**ntaHn, **naHn, **yaHn	Sf	*wife*

POM Parent and Child Term Reconstructions

Apart from the relationship between husband and wife, the parent-child relationship is the primordial relationship of kinship. In one sense, the simplest of relationships based upon the fundamental principle of filiation and embellished only by the biological facts of sex of kinsman, it becomes a most important and complex relationship, replete with affective and jural implications of greater social significance than those of any other kinship relationship. Along with the phonological and grammatical accidents of Otomanguean linguistic history, the importance of this relationship has undoubtedly contributed to the complexity of the problem in reconstructing POM parent and child terms, even though there is little doubt that just three parent-child categories existed at the POM horizon, with the primary ranges *Pm, Pf,* and *C,* respectively.

Of the three categories, the mother category shows the greatest lexical complexity, with no less than four complicated cognate sets each finding considerable support as the POM mother term. It may be that with further study of POM phonology and grammar the four sets can be shown to be but inflectional variants of one another, as may at least two of several terms for child; but such study, if possible, remains to be done, permitting here only mention of the possibility and requiring some questions to be left unanswered.

In the POM case, the social significance of the parent-child relationship appears to go beyond just kinship in that father and mother terms, particularly the latter, appear to be inextricably associated with the more generic categories of male and female, or man and woman, respectively. All four terms for mother show a strong association with such general reference to women or females.

The phonological and grammatical accidents of Otomanguean linguistic history which complicate the reconstruction of parent and child terms include stem-initial consonantal alternations which involve a large inventory of consonants, several of which occur in more than one set, as well as the backing and raising of vowels in a simple four-vowel system under certain conditions only some of which are clearly understood. As it turns out, terms for father and mother are in some cases very close to one another phonologically and share alternants of almost identical form. The problem becomes even more acute when father and mother terms combine with other material in such a way as to be placed in unstressed positions which exhibit reduced phonological complexity, and especially so for this study since very little is known of the phonological history of unstressed material, most study having been focused on the stressed syllable of Otomanguean languages.

The discussion of POM parent and child terms will proceed one category at a time, first the terms for father, then those for mother, and finally those for child.

Father

Otomanguean languages manifest at least three terms for father. One such term is **tata**; but because it is found throughout Mesoamerica in both Otomanguean and non-Otomanguean languages, it is not here considered to be of POM origin. Whatever its origin, it has spread with the currents of political and social change across Mesoamerica through the course of at least several centuries as a kind of lingua franca term, and its presence in modern Otomanguean languages requires at least passing mention. Its distribution is much more wide than indicated by the following data, especially as a term of respect for a senior male of the community.

PMn: PM 101. *tata *Pm*
PPn: I tata *Pm.*
POP 812. *tata *Pm*
PZn: PZ 1. *tata *Pm.*

A second term, ****Ytah,** is phonologically similar to **tata,** but uniformly reflects the presence of a laryngeal and often a preposed palatal. Rensch (1976:201) is justifiably suspicious that it too is a "widely disseminated loan word" (and presumably related to **tata**) but, once again, its ubiquity warrants recognition as a possible POM term. Whether or not it is of POM origin, the evidence indicates that it primarily has played a vocative role in Otomanguean languages. The following set expands the material assembled by Rensch. It includes one Tlapanec form which would have to be an ****n**-initial form, a standard POM variant of ****t**.

POM 49 **Ytah *Pm(vocative).*
  PMn 30l. *Ci-tah *Pm.* < **POM **Ytah.**
  PPn: PP 1. *?ta² *Pm.* < **POM **?ta.**
  POP: PO 289. *ta *Pm.* < **POP **ta** < **POM *ta** or ****tah.**
  PCn 76. *tiá² *Pm(vocative).* < **POM **Ytah.**
  A **co¹tyǎ¹, co¹tyé²; tá¹²; tyé?³** *(vocative) Pm.* < **POM **Ytah, **tah, **Ytah?.**
  H **téât** *Pm.* < **POM (ta-)**Ytah.**
  PTl 1. *a-na-u? *Pm.* < **POM **na.**
  PCM 34. *ngu-tá? *Pm.* < **POM **nkwi-tah?.**

The third term, ****kwin-yu-wa, **kin-yu-wa, *nwin-yu-wa** is the best candidate for a true POM term of reference for father. In addition to stem alternants, its reconstruction is complicated by its occurrence with modifying elements. Rensch lists clear cognates from PPn, POP, and PCn (third person) to which may be added cognates from PCM and, possibly, PCn (first person). PM and PZn terms are also relevant to the set as probably reflecting postposed modifiers, as suggested by **PCM 221**.

POM 361. **kwin-yu-wa, **kin-yu-wa, **nwin-yu-wa *Pm.*
    PMn: PM 102. *yu-wa *Pm.* < POM ****yu-wa.**
    PPn 227. *na⁴ʔmi³ *Pm.* < POM ****ʔnwi.**
    POP 471. *peoʔ, *meoʔ, *weoʔ *Pm.* < POM ****kwin-yu-ʔ, **nwin-yu-ʔ, **win-yu-ʔ.**
    PZn 1. *š-yu-zi *Pm.* < POM ****yu-sen.**
    PCn 359. *hmi·¹ *Pm(third).* < POM ****hnwi.**
    PCn 563. *ŋiuʔ *Pm(first).* < POM ****nkin-yu-ʔ.**
    PCn 812. *zá·²¹ŋiuʔ, *zá·²¹hmi·¹ *SPm(L).* < POM ****nsehn-kin-yu-ʔ, **nsehn-wi.**
    PCM 34. *ngu-táʔ *Pm.* < POM ****nkwi-tahʔ.**
    PCM 221. *pu-yu-wa *Pm.* < POM ****kwi-yu-wa.**

The proposed derivation of **PCn 563** from ****nkin-yu-ʔ**, with resyllabification from two syllables to one, does not find direct support in Rensch (1976) and is, therefore, to be considered a tentative proposal. Alternatively, the following derivation is possible: ***ŋiuʔ** < ***Yŋuʔ** < ****Ynkiʔn.**

The modifying elements reflected in **POM 361** above are ****yu** *person* and ****wa** *male,* with PZn 1 showing another term for male other than ****wa**, namely, ****sehn, **yehn.** (Future research should examine the hypothesis that **POM 387** (below) may be related not only to the last syllable of the proposed father term, but also to the first. Study of the kinship terms leaves a clear indication of a close affiliation between parent and sex-designating terms. While POM ****a** and ****i** are not directly related to one another, POM does show a complex pattern of vowel shifts in its derivational history, particularly in the presence of postvocalic ****n.**)

POM 421. **yu *person.*
    PMn: PM 102. *yu-wa *Pm.* < POM ****yu-wa.**
    PZn 8. *giʔ-yu *man.* < POM ****kiʔn-yu.**
    PZn 1. *š-yu-zi *Pm.* < POM ****yu-sen.**
    PCn 563. *ŋiuʔ *Pm(first).* < POM ****nkin-yu-ʔ.**
    PCn 810. *ŋiu *emPCm(0).* < POM ****nkin-yu.**
    A yu- *human.* < POM ****yu.**
    PCM 221. *yu-wa *male.* < POM ****yu-wa.**
    PCM 221. *pu-yu-wa(ʔ) *Pm.* < POM ****kwi-yu-wa.**
POM 387. **kwa, **ka, **wa *male.*
    PMn: PM 102. *yuwa *Pm.* < PMn *wa < POM ****wa.**
    PPn 318. *nta-wa *Sm.* < POM ****wa.**
    POP 389. *=tǫa-n *male.* < POM ****wa.**
    POP 490. *n-ʔǫa-n *Sm.* < POM ****wa.**
    PZn: PZ 9. *žiʔni gaʔna *Cm.* < POM ****ka.**
    PTl 21. *ahmba-Vʔ *Sm.* < POM ****nhkwa.**
    PCM 221. *nu-wa *male.* < POM ****wa.**

PCM 221. *pu-yu-wa(?) *Pm.* < POM **wa, **wa?.
POM 254. **sehn, **yehn *male.*
PMn 304. *Өe?m, *yehm *Sm.* < POM **se?n, **yehn.
PPn 227. *ši?į *Sm.* < POM **Yse?yehn.
PZn 1. *š-yu-zi *Pm.* < POM **yu-sen.
PCn 445. *zá·²¹ *male.* < POM **nsehn.
PCn 812. *zá·²¹ŋiu?, *zá·¹²hmi·¹ *SPm(L).* < POM **nsehn-kin-yu-?, **nsehn-wi.
A s?á³ *Sm.* < POM ** ?sehn.

In addition to the modern terms for father presented above as having their source in POM 361, a number of modern POM languages support the hypothesis that senior collateral male kinsmen (and reciprocally, junior collateral kinsmen) were referred to by forms based upon POM 361. The entire question of how senior and junior collateral kinsmen were classified terminologically will be discussed in a later section, but it should be noted that the following forms, referring to such kinsmen, are very likely closely related to POM 361. They are here presented as POM 361a, to show this relationship.

POM 361a. **kwin, **kin, **win *PPCm(R,G).*
PMn 244. *ӨV-kwim *mPCC(G).* < POM **sa-kwin.
PMn: PT 2. *du-?we *PPCf(G),* < POM **su-?win.
PPn 246. *ka?me *yPCC(I,1).* < POM **ka?nwin.
POP 822. *mo =*PPCm(R,G).* < POM **nwin.
POP 823. *?oe *xPPCm(R,G).* < POM **?win.
POP: CP A rabbéo?, B ábbɛo?, C wobbéo? *xPm(G,S);* či rabbéo? *xmC(G).* < POM **kwin-yu-?.
PCn 810. *ŋiu *emPCm(0).* < POM **nkin-yu.
PTl 13. *a-ma-u? *PPCm(G).* < POM **nwin.

PT 2 denotes a female kinsman rather than a male. It would seem that the uncle term has been reassigned by the addition of *Өu < POM 340 **suhn *female;* that is, at some stage PT aunts were classified as *female uncles.* Since both father and mother terms had alternate forms with initial **kw (as will be seen in the description of mother terms below), it is possible that the uncle and aunt terms coalesced phonologically in pre-PT, requiring the addition of *Өu to distinguish them.

PCn 810 is subject to the same limits of interpretation as PCn 563 above, and can have descended from **Ynkin rather than the proposed **nkin-yu.

Mother

As in the case of terms for father, a number of terms for mother are supported by data from modern OM languages. First of all, mother terms which correspond to **tata** and **Ytah** are found throughout the area. A sample of **nana** reflexes are as follows:

PMn: PM 104. *nana Pf.
PMn: PM. *nana Өa?nu PPf(1).
POP 813. *nana Pf.

The second set, corresponding to **Ytah *Pm(vocative)*, is **POM 350 **nahn *Pf(vocative)*. Sound shifts implied by this set lend credence to the hypothesis that it has considerable antiquity within the Otomanguean group. The Trique form referred to by Longacre in **PMn 156** appears to be a reflex of **350** which has been reshaped to two syllables under the influence of the lingua franca **nana** term.

**POM 350. **nahn *Pf(vocative)*.
PMn 156b: T na³nah³ *elderly lady*. < **POM **nah.
PPn 357. *n?a⁴ *Pf.* < *na?a < **POM **?nahn.
PZn 2. *ši-na?a *Pf.* < **POM **nahn.
PZn: Yt nagwe *Pf(vocative)*. < **POM **na.
PCn 287. *mï·, *ma *Pf(vocative)*. < **POM **nnan, **nna.
A ná¹² *Pf.* < **POM **nahn.
A co¹ñtɔ́³ *Pf.* < *co-ti-nɔ́ < **POM **nahn.
PCM 179. *ngu-má?, *ngi-má? *Pf.* < **POM **nkwin-nah?, **nkin-nah?.

The validity of *350* as a long-standing term for mother within Otomanguean is further attested by its relationship to additional reflexes of **350**, presented below as **350a**, which show it not only to have been a term for mother, but also a general term for *female* or *woman*. As was mentioned above, such a relationship is characteristic of several POM forms which have come down to the present as terms for mother in OM languages. **POM 350a** exhibits the well-known POM **t ~ **n ~ **y alternation.

**POM 350a. **ntaHn, **naHn, **yaHn *female*.
PMn 302. *nda?a, *ña?a *Sf.* < **POM **nta?n, **nya?n.
POP 835. *n?įą *woman*. < **POM **n?yaHn.
PZn: PZ 19. *bela, *žila *fPCf(G)*. < **POM **kwan-yan, **nsin-yan.
PZn: PZ 5. *ča?a, PZ 7. *la *female*. < **POM **ntahn, **nyan.
PZn 3. *gu-na?a *woman*. < **POM **kwi-nahn.
PCn 808. *?ya· *woman*. < **POM **?ya.
PCn 809. *siá·² ?ya·² *PPf(e₂0)*. < **POM **Ysuhn-?ya.
PCn 811. *nï· *efPCf(0)*. < **POM **ntan.
H ntáh *Sf.* < **POM **ntahn.
PTl 2. *ru-du-u? *Pf.* < **POM **nyan-sun.

A third set also represents a true POM parent term. The reconstruction of this term for mother is even more complicated than that for father, particularly in the way it is closely associated with general terms for *female*. Even the father term can be seen to reflect a general term for *male* (e.g., **PCM 158** *mbu-hwe, *nu-hwi *Sm* < **POM **hwin), but the evidence for an association between words for *mother* and *female* is much more plentiful.

Rensch's **POM 255** is here amplified and divided into three parts suggesting a relationship between a general term for *female*, a specific term for *mother*, and a reduplicated term for *aunt*.

**POM 255. **siHn, **nihn *female*.
PPn 111. *čihį *Sf.* < **POM **Ynsihn.
POP 320,375,532. *sǫ, *co *Sf, woman*. < **POM **sihn, **nsin.

PZn: V pinih *female.* < POM **nin.
POM 255a. **siHn, **nihn *Pf.*
  PMn: PT 6. *nih³ *Pf.* < POM **nihn.
  POP 473. *c?ǫ *Pf.* < POM **nsi?n.
  PZn 2. *ši-na?a *Pf.* < POM **si-nahn.
  PCn 807. *ni· *Pf(vocative).* < POM **nin.
POM 255b. **nsi-nsi *PPCf(R,G).*
  PMn 51. *Ɵi-Ɵi *efPPCf(I,G).* < POM **nsi-nsi.
  POP 824. *ci-ci =PPCf(R,G).* < POM **nsi-nsi.
  POP: CP A nc?ộk, B nc?ộk?, C nc?ộp *xPf(G,S).* < POM **nsihn.
  PZn: PZ 20. *š-ni-su *PPCf(I,I).* < POM **ni-su.
  PTl 14. *ni-yu-i? *PPCf(G).* < *ndi-yu < POM **nsi-nuhn.

Rensch also reconstructs another stem for *female* which is significantly close to the form of **POM 255**, differing essentially only in the vowel being **u rather than **i. While it is not clear what has caused this vowel alternation, it is clear that the forms are related. Rensch suggests that the stem with **u may be related to **POM 327 **(n)su** *breast, to nurse* and that the stem with **i may be related to **POM 261 **(n)si(H)(n)³** *breast, to nurse*, which two sets are probably themselves related, further supporting the hypothesis that these sets are related. The **u set in question is **POM 340 **suhn, **nuhn.** It exhibits the same sort of semantic range as **POM 255**.

POM 340. **suhn, **nuhn *female*
  PMn: PM 109. *ña-Ɵĩ?i *Sf.* < POM **nya-su?n.
  PMn: PT 2. *du-?we *PPCf(G).* < POM **su-?win.
  PPn 366. *chu⁴¹ *woman.* < POM **Ynsuhn.
  POP 320, 375, 532. *sǫ, *co *Sf, woman.* < POM **suhn, **nsun.
  PZn: Yt zo?ołi *Sf.* < POM **suhn.
  PZn: Yt no?ołi *woman.* < POM **nuhn.
POM 340a. **suhn, **nuhn *Pf.*
  PMn: PM 108. *Ɵĩ?i *Pf.* < POM **su?n.
  PCn 651. *siá·² *Pf(third).* < POM **Ysuhn.
  PCn 802. *sia *Pf(first).* < POM **Ysun.
  PCn 813. *mĩ-sia· *SPf(L).* < POM **n?kwin-sun.
  A co¹ñtɔ̃³ *Pf.* < POM **nuhn.
  PTl 2. *ru-du-u? *Pf.* < POM **nyan-sun.
POM 340b. **suhn, **nuhn *PPCf(R,G).*
  PZn: PZ 20. *š-ni-su *PPCf(I,I).* < POM **ni-su.
  PTl 14. *ni-yu-i? *PPCf(G).* < *ndi-yu < POM **nsi-nuhn.

Set **148** below is still another set proposed by Rensch and here amplified which is clearly a term for mother with all the ranges of the preceding three sets. The PCn terms are included here as well as under **POM 350** above where they can also fit; it is not clear whether they belong here or there, but it is unlikely that both derivations are correct. The PTl derivations are highly speculative. **POP 820** does not appear to have its source in **POM 148** alone, since there is at least an additional nasal preceding the stem, and **148** does not seem to be sufficient to account for the meaning of **820**.

POM 148. **kwin, **kin, **win *female.*
   PMn 13. ***Өa-kwim-xiHm** *fPCC(G).* < POM ****sa-kwin-hkiHn.**
   PMn 38. ***ku?n-gwi** *fPCf(G).* < POM ****ku?n-kwin.**
   POP 376. ***khǫ-hoe** *efPCf(G),* < POM ****kuhn-kwin.**
   POP 820. ***nkhoe** *emPCf(G).* < POM ****nhkVwin.**
   POP: PO 120. ***c?j-hwä** *CSf.* < POM ****hkwin.**
   PZn 3. ***gu-na?a** *female.* < POM ****kwi-nahn.**
   PCn 280. ***mǐ¹** *female.* < POM ****n?kwihn.**
   PCn 813. ***mǐ-sia·** *SPf(L).* < POM ****n?kwihn-sun.**
   A skú³ *Sf.* < *kuh < POM ****kwihn.**
   A škyie *female.* < POM ****Ykihn.**
   PTl 11. ***ja-gu-i?** *mPCf.* < POM ****nteHn-kwin.**
   PTl 22. ***a?gu-i?** *Sf.* < *n?ku < POM ****n?kwin.**
   PCM 159. ***na-hwí** *female.* < POM ****hkwi.**
   PCM 197. ***mba-hwi, *nu-hmi** *Sf.* < POM ****nkwa-hkwi, **hnwi.**
148a. ****kwin, **win** *Pf.*
   PMn: PC 3. ***ča-ku** *Pf.* < POM ****Ca-kwi.**
   POP: PO 177. ***me** *Pf.* < POM ****nwin.**
   PZn: Yt nagwe *Pf(vocative).* < POM ****kwin.**
   PCn 287. ***mǐ·, *ma** *Pf(vocative).* < POM ****nwin, **nwen.**
   H mǐm *Pf.* < POM ****nwin.**
   PCM 179. ***ngu-má?, *ngi-má?** *Pf.* < POM ****nkwin-nah?, **nkin-nah?.**
POM 148b. **kwin, **kin *PPCf(R,G).*
   PMn 13. ***Өa-kwim-xiHm** *fPCC(G).* < POM ****sa-kwin-hkiHn.**
   POP 825. ***hi** *xPPCf(R,G).* < POM ****hki.**

In summary then, we find several terms for mother, all associated with a generic term for *female* or *woman,* and some of them appearing as terms for *aunt* as well. Each of these terms is found to have exhibited stem-initial consonant alternations common to POM, and it is tempting to further associate the several terms phonologically into one or more supersets by recognizing even larger patterns of alternation. The **s ~ **n alternation of **POM 255,** for example, is not altogether incompatible with the **kw ~ **k ~ **w alternation of **POM 148,** but Rensch draws back from encouraging their inclusion within a single set (1976:33). We will, therefore, content ourselves to have recognized a number of POM sets, possibly related to one another, which underlie the bulk of modern OM terms for mother and which have an unquestionable historical relationship to generic terms for *female* or *woman.* In summary, the four sets are:

POM 148. **kwin, **kin, **win *Pf, PPCf(R,G), female.*
POM 255. **siHn, **niHn *Pf, PPCf(R,G), female.*
POM 340. **suhn, **nuhn *Pf, PPCf(R,G), female.*
POM 350. **ntaHn, **naHn, **yaHn *Pf(vocative), PPCf(R,G), female.*

Child

Several terms reconstruct for child at the POM horizon, but only two of them are probable kinship terms. These two terms differ in their initial consonant, one attesting **t, the other **s. While Rensch does not find these consonants in alternation in POM, the existence of the two sets suggests a connection between them. It is probably that they represent an inflectional relationship of the sort that exists, for example, in contemporary Mazahua where first person forms, such as čʔi *Cm(first)*, exhibit the presence of a palatal element while corresponding third person forms, such as tʔi *Cm(third)*, do not. Such a relationship may be presumed to have existed between **POM 308** and **57**, but the details remain obscure at present.

POM 57. **ʔntan³ *C.*
   PPn 267. *ʔntye¹ *C.* < POM **Yʔntan³.
   POP 542. *tʔoiHC *C.* < POM **ʔtan.
   A hnta²¹, hntá² *C(L).* < POM **hntan.
   A ʔnta¹ *very young person (vocative).* < POM **ʔntan.
   PTl 3. *aʔda-Vʔ *C.* < POM **ʔntan.
   PCM 37. *na-tu-me, *na-ru-me *C.* < POM **tan.
**POM 308. **Yhnsan, **hyan *C.*
   PMn 303. *Өaʔya, *Өaʔni *C.* < POM **sa.
   PPn 135. *čhą⁴ *C.* < POM **Ynsahn.
   POP 383. *mhǫ-te *Cf.* < POM **hyan.
   PCn 803. *hą· *C.* < POM **hyan.
   H kwál *C(L).* < POM **kwan-yV.
   PCM 206. *mba-ña *C.* < POM **nkwa-Yna.

POM 87 does not appear to represent a true kinship term but is rather the source of a generic child term. Because there is a known phonological relationship between **POM **an** and *u in certain daughter languages, however, it is also possible that **87** is an inflectional variant of **57**.

**POM 87. **tun, **yun *infant, baby.*
   PZn: PZ 10. *mbaʔdu *young child.* < POM **nkwa-ʔtun.
   PCn 764. *yʉ·(n) *infant.* < POM **yun.
   A tyhɔ¹² *young person (vocative).* < POM **Yhtuhn.

POM 258 is probably not a kinship term even though the cognates listed below may be used in kinship reference. Rensch includes additional cognates, not here repeated, which make reference to smallishness, youthfulness, or tenderness, indicating that reference to a young kinsman by these terms probably represents metaphorical reference based on age.

**POM 258. **siʔ *youngster.*
   POP 814. *cʔi *C.* < POM **nsiʔ.
   PZn 4. *šiʔni *C.* < POM **siʔ.
   PCn 806. *si·ʔ¹ *youngster.* < POM **siʔ³.

Finally, a few forms appear to indicate the need to reconstruct a POM diminutive term which occurred with kinship terms.

**POM 428. **nkwan, **nwan *(diminutive).*
   POP 540. *mʔai-toi *CC.* < POM **nʔwan-Ysan.

PZn: PZ 10. *mba?du *young child.* < **POM** **nkwa-?tun.**
H kwál *C(L).* < **POM** **kwan-yV.**
PCM 206. *mba-ña *C.* < **POM** **nkwa-Yna.**

Summary of the Development of POM Parent and Child Terms

POM exhibited three parent and child categories—father, mother, and child—whose primary ranges of reference were *Pm, Pf,* and *C,* respectively. Because the parent and child terms which designate these kinsmen occurred with modifiers to designate lineal ancestors and descendents, as the following section will show, it is possible to consider them to have had extended lineal ranges as well; but such extended ranges are here treated as functions of the terms only when modified. A few modern reports appear to indicate that parent or child terms may be used generically for lineals of any distance from ego. This is particularly the case where grandparent terms—formerly self-reciprocal and ranging over both grandparent and grandchild kintypes—are reduced to nonreciprocal ranges, leaving only the child term to designate all direct descendents. In such cases, which are few in number and scattered throughout Otomanguean language families, a semantic shift characterizable as the addition of Rule L (=lineal extension) is here assumed to have taken place. Clearly, it may be argued that Rule L, in fact, already existed as a part of the definition of parent and child ranges in POM times.

It may also be argued that parent and child terms ranged over collateral kintypes, under certain conditions, in POM times; but the discussion of this question is postponed until the end of the discussion of all other POM consanguineal kinsmen, since it will involve not only parent and child terms, but grandkinsman and sibling terms as well.

Apart from these matters, then, POM parent and child terms show no significant change in their patterns of reference in modern Otomanguean languages which show remarkable stability in this regard. There may be one minor trend in Otomian languages toward marking the sex of children by separate elementary terms where other languages tend not to mark the distinction unless the context calls for it.

The three POM parent and child categories are, thus, straightforward and stable; but the lexicon which distinguishes these categories is complex. It would appear that separate terms were used in reference as opposed to direct address, although the question of whether vocative terms were borrowed from outside the language group since POM times must also be considered. The following summary of the distribution of lexical material since POM times assumes a late intrusion of **tata** and **nana** into Otomanguean, but that other vocative terms (specifically **POM 49** and **350**) are very early.

In regard to **tata** and **nana,** they enter Otomanguean vocabularies at an unknown but relatively late date, usually as vocative words for senior members of the community. In Ixcatec, Chocho, and some Mixtec, Otopamean, and Zapotec communities, they enter the kinship vocabulary as primary terms for father and mother. The majority of languages, however, continue to reflect POM parent terms.

The POM vocative term for father was **POM 49** **Ytah.** It continues in all families of Otomanguean except Zapotecan. In Mixtecan, it is restricted to Trique and Cuicatec, in Popolocan to Popoloc, and in Otopamean to Otomí. Only in Chinantecan does it remain primarily a vocative term, although the evidence is not clear for PCM, where it may be vocative since a second term does exist alongside it.

The POM term of reference for father was **POM 361** **kwin-yu-wa** (and its variants). In Mixtecan, it continues as the primary term for father only in those Mixtec languages which have not adopted **tata.** Only Mazatec attests it in Popolocan, only Pame, and Chichimec in Otopamean. Zapotecan, Chinantecan, and Chiapanec-Mangue attest it; Amuzgo, Huave, and Tlapanecan do not.

Of the four POM terms for mother, **POM 350 **ntaHn** (with its variants) was most likely the term used in direct address. It continues as the primary term—even in reference—in Popolocan, Zapotecan, Amuzgo, and Chiapanec-Mangue. It may also be the source of the Chinantecan vocative term for mother, but an alternate hypothesis leads the Chinantecan term back to **POM 148 **kwin** (and its alternants).

This last form is otherwise found as a term for mother only in Cuicatec and Otomí, and the association between the modern terms and their proposed source must be considered with continuing skepticism. The evidence is thin.

Two final terms for mother appear to be but inflectional variants of each other, namely, **POM 255 **siHn ~ **niHn** and **POM 340 **suhn ~ **nuhn.** POM 255 becomes the mother term in Trique, Central Pame, and Chichimeca-Jonaz. It also is found in two Chinantec languages, but not as a primary term of reference. POM 340 becomes the mother term in Mixtec, Chinantec, and Tlapanec.

It is not clear if one or another of the two POM terms for child, **POM 57 **ʔntan** and **POM 308 **Ynsan,** was a vocative term. Such may have been the case. Another possibility is that the two forms are inflectional variants of each other, but the relationship between the consonantisms of the two terms is not of the sort regularly exhibited by inflectional sets. **POM 308** continues as the child term in Mixtecan, Popoloc, Chocho, Chinantecan, and Chiapanec-Mangue. **POM 57** continues in Mazatec, Ixcatec, Otopamean, Tlapanecan, Chiapanec-Mangue, and Amuzgo, except that the Amuzgo term can also be the result of **POM 87 **tun,** which is also continued in Chinantecan as a word for *infant.*

POM Grandkinsman Term Reconstructions

There were two ways to refer to grandkinsmen in POM times. First, there was a set of two elementary terms which we will hereafter treat as the true POM grandkinsman terms. Second, there was a set of three terms—phrases really—based on parent and child terms with postposed modifier. While these phrases are believed to have been a viable part of the kinship system in POM times, they will be referred to as phrases in the interest of clarity and to distinguish them from the elementary terms.

The two elementary terms were self-reciprocal, one used between a senior male kinsman and his junior kinsman counterpart of either sex, and one used between a senior female kinsman and her junior kinsman counterpart of either sex. The primary kintypes of these two terms were thus *PPm* and *mCC* on the one hand and *PPf* and *fCC* on the other. The terms extended in reference to lineal kinsmen beyond the second generation from ego (presumably without limit) and to all collateral kinsmen other than ego's own generation or age peers; that is, either by Rule 2 or by Rule $e^2 0$.

In the material to follow, extension Rule 2 will be listed for these terms for the simple reason that it entails a more succinct notation than does $e^2 0$. It should become clear through an examination of the data, however, that the evidence is divided in regard to the underlying principle of seniority that was present in the POM system. A number of Otomanguean languages support the hypothesis that collateral kinsmen were divided, not strictly on the basis of genealogical generation, but rather into more loosely defined, relative age categories. It is perhaps impossible to determine with any certainty which of

these principles was actually in force in POM times, but the kind of social situation
which is most likely to have obtained in a nomadic or seminomadic condition certainly
would be more compatible with a loose relative age principle than to a strictly
genealogical one.

The two grandkinsman terms and the data supporting their reconstruction are as
follows:

POM 429. **seh, **hkeh *PPm(R,2)*.

   PMn 302. *Ɵeh, *xeh *PPm(1)*. < POM **seh, **hkeh.

   PMn 156. *Ɵe-ta?m, *xe-ngwe?m, *xe-kwe?m *PPf(1)*. < POM **se-ta?n, **hke-nkwe?n,
      **hke-kwe?n.

   PMn 303. *Ɵa?ya xani, *Ɵa?ya xe?num *CC(1)*. < POM **sa?ya hkani, **sa?ya hke?num.

   POP 818. *hę́m *PPm(R,2)*. < POM **hkehn.

   PZn: PZ 11. *pi-ši-yu *PPm(1,2)*. < POM **kwi-se-yu.

   H šéèč *PPm(e₂0)*. < POM **sinseh.

   PTl 4. *ši-?nu-u? *PPm(1)*. < POM **se?nu.

POM 430. **Ynsan, **Ynan PPf(R,2).

   POP 819. *to *PPf(R,2)*. < POM **nsan.

   PZn: PZ 12. *žusa *PPf(1,2)*. < POM **Ysu-nsan.

   PCn 452. *zia-²¹² *CC(y₂0)*. < POM **Ynsa.

   H nčéy *PPf(e₂0)*. < POM **Ynsa.

   PTl 5. *ši-nu-u? *PPf(1)*. < POM **si-nan.

   PTl 6. *ši-nu-V? *CC(1)*. < POM **si-nan.

Popolocan languages do not show direct reflexes of these terms, but three cases of
loans from sister Mixtecan languages seems to be the best explanation of the following
forms from Chiquihuitlán Mazatec (Q) and Western Popoloca (O):

Q: či³ky?³¹⁴ *PPf(L)*. < PC *či-ky?y < PMn *xe-kwe?m.

O: āpá sīnõ?nâ *PPm(L,S)*. < PC *duno < PMn *Ɵendu.

O: āmá sítá?nâ *PPf(L,S)*. < PM *Ɵitą < PMn *Ɵe-ta?m.

The extended ranges of the grandkinsman terms over senior and junior collateral
kintypes overlapped the ranges of POM sibling terms as they extended to certain of these
same senior and junior kintypes, depending upon particular social contexts or particular
purposes of POM speakers in those contexts. Senior and junior collateral kintypes
constituted, therefore, a no man's land or fuzzy area between the primary areas marked
by grandkinsman and sibling terms. In order to specify a kinsman as belonging to this in-
between area it was apparently possible to juxtapose the two sets of terms in phrases,
with one or another of the grandkinsman terms followed by a sibling term. This matter
will best be discussed in detail after the POM sibling terms have been introduced, but
suffice it to say here that reflexes of the male grandkinsman term showing an ultima
which reflects POM **nu or **yu are considered reflexes of such phrases.

PMn 303 is listed under the POM male grandkinsman term, but may actually reflect
both grandkinsman terms. Although the consonantism is not clearly correct, the form of
303 supported by PM may have its source in the female term, while PT and PC forms
come from the male term.

PCn 452 can derive from **t or **s, as can the ultima of POP 540 *m?ai-(h)-to CC(1), which accounts for Rensch having included them in POM 50 as stems with initial **t. With additional data available, however, it seems best to include them here as attesting to initial **s. (POP 540 is not listed separately here since it is included within the range of POP 819, a reflex of POM 428 **nkwan (diminutive) having been preposed to 819 to specify a junior kinsman.)

The second set of terms used in POM times to refer to certain grandkinsmen consisted of three phrases based on POM terms for father, mother, and child. Parent terms were modified by words meaning big or old, of which two reconstruct at the POM horizon, whereas the child term appears to have occurred in a phrase with itself in some sort of genitive construction (my child's child which in POM would be, more literally, his/her-child my-child), although this is not certain. If the grandchild term was not of this type, the source of the modifier is not clear, although it bears a close similarity with the man's term for brother in some languages.

POM 189 and 423 represent the two terms which modified parent terms to designate grandparents. POM 50 represents the full phrase which makes up the grandchild term (but note that this interpretation of POM 50 differs considerably from the set postulated by Rensch).

POM 189. **kwe?n², **ke?n big, old.
   PMn 156. *xi-ngwe?m, *xi-kwe?m PPf(l). < POM **hke-nkwe?n, **hke-kwe?n.
   PPn 359. *hča¹ big, old. < POM **Yhken.
   PZn: I naro?ba? big. < POM **?kwen.
   PZn 6. *š-yu-zi gula PPm(L), PZn 7. *ši-na?a gula PPf(L). < *gwV-la < POM **kwen-ya.
   PCn 129. *ka-? big (plural). < POM **ke?n.
   PCn 336. *hwə-?³² big (singular). < POM **hkwe?n².
   A co¹tyá¹ cǫ¹tkie² PPm(L), co¹ñtɔ̃³ cǫ¹tkie² PPf(L). < POM **Yken.
   PTl 7. *aga? big. < POM **nke?n.
   PCM 277. *aka big. < POM **ken.
POM 423. **nu, **yu big, old.
   PMn 275. *ka?num big. < POM **ka-?nun.
   PMn 305. *tata Өa?nu, *tata ya?nu, *tata xa?nu PPm(1). < POM **sa-?nu, **ya-?nu, **hka-?nu.
   PZn: PCh 70. *ka·lu to grow; PCh: T tonų, tlyu big. < POM **nyu, **nun, **nyun.
   PCn 765. *yu·? old (male). < POM **yu?.
   PCn 766. *tiá²yu·?², *ŋiu?-yu·?², *hmi·¹yu·?² PPm(e₂0). < POM **yu?.
POM 50. **?ntan³ Yhntah³ CC(L).
   PPn 360. *?ntye¹ ntai⁴, *chǫ⁴ ntai⁴ CC(L). < *ntahi < POM **Yhntah³.
   A hntá² ka²ñthɔ̃² CC(L). < POM **hntan³ Yhntah³.

These grandkinsman phrases are considered to have designated a special subset of parents and children. We may presume, as discussed above in the section dealing with parent and child terms, that the primary ranges of parent and child terms were Pm, Pf, and C. Whether or not the unmodified parent and child terms were ever used in reference to more distantly related lineal kinsmen, the extended ranges defined by application of Rule L to these primary categories may be considered extended parent and child ranges to which specific reference can be made by use of the postposed modifiers. This may be summarized as follows:

father term	$Pm(L)$
mother term	$Pf(L)$
child term	$C(L)$
father term + modifier	$PPm(L)$
mother term + modifier	$PPf(L)$
child term + modifier	$CC(L)$

Summary of The Development of POM Grandkinsman Terms

The earliest POM grandkinsman terms were two in number. One term was used reciprocally between a grandfather and his grandchildren of either sex; the other between a grandmother and her grandchildren of either sex. Both terms extended lineal without limit and collaterally to kinsmen one or more generations (or age categories) from ego by Rule 2 (or Rule e^20). Junior grandkinsman could be specified by preposing a diminutive to either grandkinsman term. Collateral kinsman could be specified by postposing a sibling term to either grandkinsman term.

Sometime later, the self-reciprocal character of these terms began to deteriorate and in some languages was completely lost. It is probable that this shift was a direct result of another semantic shift, namely, that in some languages the principle *sex of senior kinsman* began to shift to *sex of kinsman*, always marking the sex of alter regardless of the relative age of ego and alter. That is, whereas previously each term was used reciprocally (by Rule R) between a senior kinsman of a particular sex and his or her junior kinsman of either sex, now a term denoted a senior kinsman of a particular sex or a junior kinsman of that same sex (by Rule I). At a still later date, the distinction between the two terms became confused in reference to grandchildren under the influence of the more general pattern in POM of not distinguishing the sex of younger kinsmen. The diminutive forms of the grandkinsman terms, then, began to range over the same kintypes in complete competition with each other. These two shifts may be presented graphically as follows:

	POM TIMES		POST-POM TIMES	
grandfather term	PPm	$<$	PPm	$< PPm$
grandmother term	PPf	$<$	PPf	$< PPf$
diminutive + grandfather term	mCC	$<$	CCm	$< CC$
diminutive + grandmother term	fCC	$<$	CCf	$< CC$

Grandmothers have more to do with grandchildren than do grandfathers. The grandchild term based on the grandmother term, therefore, had greater survival potential, and the term based on the grandfather term was accordingly lost everywhere except in Mixtecan; and there it apparently only survived in Trique and Cuicatec. The remaining grandchild term was also lost in Popolocan and Amuzgo, but appears to have survived as the grandchild term everywhere else.

The loss of both grandchildren terms in Popolocan and Amuzgo is merely a function of the complete loss of the two grandkinsman terms for grandparents in those languages as well, presumably in competition with the phrases based on parent and child terms, and possibly as a result of the confusion which accompanied these semantic shifts. Chinantecan also lost the terms in reference to senior grandkinsmen, although it seems to have hung on to the grandmother term in reference to grandchild.

Only Otopamean continues to the present with direct reflexes of the self-reciprocal terms according to their original definition, but Zapotecan appears to have made a successful shift from *sex of senior kinsman* to *sex of kinsman* without moving on, in all languages, to distinguishing the sex of only senior kinsman.

Mixtecan languages show an additional lexical innovation not found elsewhere in regard to the grandfather term. For some unknown reason, a phrase develops based on the grandfather term (it would seem) and a postposed modifier. Mixtec shows a modifier meaning *big* or *old*. Chinantecan gives evidence of an adjective meaning *old* as being inflected differently for male and female referent. It may be that the form reflected in Trique and Cuicatec was also a feminine form, since the phrase of which it is a part replaces the POM grandmother term in PMn with the result that an unmodified reflex of the POM grandfather term continues in PMn as the grandfather term, while a modified reflex of that same grandfather term becomes the PMn grandmother term.

Finally, the collateral ranges of the grandkinsman terms gradually became more rigidly defined along the lines of genealogical generation, in some languages, and were reduced in some cases to include only kinsmen of two or more generations distance from ego. In formal terms, if we assume Rule e^20 to be the best representation of how the original POM grandkinsman terms extended collaterally, this rule was replaced by Rule 2 everywhere except in Chinantecan and Huave, and eventually by Rule 1 in Mixtecan and Tlapanecan.

All the time these changes were taking place in the elementary terms for grandkinsmen and the phrases based upon them, they were in competition with phrases based on parent and child terms in reference to lineal ancestors and descendents. If this hypothesis is correct, such phrases have continued without semantic change down to the present, except in Chinantecan where they have lexically replaced the grandkinsman terms in reference to grandparents, but have taken over the larger extended ranges of the latter.

As mentioned above, these phrases have also completely replaced the grandkinsman terms in Popolocan and Amuzgo, but without a change in extended ranges of reference. In Mixtecan, they have not been so successful, replacing the original elementary terms in some of the modern languages, but the latter survived well into PM, PT, and PC times and into the present in some cases. In those places where the phrases have taken over, their extended ranges of reference vary from that expressed by Rule L to that of Rule 1. Zapotecan languages also show the co-existence of the phrases with the elementary terms, and the tradition of extension by Rule L remains strong for these phrases.

Within the Otopamean group, Otomian languages have lost both the elementary terms and the phrases based on parent terms in reference to grandparents. In their place, they have adopted loan words of which ***tita** and ***nita** are representative (see the POP chapter for further pairs). These terms presumably extended to collaterals by Rule 2, according to data from Mazahua, but have gradually reduced their ranges to extension by Rule 1 and even by Rule L in the various Otomí languages.

As the reflexes of POM extended ranges of reference for grandkinsmen were gradually reduced from e^20, to *2,* to *1,* and to *L* in the various daughter languages, they also became more rigidly defined in genealogical terms and more discrete in respect to the ranges of other terms for collateral kinsmen, no longer overlapping them as they formerly did. The sibling terms were, at the same time, suffering the same sort of redefinition and reduction in range as former phrases were lexicalized to specify new categories of senior and junior collateral kinsmen. The details of these changes are discussed below in the section on the development of POM sibling terms.

There is one other curious occurrence of similar forms for grandkinsmen as far from each other in time and location as among the Mazahua and the North Puebla Mixtec. The Mazahua use a term **ande** ~ **lande,** for *grandparent* which does not distinguish the sex of kinsman—an unusual situation for senior kinsman. The North Puebla Mixtec use a similar term, **lante,** for precisely the same kinsmen. A specialist in the history of Spanish will perhaps be able to help us with this situation, since we must assume these usages are corruptions of colloquial Spanish usage during the colonial period. It may be that the source is *los antepasados* (forebears).

POM Sibling Term Reconstructions

The reconstruction of POM sibling terms and a corresponding system of reference presents many obstacles. There is a good deal of similarity between modern systems within the group, and yet the diversity is sufficient to provide a variety of potential hypotheses concerning the nature of the source system. Certain aspects can be affirmed with considerable confidence. It is clear, for example, that seniority, in the form of relative age, was discriminated by at least some of the sibling terms. It is also apparent that the relative sex of ego and alter was diagnostic of some of the terms. There was at least one very generic term which marked the sibling relationship without narrowing the focus by sex or seniority. The problem lies in defining which terms, at the POM horizon, were associated with each of these principles of classification. The terms are presented below with one possible interpretation, but other alternatives are possible which would change the details.

POM 61 ****ta?n** can be interpreted as a POM sibling term in its own right. It does also appear in many modern languages, however, as a more general term for *companion, fellow, twin,* and similar concepts. The assumption is here made that ****ta?n** competed with a generic term for sibling in POM times in the sense of having been used in many contexts where the sibling term would give very nearly the same connotation, but that it was not strictly speaking a term for designating a genealogical relationship. As the POM system changed over time, some of the daughter languages incorporated reflexes of ****ta?n** into the kinship system in one way or another. The kinship-term reflexes of this word are as follows:

POM 61. **ta?n *PC(0).*
> **PMn 161. *ta?m** *PC(G).* < POM ****ta?n.**
> **PMn 156. *Ɵe-ta?m** *PPf(1).* < POM ****se-ta?n.**
> **PPn: H nco¹** *yPC(0).* < ***nsi-ta?u** < POM ****nsi-hta?n.**
> **POP 377. *khǫ-a-ta-m** *emPCm(G).* < POM ****kuhn-wa-ta?n.**
> **POP 387. *?i-ta-m** *efPCm(G).* < POM ****?ya-ta?n.**
> **PZn: PCh 304. *i-ta?a** *PC(0).* < POM ****Yhta?** or ****Ytah.**
> **PCn 758. *ru·?n** *PC(0).* < POM ****Yta?n.**
> **A tyhɔ¹², tyhe³²** *yPC(0).* < POM ****Yhta.**
> **PTl 12. *gi?ta-V?** *yPC(G).* < POM ****nki?-ta.**

Huautla **nco¹** is the only term in the PPn family which seems to fit this set, and it only fits with a fairly innovative derivation based on the supposition that ****ta?n** developed in PPn on the analogy of (or parallel to) the sister term to be presented below which shows the derivation ***khau** < ***kahu** < ****hkahn.** PP ***au** does yield H **o,** but whether or not H **nc** can result from ***nsi-t** by loss of the vowel has not been demonstrated.

The POM source of PCn *r is not known. **PCn 758,** therefore, may or may not fit here. Both it and the Amuzgo term are also discussed below as possibly fitting the second POM sibling term.

The true POM sibling term has alternants with ****u** and with ****i**. They are presented as set **159** since some of its reflexes were assigned this number by Rensch (1976), but the interpretation of the set is somewhat different from that which Rensch gave it. The reflexes which attest ****u** are presented first.

POM 159. **kuHn *PC(0).*
PMn 38. *ku?n-gwi *fPCf(G).* < POM ****ku?n-kwin.**
POP 376. *khǫ-hoe *efPCf(G).* < POM ****kuhn-kwin.**
POP 377. *khǫ-a-ta-m *emPCm(G).* < POM ****kuhn-wa-ta?n.**
POP 821. *kǫi *PC(G).* < *kǫ-wi < POM ****kuhn.**
H kóh *ePC(0).* < POM ****kuh.**
PCM 110. *ma-ngu, *ma-mba *PC(G).* < POM ****nku, **nkwen.**

PCn and A terms were discussed above as possibly belonging to this set. The uncertain source of PCn *r and the complex consonantal onset of the Amuzgo term preclude certainty at this time, but the following alternate derivations are presented for consideration.

PCn 758. *ru·?n *PC(0).* < POM ****nsi-ku?n.**
A tyhɔ¹², tyhe³² *yPC(0).* < *ci-hku < POM ****nsi-kuhn.**

The reflexes of this term which attest ****i** are as follows:

POM 159a. **nsi-kihn,·**kihn-si *yPC(0).*
PPn 361. *cikhị, *kici *PC(0).* < POM ****nsi-kihn, **kin-si.**
PZn: PZ 17. *biči? *mPCm(G).* < POM ****kwi-nsi.**
PZn: PZ l8. *šiči *PPCm(I,G).* < POM ****se-nsi.**
H čîग *yPC(0).* < *ci-gi < POM ****nsin-ki.**
PTl 12. *gi?ta-V? *yPC(G).* < POM ****kihn-ta.**

Note that **PPn 361** attests two terms which are here interpreted as (1) the ****i** form of **POM 159** with a preposed element and (2) a permutation of the term and this same element, now postposed. **PZ 17** and **H** further support the existence of such alternate sequencing of material. (PZ 18 is included here for later reference as a possible adaptation of the sibling term to designate senior and junior collateral kinsmen.)

If the interpretation of **POM 159a** as two reversible elements is correct, it would appear that both elements had a certain degree of independence in their ability to enter into syntactic relation with one another. It is not probable that the form here represented as ****nsi** was merely an inflectional element, even though the occurrence of such a form preposed to a number of other kinship terms does lend credence to such an interpretation. While it is by no means certain, it may be that this element is to be associated with **POM 258 **si?** *youngster* to mark the term as referring to a junior kinsman. It may also be that such a term was phonologically similar to but, in fact, different from a preposed inflectional element occurring with other kinship terms, and that its position as modifier of **159** provided the phonological context which triggered the alternation from ****u** to ****i**.

Another possibility is that preposed **nsi is inflectional while postposed **nsi is POM 258. As can be seen, while there are phonological details which remain to be worked out in regard to these terms, the evidence is fairly good that two closely related terms did exist, one occurring with a preposed or postposed element. The question of kinship reference of these terms is also subject to some uncertainty, but the best hypothesis would appear to be that POM 159 **kuHn, when unmodified, designated any collateral kinsman in a very generic sense, with sibling *(PC)* as its primary denotation. At the same time, it served as the reciprocal of a set of terms (to be introduced below) which specifically referred to senior siblings and other collateral kinsmen. In such a context, it had the more restricted de facto ranges y*PC(0)*.

It is at this point that POM 159a comes into play. The modifier occurring with the fronted form **kihn can be interpreted as a diminutive (perhaps related to POM 258 **si? *youngster*) and the phonological context which triggered the shift forward from **u to **i. The interplay of **kuHn with terms for elder siblings created situations in which the desire to specify a junior kinsman required the addition of such a modifier. Itself a substantive, **si? could occur freely with the sibling term in an appositive function either as the first or second element of a phrase, thus accounting for alternative orderings of the two elements.

Three POM sibling terms designated elder siblings and corresponding more distantly related collateral kinsmen. These three terms, in addition to designating senior kinsmen as the reciprocal of **kuHn in its more restricted sense (and especially when modified by a diminutive), also marked sex of ego and alter in the pattern which Murdock (1970:175) has designated Jivaran. First, a term used between male kinsmen exhibits alternants in **t, **n, and **y, as well as vowel fronting from **u to **i. Inasmuch as Rensch follows Longacre in associating reflexes of this term with POM 423 **nu, **yu *big,* it is so listed here.

POM 423. **tu, **nu, **yu *emPCm(0)*.
    PMn 24. *Θi-?num *mPCm(G)*. < POM **se-?num.
    PMn 275. *Θi-ndu, *Θa-?ndu *emPPCm(I,G)*. < POM **se-ntu, **sa-?ntu.
    PPn 362. *nci?i, *sa?u *ePCm(G)*. < POM **nsi?ni, **sa?nu.
    PPn 363. *ci³ni³ *ePPCm(I,1)*. < POM **nsini.
    POP 189. *n?io-i *emPCm(G)*. < *n?iu-wi < POM **Y?nu.
    PZn: PZ 11. *pi-ši-yu *PPm(I,2)*. < POM **kwi-se-yu.
    PCn 810. *ɲiu *emPCm(0)*. < POM **nkin-yu.
    A šiɔ²¹, šió² *ePCm(0)*. < POM **si-yu.
    PTl 8. *ji-yo-u? *mPCm*. < POM **si-yu.

POM 236 represents a term used between female siblings and female collateral kinsmen. Only PPn 84 of Rensch's original set is included in this revision of the set.

POM 236. **kwaHn, **kaHn *efPCf(0)*.
    PMn 182. *kwa?-wa *aPCb(G)* < POM **kwa?n-wa.
    PPn 84. *kHwa³ *ePPCf(I,1)*. < POM **kwaHn.
    PPn 364. *kahu *ePCf(G)*. < POM **hkahn.
    PZn: PZ 19. *bela, *žila *fPCf(G)*. < POM **kwan-ya, **nsin-ya.
    A šhɔ²¹ *ePCf(0)*. < *šuhɔ < POM **kwaHn.
    PTl 10. *j-we?-gu-u? *fPCf*. < POM **nsi-kwa?n-kuhn.

Finally, **POM 431** was used between siblings and collateral kinsmen of the opposite sex.

POM 431. **nsi-ʔya *eaPCb(0).*
 PMn: PC 12. *diʔya *efPPCm(I,G).* < **POM **si-ʔya.**
 POP 378. *ʔi-ta-m *efPCm(G).* < **POM **ʔya-taʔn.**
 PZn: PZ 21. *bi-zaʔ-na *aPCb(G).* < ***ku-zi-aʔ** < **POM **kuhn-si-ʔya.**
 PCn 231. *ʔiạ-³¹³ *eaPCb(0).* < **POM **ʔyahn.**
 PTl 9. *diya-Vʔ *fPCm.* < **POM **nsi-ʔya.**

The proposed derivational history of **PZ 21** is frankly, a shot in the dark, assuming palatal movement to the left and reinterpretation of ****kuhn** to **PZ *kwi** which is preposed to many kinship terms and related to a PZ form meaning *person.*

All POM sibling terms are considered to have had *PC* as their primary range, but to have extended to all collaterals in a manner best characterized by application of Rule 0. There is, of course, some evidence that sibling terms were restricted to kinsmen of ego's generation since some Otomanguean families exhibit sibling terms with extended ranges best characterized by Rule G; but the essentially different social context of sedentary societies in Mexico today must be considered to have had a profound effect on this matter since the time of the nomadic or seminomadic existence of small POM hunting and gathering bands.

Modern Otomanguean systems appear in most instances to have fairly discrete categories of kinsmen without very much overlap of membership between categories, but even in modern times this is not entirely the case. In POM times, it is to be assumed that small nomadic or seminomadic bands functioned more effectively with a flexible scheme which provided alternative means of classifying a kinsman of a particular kintype, depending upon the particular requirements of a particular situation. This is, in fact, the known situation in some contemporary lowland South American cultures, as for example the Dení of Brazil (Koop and Lingenfelter, in press). With this consideration in mind, along with the direct evidence from several Otomanguean sources that the wider range characterized by Rule 0 is indicated, these terms are considered to have extended as a generic term to all collateral kinsmen.

In summary, POM exhibits four sibling terms. One very generic term extends to all collateral kinsmen, but does double duty in serving as reciprocal for three Jivaran terms which designate senior collateral kinsmen. The generic term can be modified, when required, to specify a junior kinsman. A fifth word for companion was also used in kinship contexts in competition with the generic term for sibling.

POM 159. **kuHn *PC(0);* ***nsi-kihn**, ****kihn-si** *yPC(0).*
 POM 423. **tu, ****nu**, ****yu** *emPCm(0).*
 POM 236. **kwaHn, ****kaHn** *efPCf(0).*
 POM 431. **nsi-ʔya *eaPCb(0).*
 POM 61. **taʔn *companion, PC(0).*

One final note before moving on to summarize how these terms developed in the Otomanguean daughter languages. The above interpretation is put forward as the POM system for classifying siblings, and further discussion is based upon it. Nevertheless, there are other alternative possibilities which have merit, two of which will be mentioned here as hypotheses deserving further study.

The first hypothesis concerns the principle of seniority. In the analysis above, seniority is a factor in all the terms since even generic **159** (and its companion **61**) double as reciprocals of the senior sibling terms. The complexity of this relationship argues against its plausibility. Further study should look at the hypothesis that, at some stage, the Jivaran terms did not in fact mark seniority, but that a second set of terms (the so-called generic ones here) did. This hypothesis is directly supported by Huave and Tlapanec. The configuration would then be:

Set One: *mPCm(0), fPCf(0), aPCb(0)*.
Set Two: *ePC(0), yPC(0)*.

The second hypothesis concerns the number of terms which mark sex of ego and alter. A Jivaran pattern of three terms has been proposed for POM, but a Quechuan pattern of four is supported by POP and PTl. This hypothesis has been rejected for the present largely on the basis of the fact that the POP terms in question appear to show the marks of innovation through compounding (as do the PTl terms for that matter). The question of seniority apart, the configuration for POM might then have been:

mPCm(0), fPCm(0), fPCf(0), mPCf(0).

Summary of The Development of POM Sibling Terms

Almost all families of Otomanguean retain traces of the POM generic sibling term. Mixtecan and Chatino (of Zapotecan) do so by adopting the companion term **POM 61 **ta?n** for this function. Otopamean, Chinantecan, Amuzgo, and Chiapanec-Mangue retain **159 **kuHn** directly (though PCn and A reflexes may also be interpreted as the result of **POM 61**), while Popolocan retains reflexes of the diminutive forms ****nsi-kihn** and ****kihn-si**. Huautla Mazatec may also reflect **POM 61** as a term for younger sibling, while Otopamean utilizes it to restructure its Jivaran pattern of terms to Quechuan. Huave and Tlapanecan reflect both ****kuHn** and its diminutive forms in pairs of terms which distinguish elder and younger siblings, with Tlapanecan possibly incorporating **61** as an ending for its junior term. The Zapotec languages are alone in not retaining a generic term for POM.

The Jivaran pattern is maintained intact in modern Mixtec and Zapotec languages, and survived into PCn times but was lost in modern Chinantec languages where systems of sibling reference have collapsed almost completely or have been reduced to an Algonkian pattern of three terms; *ePCm, ePCf, yPC* (Murdock 1970:174), also found in Popolocan and Amuzgo. Otopamean and Tlapanecan combined terms into phrases to devise a Quechuan pattern of four terms: *mPCm, fPCm, fPCf, mPCf*.

POM sibling terms also played a role in the development of separate terms for senior and junior collateral kinsmen as distinct from siblings. This matter is discussed in detail in the next section.

The Development of Other POM Collateral Kinsman Terms

Collateral kinsmen other than those of ego's generation do not appear to have constituted a major class of kinsmen in POM times in the sense of there having been a separate and distinct set of terms to denote them. There is evidence, however, that certain senior and junior collateral kinsmen were distinguished at an early date from siblings by the use of modified parent or modified sibling terms. The evidence is not strong enough to assure that the early date in question is in fact the POM horizon, since there appears to have been continuing influence between separate Otomanguean families for a long time after their separation into several distinct language communities (Rensch 1973); but the evidence from PMn and POP, in particular, supports the hypothesis that separate categories began to be well established by these intermediate time horizons.

All of the lexical material for this collateral terminology has been introduced above in conjunction with the discussion of parent-child and sibling terms to facilitate the identification of those associations. In this section, it is reintroduced in a slightly different arrangement to facilitate an understanding of the way this area of kinship vocabulary developed from primary terms. A number of OM families, of course, do not provide evidence for ever having distinguished these senior and junior collaterals from siblings, namely: Chinantecan, Amuzgo, Huave, and Chiapanec-Mangue. Evidence from the five remaining families within our corpus is presented in Figure 4.

Looking first at the Otopamean material, inflected forms of POM father and mother terms are seen to have developed into two pairs of new terms to distinguish POP parallel and cross, male and female, first-ascending-generation kinsmen and corresponding first-descending-generation kinsmen (by Rule R). The underlying parent terms referred, in their primary senses, to kinsmen of the first ascending generation, requiring additional modifiers to designate more distantly related kinsmen (by Rule L). The new terms for collaterals did not adopt lineal extension in POP, building rather on the primary sense of the parent terms and extending only collaterally by Rule G. The self-reciprocalization of these new terms was the natural result of their encroachment into the extended ranges of earlier POM self-reciprocal grandparent terms.

These terms for collaterals, in Otopamean, are the only ones in Otomanguean which give any hint at all of bifurcate categories based on the sex of a linking kinsman, the evidence coming entirely from Central Pame and the seventeenth-Century Otomí data from Ecker. It is tempting to pounce upon these hints as all the evidence needed to show that POM also displayed such categories, and some might even wish to go further (as has been done in the past on much less information) to suggest the early presence of a unilinear (perhaps Omaha) system. But the evidence is insufficient to firmly support any such hypotheses without first assessing the possible influence of Utoaztecan, or that of other neighboring language communities which may have interacted with early Otomangueans at the northern frontiers of their expanding society. It is quite likely that northern Otomangueans—some Otopameans in particular—continued a nomadic or seminomadic existence for a much longer period of time than other Otomangueans, due to differences in their ecological setting which may have not provided the same incentives for shifting to the more settled horticultural way of life being adopted in the south. If bifurcate categories were not already recognized by these northern bands, their continuing context of hunting and gathering and interaction with similar groups of nonOtomangueans with bifurcate kinship systems could have provided the context for such a development by them.

Now turning to Mixtecan, we immediately see that the POP mother's brother and mother's sister terms find very convincing cognates in PMn, but that the other two PMn terms appear to derive from sibling terms, possibly postposed to reflexes of the POM grandkinsman term **429 **seh, **hkeh** *PPm(R,2)*. The possible causes for this development in PMn are presented below in the discussion of PMn sibling terms, but are quickly

Figure 4. The Development of POM Senior and Junior Collateral Terms.

POM	PMn	PPn	POP	PZn	PTl
Pm: **kwin,**kin,**win		yPCC(I,1) *ka?me	=PPCm(R,G) *mo		PPCm(G) *a-ma-u?
	emPPCf(I,R,1) *Θu-?we		xPPCm(R,G) *?oe		
Pf: **sihn,**nihn	efPPCf(I,R,l) *Θi-Θi		=PPCf(R,G) *ci-ci	PPCf(I,1) *š-ni-su	PPCf(G) *ni-yu-i?
kwin,kin,**win			xPPCf(R,G) *hi		
emPCm(0): **tu,**nu,**yu	emPPCm(I,R,1) *Θe-tu	ePPCm(I,1) *ci³ni³			
efPCf(0): **kwaHn,**kaHn		ePPCf(I,1) *kahu			
eaPCb(0): **nsi-?ya	efPPCm(I,R,1) *Θe-?ya				
yPC(0): **nsi-kihn				PPCm(I,1) *ši-či	

outlined here. Note first that POM father and mother terms of identical form have been proposed (**kwin, **kin, **win). These were certainly not completely identical in POM times, but were apparently close enough in some of their contexts to have been the source of confusion. One result of this confusion was the reinterpretation of *?we to denote a female kinsman by preposing a reflex of POM 340 **suhn, **nuhn *female* (which also apparently is postposed to aunt terms in PZn and PTl). A second result was the loss of any reflex of **kwin, **kin, **win as a father term in PMn and the need to coin new terms for senior male collaterals from the grandfather and postposed sibling terms.

Although four terms for senior collaterals (and their junior reciprocals) are well supported in Mixtecan, there is no evidence that sex of linking kinsman was a diagnostic feature of the system, as in Otopamean. The hypothesis that sex of ego developed (along with sex of alter) in PMn to define four aunt and uncle categories rests primarily on the contemporary presence in Cuicatec of separate men and women's terms for uncle.

Finally, while POP evidence supports a definition of seniority tied to genealogical distance by generations, some Mixtec languages retain traces of seniority defined by age relative to ego (the interaction here of *e* and Rule I) and, therefore, the lineal as well as collateral extension of the terms by Rule 1, rather than just collateral extension by Rule G as in POP.

Tlapanecan shows fairly convincing cognates of parent terms as new aunt and uncle terms, while corresponding Popolocan terms appear to derive from sibling terms. None of these terms shows signs of having been self-reciprocal, unless the Popolocan term for junior collateral is the result of the aunt term with diminutive ending rather than harking back to a parent term. The Zapotecan term for aunt can be the result of POM mother terms; but the uncle term, if it does hark back to any of the sources being discussed here, can only come from the POM younger sibling term, not a particularly convincing possibility. Zapotecan evidence does, however, support self-reciprocal ranges (by Rule I) for these terms.

In summary, then, five Otomanguean families attest the development of separate categories of senior and junior collaterals, but do not show consistent enough sources to convince us that a common POM pattern has given rise to them. The confusing array of alternate treatments of collateral kinsmen as a whole, including siblings, indicates a good deal of instability in this area for a long time and much innovation. A single hypothesis is adopted for the purposes of this presentation, but any number of alternatives continue to merit further consideration.

POM Affinal Term Reconstructions

POM data attest a very elementary system for classifying affinal kinsmen, indicating the probable absence of any real emphasis upon distinguishing subclasses of kinsmen related through marriage. A few modern languages in the group exhibit fairly large inventories of affinal terms, but these all appear to be innovations and are so treated in the absence of clear comparative evidence to demonstrate their antiquity.

It is not really possible at present to propose a POM affinal system with any degree of confidence, but a suggestion is made which at least will be a starting point for future study. A number of generalizations can be made which are the basis for such a suggestion.

First of all, the primary kintypes which need to be considered are *SP* and *CS*. Only Otopamean and Zapotecan languages show elementary terms for collateral affinals and these two traditions do not appear to be cognate. The majority of Otomanguean languages either extend the parent-in-law and child-in-law terms to collateral affinals, with or without the use of modifiers, or utilize terms borrowed from Spanish to denote such kinsmen. Secondly, two phonological forms turn up repeatedly, having the kernel forms *ka and *sa, respectively. There is sufficient phonological similarity in these forms to suggest that they represent variously inflected forms of two POM affinal terms. Thirdly, elementary terms distinguish children-in-law by sex more frequently than parents-in-law; and finally, two Otomanguean families attest to self-reciprocal parent-in-law and child-in-law terms, with Huave clearly marking sex of only the junior member of these dyads.

On the basis of these generalizations, I suggest that POM had just two affinal terms, with primary ranges *CSm(R)* and *CSf(R)*, respectively. The two terms probably extended widely to other affinals, at least by Rule 2, but in the absence of clearer evidence I leave the extension unlimited (by Rule 0). The proposed cognate sets are as follows:

POM 432. **kah *CSm(R,0)*.
  PMn 137. *kahΘa *CSm(2)*. < POM **kahsa.
  PPn 124. *čha⁴, *ʔča¹ *SP(2)*. < POM **Ykah, **Yʔka.
  PPn 263. *kha⁴ʔnta³ *CS(2)*. < POM **kah-ʔnta¹/².
  PCn 814. *ŋá· *CSm(y0)*. < POM **nkahn.
  A šę³ *SP(0)*. < POM **Yʔkahn.
  A lko² *CSm(0)*. < POM **Ykan.
  H òkwáàc *CSm(R,L)*. < POM **kahnsa.
  PTl 17. *hmegu-iʔ *SPm*. < POM **hnwin-kan.
  PTl 18. *žagu-iʔ *SPf*. < POM **Ynsan-kan.

POM 433. **nsan, **nyan *CSf(R,0)*.
  PMn 276. *xanam *CSf(2)*. < POM **nan.
  PMn 309. *xihΘam *SP(2)*. < POM **san.
  PPn 124. *čha⁴, *ʔča¹ *SP(2)*. < POM **Ynsah, **Yʔnsa.
  POP 827. *n-toe-ca *mCSf(R)*. < POM **ntan-win-nsa.
  PCn 812. *zá·¹²ŋiuʔ, *zá·¹²hmi·¹ *SPm(L)*. < POM **nsah³.
  PCn 815. *lá· *CSf(y0)*. < POM **nyah.
  A šę³ *SP(0)*. < POM **Ysahn.
  A n¹nca² *CSf(0)*. < POM **n-nsa.
  H ápìw *CSf(R,L)*. < POM **kwan.
  PTl 18. *žagu-iʔ *SPf*. < POM **Ynsan-kan.

PCn 812 is listed as a possible reflex of the daughter-in-law term; but if this is so, it was subsequently reinterpreted as **PCn 445** *zá·²¹ *male* and a corresponding mother-in-law term was coined analogically from **PCn 280** *mĩ¹ *female*. It is more likely that the two parent-in-law terms were coined at the same time as Rule R was being lost from the child-in-law terms in Chinantec.

Since both PPn *č and Amuzgo *š can result either from POM **s or **k in certain contexts, **PPn 124** and **A šę³** are listed in both sets above to indicate two possible derivations or even perhaps, coalescence of the two terms in reference to spouse's parents. **POP 827** is listed as a reflex of the daughter-in-law term, but its paraphrastic form probably dates only back to the Otopamean horizon which argues against its relevance here. Huave ápìw is even less likely a reflex of the daughter-in-law term, but is included as a very slim possibility to be studied further in light of known stem alternations between POM **kw, **y, and **s.

Summary of The Development of POM Affinal Terms

It is entirely possible that external influence has obliterated the evidence of a more complex POM system for classifying affinal kinsmen, but if the picture we have been able to put together is at all valid, it would seem that little attention was given to distinguishing varieties of affinals. Such a situation does not appear to be inconsistent with the probable needs of small, highly mobile bands of the sort we are undoubtedly speaking. The differences between father-in-law, brother-in-law, and son-in-law were undoubtedly real and their roles distinguishable both socially and terminologically when the occasion demanded, but complex institutions demanding a high degree of attention to such distinctions did not probably exist at the earliest horizon of our study.

The self-reciprocal ranges of the terms paralleled similar usage between consanguineal kinsmen and, so, was not unusual. The fact that the sex of the junior member of the dyad was marked, rather than that of the senior member if we are correct in giving such weight to the Huave data at this point, is a unique pattern; but there is probably no profound conclusion to be drawn from it. Self-reciprocal ranges gradually gave way to lexicalized differences in terms for spouse's kinsman and kinsman's spouse, differences which in their earlier form were merely inflectional accoutrements to mark sex, seniority, affection, or respect. In the process of this shift, the several Otomanguean families developed their own unique systems.

The reciprocal form of the daughter-in-law term appears to have been extended to all parents-in-law without reference to sex of ego in Mixtec, while the son-in-law term appears to have been so extended in Tlapanec. In Amuzgo and Popolocan, the present parent-in-law terms can derive equally well from either of the two child-in-law terms, so that it is not clear which they hark back to. As mentioned above, it is possible that they represent a phonological coalescence of the two terms with only minor reshaping. The parent-in-law terms in Zapotec languages are clear innovations with a shift to four descriptive phrases which employ parent terms and reference to spouse. Chinantec probably also represents a unique innovation, although the father-in-law term is phonologically close to the daughter-in-law term. Similarly, Otopamean develops a completely new set of terms, four in all, each self-reciprocal and marking sex of both ego and alter.

Zapotec and Otopamean also develop special sibling-in-law terms, three Jivaran terms in Zapotec and four Quechuan terms in Otopamean, matching the Jivaran and Quechuan patterns for classifying siblings in those languages. Other languages adopt Spanish terms for sibling-in-law and reduce the ranges of the original terms accordingly.

Son-in-law continues to be distinguished from daughter-in-law in all modern languages, although lexical replacement does occur in Otopamean, Zapotecan, and Tlapanecan. Popolocan loses the daughter-in-law term, replacing it with an inflected form of the son-in-law term.

POM Spouse Term Reconstructions

While Proto Mixtecan, Proto Zapotecan, and Proto Chinantecan all support a special term for spouse which is used reciprocally between the two members of the spouse dyad, without marking sex of husband or wife, they do so in separate and noncognate traditions which do not provide the necessary assurances that such a term existed at the POM horizon. At the same time, these three families of languages also exhibit the special use of more generic words meaning *male* and *female* to denote husband and wife, respectively, when inflected for person of possessor as do all other families of

Otomanguean languages. It is therefore suggested that at least the latter pattern was present at the POM horizon.

As was indicated above in the discussion of parent terms, a variety of POM forms are proposed as having such general reference to male and female persons, all of which seem to play a role in naming parents and certain collateral kinsmen within POM. These same terms appear as terms for husband and wife also. Three such terms receive fairly even support as terms for husband.

POM 254. **sehn, **yehn *male.*
　PMn 307. *Өeʔm, *yehm *Sm.* < POM **seʔn, **yehn.
　PPn 227. *šiʔį *Sm.* < POM **Yseʔyehm.
　A sʔáᶟ *Sm.* < POM **ʔsehn.
POM 387. **kwa, **ka, **wa *male.*
　PPn 318. *nta-wa *Sm.* < POM **wa.
　POP 490. *n-ʔǫa-n *Sm.* < POM **wa.
　PTl 21. *ahmba-Vʔ *Sm.* < POM **hnkwa.
POM 361. **kwin, **kin, **nwin *male.*
　PZn 8. *giʔ-yu *male, Sm.* < POM **kiʔn-yu.
　PCM 158. *mbu-hwe, *nu-hwi *Sm.* < POM **hwin, **hwi.

Similarly, the four terms for a female introduced above as playing a role in naming *mother* and other female kinsmen are also supported widely as terms for *wife.*

POM 255. **siHn, **niHn *Pf, PPCf(R,G), female.*
　PPn 111. *čihį *Sf.* < POM **Ynsihn.
POM 340. **suhn, **nuhn *Pf, PPCf(R,G), female.*
　PMn: PM 109. *ña-Өíʔĩ *Sf.* < POM **nya-suʔn.
　PPn 364. *čhų⁴¹ *Sf.* < POM **Yn-suhn.
　POP 320. *sǫ, *co *Sf.* < POM **suhn, **nsun.
POM 148. **kwin, **kin, **win *Pf, PPCf(R,G), female.*
　A skúᶟ *Sf.* < *kah < POM **kwihn.
　PTl 22. *aʔgu-iʔ *Sf.* < POM **nʔkwi.
　PCM 197. *mba-hwi, *nu-hmi *Sf.* < POM **hwi, **hnwi.
POM 350. **ntaHn, **naHn, **yaHn *Pf(vocative), PPCf(R,G), female.*
　PMn 302. *ndaʔa, *ñaʔa *Sf.* < POM **ntaʔn, **nyaʔn.
　POP 835. *nʔią *Sf.* < POM **yaHn.
　PZn 3. *gu-naʔa *woman, Sf.* < POM **kwi-nahn.
　H ntáh *Sf.* < POM **ntah.

CHAPTER 2
PROTO MIXTECAN
KINSHIP TERMS

This chapter proposes a set of Proto
Mixtecan kinship terms with corresponding ranges of reference, presents
and discusses the evidence upon
which the proposal is made, and
summarizes a possible sequence of
development through Proto Mixtec,
Proto Trique, and Proto Cuicatec horizons to contemporary Mixtecan
languages.

PMn KINSHIP TERMS

While there is some lexical variation across modern Mixtecan languages, and some slight differences in systems of kinship reference, a comparison of modern data reflects a stable situation of considerable time depth.

PMn Parent and Child Terms

All Mixtecan languages uniformly support a system of three categories for parents and children, distinguishing the sex of parents by elementary terms but not that of children. The terms that name these categories appear to be of POM origin, but there is nevertheless considerable variety from language family to language family. Proto Mixtec is alone in attesting the primary POM father term of reference, while Trique and Cuicatec support an old vocative term as their modern term of reference. Each of the three families supports a separate term for mother, all of which have POM sources. Mixtec and Cuicatec agree on a child term while Trique probably reflects the same term but with a slightly different ending.

*yu-wa, *Ci-tah	*Pm*	*father*
*Өĩʔĩ, *nih³, *čaku	*Pf*	*mother*
*Өaʔya, *Өaʔne	*C*	*child*

49

PMn Grandkinsman Terms

The pattern of three parent and child terms, distinguishing the sex of parents but not of children, is duplicated by three Proto Mixtecan grandkinsman terms with the same configuration. These latter terms extended beyond primary denotation both lineally and collaterally by Rule 1. The grandmother term appears to be a modified form of the grandfather term and is a PMn innovation. The two forms of the grandchild term—also PMn innovations—are based on the child term.

*Ɵeh, *xeh	*PPm(1)*	*grandfather*
*Ɵe-taʔm, *xe-ngweʔm, *xe-kweʔm	*PPf(1)*	*grandmother*
*Ɵaʔya xani, *Ɵaʔya xeʔnum	*CC(1)*	*grandchild*

As will be discussed below in greater detail, the modifier of the first grandmother term above (attested by Proto Mixtec) is from a word meaning *companion,* while the second and third forms are variants of a word meaning *old.*

PMn Sibling Terms

Collateral kinsmen more than one generation distant from ego are classified as grand-kinsmen in Proto Mixtecan, and the rest are further divided into two groups: those of ego's generation and those of one generation distant from ego. In each case, terms extend collaterally without known limit.

In ego's generation, there were three terms which distinguished the sex (or relative sex) of ego and alter in Jivaran fashion, one term being used between males, one between females, and one between kinsmen of the opposite sex. Of the three terms, that used between males has two forms, the first attested by Proto Mixtec and the second by Proto Trique and Proto Cuicatec. While the phonology is unclear they are considered variants of a single PMn term.

*ya-ni, *Ɵiʔ-nu	*mPCm(G)*	*man's brother*
*kuʔn-gwi	*fPCf(G)*	*woman's sister*
*kwaʔwa, *kaʔwa	*aPCb(G)*	*cross-sex sibling*

A fourth term classified all siblings together without reference to sex. It most likely originated outside the kinship system, but was drawn into PMn terminology by adjustments from POM times in the classification of siblings. The term in question probably had an earlier more general meaning of *companion,* and was seen above as the PM modifier in the grandmother term.

*taʔm	*PC(G)*	*sibling*

PMn Terms for other Collateral Kinsmen

There is one final group of collateral kinsmen in Proto Mixtecan, those of the first ascending and first descending generations from ego. These kinsmen appear to have been grouped together by compound terms into four classes which distinguished the sex of ego and alter in such a way that the sex of the elder member of the ego-alter dyad was also specifically marked. This is very definitely a PMn innovation in which earlier terminology is combined to form these new lexical formations. Details of the development of these terms is discussed later in this chapter.

Since ego and alter are of different generations, and since seniority by relative age may or may not correspond with seniority by generation in any given case, reciprocal rules I and R are both required to define the ranges of these terms. This too is discussed in greater detail later in the chapter.

Finally, although grandkinsman terms extend to collaterals more than one generation distant from ego, there is evidence that these four terms may have overlapped such collateral ranges of the grandkinsman terms. There were presumably particular social situations in which these terms were used for a kinsman of more than one generation distance where a different context would invoke a grandkinsman term. The specifics of such social situations are not known, but the extension rule in question is Rule 1.

*Өe-tu	emPPCm(I,R,1)	man's uncle
*Өe-ʔya	efPPCm(I,R,1)	woman's uncle
*Өi-Өi	efPPCf(I,R,1)	woman's aunt
*Өu-ʔwe	emPPCf(I,R,1)	man's aunt

In anticipation of the discussion below of the extension of these terms by Rules I and R (apart from Rule 1 which is quite straightforward), the primary kintypes of the above terms may be read as follows:

emPPCm(I,R)	→	emPPCm, emPCCm, ymPPCm, ymPCCm.
efPPCm(I,R)	→	efPPCm, efPCCm, ymPPCf, ymPCCf.
efPPCf(I,R)	→	efPPCf, efPCCf, yfPPCf, yfPCCf.
emPPCf(I,R)	→	emPPCf, emPCCf, yfPPCm, yfPCCm.

Although the terms were self-reciprocal as indicated, it was undoubtedly possible to modify them so as to specify the senior or junior member of the dyad.

PMn Affinal Terms

There were three categories of affinals in Proto Mixtecan. A single term classified together all kinsmen of spouse who were of spouse's generation or above; the other two terms distinguished the sex of spouse of any kinsman of ego who were of ego's generation or below. The first term is thus the direct reciprocal of the other two.

*xihӨam	SP(2)	spouse's kinsman
*kahӨa	CSm(2)	kinsman's husband
*xanam	CSf(2)	kinsman's wife

PMn Spouse Terms

Husband and wife were referred to by possessed forms of words meaning *male* and *female*, respectively, in PMn times.

*Өeʔm, *yehm	Sm	husband
*ndaʔa, *ñaʔa	Sf	wife

PM Kinship Terms

In Proto Mixtec times, the PMn system of reference continues intact but a few lexical adjustments have been made. In regard to parent terms, for example, **nana** and **tata** have been incorporated into Mixtec in heavy competition with the parent terms of POM origin.

*yu-wa, *tata	*Pm*	*father*
*Өĩʔĩ, *nana	*Pf*	*mother*
*Өaʔya	*C*	*child*

These same borrowed forms with modifiers also form neologisms which compete in some Mixtec languages with the older grandparent terms, though no change seems to occur in regard to the grandchild term which was an innovation at the PMn level.

*Өii; *tata Өaʔnu, *tata yaʔnu, *tata xeʔnu		
	PPm(1)	*grandfather*
*Өitą; *nana Өaʔnu, *nana yaʔnu, *nana xeʔnu		
	PPf(1)	*grandmother*
*Өaʔya te-xani	*CC(1)*	*grandchild*

Sibling terms continue without significant change.

*yani	*mPCm(G)*	*man's brother*
*kuʔ-vi	*fPCf(G)*	*woman's sister*
*kwaʔwa	*aPCb(G)*	*cross-sex sibling*
*tą̃ʔą̃	*PC(G)*	*sibling*

Considerable simplification takes place in the Mixtec system of reference for collateral kinsmen other than siblings. Seniority is now reinterpreted almost everywhere according to genealogical generation rather than by relative age; and only sex of kinsman is now distinguished, ignoring sex of ego or sex of the elder member of the ego-alter dyad. Four terms do continue to constitute the basic vocabulary for this area of reference, but two distinguish the sex of senior collaterals and two the sex of junior collaterals.

*Өito	*PPCm(1)*	*uncle*
*ӨiӨi	*PPCf(1)*	*aunt*
*Өaxį	*PCCm(1)*	*nephew*
*Өiku	*PCCf(1)*	*niece*

Affinal and spouse terms continue without change in patterning.

*tiӨo	*SP(2)*	*spouse's kinsman*
*kaӨa	*CSm(2)*	*kinsman's husband*
*xanu	*CSf(2)*	*kinsman's wife*
*yïï	*Sm*	*husband*
*ña-Өĩʔĩ	*Sf*	*wife*

PT Kinship Terms

The Proto Trique system of kinship reference develops to finally form a system differing from that of Proto Mixtec in only three places. First, the generic sibling term is lost in PT. Second, PT affinal terms retain the earlier POM system of unlimited extension (by Rule 0) rather than the more limited extension by Rule 2 which appears to characterize Pm and even PMn. Third, a generic spouse term is coined in PT which does not distinguish the sex of spouse.

Proto Trique does show a different set of lexical innovations from those of Proto Mixtec, however, indicating that different directions were taken in the development from PMn before a stable period of broad areal influence caused the neighboring systems to settle down with similar configurations which continue in most languages to the present. The largest differences of this sort are found in the lexical formations which designate collaterals other than siblings. PM and PT have arrived at different lexical forms for such kinsmen, but the respective systems of classification are isomorphic.

*reh³	Pm	father
*nih³	Pf	mother
*daʔni	C	child
*ši	PPm(1)	grandfather
*žugwąʔąh	PPf(1)	grandmother
*daʔni ziʔnu	CC(1)	grandchild
*dinu	mPCm(G)	man's brother
*žugwih	fPCf(G)	woman's sister
*žugweh	aPCb(G)	cross-sex sibling
*daʔnuʔ	PPCm(1)	uncle
*duʔwe	PPCf(1)	aunt
*dukų?	PCCm(1)	nephew
*dagwači?	PCCf(1)	niece
*žičeh	SP(0)	spouse's kinsman
*zigatah	CSm(0)	kinsman's husband
*žakoh	CSf(0)	kinsman's wife
*nika	S	spouse

PC Kinship Terms

As was true of Proto Trique, Proto Cuicatec develops a system of reference different from Proto Mixtec only in minor points, but shows some independence particularly in the way it has developed neologisms in the revised scheme for naming collaterals not of ego's generation. PC uniquely continues to distinguish sex of ego in the classification of uncles, and develops a lexical distinction to specify the wife of a brother as opposed to the wife of a junior lineal kinsman. (It is yet unclear as to how the wife of a junior collateral kinsman was classified in PC.) It also coins a second term for spouse's (male) kinsman, narrowing the earlier term to designate only female kinsman of spouse.

*čida	Pm	father
*čaku	Pf	mother
*daya	C	child
*čęʔę	PPm(1)	grandfather
*čikų?ų	PPf(1)	grandmother

*daya xi?nu	CC(1)	grandchild
*di?nu	mPCm(G)	man's brother
*ku?wi	fPCf(G)	woman's sister
*ka?we	aPCb(G)	cross-sex sibling
*dunu	mPPCm(1)	man's uncle
*di?ya	fPPCm(1)	woman's uncle
*dudi	PPCf(1)	aunt
*dakwa	PCCm(1)	nephew
*kuči	PCCf(1)	niece
*nča?ą ndiku	SPm(2)	spouse's male kinsman
*?indą?ą	SPf(2)	spouse's female kinsman
*dada	CSm(2)	kinsman's husband
*dakunu	CSf(2)	kinsman's wife
*?insą?ą	Sm	husband
*nda?ata	Sf	wife

The Development of PMn Parent and Child Terms

All three of the terms for father which are supported by OM languages find reflexes in PMn materials. Lingua franca **tata** has made major incursions into Mixtec by becoming the primary term for father in several contemporary languages. The term is sufficiently widespread to posit it as a part of the Proto Mixtec inventory although its introduction into Mixtec is certainly quite late.

PM 101. *tata *Pm.*
At tátá *Pm;* D 'tá *Pm(L);* P tătá *Pm(S-);* tátí, tátáì *Pm;* SM táã *Pm;* Y tātà *Pm.*

POM 49 **Ytah *Pm(vocative)* is also found in Mixtecan, but not in Mixtec. Longacre and Millon (1961:20) speculate that PT 1 below is borrowed from Spanish **padre,** which may be the case; but Rensch (1976:80) suggests that Trique r may reflect POM **Yt. PC 1 is here considered a cognate of PT 1, although PC *d normally reflects PMn *Θ and POM **s. The possibility that PC *d might reflect POM **ht in some cases is worthy of investigation.

POM 49. **Ytah *Pm(vocative).*
PMn 301. *Ci-tah *Pm.* < POM **Ytah.
PT 1. *reh³ *Pm.* < PMn *Ci-tah.
Ch dreh³ *Pm,* Cp reh³ *Pm.*
PC 1. *čida *Pm.* < PMn *kiΘa or *xiΘa.
Tp čiidá *Pm,* Tt či³da³ *Pm.*

Finally, **POM 361** **kwin-yu-wa, **kin-yu-wa, **nwin-yu-wa is also found in Mixtecan, both in its specific reference to father and in reference to collateral kinsmen as well.

POM 361. **kwin-yu-wa, **kin-yu-wa, **nwin-yu-wa *Pm,* PPCm(R,G).
PM 102. *yu-wa *Pm.* < POM **yu-wa.
Ay yùvā? *Pm,* Ct ùbă *Pm(L),* M yūvá *Pm,* O žūbá *Pm,* SP žūā *Pm.*
PT 2. *du?we PPCf(G).* < POM **su-?win.

Ch du³ʔwi³ *PPCf(G)*, **Cp duʔwę³** *PPCf(G)*.
PMn 244. *Θa-kwim *ymPCC(I,1)*. < **POM **sa-kwin.**
PM 103. *Θi-ku *PCCf(1)*. < **PMn *Θi-kwim.**

At **šīkù** *PCCf*, Ay **šīkù** *PCCf(G,S)*, D **dí′kú** *yPCCf(1,1,S-)*, M **šīkū** *PCCf(G)*, O **šìkù** *PCCf(1,S-)*, P **díkú** *PCCf(1,S)*, S **xùkù** *PCCf(1)*, SM **šīkù** *PCCf(G,S-)*, SP **dīkū** *PCCf(G,S)*, Y **sīkù** *PCCf(1,S)*.
PT 3. *du-kų̀ *PCCm(G)*, < **PMn *Θu-kwiʔm.**
Ch du³kų̀ʔ⁴⁵ *PCCm(G)*, **Cp židukų̀ʔ³** *PCCm(G)*.
PC 2. *da-kwa *PCCm(1)*. < **PMn *Θa-kwim.**
Tp daakú *PCCm(G)*, **Tt da³kwa⁴** *PCCm(1,-S)*.

Turning now to Mixtecan terms for mother, we find that with the exception of Diuxi Mixtec, reflexes of the lingua franca **nana** term are found in all the same languages which manifest **tata.**

PM 104. *nana *Pf.*
At **náná** *Pf;* P **nǎna** *Pf(S-);* S **nání, nánâì** *Pf;* SM **náá** *Pf;* Y **nānà** *Pf.*

All four POM terms for mother are also supported by Mixtecan evidence, both in their specific use for mother as well as in their more general reference to any woman or female person.

POM 148. **kwin, **kin, **win *Pf, PPCf(R,G), female.*
PC 3. *čaku *Pf.* < **POM **Ca-kwi.**
Tp čääkú *Pf,* **Tt čä³ko³** *Pf.*
PMn 13. *Θa-kwim-xiHm *yfPCC(I,1)*. < **POM **sa-kwin-hkiHn.**
PM 105. *Θaxį̀ *PCCm(1)*. < **PMn *Θa-xiHm.**
At **sāhį̄** *PCCm,* Ay **sāšį̀** *PCCm(G,S)*, Ct **ákwécì** *PCC(1)*, D **dà′ší,** *yPCCm(I,1,S-)*, M **sāšį̄** *PCCm(G)*, O **sà̀xį̀** *PCCm(1,S-)*, P **dášį̀** *PCCm(1,S)*, S **xàšì** *PCCm(1)*, SM **sāhį̀** *PCCm(G,S-)*, SP **dáši** *PCCm(G,S)*, J **sačį̀** *PCC(2)*, Y **sāxį̀** *PCCm(1,S)*.
PT 4. *da-gwa-čiʔ *PCCf(G)*. < **PMn *Θa-kwim-xiʔ.**
Ch du³gwa³čiʔ³⁴ *PCCf(G)*, **Cp dagwačiʔ³** *PCCf(G)*.
PC 4. *ku-či *PCCf(1)*. < **PMn *kwi-xim.**
Tp nguučí *PCCf(G)*, **Tt rʔu³če⁴** *PCCf(1,-S)*.
PMn 38. *kuʔn-gwi *fPCCf(G)*. < **POM **kuʔn-kwin.**
PM 106. *kuʔ-vi *fPCCf(G)*. < **PMn *kuʔm-gwi.**
At **kūʔù** *fPCf,* Ay **kūʔvà** *fPCCf(G,-S)*, D **kú′ʔú** *fPCCf(G)*, M **kūʔvī** *fPCCf(G)*, O **kùʔù** *fPCCf(G)*, P **kúʔú** *fPCCf(G)*, S **kìʔvî** *fPCf,* SM **kūʔà** *fPCCf(G)*, SP **kùʔì** *fPCf,* J **kuʔwi** *fPCf,* Y **kūʔà** *fPCCf(G)*.
PT 5. *žu-gwih *fPCCf(G)*. < **PMn *Cuʔm-gwi.**
Ch žu³gwih³⁴ *fPCCf(G)*, **Cp žuʔwih³⁴** *fPCCf(G)*.
PC 5. *kuʔ-wi *fPCCf(G)*. < **PMn *kuʔm-gwi.**
Tp viʔí *PC(G)*, **Tt ko³ʔo⁴** *fPCCf(G)*.
POM 255. **siHn, **niHn *Pf, PPCf(R,G), female.*
PT 6. *nih³ *Pf.* < **POM **nihn.**
Ch n-i³ *Pf,* **Cp ni³** *Pf.*
PMn 51. *Θi-Θi *efPPCf(I,1)*. < **POM **nsi-nsi.**
PM 107. *Θi-Θi *PPCf(1)*. < **PMn *Θi-Θi.**

At šiši *PPCf*, Ay šìšì *PPC(G,S)*, Ct dídí *PPCf(1)*, D 'dìdí *ePPCf(1,1,-S)*, M šìšì *PPCf(G)*, O šìšì *PPCf(1,-S)* P dìdī *PPCf(1,S)*, S xìxì *PPCf(1,S)*, SM šñ *PPCf(G,-S)*, SP dīdī *PPCf(G,S)*, J čiši *PPCf(1)*, Y šìšì *PPCf(1,S)*.

PC 6. *du-di *PPCf(1)*. < PMn *Өi-Өi.

Tp duudí *PPCf(G)*, Tt du³de³ *PPCf(1,-S)*.

POM 340. **suhn, **nuhn *Pf*, *PPCf(R,G)*, *female*.

PM 108. *Ө**ï?ï *Pf*. < POM **su?n.

Ay sì?ì? *Pf*, Ct dì?ì *Pf(L)*, D dí'?ì *Pf(L)*, M sī?ī *Pf*, O sì?ì *Pf*, SP dī?ì *Pf*, J si?i *Pf*.

PM 109. *ña-Өï?ï *Sf*. < POM **nya-su?n.

At ñasî?ì, Ay ñāsì?ī *Sf*, Ct ñàdì?ì *Sf*, D 'ñàdí *Sf*, M ñásî?ī *Sf*, O ñasí?í, *Sf*, P ñadì?ì *Sf*, S ñaxí?ì *Sf*, SM ñàsî?ì *Sf*, SP ñā?à dì?ì *Sf*, J ña si?i *Sf*, Y ñàsî?ì *Sf*.

POM 350. **ntaHn, **naHn, **yaHn *Pf(vocative)*, *PPCf(R,G)*, *female*.

PMn 156b: T na³nah³ *elderly lady*. < POM **nah.

PMn 302. *nda?a, *ña?a *Sf*. < POM **nta?n, **nya?n.

PM 109. *ña-Өï?ï *Sf*. < PMn *ña-Өï?ï.

(See immediately above for data listing.)

PM: SM ñā?ā úù *second Sf*. < PMn *ña?a.

PC 7. *nda?a-ta *Sf*. < PMn *nda?a.

Tp n?daatá *Sf*, Tt nd?a³ta³ *Sf*.

One minor note on the Coatzospan Mixtec reflex of **PM 105** (of **POM 148**): Since àkwècì appears to be based upon a word for small, it may not in fact be cognate with other Mixtec nephew terms.

Contemporary Mixtecan languages uniformly show reflexes of **POM 308 **Yhnsan** as their terms for child, although Trique exhibits an ending different from that shown by Mixtec and Cuicatec (Mixtec and Cuicatec forms are discussed in Longacre and Mak 1960:39).

POM 308. **Yhnsan, **hyan *C*.

PMn 303. *Өa?ya, *Өa?ne *C*. < POM **sa.

PM 110. *Өa?ya *C*. < PMn *Өa?ya.

At sè?ē *C*, Ay sï?è *C*, Ct ï?šá *C(L)*, D dá'?yá *C(L)*, M sē?ē *C(1)*, O sè?ē *C*, P dé?e *C*, S xà?ži *C*, SM sè?ē *C*, SP dè?ē *C*, J se?e *C*, Y sē?ē *C*.

PC 8. *daya *C*. < PMn *Өaya.

Tp daiyá *C*, Tt da³ya³ *C*.

PT 7. *da?ni *C*. < PMn *Өa?ne.

Ch da³?ni²¹ *C*, Cp da?ni²¹ *C*.

The POM vocative term **350** is not used in reference by Mixtecan languages nor do the data include reports of its presence as a vocative term apart from the possible Chicahuaxtla form na³nah³ suggested by Longacre (1957:135).

No rule of extension appears to have applied to the parent and child terms when they occurred unmodified. It is possible to consider them as having extended ranges to encompass all lineal ancestors and lineal descendents on the basis of their occurrence with modifiers, as is discussed below in connection with terms for grandkinsmen, but such extension is not overtly marked in this study when the modifiers are absent. There was no semantic shift in the ranges of the parent and child terms from POM to PMn times. Thereafter, however, some of the Mixtec languages appear to have adopted Rule L for parent and child terms and one has adopted Rule 1 for the child term in conjunction with the loss of the POM term for grandchild. The following statements represent these shifts, assuming a two-step shift from L to 1 in Metlatonoc.

$ø → L /$ $\begin{cases} P & \text{(Ct D).} \\ C & \text{(Ct D M).} \end{cases}$

$L → 1 /$ $\quad C \quad$ (M).

The Development of PMn Grandkinsman Terms

The POM grandfather term continues into PMn and post-PMn times in all three branches of the family, but only in reference to senior kinsmen, losing its self-reciprocal range which is also further narrowed to kinsmen of more than one generation from ego. Both **s-initial and **hk-initial stems are supported by Mixtecan languages, **s by Mixtec, **hk by Trique and Cuicatec.

POM 429. **seh, **hkeh *PPm(R,2)*.

  PMn 304. *Ɵeh, *xeh *PPm(1)*, < POM **seh, **hkeh.

   PM 111. *Ɵii *PPm(1)*. < PMn *Ɵeh.

   Ay šīi *PPm(1,S)*; M šīi *PPm(1,S-)*; P šíi *PPm(S-)*; S táčéʔê *PPm(L)*, náčéʔê *PPf(L)*.

   PT 8. *ši *PPm(1)*. < PMn *xeh.

   Ch ši³ *PPm(1,-S)*, Cp ži⁵³ *PPm(1,-S)*.

   PC 9. *čęʔę *PPm(L)*. < PMn *xeʔm.

   Tp čʔę́ *PPm(L)*, Tt či³da³ čʔän² *PPm(L)*.

While the POM grandfather term continues into PMn and post-PMn times in all three branches of the family in reference to senior kinsmen, the POM grandmother term does not seem to do so. Rather, it would appear that the grandfather term extends not only to male grandparents but also to female grandparents when modified by the PM form of **POM 61 **taʔn** *companion* or the PT or PC forms of **POM 189 **kweʔn²** *old*. POM 189 continues as a verbal form in Mixtec languages, but did not become a part of the grandmother term as in PT and PC.

PMn 156. *Ɵe-taʔm, *xe-ngweʔm, *xe-kweʔm *PPf(1)*. < POM **se-taʔn, **hke-nkweʔn, **hke-kweʔn.

   PM 112. *Ɵitą *PPf(1)*. < PMn *Ɵi-taʔm.

   Ay šītą̀ʔ *PPf(1,S)*, M šìtà *PPf(1,S-)*, P šìtą́ *PPf(S-)*.

   PM 113. *kweʔe *sick*. < POM **kweʔ.

   Ay tà-kwīʔè *old man*; Ct ùbǎ kwìʔí *PPm(L)*, kwìʔí *sickly*; SM kū̃ʔù *sick*.

   PT 9. *žu-gwąʔąh *PPf(1)*. < PMn *xe-ngweʔm.

   Ch žugwą̀ʔ³ah³⁴ *PPf(1,-S)*, Cp žu³gwaʔąh⁵³ *PPf(1,-S)*.

   PC 10. *či-kųʔų *PPf(L)*. < PMn *xe-kweʔm.

   Tp čikųʔų́ *PPf(L)*, Tt če²ku²ʔun² *PPf(L)*.

The phonological reconstruction of the grandfather term in this unstressed position is, of course, uncertain since most of the serious work on the subject has dealt primarily with the stressed syllable. It is not beyond the realm of possibility that this unstressed material actually reflects the POM grandmother term, but the grandfather term is the better bet at this stage of our understanding.

As indicated, the POM grandparent terms lost their self-reciprocal ranges in PMn, but it is possible that reflexes of the old grandparent terms continue in the penultimate syllable of modifiers which, when postposed to child terms in PMn, specify grandchildren. Once again, we are here dealing with unstressed material which is not well understood, but the possibility is worth mentioning that the penult of the PM modifier harks back to the grandmother term while that of the PT and PC modifiers harks back to the grandfather term. The PM grandchild term seems to have been influenced by the PM term for a man's brother and the initial consonant is a problem. The PT and PC forms occur with an ending which also suggests influence from sibling terms in those languages.

PMn 305. *Өa?ya xani, *Өa?ya xe?num CC(1). < POM **sa?ya hkani, **sa?ya hke?num.

    PM 114. *Өa?ya te-xani CC(1). < PMn *Өa?ya te-xani.

        At sè?ē čání CC(1,S), Ay sī yànī CC(1,S), D dá'?yá 'ñànì CC(L), M sē?ē yání CC(1), P dé?e ñani CC(-S), S xà?šī ñání CC, SM sè?ē tíhání CC(G,S-), SP dè?ē ñānī CC, J se yani CC, Y sē?ē čání CC(L,S).

    PT 10. *da?ni zi?nu CC(1). < PMn *Өa?ne xi?num.

        Ch da³?ni⁴⁵ zi⁵?nɨ⁵ CC(1,S-), Cp da?nih³ zi?nǫ⁵ CC(1,S-).

    PC 11. *daya xi?nu CC(L). < PMn *Өa?ya xe?nu.

        Tp daiyíínú CC(L), Tt da³ya³ i²no² CC(L).

The POM grandparent terms received heavy competition in PMn, particularly in Mixtec, from the modified parent terms. Even in the reflexes of the grandfather term presented above, it is seen that Silacayoapan Mixtec and Teutila Cuicatec have converted the grandfather term itself into a modifier of the father term. The development of grandchild terms—no longer self reciprocal with the grandparent terms but being based on the child term with postposed modifier—also reflects this competition. The result of this competition is the loss of grandparent terms in several Mixtec languages, with modified parent terms replacing them altogether.

In the same way that the penultimate syllable of the modifier in grandchild terms may reflect the grandparent terms, it is also possible that the corresponding syllable of these new grandparent terms does so as well. A number of terms for collateral kinsmen emerge in several Otomanguean languages which appear to hark back to POM **sa?nu and **hke-?nu. Such terms look like the old grandparent terms with postposed **?nu, which can either be a sibling term (man's brother) or adjectival big. The PM grandparent terms reflect these same forms.

PM 115. *tata Өa?nu, *tata ya?nu, *tata xe?nu PPm(1).

    At tátá xě?nū PPm(1,S), D tà šá'tnú PPm(L), O tātá ñá?nú PPm(1,S), S tá sá?nūi PPm(L), J sutu ča?nu PPm(L).

PM 116. *nana Өa?nu, *nana ya?nu, *nana xe?nu PPf(1).

    At nana xě?nū PPf(1,S), D dì šá'tnú PPf(L), O nāná ñá?nú PPf(1,S), S ná sá?nūi PPf(L), J si?i ča?nu PPf(L).

Some Mixtec languages simply use unmodified parent terms for grandparents (Ct D) or loan words (SP Y), while the following languages use modifiers with the parent terms which are not cognate with the modifiers above. Longacre suggests that the SM modifier may be a reflex of **PMn 156** (1957:135), as is the second Ct modifier.

Ct ùbǎ àtǎ, ùbǎ kwìʔí *PPm(L); SM* **tātá ñúù** *PPm(1,-S).*

The assumption is here made that POM modified parent and child terms originally extended only to lineal ancestors and descendents, and that the replacement of the POM grandparent terms by these phrases left its mark on the latter in a few Mixtec languages in the form of extended ranges which included collateral kinsmen of more than one generation from ego. This semantic shift may be characterized as follows:

$$L \to l \; / \qquad \begin{cases} P + \textit{modifier} & \text{(At O SM).} \\ C + \textit{modifier} & \text{(At O SM).} \end{cases}$$

This shift to increase the range of reference of modified parent and child terms is just the reverse of the semantic shift which took place for the original grandparent terms in those languages where they survive. In the first place, the reciprocal range of the terms was lost. Then the extension of the terms to collateral kinsmen was aligned more closely to genealogical considerations in PMn, restricting the ranges of grandparent terms to kinsmen of more than one generation distance from ego. Cuicatec then further narrowed the range of the terms to lineal ancestors, while Peñoles restricts them to lineals of the second generation from ego (assuming the data to be complete on this point). These semantic shifts may be characterized as follows:

$R \to \o \,/\, PP$ (Ay M P Ch Cp Tp Tt).
$2 \to l \,/\, PP$ (Ay M P Ch Cp Tp Tt).
$l \to L \,/\, PP$ (P Tp Tt).
$L \to \o \,/\, PP$ (P).

In summary, the grandfather term with POM ranges *PPm(R,2)* survives with reduced range *PPm(1)* in PMn and on into PM and PT, but is reduced further to *PPm(L)* in PC. The corresponding grandmother term is lost, but the grandfather term with modifier appears in PMn for the range *PPf(1)* and extends on into PM and Pt, with correspondingly reduced range *PPf(L)* in PC. At the same time, the POM parent terms with modifiers compete heavily with the grandparent terms, replacing them completely in the majority of Mixtec languages with the range *PPm(L)* and *PPf(L),* except that Rule L is replaced by Rule 1 in a few places under the influence of the original grandparent terms. The POM child terms with modifiers, on the otherhand, completely take over the reciprocal ranges of the original grandparent terms by PMn times.

The Development of PMn Sibling Terms

All of the POM sibling terms survive in PMn, including the word for companion, but the development of a distinction between ego's generation peers and other collaterals in PMn precipitates a number of lexical shifts and new morphological structures. First, the POM man's term for elder brother divides in PMn into a man's term for brother, on the one hand, and a man's term for uncle, on the other, as reflected in the final syllable of **PMn 24** and **275,** by postposing it to a diminutive in the case of **24** and to grandparent terms in the case of **275.**

POM 423. **tu, **nu, **yu *emPCm(0)*.
PMn 24. *ya-ni, *Өiʔ-nu *mPCm(G)*. < POM **ya-ni, **siʔ-nu.
PM 117. *yani *mPCm(G)*. < PMn *ya-ni.
At ñānī *mPCm(G)*, Ay ñànì *mPCm(G,-S)*, Ct énî *mPCm(G)*, D 'ñànì *mPCm(G)*, M yānī *mPCm(G)*, O ñànì *mPCm(G)*, P ñanî *mPCm(G)*, S ñànî *mPCm*, SM ñānì *mPCm(G)*, SP ñānī *mPCm*, J yani *mPCm*, Y ñānī *mPCm(G)*.
PT 11. *dinu *mPCm(G)*. < PMn *Өiʔ-num.
Ch di³ni²¹ *mPCm(G)*, Cp dinu²¹ *mPCm(G)*.
PC 12. *diʔnu *mPCm(G)*. < PMn *Өiʔ-nu.
Tp ʔdiinú *mPCm(G)*, Tt dʔi²no⁴ *mPCm(G)*.
PMn 275. *Өe-tu, *Өaʔ-ndu, *Өe-nu *emPPCm(I,R,1)*. < POM **se-tu, **saʔn-tu, **se-nu.
PM 118. *Өito *PPCm(1)*. < PMn *Өe-tu.
At stōō *PPCm*, Ay šìtò *PPCm(G,S)*, Ct dító *PPCm(1)*, D 'dìtò *ePPCm(I,1,-S)*, M šìtò *PPm(G)*, O šītò *PPCm(1,-S)*, P ditó *PPCm(1,S)*, S xìtòì *PPCm(1,S)*, SM stóō *PPCm(G,-S)*, SP dītō *PPCm(G,S)*, J šito *PPCm(1)*, Y šitō *PPCm(1,S)*.
PT 12. *daʔnuʔ *PPCm(G)*. < PMn *Өaʔndu.
Ch da³ʔniʔ⁴⁵ *PPCm(G)*, Cp daʔnuʔ³ *PPCm(G)*.
PC 13. *dunu *mPPCm(G)*. < PMn *Өe-nu.
Tp duunū *mPPCm(G)*, Tt du³no⁴ *mPPCm(1,-S)*.

The limits of our knowledge concerning the development of POM unstressed syllables (and perhaps even more important, the limits such material imposes upon reconstruction in any case) necessarily reduces the level of confidence we can place in the foregoing hypothesis regarding the sources of the pretonic PMn data above but it is a reasonable one from both phonological and semantic points of view. The diminutives occurring in **PMn 24** differ in PM from PT and PC. PM *ya can derive from **POM 308 **hyan** *C*, while PT *di and PC *diʔ can result from **POM 258 **siʔ** *youngster*. In the case of **PMn 275,** PT *daʔn can result from the POM grandmother term while PM *Өi and PC *du appear to hark back to the POM grandfather term. (This differs in configuration from the PMn grandchild terms, as discussed above, in which the PM term is based on the grandmother term while the PT and PC terms are based on the grandfather term.) The variation between PM *i and PT and PC *u in the ultima is known to occur elsewhere, and Trique support for final *m is not without precedent (Longacre 1957:47, Rensch 1967:84).

The POM cross-sex term for sibling turns up in PMn only in Cuicatec as **PC 12**—a term for a woman's uncle—where it is postposed to a reflex of the POM grandfather term, parallel to the development of a man's term for uncle. PT and PC unaccountably show palatal influence of the final vowel in this term.

POM 431. **ʔya *eaPCb(0)*.
PC 14. *diʔya *efPPCm (I,R,1)*. < POM **se-ʔya.
Tp diiʔyá *fPPCm(G)*, Tt dʔi³ya³ *fPPCm(1,-S)*.

The loss of a reflex of **POM 431** from the set of PMn terms to denote siblings results in the restructuring and reinterpretation of two other POM sibling terms to accomodate the loss. First, a reflex of **POM 236,** the woman's term for sister in POM, is combined with a reflex of **POM 387 **wa** *male* to provide a cross-sex term for sibling in PMn; and, second, a reflex of the general POM sibling term, **POM 159** ****kuHn,** is combined with a reflex of **POM 148** ****kwin** *female* to narrow its focus to sisters by female speaker.

POM 236. ****kwaHn** *efPCf(0)*.
　PMn 182. **kwaʔwa, *kaʔwa aPCb(G)*. < POM ****kwaʔ-wa.**
　　PM 119. **kwaʔwa aPCb(G)*. < PMn **kwaʔwa.*
　　At **kwàʔā** *aPCb,* **D kúʔá** *aPCb(G),* **M kūʔvā** *aPCb(G),* **O kwàʔā** *aPCb(G),* **P kúʔa**, *aPCb(G),* **S kyàʔvàì** *aPCb,* **SM kwàʔá** *aPCb(G),* **SP kùʔā** *aPCb,* **J kuʔwa** *aPCb,* **Y kwāʔā** *aPCb(G).*
　　PT 19. **žugweh aPCb(G)*. < PMn **Cuʔn-gwam.*
　　Ch **žu³gweh³⁴** *aPCb(G),* Cp **raʔwih³⁴** *aPCb(G).*
　　PC 15. **kaʔwe aPCb(G)*. < PMn **kaʔwa.*
　　Tt **kʔä²be** *aPCb(G).*
POM 159. ****kuHn** *PC(0)*.
　PMn 38. **kuʔn-gwi fPCf(G)*. < POM ****kuʔn-kwin.**
　　(See **POM 148** *under parent terms for data listing.)*

The Trique penult in **PMn 182** can either represent a sequence of **Cwa* < **Cu* and reflect **kwaʔ,* as proposed, or can show a direct relationship with a PMn reflex of ****kuHn,** indicating confusion between ****kuHn** and ****kwaHn** in the development of the PMn configuration of terms.

Finally, the shifting of reference of PMn terms resulted in the adoption of **PMn 161** into the system as a true sibling term in a few isolated cases. In Coatzospan, it replaces the function of **kuʔn* which combines with a *female* term to denote *sister.* In Ayutla, it fills in for **ʔya* which denotes *aunt.*

POM 61. ****taʔn** *PC(0)*.
　PMn 161. **taʔm PC(G)*. < POM ****taʔn.**
　　PM 120. **tạ̧ʔạ:* Ay **tạ̧ʔạ̧ʔ** *aPCb(G,-S),* Ct **tạ̧ʔạ̧** *PC(G).*

The general system of reference for siblings in PMn (and in PM, PT, and PC) thus remains substantially the same as the prior POM system. There is, in at least some cases, a general sibling term, and then three Jivaran terms denoting *mPCm, fPCf,* and *aPCb,* respectively. But the lexical material which labels these categories does shift about some, and the extended ranges of reference are reduced from those characterized by Rule 0 to those characterized by Rule G, ascending- and descending-generation collaterals being separated into a distinct class of senior and junior collateral kinsmen. This semantic split can be stated as follows:

$$ePC(0) \rightarrow \quad \left\{ \begin{array}{l} ePPC(I,R,1) \\ PC(G) \end{array} \right\} \quad \text{(PMn).}$$

Of the modern languages, Coatzospan uniquely loses terms for *aPCb* and *fPCf,* retaining only the general reference to *PC* (by **tạ̧ʔạ̧**) and the specific term for *mPCm.*

There are also a few reports that cousins are no longer included within sibling ranges, reducing the latter to primary ranges only.

$$G \rightarrow \emptyset \ / \ PC \qquad \text{(S SP J).}$$

The Development of Other PMn Collateral Kinsman Terms

As mentioned, PMn lexical shifts in the system of reference for siblings were precipitated by the development of a terminological distinction between collaterals of ego's generation and all other collaterals. PMn evidence attests the adoption of four collateral terms for aunt and uncle, distinguishing sex of both ego and alter, by adapting existing terms of the system to designate these new categories. All these new terms have been introduced above in connection either with discussion of parent and child terms or in the discussion of sibling terms. The development in PMn can be summarized as follows, using only citation forms and not all possible variants.

POM **seh *PPm* + **tu *emPCm*   → PMn *Өe-tu *emPPCm(I,R,1)*.
POM **seh *PPm* + **?ya *eaPCb*   → PMn *Өe-?ya *efPPCm(I,R,1)*.
POM reduplication of **siHn *Pf*   → PMn *Өi-Өi *efPPCf(I,R,1)*.
POM **suhn *female* + **win *Pm*   → PMn *Өu-?we *emPPCf(I,R,1)*.

Two kinds of reciprocal ranges are supported by the data. The shift from *ePC* to *ePPC* naturally invokes the use of Rule I, since the addition of *P* to *PC* (*P + PC → PPC*) is not meant to introduce a second principle of seniority (in addition to *e*), but rather to introduce the principle of generation, distinguishing kinsmen of ego's generation from all other kinsmen. *ePPC(I)* thus yields all the older kinsmen not of ego's generation (including *ePCC*). Rule I is still in use in Diuxi and is known to have been a rule of Proto Zapotec because of modern data from Amatlán.

The second reciprocal rule, Rule R, also came into play with these terms in a natural way, since it was earlier associated with these same collateral kintypes through the pre-Mixtecan grandkinsman terms which had ranges *PPm(R,2)* and *PPf(R,2)*, respectively. Taking the ranges of just one of the four collateral categories as an example, the interaction of Rules I and R yields the following kind of results:

emPPCf(I,R) → *emPPCf, emPCCf, yfPCCm, yfPPCm.*

Evidence such as **PMn 244 *ӨV-kwim** *mPCC(1)*, a derivative of the father term, also points to the aunt and uncle terms as having been self-reciprocal by Rule R. In this case, a reflex of **POM 308 **Yhnsan** *C* is proposed to an *uncle* term to designate a man's junior collateral kinsman. The corresponding term for a woman's junior collateral kinsman is **PMn 13 *Өa-kwim-xiHm** *fPCC(1)*. The reconstruction of these forms is somewhat speculative, but the following derivation is suggested:

As indicated, the four collateral terms were at first self-reciprocal. Nevertheless, by preposing a diminutive, the junior kinsman of the dyad could be specified. Unaccountably, reflexes of only two nephew and niece terms are found in PMn, where we might expect at least a trace of the four aunt and uncle terms. One reason for this was the tendency in Otomanguean not to mark the sex of junior kinsman unless required by context. This principle would naturally lead to just two terms at this point, one for the dyad with a male senior member, and one for the dyad with a female senior member. But this does not explain why both surviving terms reflect **POM 361 **kwin-yu-wa** *father,* while none of the other sources of aunt and uncle terms are so reflected in any Mixtecan nephew or niece term.

Acknowledging this as a problem, it is possible to see how *xiHm* could have developed as the ending of the second term. Both father and mother terms in POM exhibit the form **kwin. (This close phonological relationship may have been a factor in PMn dropping *kwim as the antepenult of its reflex of POM 361, where POM **kwin-yu-wa *Pm* yields PMn *yu-wa *Pm*.) The PMn sequence *ΘV-kwim, while based on a father term, could easily have become confused with a reflex of the term for mother, resulting in the further marking of sex of senior kinsman as specifically being female by the ending *xiHm, which derives from **hkiHn, a possible alternant of POM 148 **kwin *female.*

With the development of these two terms for junior collaterals, Rule R was lost in respect to the terms for senior collaterals. In this process of change, PM separates from PT and PC in its interpretation of the junior terms, resulting in a semantic flip-flop of ranges. It is easy to see how this could have happened with a shift to mark the sex of junior kinsman, not previously marked.

Let's say, for example, that because of confusion between certain forms of the parent terms, the ending described above had been added to *Θa-kwim, as indicated, and that subsequently only the two new terms were used (perhaps there were a full set of four terms for a short period) for junior kinsmen, the original forms being restricted to senior kinsmen. At this stage then, we have the following configuration:

*Θe-tu	emPPCm(I,1)	man's elder male collateral
*Θe-?ya	efPPCm(I,1)	woman's elder male collateral
*Θi-Θi	efPPCf(I,1)	woman's elder female collateral
*Θu-?we	emPPCf(I,1)	man's elder female collateral
*ΘV-kwim	ymPCC(I,1)	man's younger collateral
*Θa-kwim-xiHm	yfPCC(I,1)	woman's younger collateral

This means that anyone (male or female), when speaking to a woman, would use *Θa-kwim-xiHm to say *your nephew* or *your niece,* but would use *ΘV-kwim to say the same things to a man. As the principle *sex of elder kinsman* shifted to that of *sex of kinsman* (and assuming that the association of *xiHm to a term for female had eventually become obscure), it would have been possible for Mixtec to re-assign *Θa-kwim-xiHm the range *yPCCm(I,1)* for both male and female speakers and *ΘV-kwim the range *yPCCf(I,1),* also for both male and female speakers, while Trique and Cuicatec made the opposite assignments. At some stage, Ct and J lost the second term altogether, conforming to the pattern of not distinguishing the sex of junior kinsman unless especially required by context. These shifts can be characterized as follows:

$$ymPCC(I,1) \rightarrow \begin{cases} yPCCm(I,1) & \text{(PM)} \\ yPCCf(I,1) & \text{(PT PC).} \end{cases}$$

$$yfPCC(I,1) \rightarrow \begin{cases} yPCCm(I,1) & \text{(PT PC)} \\ yPCCf(I,1) & \text{(PM).} \end{cases}$$

And later:

$$yPCCm(I,1) \rightarrow yPCC(I,1) \quad \text{(Ct J).}$$
$$yPCCf(I,1) \rightarrow \emptyset \quad \text{(Ct J).}$$

The corresponding terms for senior collaterals lose Rule R and the principle *sex of ego* is dropped everywhere except for PC uncles.

$R \rightarrow \emptyset /$ $ePPC(I,1)$ (PM PT PC).

$m \rightarrow \emptyset /$ $\begin{cases} \_PPCm & \text{(PM PT)} \\ \_PPCf & \text{(PM PT PC).} \end{cases}$

$f \rightarrow \emptyset /$ $\begin{cases} \_PPCm & \text{(PM PT)} \\ \_PPCf & \text{(PM PT PC).} \end{cases}$

Rule I is then also lost (everywhere except in Diuxi) in the process of shifting from seniority by age to seniority by generation.

$e(I) \rightarrow \emptyset / PPC$ (PM PT PC, except Dx).

$y(I) \rightarrow \emptyset / PCC$ (PM PT PC, except Dx).

Finally, a few reports indicate that the ranges of senior and junior collaterals have been reduced to extension by Rule G.

$I \rightarrow G /$ $\begin{cases} PPC & \text{(Ay M SM SP Ch Cp TP)} \\ PCC & \text{(Ay M SM SP Ch Cp Tp).} \end{cases}$

The Development of PMn Affinal Terms

Both POM child-in-law terms are preserved in each of the three Mixtecan families, the daughter-in-law term being tentatively considered the source of both parent-in-law and daughter-in-law terms in the daughter languages.

POM 432 **kah $CSm(R,0)$.
  PMn 137. *kahΘa $CSm(2)$. < POM **kahsa.
    PM 122. *kaΘa $CSm(2)$. < PMn *kahΘa.
      At kàsá $CSm(?)$, Ay kàsā? CSm, Ct kàdá $CSm(2)$, D kà'dá $CSm(2)$, M kāsā $CSm(2)$, O kàsá $CSm(2)$, P kada $CSm(G2)$, S kàxáì CSm, SM kāsá $CSm(2)$, SP kādà CSm, J kasa $CSm(0)$, Y kàsà $PCSm(G,V,S-)$.
    PT 15. *zi-gatah $CSm(0)$. < PMn *Θi-kahΘa.
      Ch zi³ ga³tah³⁴ $CSm(3)$, Cp zigatah³⁴ $CSm(3,yS-)$.
    PC 17. *dada $CSm(2)$. < PMn *Θahθa.
      Tp daadá $CSm(G2)$, Tt da³da³ $CSm(L,G2)$.
POM 433. **nsan, **nyan $CSf(R,0)$.
  PMn 276. *xanam $CSf(2)$. < POM **nan.
    PM 123. *xanu $CSf(2)$. < PMn *xanam.
      At xènū $CSf(?)$, Ay šànù CSf, Ct ènú $CSf(2)$, D šà'nú $CSf(2)$, M šànù $CSf(2)$, O xànū $CSf(2)$, P sánu $CSf(G2)$, S sànuì CSf, SM hànù $CSf(2)$, SP sànū CSf, J čanu $CSf(0)$, Y xānū $PCSf(G,V,S-)$.
    PT 16. *žakoh $CSf(0)$. < PMn *xahku.
      Ch ža⁵ko?⁵ $CSf(3)$, Cp žo³ko?⁵ $CSf(3,yS-)$.
    PC 18. *dakunu $CSf(L)$. < PMn *Θahku-nam.
      Tp adakų̀ų̀nú CSf, Tt de⁴ku³¹no⁴ $CSf(L)$.
    PC 19. *čanu $PCSf(G)$. < PMn *Yxanam.
      Tp čäänú $PCSf(G)$, Tt čä³no³ $PCSf(G)$.
  PMn 309. *xihΘam $SP(2)$. < POM **san.
    PM 121. *tiΘo $SP(2)$. < PMn *xihΘam.

At čìsō *SP(?);* **Ay** tìsò *SP;* **dì'dó** *SP(2);* **M** sīsó *SP(2);* **O** čìsō *SP(2);* **P** šído *fSPCm(G);* **S** šòxòì *SP;* **SM** čisó *SP(2);* **SP** dìdō *SP;* **J** čiso *SP(C);* **Y** tātā čìsò *SPm,* nānà čìsò *SPf.*
PT 14. **žičeh *SP(0),* < PMn **xihΘam.*
Ch ži³če²¹ *SP(3),* dreh³ ži⁵čeh⁵ *SPm,* n·i³ ži⁵čeh⁵ *SPf;* **Cp** žiče²¹ *ySP(3),* reh³ čeh⁵ *eSPm(3,-S),* ni³ čeh⁵ *eSPf(3,-S).*
PC 16. **?indą?ą *SPf(2).* < PMn **?im-Θa?m.*
Tp indą́?ą́ *SPf, SPCm;* **Tt** ?i⁴nda²?an² *SPf(L,G2).*

PMn 137 is presented as a reflex of **POM 432** through its penultimate syllable rather than through its ultima. This is highly questionable, and the association is, in fact, not very likely. Longacre (1959:39f) suggests that the Chicahuaxtla Trique son-in-law term has its source in a phrase meaning *he who spoke,* in reference to the request for the daughter's hand in marriage, and that the daughter-in-law term probably can be associated with the first plural form of a verb meaning *take* (which harks back to **POM 126** ****hkan**). These are very plausible suggestions.

Longacre (1957:132) also suggests that the penult of **PC 17** represents reduplication of the ultima. This may be the case, or it may be the same formative which occurs with **PC 8** **daya C* and **PC 18** **dakunu CSf(L).*

The consonantism of **PC 16** can be considered a result of PMn **nt* rather than **Θ*, in which case the term could be interpreted as an inflected form of a term meaning *female* harking back to **POM 350** ****ntaHn**. The corresponding Cuicatec term for father-in-law does appear to reflect a term of respect for a male and is clearly a Cuicatec innovation.

PC 20. **n-čą?ą ndiku SPm(2).*
Tp inčą ndiikú *SPm,* **Tt** nča³?an³ ndi⁴ko⁴ *SPm(L,G2).*

In summary, there are several unclear associations in attempting to relate the Mixtecan data to the proposed analysis of POM affinal terms. The PMn system which emerges, however, is quite clear and stable, continuing to the present with only minor changes. A single term with primary sense *SP* designated the consanguineal kinsmen of spouse, while two terms with primary senses *CSm* and *CSf* designated the spouses of ego's own consanguineal kinsmen. It is probable that these three terms occurred in phrases to further specify sub-groupings of affinal kinsmen. What is not so clear is the basis upon which the various sub-groupings were defined or if there was a clear boundary past which the ranges of these terms for affinals did not extend.

In regard to extension of terms, it may be that Rule 0, unlimited extension, applied to these terms so that in their widest sense they extended to all consanguineal kinsmen of spouse and to spouses of all of ego's consanguineal kinsmen. That appears to be the Western Jamiltepec situation today, at least for the two child-in-law terms if not also for the parent-in-law term (where the unique limitation of the term to *SP* and *SPC* may simply reflect incomplete data).

Trique languages are reported to limit extension of these terms by Rule 3, which in effect encompasses all the affinals in question other than those who qualify as grand-kinsmen. This limitation implies a clear division between affinals and grandkinsmen which is a question which might bear further investigation. It may be that alternate means of classifying kinsmen of that distance are available which depend upon social and linguistic contexts.

In Cuicatec languages, apart from affinals of ego's generation, it would appear that the extended ranges of affinal terms have been reduced by the extension of consanguineal terms to include collateral affinals. Otherwise, Cuicatec supports the strong pattern in Mixtec languages suggesting that affinals included only kinsmen-in-law as opposed to step-kinsmen in the senses defined by Lounsbury (1965:163). This limitation is expressed here by Rule 2 such that the parent-in-law term extends to all of spouse's direct ancestors and to spouse's collateral kinsmen of spouse's generation and above, while the child-in-law terms extend to spouses of all of ego's lineal descendants and to spouses of all of ego's collaterals of his (or her) generation or below. The step-kinsmen—spouse's collateral kinsmen of descending generations and spouses of ego's ascending-generation collateral kinsmen—are typically treated as consanguineal kinsmen by modern Mixtec languages. Whether that pattern existed at the PM or PMn horizons or not is not at all clear. Step-kinsmen may have fallen outside the scope of kinship altogether, if Rule 2 does in fact express the scope of the extended range of these terms at one or another of these horizons.

In light of the above, the extended ranges of affinal terms at the depth of PMn are best expressed either by Rule 0 or Rule 2. The implication of Rule 0 is, of course, that any kinsman of spouse or any spouse of a kinsman is to be acknowledged as an affinal. The implication of Rule 2, on the otherhand, is that the affinal relationship is one which is established *only between adults,* i.e., persons of marriageable age, and *only at the time of a specific marriage.* The kinsmen of spouse who are of spouse's generation or above is a de facto way of saying kinsmen of spouse who are at least of marriageable age and, therefore, adults. The spouses of kinsmen of ego's generation or below is another way of saying spouses of kinsmen who do not marry until ego is himself of marriageable age and, therefore, an adult.

Since Rule 2 implies that both parties of an affinal relationship must be adults *at the time of the marriage which establishes that relationship,* excluding those persons from the relationship who become adults subsequent to the celebration of the marriage which would otherwise so relate them, it seems safe to presume that the relationship also entails rights and obligations between the parties of the relationship which pertain directly to the transaction of the marriage itself. Unfortunately, information regarding the nature of such possible rights and obligations is not available to us, even though several Mixtecan systems currently employ the principle of Rule 2 in defining the ranges of affinal kinsmen. Without such information, it is difficult to decide the significance of choosing Rule 2 over Rule 0, or vice versa, as the more probable one to have been in effect at the PMn horizon.

In the absence of other evidence, then, we must rely on the overriding frequency of the occurrence of Rule 2 within Mixtecan languages to suggest that it most probably represents the principle of extension which the languages shared at the time they separated from other Otomanguean groups. The following statements, therefore, begin with this assumption in their attempt to represent a possible history of semantic shifts from PMn times to the present.

The exception is Proto Trique which is best considered to have retained unlimited extension (Rule 0), as in POM. Modern Trique languages have subsequently narrowed the affinal categories to extension by Rule 3, considering more distant affinals as grand-kinsmen.

Q

$0 \rightarrow 3$ / $\begin{cases} SP \\ CS \end{cases}$ (Ch Cp)

(Ch Cp).

Copala Trique further evidences attention to relative age in the subgrouping of affinals and the extension of affinal relationships to the spouses of affinals. Disregarding the matter of relative age, the latter extension may be expressed as follows:

$\emptyset \rightarrow$ $\begin{cases} -S \ / \ SP \\ S- \ / \ CS \end{cases}$ (Cp).

(Cp).

Certain Mixtec and Cuicatec languages have shifted from the Mixtecan pattern by reducing affinal ranges to lineal affinals and affinals of ego's or spouse's generation. All other collateral affinals now fall within the extended ranges of terms for consanguineal kinsmen. In certain cases, lineal affinals are distinguished by modifiers from affinals of ego's or spouse's generation, but the general semantic shift may be expressed as follows:

$2 \rightarrow L,G2$ / $\begin{cases} SP \\ CS \end{cases}$ (Ay P S SP J Y Tp Tt)

(Ay P S SP Y Tp Tt).

Western Jamiltepec was mentioned above as evidencing a wider extension of terms for junior affinals than for senior, creating a skewed situation as regards reciprocals. This may be due to incomplete data which results in the apparent participation of J in only the first part of the above shift. J apparently does participate in the following shifts.

$2 \rightarrow \emptyset$ / $\begin{cases} SP \\ CS \end{cases}$ (J?)

(J).

The extension of grandkinsman terms has further reduced affinal areas of most of the languages adopting the above shifts, the exceptions being Teutila Cuicatec and Western Jamiltepec Mixtec (for junior affinals).

$L \rightarrow \emptyset$ / $\begin{cases} SP \\ CS \end{cases}$ (Ay P S SP J Y Tp)

(Ay P S SP Y Tp).

Three of the above languages (Ay S SP) retain the area of extension which results from the above loss of Rule L, but divide the lineal affinals from collaterals by introducing loan words from Spanish for the latter, and reducing the ranges of the Mixtec lexical material accordingly. Yosondua shows a unique pattern in reducing the range of the parent-in-law terms to lineal affinals, and extending the child-in-law terms to fill the void created thereby.

$G2 \rightarrow \emptyset$ / SP   (Y).

$\emptyset \rightarrow V$ / PCS   (Y).

There are a few additional shifts which are unique to individual systems because of the encroachment of Spanish terms, but these are not of general interest to the family. In Peñoles, for example, all lineal affinals except those of the first descending generation are referred to by consanguineal terms, and male ego uses Spanish terms for his wife's kinsmen of her generation. The parent-in-law term is used only by female ego, and only for her husband's male kinsmen of his generation, a descriptive phrase being used for her husband's corresponding female kinsmen.

The rules have been presented for the reduction of ranges of affinal terms where certain consanguineal terms extended into affinal areas. The corresponding extension of ranges of consanguineal terms may be summarized as follows:

$\emptyset \rightarrow S$- /
- P   (P)
- PP   (Ay M O P Y)
- CC   (Ay O SM Y Ch Cp).

$\emptyset \rightarrow$ -S /
- PP   (Ay O Sm Y Ch Cp)
- CC   (Ay O P Y)
- PC   (Ay).

The Development of PMn Spouse Terms

Trique languages support a generic term for spouse, but Mixtec and Cuicatec support the use of terms meaning *male* and *female* to designate husband and wife, respectively. These latter terms hark back to POM terms, all of which were first discussed above under the discussion of POM and PMn parent terms.

PT 17. *nika *S.*
    Ch ni³ka⁴, Cp ni³ka̧⁴.
POM 254. **sehn, **yehn *male.*
    PMn 307. *Өeʔm, *yehm *Sm.* < POM **seʔn, **yehn.
        PM 124. *yïï *Sm.* < PMn *yehm.
        At žä̃, Ay ñ̃, Ct šñ̃, D 'žä̃, M ñ̃, O žñ̃, P žä̃, S žñ̃, SM žñ̃, SP ʔñ̃, J ii, Y žä̃.
        PC 21. *ʔin-sa̧ʔa̧ *Sm.* < PMn *Өeʔm.
        Tp isáʔà, Tt ʔi⁴nča³ʔan³.
POM 340. **suhn, **nuhn *Pf, PPCf(R,G), female.*
    PM 109. *ña-Өïʔï *Sf.* < POM **nya-suʔn.
    (See above for data listing.)
POM 350. **ntaHn, **naHn, **yaHn *Pf(vocative), PPCf(R,G), female.*
    PMn 302. *ndaʔa, *ñaʔa *Sf.* < POM **ntaʔn, **nyaʔn.
        PC 7. *ndaʔa-ta *Sf.* < PMn *ndaʔa.
        Tp nʔdaatá *Sf,* Tt ndʔa³ta³ *Sf.*

CHAPTER 3
PROTO POPOLOCAN
KINSHIP TERMS

This chapter proposes a set of Proto
Popolocan kinship terms with corresponding ranges of reference, presents and discusses the evidence
upon which the proposal is made,
and summarizes a possible sequence
of development through Proto
Mazatec and Proto Popoloc horizons
to contemporary Popolocan languages.

PPn KINSHIP TERMS

The Proto Popolocan kinship system distinguished twelve categories of consanguineal kinsmen, six of them lineal and six of them collateral. Lineal kinsmen were divided between senior and junior kinsmen with two degrees of distance being distinguished, although additional degrees could also be specified by the cumulative addition of modifiers. Elementary terms distinguished the sex of senior lineals whereas junior lineals were classified together without reference to sex apart from the use of specific sex-marking material which could be added.

PPn Parent and Child Terms

There were, thus, three categories of first generation lineals—father, mother, and child. Proto Mazatec and Ixcatec attest the first father and child terms listed below, while other languages support the second.

*na⁴ʔmi³, *tʔa¹	Pm	father
*nʔa⁴	Pf	mother
*ʔntye¹, *čhą⁴	C	child

In one sense, it is correct to think of the parent and child terms as extending their ranges to all lineals by Rule L, since grandkinsmen are designated by appending modifiers to these same terms. It is not clear, however, that parent and child terms are used generically for such more distant lineals in the absence of such modifiers. For this reason, Rule L is assigned to grandkinsman terms only.

ꝒPn Grandkinsman Terms

Three categories of grandkinsmen are distinguished by the use of the parent terms and a postposed modifier. The modifier *hča¹ *old* is appended to parent terms, while the modifier of the child terms is probably a form of the first child term which at an earlier time combined in a descriptive phrase of the form *child's child* but later was reshaped and lexicalized to mean *grandchild*.

*na⁴ʔmi³ hča¹, *tʔa¹ hča¹	PPm(L)	grandfather
*nʔa⁴ hča¹	PPf(L)	grandmother
*ʔntye¹ ntai⁴, *čhą⁴ ntai⁴	CC(L)	grandchild

PPn Terms for Collateral Kinsmen

As in the case of lineal kinsmen, there are also six categories of collateral kinsmen in Proto Popolocan, also further divided into two sets of three on the basis of distance. Distance is here defined genealogically but, as will be discussed briefly below, there is evidence that sociological factors may have resulted in a reinterpretation of the genealogical facts in some instances.

All kinsmen of ego's generation were divided into three categories in Algonkian fashion, marking the sex of elder kinsmen but not of younger. The third term appears to have extended beyond ego's generation as a generic term for collateral kinsmen and, in this sense may not have been limited to junior collaterals only. Proto Mazatec attests different variants of two of these terms from those attested by Proto Popoloc.

*nciʔi, *saʔu	ePCm(G)	elder brother
*kahu	ePCf(G)	elder sister
*cikhį, *kici	yPC(G), PC(0)	younger sibling

Remaining collateral kinsmen—those not of ego's generation—were also divided in Algonkian fashion into three categories, apparently extending to several generations without specific limit. Since seniority is defined by relative age and, yet, kintypes of ego's generation must be excluded from the ranges of these terms, they are defined by use of Rule I which has the effect of including inverse ranges within their scope. In particular, ePPC(I) includes ePPC and ePCC while yPCC(I) includes the corresponding yPPC and yPCC.

*ci³ni³	ePPCm(I,I)	elder distant brother
*kHwą³	ePPCf(I,I)	elder distant sister
*kaʔme	yPCC(I,I)	younger distant sibling

As indicated above, the division between kinsmen of ego's generation and other collaterals may have been blurred by sociological factors. Popoloc, in particular, supports the idea that sociologically *near* kinsmen—those perhaps who lived in the same home or extended family compound, or who worked or played together on a regular basis—may have ignored genealogical distance by referring to one another as *siblings* even though of different generations. If this hypothesis is correct, the ranges of these terms would be defined more directly by defining sociological concepts *near (N)* and *distant (D)* as parameters of the system of reference. Taking the two terms for elder male kinsmen as examples, their respective ranges could then be defined as *eNPCm(0)* and *eDPCm(0)*.

PPn Affinal Terms

Just two categories of affinals are defined by PPn terms, although several subcategories must necessarily have been distinguishable by the use of further inflection or modification. One term designates any kinsman of spouse who is of his or her generation or above. The other term designates the spouse of any of ego's kinsmen who is of ego's generation or below. In light of the fact that seniority is defined for PPn consanguineal kinsmen in terms of relative age, it may be more correct to consider the limits of these ranges as relating to the relative age of ego and spouse rather than to their generation, but the modern data specifically tie them to generation. Ranges for these terms defined by relative age presumably would be *eSP(0)* and *yCS(0)*, respectively.

*ʔča¹, *čha⁴	SP(2)	spouse's kinsman
*kha⁴ʔnta³	CS(2)	kinsman's spouse

PPn Spouse Terms

No single term for husband or wife reconstructs at the Proto Popolocan horizon, but there is considerable support for the hypothesis that possessed forms of general terms for male and female distinguished spouses by their sex.

*šiʔį, *nta-wa	Sm	husband
*ʔkwa, *čihį, *čhų⁴¹	Sf	wife

PMz Kinship Terms

Proto Mazatec differs from Proto Popolocan only in minor lexical innovations and a few semantic shifts in the definition of collateral kinsmen.

There are no significant changes in the system of reference for lineal kinsmen.

*na⁴ʔmi³	Pm	father
*na⁴	Pf	mother
*ʔnti¹	C	child
*na⁴ʔmi³ hča¹	PPm(L)	grandfather
*na⁴ hča¹	PPf(L)	grandmother
*ʔnti¹ntai⁴	CC(L)	grandchild

Collateral kinsmen are redefined in Mazatec strictly along genealogical lines with no evidence of relative age or social proximity affecting their classification. With the loss of relative age as a factor, the younger sibling term retains only its more generic usage to refer to any collateral kinsman without reference to age or generation.

*nce⁴ʔe⁴	PCm(G)	brother
*nti³čha³	PCf(G)	sister

*ši²khį¹	PC(0)	collateral kinsman
*ci³ni³	PPCm(1)	uncle
*nču³khwą³	PPCf(1)	aunt
*kha⁴?me³	PCC(1)	junior collateral

Through lexicalization of phrase and inflectional material, the PPn term for spouse's kinsman splits in Proto Mazatec to distinguish father, mother, and sibling of spouse. The available data argue (from silence, but perhaps only from incompleteness) that affinal ranges were more limited in PMz than those proposed for PPn.

*na⁴?mi³č?a¹	SPm	father-in-law
*na⁴č?a¹	SPf	mother-in-law
*čha⁴	SPC(G)	sibling-in-law

The term for kinsman's spouse also splits in PMz by the addition of *š- to designate a male affinal. The extended range (by Rule 2) has probably not changed for junior affinals, which would also indicate that the PMz ranges for senior affinals were actually larger than indicated above.

*škha³?nta³	CSm(2)	son-in-law
*kha⁴?nta³	CSf(2)	daughter-in-law

Husband and wife continue to be distinguished by two terms meaning male and female respectively.

*ši⁴?į³	Sm	husband
*čhụ⁴¹	Sf	wife

PP Kinship Terms

Proto Popoloc continues to reflect Proto Popolocan kinship reference without significant change other than lexical replacement and regular sound change.

*t?a¹	Pm	father
*n?a³	Pf	mother
*čhą³	C	child
*t?a¹či³	PPm(L)	grandfather
*n?a¹či³	PPf(L)	grandmother
*čhą³nti²	CC(L)	grandchild
*s?au	ePCm(G)	elder brother
*khau	ePCf(G)	elder sister
*kiči	yPC(0)	younger sibling
*ci³ni³	ePPCm(I,I)	uncle
*khwa	ePPCf(I,I)	aunt
*šą-kwę?ę	yPCC(I,I)	junior collateral
*č?a¹	SP(2)	spouse's kinsman
*ki²nta²	CS(2)	kinsman's spouse
*ši	Sm	husband
*čihį	Sf	wife

The Development of PPn Parent and Child Terms

Mazatec and Ixcatec retain reflexes of POM 361 **kwin-yu-wa, but in some of the languages it has shifted in its use. It shows up in Ixcatec as the basis for the grandfather term, and in Huautla and Ixcatec as a term for (Roman Catholic) priest. Otherwise, the Popoloc languages have adopted POM 49 **Ytah as their father term, and Ixcatec has gone to lingua franca tata, as has Chocho. All Popolocan languages reflect the POM term for mother **naHn which, together with POM 49 **Ytah, have been influenced heavily by nana and tata, respectively.

POM 49. **Ytah *Pm(vocative)*.
 PP 1. *t?a¹ *Pm*. < POM **?ta.
  A t?a²na¹³ *Pm(L)*, t?a¹či⁴na²³ *PPm(L)*; O t?ánâ *Pm*; T ntodana *Pm*, ntoda?a *Pm(unpossessed)*, ntončana *SPm*, ntooešina *CSPm*, ntooelitona *PPm(G,S)*.
  I tata *Pm*.
  C tatána *Pm*, tačína *PPm*. < tata, POM **ta.
POM 361. **kwin-yu-wa, **kin-yu-wa, **nwin-yu-wa *Pm*.
 PPn 227. *na⁴?mi³ *Pm*. < POM **?nwi.
  PMz 282. *na⁴?mi³ *Pm*. < PPn **na⁴?mi³.
  H n?ai³ *Pm*, na⁴?mi³ *priest;* J na³?mi² *Pm;* Q na⁴?mi³⁴ *Pm*.
  I na²?mi¹ci¹ *PPm*, na³?mi¹ *priest.*
POM 350. **ntaHn, **naHn, **yaHn *Pf(vocative)*, *PPCf(R,G)*, *female*.
 PPn 357. *n?a⁴ *Pf*. < *na?a < POM **?nahn.
  PMz 253. *na⁴ *Pf*. < PPn *na.
  H na⁴ *Pf,* J na³ *Pf,* Q na·³⁴ *Pf*.
 PP 2. *n?a³ *Pf*. < PPn *n?a⁴.
  A na⁴na¹³ *Pf(L)*; O n?ánâ *Pf;* T hanana *Pf,* hana?a *Pf(unpossessed)*.
  I na²?a¹ *Pf*. < PPn *n?a.
  C nanána *Pf*. < nana.

Both POM child terms are attested in PPn, POM 57 being reflected in Mazatec and Ixcatec while POM 308 is reflected in Popoloc and Chocho. Huautla Mazatec has two specific son and daughter terms, ti³ *Cm* and co²ti³ *Cf*, which lack preposed laryngeal and nasal. co² harks back to an unstressed form of POM 340 **suhn *female*.

POM 57. **?ntan³ *C*.
 PPn 267. *?ntye¹ *C*. < POM **Y?ntan³.
  PMz 714. *?nti¹ *C*. < PPn *?nti¹.
  H ?nti¹ *C*, ?nti¹ntai⁴ *CC(L);* J nti¹, ti¹ *C;* Q ki³?nti² *C(sing)*, ni⁴šti³⁴ *C(plural)*.
  PMz: H ti³ *Cm*, co²ti³ *Cf;* J ti² *fCm*. < PPn *ti, *co-ti.
  I ?nje¹ *C*, ?nje¹ye¹ *CC*, ?nje⁴ *little (of animals)*.
POM 308. **Yhnsan, **hyan *C*.
 PPn 135.* čha⁴ *C*. < POM **Ynsahn.
  PMz: J hmi²nčha¹ *fCm(plural)*.   ‿ PPn *nčha.
  PP 3. čha³ *C*. < PPn *čha⁴.
  A šha⁴na²³ *C*, O čhà?nà *C*, T ša?na *C*.
  C šana *C*, šandína *CC(G2)*.

There is no change of reference in Popolocan parent and child terms from that of their POM sources.

The Development of PPn Grandkinsman Terms.

The two POM grandkinsman terms are lost almost without a trace in PPn. The exceptions are as follows:

Chiquihuitlán Mazatec exhibits a grandmother term či³ky?³¹⁴ which is cognate with the PMn grandmother term innovation, but which is clearly a loan from nearby Cuicatec. Western Popoloca has two sets of grandparent terms, one which adds sīnō and sítá to parent terms to designate grandfather and grandmother, respectively. These forms are also reminiscent of Mixtecan formations, particularly, the grandmother term which appears to be a PM innovation.

Apart from these apparent borrowings, PPn utilizes phrases to designate grandkinsmen, retaining intact the POM pattern of adding a modifier meaning *old* to parent terms for grandparents and a *child's child* phrase for grandchildren. The POM pattern of extension by Rule L is also continued in PPn.

POM 189. **kwe?n², **ke?n *big, old.*
  PPn 359. *hča¹ *big, old.* < POM **Yhken.
    PMz 454. *hča¹: H n?ai³hča¹ *PPm(L)*, na⁴hča¹ *PPf(L)*; J na³?mi²ča¹ *PPm(L)*, na³ča¹ *PPf(L)*; Q nča³wa¹⁴ *PPm(L)*.
    PP 4. *či³: A t?a¹či⁴na²³ *PPm(L)*, na¹či⁴na²³ *PPf(L)*; O t?áčí?nà *PPm(L,S)*, n?áčí?nà *PPf(L,S)*.
      I na²?mi¹ci¹ *PPm(?)*, na²ci¹ *PPf(?)*; C tačina *PPm(?)*, načina *PPf(?)*.
POM 50. **?ntan³ Yhntah³ *CC(L)*.
  PPn 360. *?ntye¹ ntai⁴, *chạ⁴ ntai⁴ *CC(L)*. < POM **Y?ntan³ ntahi, **Ynsahn Yhntah³.
    PMz 733. *ntai⁴: H ?nti¹ntai⁴ *CC(L)*, Q ki³?nti²ntai²⁴ *CC(L)*.
    PP 5. *nti²: A šhạ⁴nti²na¹³ *CC(L)*, O čhạ́ndínâ *CC(L,S)*, T sạntina *CC(1,S)*.
      I ?nje¹ye¹ *CC(?)*, C šandína *CC(G2)*.

With the loss of POM grandkinsmen terms, there was a corresponding shift in the categorization of distant collateral kinsmen in PPn, there no longer being terms which classified them with distant lineal kinsmen. All lineal kinsmen were now classified as subclasses of parents or children; all collateral kinsmen were classified as kinds of sibling. (The child term in Chocho seems to contradict this pattern, but the rules of extension in Chocho and Ixcatec have really not been worked out for lack of data, so that the more complete information from Mazatec and Popoloc must be given greater weight.) The PPn pattern continues uniformly in all contemporary Mazatec and Popoloc languages reported.

The Development of PPn Terms for Collateral Kinsmen

Like PMn, PPn also shows a division of the POM range of collateral kinsmen—definable most generically as *PC(0)*—into generation peers of ego as opposed to all other collaterals. In the case of PPn, however, the development shows no sign of any of the terms developing self-reciprocal ranges by Rule R, and is therefore much more straightforward. Rule I is introduced, nevertheless, in association with the definition of seniority by relative age, as in PMn.

$$epC(0) \rightarrow \begin{cases} ePPC(I,1) \\ epC(G) \end{cases}$$

The derivation is further simplified in PPn by the loss of the POM cross-sex sibling term and the principle of *sex of ego* as a feature of the system. The man's term for elder brother becomes a term for elder brother regardless of ego's sex; the woman's term for elder sister becomes a term for elder sister without reference to ego's sex.

$$m,f \rightarrow \emptyset \,/\, \_\_PC$$
$$aPCb \rightarrow \emptyset$$

The inflectional details upon which the elder brother and elder sister terms divided into four terms are not known. The association of these terms with POM sources is even somewhat speculative since all the phonological details have not been worked out. The hypothesis is nevertheless put forward that each of the two terms divided and hark back to POM brother and sister terms. **PPn 362** unaccountably loses an alveolar consonant if the association is correct, perhaps on the analogy of **PP 8** *khau < *kahu < **hkahn, which shows only a laryngeal between vowels. The penult of **PMz 307** harks back to **POM 340** **suhn *female*.

POM 423. **tu, **nu, **yu *emPCm(0)*.
  PPn 362. *nci?i, *sa?u *epCm(G)*. < *nci?ni, *sa?nu < POM **nsi?ni, **sa?nu.
   PMz 286. *nce⁴?e⁴ *PCm(G)*. < PPn *nci?i.
      H nc?e⁴ *PCm(G)*, J nda³nc?e¹ *PCm(singular)*, Q ?ncä⁴ *PCm(G)*.
   PP 7. *s?au *ePCm(G)*. < PPn *sa?u.
      A sa⁴na¹³ *ePCm(0,S)*, O s?ónâ *ePCm(S)*, T saona *ePCm*.
  PPn 363. *ci³ni³ *ePPCm(I,1)*, < POM **nsini.
   PMz 34. *ci³ni³ *PPCm(1)*. < PPn *ci³ni³.
      H ci³ni³ *PPCm(1)*, J ci²ni² *PPCm*, Q ci³ni³⁴ *PPCm(1)*.
   PP 8. *ci³ni³ *ePPCm(I,1)*. < PPn *ci³ni³.
      A ši⁴ni²na¹³ *ePPCm(I,0,S)*, O çí?nínâ *ePPCm(I,0,S)*, T činina *PPCm(G,S)*.
      I ci²ña¹ *PPCm*, C šnina *PPCm*.
POM 236. **kwaHn, **kaHn *efPCf(0)*.
  PPn 364. *kahu *ePCf(G)*. < POM **hkahn.
   PMz 387. *nti²čha³ *PCf(G)*. < PPn *Yhkah.
      H nti³čha³ *PCf(G)*, J ni²čha² *PCf(singular)*, Q ti³čha³ *PCf(G)*.
   PP 9. *khau *ePCf(G)*. < PPn *kahu.
      A kha³na¹³ *ePCf(0,S)*, O khǒnâ *ePCf(S)*, T haona *ePCf*.
  PPn 84. *kHwą³ *ePPCf(I,1)*. < POM **kwaHn.
   PMz 307. *nču³khwą³ *PPCf(1)*. < PPn *khwą.
      H nčo³khoą³ *PPCf(1)*, J ču²kwhą² *PPCf*, Q nču³khuą³⁴ *PPCf(1)*.
   PP 10. *khwa *ePPCf(I,1)*. < PPn *khwa.
      A khoa⁴na³ *ePPCf(I,0,S)*, O khoã?nà *ePPCf(I,0,S)*, T hoa?na *PPCf(G,S)*.
      I kwa²?a² *PPCf*, C bana *PPCf*.

Rule G appears to best represent the extended range of sibling terms in PPn, as attested in PMz. In Popoloc, sibling terms range more widely by Rule 0 for those kinsmen who are socially close to ego. The rule here appears to have more of a sociological definition than a genealogical one, as discussed earlier. Although this is unique to PPn, it may be a direct reflection of the former flexibility of POM terms as they ranged over collateral kintypes. Two Popoloc languages show reduction of the ranges of sibling terms to their primary denotations. PMz and T lose relative age as a principle for classifying collateral kinsman (which also entails the loss of Rule I, when present).

$$G \rightarrow \begin{cases} 0 & / PC \\ \emptyset & / PC \end{cases} \qquad \text{(A)} \\ \qquad\qquad\qquad\qquad \text{(O T).}$$

$e(I), y(I) \rightarrow \emptyset / PC, PPC, PCC$ (PMz T).

$l \rightarrow G / PPC, PCC$ (T).

With the split of elder sibling terms in PPn to designate elder siblings and senior collaterals of ascending generations, an additional term develops to designate junior collateral kinsmen not of ego's generation, while a reflex of the POM generic term for siblings becomes its counterpart for younger collaterals who are of ego's generation. The source of the first of these terms is not at all certain. It is clearly a phrase based on child terms, but the final two syllables are of most importance. Of these, the ultima is tentatively considered to be associated with **POM 361 **kwin** *father*, following the same pattern as was discussed for PMn. The penultima may be an unstressed form of **PPn 84 *kHwą³** *ePPCf(I,1)*.

Gudschinsky reconstructs *n as the nasal in **PPn 246** in spite of the occurrence of m in Huautla forms because of a supposed relationship between **PPn 246** and the Mixtecan grandchild term of **PMn 27** which shows an alveolar nasal. This relationship is unlikely even though range *CC* extends to *PCC* (by Rule 2) in POM.

POM 361. **kwin-yu-wa, **kin-yu-wa, **nwin-yu-wa *Pm, PPCm(R,G) male*.
   PPn 246. *kaʔme yPCC(I,1)*. < POM **kaʔnwin.
   PMz 734. *kha⁴ʔme³ PCC(1)*. < PPn *kaʔme.
     H ti³kha⁴ʔme³ *PCCm(1)*, co²ti³kha⁴ʔme³ *PCCf(1)*; Q ki³ʔnti² nču²⁴ʔme² *PCC(1)*.
   PP 11. *šą-kwęʔę yPCC(I,1)*. < PPn *kaʔwe.
     O čāwʔę̀ *yPCC(I,1,S)*, T šąkoęʔę *PCC(G,S)*.
POM 159. **nsi-kihn, **kihn-si *yPC(0)*.
   PPn 361. *cikhį, *kici *yPC(0)*. < POM **nsi-kihn, **kin-si.
   PMz 735. *ši²khį¹ *PC(0)*. < PPn *cikhį.
     J ca³khį¹, ʔi³khį¹ *Cf*; J ši²nkhįą¹ *PPCC*; Q ši²khį² *PC(0)*.
   PP 6. *kiči *yPC(0)*. < PPn *kici.
     A ki¹či²na¹³ *yPC(0,S)*, O ʔičą̀ *yPC(S)*, T šąčįą *PC*.
     I ki²či¹ *PCm*, kwa²ki²či¹ *PCf*; C kečana *PC*.

Huautla shows an additional term for younger sibling the source of which is not clear. In the POM chapter it was presented as possibly stemming from **POM 61,** but the derivation assumes analogic change on the model of *khau < *kahu < **hkahn and the reduction of *nsit to nc which is not attested elsewhere.

POM 61. **taʔn *PC(0)*.
   H nco¹ *yPC(0)*. < *nsi-taʔu < POM **nsi-htaʔn.

The Development of PPn Affinal Terms

Within the Popolocan family of languages, a simple system of reference for affinals is strongly supported with very little internal diversity. Affinals are basically divided into two groups by two lexical items, with further inflection distinguishing the sex of kinsmen within each group and, in at least one case, generational distinctions. The two major groups are spouse's kinsmen and kinsmen's spouses.

The latter group is designated by a Popolocan form which appears to hark back to **POM 432** ****kah** *CSm(R,0)* followed by what may be a diminutive (related perhaps to **PPn 267** ****?ntye** *little*) and preceded by ***š-** to distinguish female affinal from male affinal. The former group is designated by a Popolocan form which may hark back either to this same source or to **POM 433** ****nsan** *CSf(R,0)* since **PPn *č** may be a palatal reflex of **POM **k** or ****ns**. Mazatec languages attest to a slightly different form of this term for use in reference to collateral kinsmen of spouse as opposed to lineal kinsmen of spouse, the latter being specified by collocating the affinal term with parent terms.

POM 432. ****kah** *CSm(R,0)*.
  PPn 263. **kha⁴?nta³ CS(2).* < POM ****kah-?nta¹/².**
    PMz 186. **kha⁴?nta³ CSf(2).* < PPn **kha⁴?nta³.*
      H ha⁴?nta³ *CSf(G2),* J n³nta² *CSf,* Q ha⁴?nta³⁴ *CSf(G2).*
    PMz 533. **škha³?nta³ CSm(2).* < PPn **škha³?nta³.*
      H ška⁴?nta³ *CSm(G2),* J ška²nta² *CSm,* Q ška³?nta³⁴ *CSm(G2).*
    PP 13. **ki²nta² CS(2).* < PPn **ki-?nta.*
      A ki¹nta⁴ *CSm(L),* ti¹ki¹nta⁴ *CSf(L);* O gīndā?nà *CSm(G2),* tàgīndā?nà *CSf(G2);* T šą̊kįnta?na *CSm,* sądąinta?na *CSf.*
      I ška¹?nda¹ *CS,* C kanda *CS.*
  PPn 124. **čha⁴, *?ča¹ SP(2).* < POM ****Ykah, **Y?ka.**
    (See immediately below for full data listing.)
POM 433. ****nsan, **nyan** *CSf(R,0)*.
  PPn 124. **?ča¹, *čha⁴ SP(2).* < POM ****Y?nsa, **Ynsah.**
    PMz 60. **č?a¹ SP.* < PPn **?ča¹.*
      H n?ai³ča¹ *SPm,* na⁴ča¹ *SPf;* J na³?mi²nči¹?ya² *SPm,* na³nči¹?ya² *SPf;* Q na⁴?mi³⁴ nča³?ya³⁴ *SPm,* na⁴?ya³⁴ *SPf.*
    PMz 73. **čha⁴ SPC(G).* < PPn **čha⁴.*
      H čha⁴ *SPCm(G),* J -che⁴ *SPC(G),* Q čha⁴ *SPCm(G).*
    PP 12. **č?a¹ SP(2).* < PPn **?ča¹.*
      A č?a⁴ *SP(L);* O č?ánâ *SP;* T ntončana *SPm,* hąnčana *SPf.*
      I na²?mi¹č?a¹ *SPm,* na²č?a¹ *SPf;* C tažana *SPm,* nažana *SPf.*

Gudschinsky (1958:263) focuses upon the reconstruction of the final syllable of **PPn 263** which, as the tonic syllable, is the place we would expect to find the modern phonological reflex of the earlier child-in-law term. Unfortunately, the PPn ultima does not appear to be cognate with any other Otomanguean child-in-law term, forcing us to attempt an association with the penultimate syllable as is done above. This is not entirely satisfactory, but is the best hypothesis available for tying PPn into the reconstruction at this point.

Association with Spanish kinship terms and Hispanic marriage practices has resulted in some adjustments in the way affinal terms extend beyond their primary ranges of reference. This is particularly the case in regard to collateral kinsmen of other than ego's (or spouse's) generation. Affinals who fall within this area were probably originally so classified—as affinals—but more recently have been drawn into the ranges of reference of consanguineal terms. The reduction of affinal ranges in this respect may be stated as follows:

$SP(2) \rightarrow SP(L,G2)$.
$CS(2) \rightarrow CS(L,G2)$.

The data also indicate the loss of extension by Rule L in some languages, but this may simply be due to lack of information in some cases. Mazatec languages then divide the SP ranges by separate inflectional forms *čha⁴ and *ʔča¹, as follows:

$SP(G2) \rightarrow SP, SPC(G)$.

The corresponding extension of consanguineal ranges into these earlier affinal ones, in terms of the data introduced in previous sections of this chapter, may be summarized as follows:

$\emptyset \rightarrow S\text{-},\text{-}S$ / $\begin{cases} PP,CC \\ PC \end{cases}$ (O T) (A O T)

The Development of PPn Spouse Terms

There seems to have been no special term for spouse at the PPn horizon. Rather, a variety of possessed forms of words meaning *male* and *female* are attested, all but one being clearly of POM antiquity. Even the one term for wife for which no sure POM source is here cited is very likely of POM origin and may be inflectionally related to PPn **84. *kHwą³** *ePPCf(I,1)*.

POM 254. **sehn, **yehn *male.*
    PPn 227. *ši?į *Sm.* < POM **Yse?yehn.
        PMz 522. *ši⁴?į³ *Sm.* < PPn *ši?į.
        H š?į⁴ *Sm*, J š?i³ *Sm*, Q šį?³⁴ *Sm*.
        PP 14. *ši *Sm.* < PPn *ši.
        A ši¹⁴ *Sm*, O ší?nà *Sm*, T šiši?na *Sm*.
POM 387. **kwa, **ka, **wa *male.*
    PPn 318. *nta-wa *Sm.* < POM **wa.
        I nda²ba¹ *Sm.*
    PPn 365. *?kwa *Sf.*
        I k?wa¹ *Sf*, kwa²ki²či¹ *PCf*, kwa²?a² *PPCf*.
POM 340. **suhn, **nuhn *Pf, PPCf(R,G), female.*
    PPn 366. *čhų⁴¹ *Sf.* < POM **Ynsuhn.
        PMz 86. *čhų⁴¹ *Sf.* < PPn *čhų⁴¹.
        H čhǫ⁴² *Sf*, J čhų³¹ *Sf*, Q čhų⁴² *Sf*.
POM 255. **siHn, **niHn *Pf, PPCf(R,G) female.*
    PPn 111. *čihį *Sf.* < POM **Ynsihn.
        PP 15. *čihį *Sf.* < PPn **čihį.
        A čhį² *Sf*, O čí?nà *Sf*, T či?na *Sf.*

CHAPTER 4
PROTO OTOPAMEAN
KINSHIP TERMS

This chapter proposes a set of Proto Otopamean kinship terms with corresponding ranges of reference, presents and discusses the evidence upon which the proposal is made, and summarizes a possible sequence of development through a Proto Otomí horizon to contemporary Otomí and to other Otopamean languages.

POP KINSHIP TERMS

The Proto Otopamean system of kinship reference exhibits the largest inventory of terms of any branch of Otomanguean, having heavily exploited both the principle *sex of ego* and the principle *sex of alter,* particularly in reference to collateral and affinal kinsmen.

POP Parent and Child Terms

There were three categories of first-generation lineals in POP, as in almost all Otomanguean languages past and present, namely, *father, mother,* and *child.* The original POM term for father continues to show stem initial alternations in POP, and two forms of the mother term also persist. It may be that the two child terms are also merely alternates of a single term of a pre-POM time. In addition, at some time in the development of POP languages, the lingua franca terms tata and nana were introduced into almost all Otopamean vocabularies in some form or other. It is not clear how early this intrusion occurred and it may not have happened as early as POP; but all the daughter languages of POP show the terms to be firmly entrenched in their vocabularies, and so are included here as having appeared some time during the intervening period.

*peo?, *meo?, *weo?; *tata	*Pm*	*father*
*win, *c?ǫ; *nana	*Pf*	*mother*
*t?oiHC, *c?i	*C*	*child*

POP Grandkinsman Terms

Grandkinsmen appear to have encompassed all kinsmen more than one generation distant from ego, whether lineal or collateral, and collateral kinsmen of just one generation distant from ego at least in some social contexts (discussed below). Just two terms, both self-reciprocal, distinguished the sex of the senior grandkinsman in each dyad, although either of the terms could occur with preposed *?mai- to specify the junior member as well.

*hęm	*PPm(R,2)*	*grandfather*
*to	*PPf(R,2)*	*grandmother*

POP Sibling Terms

Four sibling terms classified siblings in Quechuan fashion by distinguishing the sex of both ego and alter. A fifth very generic term ignored sex altogether. There is evidence that the four terms may have been used only for elder sibling and this is the position taken in their presentation below, but modern witnesses are not consistent on this point. Two distinct terms compete with one another in various languages to denote a man's brother.

*khǫ-a-ta-m, *n?io-i	*emPCm(G)*	*man's elder brother*
*?į-ta-m	*efPCm(G)*	*woman's elder brother*
*khǫ-hoe	*efPCf(G)*	*woman's elder sister*
*nkhǫe	*emPCf(G)*	*man's elder sister*
*kǫ-i	*PC(G)*	*sibling*

POP Terms for Other Collateral Kinsman

Between terms for siblings and terms for grandkinsmen, all collateral kinsmen are covered. There is, nevertheless, an important third set of terms which classifies collateral kinsmen of the first ascending and descending generations, overlapping the ranges of grandkinsman terms. It may be that these terms extended even beyond the first generation from ego, overlapping even more grandkinsman kintypes, but the evidence for this is not as sure as that the grandkinsman terms did encompass kintypes of the first generation from ego.

The position is here taken that social considerations apart from genealogy entered into the classification of collaterals other than siblings (and perhaps even of siblings), so that a particular kinsman was classified as a *grandfather* or as an *uncle* depending upon some sliding measure of social distance which kinsmen tended to manipulate to their social advantage. As intimated above, this kind of flexibility may have been employed even in the use of sibling terms. A rigid classification of collaterals into discrete, well-defined classes based on a strict genealogical interpretation came later, as the POP populations settled into more permanent, sedentary communities.

As in the case of siblings, four classes of first-generation collaterals are distinguished by sex. In this case, however, the evidence is fairly compelling that bifurcate categories had developed, distinguishing the sex of linking kinsman and of the senior member of the ego-alter dyad. In the absence of specific detail on the subject, bifurcation is taken to be of the Seneca type in which parallel and cross categories are defined on the basis of the relative sex of kinsmen of the first generation above that of the junior member of the ego-alter dyad (Merrifield 1980). The terms were self-reciprocal (by Rule R) in which a junior kinsman used the same term for his senior alter ego as the latter did for him or her, although the younger member of the dyad could be specified as in the case of grandkinsman terms by preposing *?mai-.

*mo	=PPCm(R,G)	father's brother
*?oe	xPPCm(R,G)	mother's brother
*ci-ci	=PPCf(R,G)	mother's sister
*hi	xPPCf(R,G)	father's sister

POP Affinal Terms

The elaboration of the POP system of reference for siblings and for other collateral kinsmen—by two sets of four terms—is matched by two additional sets of four terms for affinal kinsmen. Four terms are used self-reciprocally (by Rule R) between parent-in-law and child-in-law, distinguishing the sex of both. It is not clear that the terms extend at all beyond their primary ranges of denotation.

*n-toe-n?ią	mSPm(R)	man's father-in-law
*n-toe-ca	fSPm(R)	woman's father-in-law
*kao	fSPf(R)	woman's mother-in-law
*to	mSPf(R)	man's mother-in-law

The second set of four terms, this time reciprocal by Rule V, classify siblings-in-law, distinguishing sex of both ego and alter and extending to all affinals of ego's and spouse's generation.

*koa?	mPCSm(V,G)	man's brother-in-law
*mo	fPCSm(V,G)	woman's brother-in-law
*mǫtǫ	fPCSf(V,G)	woman's sister-in-law
*po	mPCSf(V,G)	man's sister-in-law

POP Spouse Terms

Spouses are referred to by possessed forms of words meaning *male* or *female* in Proto Otopamean.

*=tǫa-n, *n-?ǫa-n	Sm	husband
*n?ią, *sǫ, *co	Sf	wife

PO Kinship Terms

Proto Otomí exhibits a number of innovations from the earlier POP system. One of the child terms becomes a specific term for male child unless occurring with a female marker to specify a daughter.

*ta	Pm	father
*me	Pf	mother

*baci	C	child
*tʔi	Cm	son
*tʔįšų	Cf	daughter

The POP self-reciprocal grandkinsman terms continue only in their diminutive forms to designate grandchildren, marking sex of ego only (i.e., senior member of the ego-alter dyad). New grandparent terms are then introduced, one pair of terms based on *-ta with differing penult to distinguish sex of kinsman, and a second pair based on *-ta for males and *-cu for females with the penult varying from language to language without known semantic significance. Most modern witnesses support Rule 1 as the limit of extension of these terms, but Mazahua shows the grandparent terms continuing to extend by Rule 2 which implies the grandchild terms must have also extended (reciprocally) by the same rule into PO times.

*tita; *cita, *tạta, *pota	PPm(2)	grandfather
*nita; *cicu, *tạcu	PPf(2)	grandmother
*ʔbä-hịạ	mCC(2)	man's grandchild
*ʔbä-to	fCC(2)	woman's grandchild

The six sibling terms of POP survive intact in PO without significant change in form or in referential ranges.

*khwạda, *ʔñowi	emPCm(G)	man's elder brother
*ʔịdạ	efPCm(G)	woman's elder brother
*khụhwä	efPCf(G)	woman's elder sister
*nkhụ	emPCf(G)	man's elder sister
*kụ	PC(G)	sibling

The bifurcate categories of POP reference to collateral kinsman other than siblings is gone by PO times through the loss of two of the four uncle and aunt terms, the remaining terms occurring alone to refer to senior collaterals and with diminutive to refer to junior collaterals.

*ʔwe	PPCm(G)	uncle
*zici	PPCf(G)	aunt
*ʔbä-ʔwe	mPCC(G)	man's junior collateral
*ʔbä-zici	fPCC(G)	woman's junior collateral

Four parent-in-law terms distinguish sex of ego and alter, as in POP times, but two neologisms appear for son-in-law and daughter-in-law.

*ntë-hñạ	mSPm	man's father-in-law
*ntë-ca	fSPm	woman's father-in-law
*kɔ	fSPf	woman's mother-in-law
*to	mSPf	man's mother-in-law
*m-ʔbä-ʔạhạ	CSm	son-in-law
*cʔị-hwä	CSf	daughter-in-law

Four terms designate siblings-in-law, defining both sex of ego and of alter, and include the spouses of all of ego's generation peers as well as all the generation peers of spouse.

*ko	mPCSm(V,G)	man's brother-in-law
*mo	fPCSm(V,G)	woman's brother-in-law
*mųdų	fPCSf(V,G)	woman's sister-in-law
*ʔbä-po	mPCSf(V,G)	man's sister-in-law

The sex of spouse is specified by separate terms based on words for man and woman, respectively.

*ntë-me	Sm	husband
*ʔbä-hñą, šicu	Sf	wife

POP Parent and Child Terms

Lingua franca **tata** and **nana** are found in the Mesquital, in Mazahua, in Central Pame, and in Chichimeca-Jonaz. They quite possibly exist in other Otopamean communities as well, but were not reported as being of native interest. It seems appropriate to take note of their introduction into OP languages by postulating recent source words adopted by at least some members of the OP language community. It is not clear that such sources date to the POP horizon, but for lack of a better way to tag them they are so named.

POP 812. *tata *Pm.*
  PO: Ms dǎdá *Pm.*
  Mz tata *Pm.*
  CP tát =*Pm(G,S-).*
  Ch tátá *Pm.*
POP 813. *nana *Pf.*
  PO: Ms nǎná *Pf.*
  Mz nana *Pf.*
  CP nán =*Pf(G,S-).*
  Ch náná *Pf.*

Turning now to terms having their sources in POM, both POM father terms are reflected in Otopamean languages. Vocative **POM 49 **Ytah** appears to be the source of Otomí father terms, although one cannot be sure that they do not reflect reduced forms of **tata**. This father term is matched in just these same Otomí languages by a term for mother which can be the result of **POM 148 **win** *Pf.* It is by no means certain that **148** is the true source of this mother term, but it is the best candidate among POM terms. **POM 148** also shows up as a possible source of the CP first person term for mother and of a POP term for aunt which will be discussed in more detail after all POP terms have been introduced.

POM 49. **Ytah *Pm(vocative).*
  PO 289. *ta *Pm.* < POM **ta or **tah.
    E htä *Pm,* **H hta** *Pm,* **J tá** *Pm,* **T ta** *Pm.*
POM 148. **kwin, **kin, **win *Pf, PPCf(R,G), female.*
  PO 177. *me *Pf.* < POM **nwin.

E mé *Pf*, H mbe *Pf*, J mé *Pf*, T me *Pf*.
CP A rawí =*Pf(G)*. < POM **win.
POP 825. *hi *xPPCf(R,G)*. < POM **hki.
PO: E hi *xPPCf, PPCf;* E bähi *xfPCC*. < POP *hi, *mʔai-hi.
Ch A nàhí, C ènhí *fPCf(G), fPCCf*. < POP *hi.

The remaining contemporary OP parent terms result from POM 361 **kwin-yu-wa, for father, and POM 255 **siHn, for mother, as do certain aunt and uncle terms which parallel and complement POP 825 in the set above.

POM 361. **kwin-yu-wa, **kin-yu-wa, **nwin-yu-wa *Pm, PPCm(R,G)*, male.
POP 471. *peoʔ, *meoʔ, *weoʔ *Pm*, < POM **kwin-yu-ʔ, **nwin-yu-ʔ, **win-yu-ʔ.
CP A rawéʔ, B wíeoʔ, C wómmeoʔ =*Pm(G)*.
Ch B úngwè, C émè, D búpè *Pm*.
POP 822. *mo =*PPCm(R,G)*. < POM **nwin.
PO: E mo *PPCm*, bämo =*mPCC*.
POP 823. *ʔoe *xPPCm(R,G)*. < POM **ʔwin.
PO 506. *ʔwe *PPCm(G)*. < POP *ʔoe.
E ue *PPCm*, H ntëʔwe *PPCm(1,S)*, T ʔwe *PPCm(1)*.
PO 507. *ʔbä-ʔwe *mPCC(G)*. < POP *mʔai-ʔoe.
E bäue *xmPCC, PCCm;* H ʔbäʔwe *PCC(1,S);* T ʔbäʔwe *PCC(G)*, bʔähto ʔbäʔwe *PCCC(1)*.
Mz ʔwe *xPPCm*. < POP *ʔoe.
POP: CP A rabbéoʔ, B ábbeoʔ, C wobbéoʔ *xPm(G,S);* či rabbéoʔ *xmC(G)*. < POM **kwin-yu-ʔ.
POM 255. **siHn, **niHn *Pf, PPCf(R,G)*, female.
POP 473. *cʔọ *Pf*. < POM **nsiʔn.
CP B ácʔọ, C wacʔọ̀ =*Pf(G)*.
Ch B úcʔù̀, C ècʔú, D búcʔừn *Pf*.
POP 824. *ci-ci =*PPCf(R,G)*. < POM **nsi-nsi.
PO 508. *zici *PPCf(G)*. < POP *ci-ci.
H cìhci *PPCf(1,S)*, J zìhci *PPCf(G)*, T zisi *PPCf(1)*.
PO 509. *ʔbä-zici *fPCC(G)*. < POP *mʔai-ci-ci.
E bäzici =*fPCC*, Ms ʔbằdàʔci *PCC(1,S)*, Tm ʔbằdìcí *PCC(G)*.
Mz zizi =*PPCf*. < POP *ci-ci.
POP: CP A ncʔộk, B ncʔộkʔ, C ncʔộp *xPf(G,S)*. < POM **nsihn.

The primary data upon which this research is based support the reconstruction of two child terms from POM sources, one from POM 57, a true kinship term in POM times, the other from POM 258 which would appear to have been a generic term for *youngster* in POM times, rather than a true kinship term. The strongest term today, in the sense that reflexes are found in a wide area, is POP 542 from the POM child term (57). In Otomí languages, this term refers only to male offspring unless occurring with a modifier marking it as a female term. Otomí postposes and Mazahua preposes reflexes of POM 340 **suhn *female* for this purpose, but Mazahua also shows alternate female terms with reflexes of POM 148 **kwin *female* as modifier. The *youngster* term is limited to Otomian languages, as far as their systems of kinship terminology is concerned .

POP Terms   89

POM 57; **ʔntan³ *C.*
  POP 542. *tʔoiHC *C.* < **POM **ʔtan.**
   PO 285. *tʔĭ *Cm* < **POP *tʔoiHC.**
   E tʔĭ *Cm,* H cʔĭntʔĭ *Cm,* J tʔĭ *Cm,* Ms tʔĭ *Cm,* T cʔĭntʔĭ *Cm.*
   PO 286. *tʔįšų *Cf.* < **POP *tʔi-sǫ.**
   E tʔįšų *Cf,* H tʔįšų *Cf,* J tʔįšų́ *Cf,* Ms tʔĭšú *Cf,* T tʔįšų *Cf.*
   Mz čʔi, tʔi *C(1);* šuntʔi, čʔihwä, tʔihwä *Cf(1).* < **POP *Ytʔoi, *tʔoi, *sǫ-tʔoi, *Ytʔoi-hoe, *tʔoi-hoe.**
   CP A naʔí, B ŋgodwì, C ŋgodwí, D ŋgolʔwép =*C(G),* xf*C(G).* < **POP *ʔoi, *toi, *tʔoi.**
  Ch útʔų́ *Cm,* undü *Cf,* bùrʔų́ *C.* < **POP *tʔoi, *ntoi, *tʔǫi.**
POM 258. **siʔ *youngster.*
  POP 814. *cʔi *C.* < **POM **nsiʔ.**
   PO 37. *bącí *C* < **POP *mʔai-cʔi.**
   E bącį *C,* šųbącį *Cf;* J bàhcí *C;* Ms bącí *C;* T bąsi *C.*
   Mz čʔi, tʔi *C(1);* šuntʔi, čʔihwä, tʔihwä *Cf(1).* < **POP *cʔi, *tʔi, *sǫ-tʔi, *cʔi-hoe, *tʔi-hoe.**

The Mazahua data are included in both of the sets above, each with an acceptable derivational history. The existence of palatal and nonpalatal alternants of these forms—paralleled, by the way, in other OM families—reenforces the need to examine the possible relationship between forms ascribed to POM **s and those ascribed to POM **t. The OM kinship data press this issue time and time again. In the present instance **POM 57** and **POM 308 **Yhnsan** show the possibility of being related to each other and also to **POM 258** as a general term for youngster as well as an even more general diminutive adjective of animate objects.

Bartholomew reconstructs an additional daughter term from Southern Otomian languages not included within my corpus. It may be related to **POM 308,** as follows:

POM 308. **Yhnsan, **hyan *C.*
  POP 383 *mhǫ-te *Cf.* < **POM **hyan.**

The primary ranges of reference of POM parent and child terms—*Pm, Pf,* and *C*—do not change in POP. The use of inflected forms of the parent terms to designate collateral kinsmen is discussed below after the introduction of all POP terms. The extension of parent and child terms to lineal ancestors and descendents remains a viable concept in POP times, but as the discussion of grandkinsman terms below will show, OP languages are lexically innovative in this regard, not simply following POM patterns of modifying parent and child terms to extend their ranges by Rule L.

Otomí appears to innovate in narrowing the range of reference of the unmodified child term to sons, requiring a modifier to mark daughters. Mazahua marks daughters in this same way, but does not appear to narrow the range of the unmodified form. It is possible that this pattern antedates POP, but the evidence for it really only becomes firm in PO. There is another reflex of this pattern in Huautla Mazatec which could speak for a pre-POP origin of this usage, but it is not outside the realm of possibility that Huautla has adopted this pattern at a late date from Otomí communities to the north. Its absence from any other PPn languages suggests such an intrusion from outside of the Popolocan community. The shift can be stated as follows:

$\emptyset \rightarrow m \ / \ C\_\_$ (E H J Ms T).

The extension of the Mazahua term for child by Rule 1 and of the Central Pame term by Rule G is a function of the use of parent terms for collateral kinsmen to be discussed at the end of this chapter.

POP Grandkinsman Terms

The POM terms for grandfather and grandmother, self-reciprocal by Rule R in POM, retain their self-reciprocal ranges in Central Pame and Chichimeca-Jonaz, but continue in Proto Otomi and Mazahua only for grandchildren and marked with preposed diminutive. Most Otomi languages retain the grandmother term for grandchild, but the seventeenth-century data recorded by Ecker also include the grandfather term as being used for grandchildren by male ego, thereby supporting the hypothesis that both terms continued to the PO horizon with primary ranges *mCC* and *fCC*, respectively. Mazahua retains only the diminutive form of the grandfather term. (The Otomian diminutive is from **POP 537** ***ʔoai-ne** *infant* which is also the source of the penult of **PO 37** ***bąci** *child*.)

POM 429. ****seh, **hkeh** *PPm(R,2)*.
  POP 818. ***hę̨m** *PPm(R,2)*. < POM ****hkehn.**
    PO: E bähią *CC(1)*. < POP ***mʔai-hęm.**
    Mz bʔäče *CC(L,-S)*. < POP ***mʔai-ke.**
    CP A ràhę́ŋ, B wahę̀ŋ, C wanhę́ŋ *PPm(R,G)*. < POP ***hęm.**
    Ch A náhę́, B ùmhę́, C ènhę́, D bùmhę́ʔr *PPm(R,2,S)*. < POP ***hęm.**
POM 430. ****Ynsan, **Ynan** *PPf(R,2)*.
  POP 819. ***to** *PPf(R,2)*. < POM ****nsan.**
    PO 431. ***ʔbäto** *fCC(2)*. < POP ***mʔai-to.**
      E bähto *fCC(1)*, *mCCm(?)*; **H ʔbä̀hto** *CC(L)*; **J ʔbä̀htó** *CC(L)*; **Ms ʔbä̀tó** *CC(L)*; **T ʔbähto** *CC(L)*.
    CP A rattòi, B attòi, C watòi *PPf(R,G)*. < POP ***to-wi.**
    Ch A nàtǘ, B ùtǜ, C èrǘ, D bǜtǘ *PPf(R,2,S)*. < POP ***tǫ-wi.**
    Ch B ùtǘ èléʔ, C èrǘ èléʔ, D bùtǘ èléʔ *PPf.* < POP ***to-wi.**

While Otomian languages retain reflexes of the POM grandparent terms in reference to junior grandkinsmen, they exhibit a strong innovative tradition that has swept over the entire group of languages in reference to senior grandkinsmen in the form of two closely similar sets of terms reminiscent of but not the same as the lingua franca tata/nana terms. Both sets consist of two bisyllabic words which distinguish the sex of the senior kinsman.

The first set appears to be based on father and mother terms with preposed modifier, not to be confused with the POM pattern of reference for lineal grandparents by the use of parent terms and postposed modifier. The father term upon which this grandfather term is based is apparently **POM 49** ****Ytah** (if not ***tata**) while the basis of the grandmother term is **POM 340** ****suhn** *Pf*, *PPCf(R,G)*, *female*. The preposed modifiers vary from language to language: ***po** has not been reconstructed for PO, but **PO 53** ***ci** *small* is a diminutive, while **POP 354** ***n=tąi** < **PO *dą** *big* is an augmentative. Ms simply reduplicates the mother term.

PO 501. *cita, *tạta, *pota *PPm(2)*.
    E dạhta, šihta *PPm(1)*; H pẽhta *PPm(L)*; Ms šítá *PPPm(L)*; T šita *PPm(L)*.
PO 502. *cicu, *tạcu *PPf(2)*.
    E dạcu *PPf(1)*, J čùhčú *PPf(1)*, Ms čúčú *PPPf(L)*, T su *PPf(L)*.

The second set has **ta** as its second syllable which, therefore, does not appear to reflect **POM 49** ****Ytah**. It would seem that these terms were adopted without separate semantic value having been associated with individual syllables.

PO 503. *tita *PPm(2)*.
    J tìtá *PPm(1)*, Ms títá *PPm(L)*, Mz títa *PPm(2)*.
PO 504. ·*nita *PPf(2)*.
    Ms nítá *PPf(L)*, Mz níta *PPf(2)*.

The incursion of these two sets of grandparent terms dates to a general Otomian horizon which encompasses both Otomi languages and Mazahua, as the set above shows. This lexical replacement in Otomian coincides with the semantic shift characterized by a loss of Rule R as a rule of extension associated with the POM grandparent terms, these terms continuing in Otomian only in their diminutive forms.

$R \rightarrow \emptyset \,/\, PP$ (E H J Ms T Mz).

The extended ranges of terms for grandkinsmen were further curtailed in Otomian times from extension by Rule 2 to extension by Rule 1, and later to extension by Rule L in some languages, more so for junior grandkinsmen than for senior grandkinsmen. Central Pame has uniquely restricted the range of grandkinsmen terms to that of Rule G.

$2 \rightarrow 1 \,/$	PP	(E H J Ms T CP)
	CC	(E H J Ms T Mz).
$1 \rightarrow L \,/$	PP	(H Ms T)
	CC	(H J Ms T Mz).
$1 \rightarrow G \,/$	PP	(CP).

POP Sibling Terms

The Jivaran pattern of three POM elder sibling categories is redistributed in POP and further differentiated into four categories which distinguish sex of both ego and alter, the pattern named Quechuan by Murdock (1970:174). The pattern continues in POP to relate only to elder siblings, following the POM pattern. Younger siblings continue to be designated by a generic sibling term which marks neither sex nor seniority.

The switch to four terms is accomplished through several new lexical formations. Only one of the POM Jivaran terms, **POM 423** ****nu** *emPCm(0)*, continues directly into POP without radical reshaping, and it only does so in a few of the Otomi languages. The remaining Otomí languages attest a new term based on **POM 159** ****kuHn** *PC(0)* and **POM 61** ****ta?n** *companion* which matches a second phrase also based on **POM 159,** but with final reflex of **POM 148** ****kwin** *female*, and a third phrase based on **POM 431** ****?ya** *eaPCb(0)* and **POM 61** ****ta?n** *companion*. Where we would have expected a reflex of **POM 236** ****kwaHn** *efPCf(0)*, we apparently get one of the very similar **POM 148** ****kwin** *female*, for man's sister.

POM 423. **tu, **nu, **yu *emPCm(0)*.
POP 189. *nʔio-i *emPCm(G)*. < *nʔiu-wi < POM **Yʔ-nu.
PO 10. *ʔño, PO 321 *-wi *(dual)*.
H nʔyŏhï *MPCm(G)*, nʔyŏʔbe *companion, spouse,* J ʔñŏwí *PC(G)*, T nʔyohï *mPCm(G)*.
CP A hoèo, B nhô, C nhèo *PC(G), PPP(R)*. < POM *hio.
CP wí *yPCf(G), CCCf*. < POP *wi.
POM 61. **taʔn *companion*.
POM 159. **kuHn *PC(0)*.
POM 431. **nsi-ʔya *eaPCb(0)*.
POM 148. **kwin, **kin, **win *Pf, PPCf(R,G), female*.
POP 376. *khǫ-hoe *efPCf(G)*. < POM **kuhn-kwin.
PO 155. *khųhwä *efPCf(G)*. < POP *hkǫ-hoe.
E khųhuä *efPCf(0)*, H khų̀hwä *fPCf(G)*, J khų̀hwä̌ *fPCf(G)*, Ms xúxwä̌ *fPCf(G)*, T xųhwä *fPCf(G)*.
Mz chįhhwä, khųhhwä *fPCf(G)*. < POP *nkho-hoe.
CP hóc *efPCf(G), fPPPf*. < POP *ho-cʔ.
Ch A nàhí, B únhò, C ę̀nhí *fPCf(G), fPCCf*. < POP *hoe.
POP 377. *khǫ-a-ta-m *emPCm(G)*. < POM **kuhn-wa-taʔn.
PO 154. *khwą̊da *emPCm(G)*. < POP *khǫ-a-ta-m.
E khuą̊dą *emPCm*, J khwą̊dą́ *mPCm(G)*, Ms xwą̊dá *mPCm(G)*.
Mz khwą̊rhmą *mPCm(G)*. < POP *khǫ-a-ta-m.
CP A láiʔ, B lyài, C wanái *ePCm(G), PPPm*. < POP *ta-i.
Ch A úré, B ùré, C éné *ePCm(G)*. < POP *ta-i.
POP 378. *ʔį-ta-m *efPCm(G)*. < POM **ʔya-taʔn.
PO 6. *ʔįdą *efPCm(G)*. < POP *ʔį-ta-m.
E įdą *efPCm*, H ʔį̀ta *fPCm(G)*, J ʔį̀dą́ *fPCm(G)*, Ms ìdą́ *fPCm(G)*, T ʔį̀dą *fPCm(G)*.
Mz ʔñinž̧mï, ʔinž̧mï *fPCm(G)*, sę̧ʔę *ePCm*. < POP *n-ʔį-ta-m, *ce-ʔę.
CP A láiʔ, B lyài, C wanái *ePCm(G), PPPPm*. < POP *ta-i.
Ch A úré, B ùré, C éné *ePCm(G)*. < POP *ta-i.
POP 820. *nkhǫe *emPCf(G)*. < POM **nhkVwin.
PO 455. *nkhų *emPCf(G)*. < POP *nkhǫe.
E nkhų *emPCf*, H nkhų́ *mPCf(G)*, J nkhų́ *mPCf(G)*, Ms nkhų́ *mPCf(G)*, T nkhų *mPCf(G)*.
Mz khų *mPCf(G)*, sïngï *ePCf*. < POP *nkho, *co-nkǫ.
CP A kǫ́e, C ŋgǫ́e *emPCf(G), mPPPPf*. < POP *kǫe.
Ch A mánthừ, B mànthừ, C énkữ *mPCf(G)*. < POP *nʔ-hkoe, *n-khoe.

The generic younger sibling term from POM continues in POP without significant phonological reshaping or semantic shift, as the reciprocal of the elder sibling terms and as a general term which does not focus upon seniority.

POM 159. **kuHn *PC(0)*.
POP 821. *kǫ-i *PC(G)*. < *kǫ-wi < POM **kuhn.
PO 159. *kų *PC(G)*. < POP *kǫ.
E hkų *yPC*, H hkų *PC(G)*, Ms kų́ *yPC(G)*, T kų *PC(G)*.

CP kyôi? *yPCm(G), CCCm, PCCm.* < POP *koi?.
Ch A úkų̂, B ùkų̂, C égų̂ *yPCm(G), PCCm.* < POP *kǫi.

All the POP sibling terms show a reduction in extended range to kinsmen of ego's generation from the presumed wider range represented by Rule 0 for the POM horizon. As the POP population began a more settled existence, the distinction between kinsmen of ego's generation and those of greater genealogical distance began to be emphasized and the overlap of extended ranges of various terms was eliminated.

$ø → G / PC$ (POP).

The two terms for elder brother are clearly compounds with common ultima from **POM 61 **ta?n** *companion.* The Pamean languages retain only this ultima, thereby suppressing the distinction between male and female speakers for these terms, but attesting the POP dual ending ***-wi** (Bartholomew 1965:216).

$m,f → ø / \_\_PCm$ (CP Ch).

The development of **POP 189** and **377** as synonymous terms for a man's brother has its source in the **POM 61** use of ****ta?n** *companion* as a sibling term of very similar meaning to that of **POM 159 **kuHn** *PC(0).* Whereas reflexes of **POM 61** turn up in PMn as general terms for *companion,* the reverse is true in POP where Bartholomew lists two sets, **POP 189** and **708**, unaccountably dividing the morphemes differently in each case but otherwise showing the same phonemes. **189** is glossed *companion* while **708** is glossed *sibling.* There is thus a switch in POP between the two POM terms. ****ta?n** is taken into the system of kinship reference and, in some Otomí languages, the POM term for man's brother becomes a term for *companion.*

The CP term included in POP set **189** is placed there on the basis of its meaning in spite of a troublesome consonantism. Bartholomew placed it with the Chichimec term of **POP 376** where the consonantism fits and the vocalic element can also fit, but the meaning of the term is counter to their equation. Huehuetla and Tenango forms of **PO 10** show an ending other than the dual, indicating probable influence on this term from **PO 12 *?ñëhë** *man.*

The relative age distinction has been suppressed for the sibling terms in some Otomian languages and for female siblings in Ch. The two cross sex sibling terms (*mPCf* and *fPCm*) appear to have split in Mazahua, resulting by the addition of ***cV-** in special terms for eldest brother and eldest sister.

$e → ø /$ $\begin{cases} \_\_PCf & \text{(Ch)} \\ \_\_PC & \text{(H J T Mz)} \end{cases}$

CP shows an equation between siblings and kinsmen of the third ascending and third descending generations. Lack of any corresponding pattern in other languages makes it difficult to assess the significance of this for POP, but the equation would seem to place emphasis upon the distinction between particular generations within the system and, in turn, upon the likelihood that rules of extension within generations (Rule G), rather than between them (Rules like 1 or 0), were in force, with the relationship between non-contiguous generations as an additional rule.

POP Senior and Junior Collateral Kinsmen

In addition to the foregoing sibling terms, POP reflects the existence of self-reciprocal terms, by Rule R, for senior and junior collateral kinsmen. Otomian languages support bifurcate collateral terms, with preposed diminutive *m?ai to designate the junior member of the dyad; Central Pame supports bifurcate merging terms, with preposed diminutive *c?i to designate junior kinsman. A single Chichimec form is tentatively associated with the Otomian forms of POP 825 on the basis of its range of reference. This form is also included above in POP 376 *khǫ-hoe efPCf(G) because of its reference to fPCf(G) as well as to fPCCf. It is possible to derive it from both *hoe and from *hi, suggesting that two forms may have coalesced in Ch, retaining both ranges of reference in a single form.

All the collateral terms can be derived from inflected forms of POM parent terms. Those for male collateral kinsmen appear to be the result of POM 361; those for females appear to derive from POM 148 and POM 255. The data were presented above in discussing parent and child terms, but are repeated here as well.

POM 361. **kwin-yu-wa, **kin-yu-wa, **nwin-yu-wa *Pm, PPCm(R,G), male*.

POP 822. *mo =PPCm(R,G). < POM **nwin.

    PO: E mo *PPCm*, bämo =mPCC.

POP 823. *?oe xPPCm(R,G). < POM **?win.

    PO 506. *?we *PPCm(G)*. < POP *?oe.

    E ue *PPCm*, H ntë?we *PPCm(1,S)*, T ?we *PPCm(1)*.

    PO 507. *?bä-?we *mPCC(G)*. < POP *m?ai-?oe.

    E bäwe xmPCC, PCCm; H ?bä̀?we *PCC(1,S)*; T ?bä?we *PCC(G)*, b?ähto ?bä?we *PCCC(1)*.

    Mz ?we xPPCm. < POP *?oe.

POP: CP A rabbéo?, B ábbeo?, C wobbéo? xPm(G,S); či rabbéo? xmC(G), < POM **kwin-yu-?.

POM 255. **siHn, **niHn *Pf, PPCf(R,G), female*.

POP 473. *c?ǫ *Pf*. < POM **nsi?n.

    CP B ác?ǫ, C wac?ǫ̀ =Pf(G).

POP 824. *ci-ci =PPCf(R,G). < POM *nsi-nsi.

    PO 508. *zici *PPCf(G)*. < POP *ci-ci.

    H cìhci *PPCf(1,S)*, J zìhcí *PPCf(G)*, T zisi *PPCf(1)*.

    PO 509. *?bä-zici fPCC(G). < POP *m?ai-ci-ci.

    E bäzici =fPCC, Ms ?bä̀dà?ci *PCC(1,S)*, Tm ?bä̀dìcí *PCC(G)*.

    Mz zizi =PPCf. < POP *ci-ci.

POP: CP A nc?ǫ̂k, B nc?ǫ̂k?, C nc?ǫ̂p xPf(G,S). < POM **nsihn.

POM 148. **kwin, **kin, **win *Pf, PPCf(R,G), female*.

POP: CP A rawí =Pf(G). < POM **win.

POP 825. *hi xPPCf(R,G). < POM **hki.

    PO: E hi xPPCf, PPCf; E bähi xfPCC. < POP *hi, *m?ai-hi.

    Ch A nàhí, C ę̀nhí fPCf(G), fPCCf. < POP *hi.

The reference of the Otomí terms has shifted radically since POP times and would be difficult to discern were it not for the seventeenth-century material from Ecker and the existence of bifurcate categories in CP through the use of modified parent terms for cross kinsmen of first ascending and first descending generations. The Ecker material, however, does provide a consistent enough picture to indicate that sex of senior kinsman (in the ego-alter dyad) and sex of senior kinsman's generation peer were diagnostic in defining the ranges of the POP sources of these terms.

Apart from extended ranges of reference, semantic shifts for these four terms in Otomí languages can be shown as follows, looking first at the ranges for senior collateral kinsmen.

*mo	=PPCm	→	PPCm	→	*no change*	(E)
					Spanish replacement	(J Ms)
					loss	(H T).
*cici	=PPCf	→	PPCf	→	*no change*	(H J T)
					Spanish replacement	(Ms)
					loss	(E?).
*ʔoe	xPPCm	→	PPCm	→	*no change*	(E H T)
					Spanish replacement	(J Ms).
*hi	xPPCf	→	*no change*			(E)
			PPCf	→	*no change*	(E)
					Spanish replacement	(Ms)
					loss	(H J T).

The parallel-cross distinction was lost almost everywhere, with only one reference in the material from Ecker to *xPPCf* for **hi** (and that in competition even there with the more general reference *PPCf*). E retains all of the terms except ***cici** (which may simply be an oversight by the seventeenth-century source), the two terms for senior male kinsmen overlapping in range. H and T retain ***ʔoe** for senior male kinsman, while J and Ms introduce the Spanish term for uncle. Ms also uses the Spanish aunt term for senior female kinsmen, while H J T retain ***cici**. ***mo** and ***hi** are lost everywhere except in E, ***cici** is lost in E (?) and Ms, and ***ʔoe** is lost in J and Ms.

There is a greater degree of retention of the four terms in reference to junior collaterals.

*mʔai-mo	=mPCC	→	*no change*				(E)
			PCC	→	*Spanish replacement*		(J)
					loss		(H Ms T).
*mʔai-cici	=fPCC	→	*no change*				(E)
			PCC	→	*no change*		(Ms)
					Spanish replacement		(J)
					loss		(H T).
*mʔai-ʔoe	xmPCC	→	*no change*				(E)
			PCCm?				(E)
			PCC	→	*no change*		(H T)
					Spanish replacement		(J)
					loss		(Ms).
*mʔai-hi	xfPCC	→	*no change*				(E)
			PCC	→	*Spanish replacement*		(J)
					loss		(H Ms T).

Once again, the parallel-cross distinction was lost almost everywhere, but E gives strong attestation to its survival to the seventeenth century. E also gives a dubious reference to *PCCm* as a range for **bäue** (< ***m?ai-?oe**) which, while probably not untrue, is almost certainly an incomplete statement of the more general range *PCC*. Sex of senior kinsman was apparently also suppressed when the parallel-cross distinction was lost, resulting in all four terms being homonymous. H and T retained ***m?ai-?oe**, Ms retained ***m?ai-cici**, and J introduced Spanish nephew and niece terms.

There is little significance in the difference between merging terminology in Pame and collateral terminology in Otomí inasmuch as the terms for parallel collaterals are based on parent terms even in Otomí, thereby implying a close association of such kinsmen with parents. In the case of Pame junior cross kinsmen, however, there has been a special merger, through probable loss of a term. Female ego classifies her junior cross kinsman with her child and her junior parallel kinsman, resulting in a disjunctive definition of the ranges of the child terms, *viz.* =*C(G)*, *xfC(G)*, and a complete suppression of any modified form of the mother term to designate junior cross kinsman of a woman, if such a term ever existed.

There are no direct data available concerning the extension of bifurcate categories in POP, but the Seneca variety (Merrifield 1980) seems the most likely candidate:

PARALLEL (SENECA): Within the genealogical chain that links ego to a designated kinsman, the two kinsmen of the generation immediately above ego or alter, whichever is the junior member of this dyad, are of the same sex.

CROSS (SENECA): Within the genealogical chain that links ego to a designated kinsman, the two kinsmen of the generation immediately above ego or alter, whichever is the junior member of this dyad, are of the opposite sex.

If alter is of the first ascending generation from ego, ego is the junior member of the dyad and the two kinsmen whose sex is relevant are ego's parent and alter. Conversely, if alter is of the first descending generation, he is the junior member of the dyad and the two relevant kinsmen are ego and alter's parent. (These are the only two situations where bifurcation plays a role in Otopamean.)

POP Affinal Terms

POP (particularly Otomí) has greatly expanded its inventory of affinal terms and shows no clear relationships with other Otomanguean languages. As with POP terms for siblings and other collateral kinsmen, affinal terms occur in two sets of four terms which distinguish sex of both ego and alter. The first set is made up of four self-reciprocal terms used between parent-in-law and child-in-law. Although the terms do appear to be self-reciprocal, the parent-in-law is often distinguishable from the child-in-law through inflectional additions to basic terms.

POP 826. ***n-toe-n?ią** *mSPm(R)*.
> PO 106. ***ntë-hñą** *mSPm*. < POP ***nto-n?ią**.
> E **hią** *mSPm*, H **ntëhyą** *mSPm*, J **ndëhñą́** *mSPm*, Ms **ndëhñą́** *mSPm*, T **ndëhya** *mSPm*.
> Mz **?męñ?ę** *CSm*. < POP ***m?ai-n?e**.
> CP A **légŋ**, B **lyègŋ**, C **wanégŋ** *SP*. < POP ***toe-n?**.
> CP A **wat?ę̀**, B **ma?ę̀**, C **ma?ę̀** *CSm*. < POP ***?ią**.
> Ch A **úrí**, B **ùrí**, C **éní**, D **bùrí** *SP(R)*. < POP ***toe**.

POP 827. *n-toe-ca *fSPm(R)*.
  PO 46. *ntë-ca *fSPm*. < POP *nto-ca.
    E cä *fSPm*, H ntëhca *fSPm*, J cä *fSPm*, T ndësa *fSPm*.
    Mz nžą̃ʔą, ndą̃ʔą *SPm*. < POP *Yn-ta-ʔ, *n-ta-ʔ.
    CP A légŋ, B lyègŋ, C wanégŋ *SP*. < POP *toe-n?.
    Ch A úrí, B ùrí, C éní, D bùrí *SP(R)*. < POP *toe.
POP 727. *kao *fSPf(R)*.
  PO 158. *kɔ *fSPf*. < POP *kao.
    E hkɔ *fSPf*, H ëhkɔ *fSPf*, J kɔ̀ *fSPf*, T kɔ *fSPf*.
    Mz cɔʔɔ, kɔʔɔ *SPf*; chɔʔɔ, khɔʔɔ *CSf*. < POP *kao-ʔ, *khao-ʔ.
    CP A waŋkháo, B makâo, C ŋgoáo *CSf*. < POP *kao.
POP 728. *to *mSPf(R)*.
  PO 315. *to *mSPf*. < POP *to.
    E hto *mSPf*, H hcùhto *mSPf*, J tǒ *mSPf*, Ms tǒ *mSPf*, T to *mSPf*.
    Mz čoʔo, toʔo *mSPf*. < POP *to-ʔ.

The two POP mother-in-law terms are apparently morphologically simple; but the father-in-law terms are compound, with the final element of at least one of them making reference to the spouse through whom the relationship to father-in-law is traced. Specifically, POP 835 *n?ią may be associated with the ultima of POP 826 above and is a word for *woman* from POM 350 **yaHn *female* which also shows up as a POP term for *wife*, as will be discussed below. The final element *ca of POP 827, however, has not been traced to a corresponding Otomanguean or Otopamean term for a *male*. The penultimate element of the two father-in-law terms is possibly related to the mother-in-law term used by male ego, and may itself hark back to a morphologically complex source, one possible derivation being POP *to-e < POM **tan-win, in which the second element could be associated with POM 361 **win *male*.

The self-reciprocal ranges of the four terms seem to be fairly well supported by the data. Chichimeca-Jonaz continues to show such a range, if only with a single term. Central Pame has a parent-in-law term which reflects either the man's mother-in-law term or the penult of the father-in-law terms, and has a child-in-law term which reflects the ultima of the man's father-in-law term. The Mazahua daughter-in-law term appears to be an inflectional variant (historically) of the mother-in-law term. Nevertheless, the shift away from self-reciprocal ranges would also appear to have considerable time depth.

Otomí languages attest the development of completely new child-in-law terms based on elements reconstructable at the POP horizon but not necessarily representing usage of that period. A son-in-law term harks back to POP 537 *m?ai *child* and POP 274 *?iąh *sleep* while the daughter-in-law term is the result of POP 814 *c?i *child* and POM 148 **kwin *female*.

PO 181. *m-ʔbä-ʔą̀hą *CSm*. < POP *m?ai-?ią̀h.
    E bëąha *CSm*, H mʔbä̀hą *CSm*, J ʔmähą́ *CSm*, Ms ʔmä̀ʔhą́ *CSm*, T mʔbähą *CSm*.
PO 120. *c?ĵ-hwä *CSf*. < POP *c?ĵ-hoe.
    E cʔĵhuä *CSf*, H cʔĵhwä *CSf*, J cʔĵhwä́ *CSf*, Ms cʔĭhä́ *CSf*, T cʔĵhwä *CSf*.

The second set of four POP terms which mark both sex of ego and of alter is used between siblings-in-law, either generation peer of spouse or spouse of ego's own generation peer. The development of four terms for these kinsmen clearly seems to be a

POP innovation to match the development of a corresponding set of four sibling terms. There is no convincing way to associate these four terms with corresponding affinal terms in other Otomanguean languages. Two of these terms are supported widely within Otopamean while the other two are supported only within Otomian (Otomí and Mazahua).

POP 828. *koaʔ *mPCSm(V,G).*
    PO 156. *ko *mPCSm(V,G).* < **POP *ko.**
    E hkó *mPCSm(V,G);* H ntëhko *mPCSm(V,G);* J kǒ *mPCSm(V,G), fPCSm(G);* Ms kǒ *PCSm(V,G);* T ko *mPCSm(V,G).*
    Mz choʔo, khoʔo *mPCSm(V,G), fPCSm(G);* chorišy̨, khorišy̨ *mPCSf(G).* < **POP *kho-ʔ, *kho-nti-sǫ.**
    CP A akkoáʔ, B ákkoaʔ, C wakoáʔ *mPCSm(V,G).* < **POP *koaʔ.**
    Ch A úkúʔ, B úkùʔ, C égúʔ, D bùkúʔ *PCSm(V).* < **POP *koaʔ.**
POP 829. *mo *fPCSm(V,G).*
    PO 514. *mo *fPCSm(V,G).* < **POP *mo.**
    E mɔ *fPCSm(V,G),* H mbèke *fPCSm(V,G),* J mó *fSPCm(G),* T mege *fPCSm(V,G).*
    Mz meʔe *fPCSm(V,G).* < **POP *me-ʔ.**
    CP A kommò, B kimy̨ǫ̀, C kamò *fPCSm(V,G), PCSf(V,G).* < **POP *mo.**
    Ch A kàmy̨ú, B kàmy̨ú, C kàmy̨ú *PCSf(V).* < **POP *mo.**
POP 830. *mǫtǫ *fPCSf(V,G).*
    PO 515. *my̨dy̨ *fPCSf(V,G).* < **POP *mǫtǫ.**
    E mudu *fPCSf(V,G),* H my̨tu *fPCSf(V,G),* J my̨dy̨ *fPCSf(V,G),* Ms my̨dy̨ *fPCSf(V,G),* T my̨ty̨ *fPCSf(V,G).*
    Mz my̨rį̀ *fPCSf(V,G).* < **POP *mǫtǫ.**
POP 831. *po *mPCSf(V,G).*
    PO 174. *ʔbä-po *mPCSf(V,G).* < **POP *mʔai-po.**
    E bähpo *mPCSf(V,G),* H ʔbǎhpo *mPCSf(V,G),* J ʔbǎhpó *mPCSf(V,G),* Ms ʔbǎpó *mPCSf(V,G),* T ʔbähpo *mPCSf(V,G).*
    Mz bʔähpe *mPCSf(G).* < **POP *mʔai-pe.**

There are a few problems with these sets. Otomí does not reflect the cluster *oa in the man's term for brother-in-law. The final glottal, missing in Otomí, may be a suffix. In the woman's term for brother-in-law, H T Mz reflect either *e or *ai, which could be the result of influence by an adjacent morpheme. H reflects *p rather than *m. This adds force to the question which arises in any case as to whether **POP 829** is not a variant of **POP 831.** Without evidence from other languages, however, the vowel of **831** may be incorrect, as is also the case with **POP 830.** Any of these vowels can be the result of POP clusters.

There is little to be said concerning the ranges of reference of these terms. As has been mentioned above, this group of terms appears to have developed to match the four sibling terms which also extend by Rule G. There is ample support for the hypothesis that they were self-reciprocal in the sense of Rule V—that is, that they were used for both the sibling of spouse and the spouse of sibling. There appears to have been a certain amount of instability in the use of these terms as indicated by slightly different ranges in some Otomí languages and, in particular, in Mazahua.

A few modern consanguineal terms have extended their ranges of reference over certain affinal kintypes. In particular, certain terms for collateral kinsmen other than siblings have done this. In Central Pame, current usage appears to be assymmetrical. Aunt and uncle terms are reported to extend both to spouse's collateral kinsmen of the first ascending generation and to the spouses of ego's own kinsmen of the first ascending generation. Conversely, however, the diminutive form of the uncle term which denotes a man's cross kinsman of the first descending generation is not stated to include any affinals within its ranges. Rather, separate child-in-law terms extend to the spouses of ego's first descending generation collateral kinsmen while the first descending generation collateral kinsmen of spouse are not mentioned.

In Otomí, H and Ms extend senior and junior collateral terms to corresponding affinals. J extends the Spanish uncle term to spouse of aunt, employing the Spanish aunt term for spouse of uncle but not so extending its reflex of the POP aunt term. (Data regarding junior collateral affinals are not reported for J.)

$\emptyset \rightarrow S$- / xP	(CP).
$\emptyset \rightarrow$ -S / xP	(CP).
$\emptyset \rightarrow S$- / PPC	(H Ms).
$\emptyset \rightarrow$ -S / PCC	(H Ms).
$\emptyset \rightarrow$ -S / PPC	(H J Ms).
$\emptyset \rightarrow S$- / PCC	(H Ms).

Otomian Co-affinal Terms

Otomian languages have further elaborated the affinal system of reference through the development of one term used between men who marry sisters, one for women who marry brothers, and a third term for persons whose children marry each other. Such terms exist in other Otomanguean languages, but these terms do not appear to be cognate with any of them.

POP 832. *miki $mSPCSm(G)$.
> **PO 516.** *miki $mSPCSm(G)$.
> E mihkí $mSPCSm$, H mmìhki $mSPCSm$, J mĵhkí $mSPCSm(G)$, Ms mìkí $SPCS(G)$, T mĵkĵ $mSPCSm(G)$.
> Mz mic?meñ?e $mSPCSm(G)$.

POP 833. *minkhao $fSPCSf(G)$.
> **PO 517.** *minkhɔ $fSPCSf(G)$.
> E min makhɔ $fSPCSf$; H mìnkhɔ $fSPCSf$; J mìmìnkhɔ, mìnkhɔ́ $fSPCSf(G)$; T miŋkhɔ $fSPCSf(G)$.
> Mz minkhɔ $fSPCSf(G)$.

POP 834. *cheohni CSP.
> **PO 518.** *chëhni CSP.
> E chɔni CSP, H chĕhni CSP, J chĕhní CSP, Ms sĕhní CSP, T hsĕhni CSP.
> Mz shëhnë CSP.

POP Spouse Terms

POP terms for husband and wife hark back to POM terms for man and woman, respectively. Bartholomew reconstructs two separate husband terms but they are both from the same POM root. There are two unrelated terms for wife, the second having at least two inflected forms.

POM 387. **kwa, **ka, **wa *male.*

POP 389. *=tǫa-n *man.* < POM **wa.

  PO 519. *ntë-me *Sm.* < POP **ntoe.

    E dąmé *Sm,* H ntë *Sm,* J dą̀mé *Sm,* Ms dą́mé *Sm,* T ndë *Sm.*

  Mz írý *man.* < POP *tǫan.

  CP kyoą́ŋ *man.* < POP *kǫan.

POP 490. *n-ʔǫa-n *Sm.* < POM **wa.

  CP A ʔyą́ŋ, B nʔoą́ŋ, C wanʔoą́ŋ *Sm.* < POP *n-ʔǫa-n.

  Ch A náʔý, B ùnʔý, C únʔý, D bùrʔý *Sm.* < POP *n-ʔǫa-n.

POM 350. **ntaHn, **naHn, **yaHn *Pf(vocative), PPCf(R,G), female.*

POP 835. *nʔią *woman.* < POM **nʔyaHn.

  PO 172. *ʔbä-hñą *Sf.* < POP *mʔai-nʔią.

    J ʔbǎhñą́ *Sf,* Ms ʔbä̂hñą́ *Sf.*

  CP A ʔią́ʔai, B nʔią́ʔa, C wánʔią́ʔa *Sf.* < POP *nʔią.

  Ch B ùníʔí, C úníʔì, D bùníʔín *Sf.* < POP *nʔią.

POM 340. **suhn, **nuhn *Pf, PPCf(R,G), female.*

POP 320. *sǫ, *co *Sf.* < POM **suhn, **nsun.

  PO 261. *šicu *Sf.* < POP *co.

    H šĭhcu *Sf,* T šisu *Sf.*

  Mz suʔu *Sf.* < POP *co.

  Ch masý *Sf.* < POP *sǫ.

CHAPTER 5
PROTO ZAPOTECAN
KINSHIP TERMS

This chapter proposes a set of Proto Zapotecan kinship terms with corresponding ranges of reference, presents and discusses the evidence upon which the proposal is made, and summarizes a possible sequence of development through Proto Zapotec and Proto Chatino horizons to contemporary Zapotecan languages.

PZn KINSHIP TERMS

In the absence of a thoroughgoing phonological reconstruction of Proto Zapotecan, it is possible only to posit tentative phonological reconstructions of PZn terms by extrapolation from the information provided by Miranda de Fernández and from the discussion of PZn in Rensch (1976). Nevertheless, the lexical data provide the opportunity to make a reasonable hypothesis concerning PZn terms and their probable ranges of reverence. In some cases reconstruction of terms is limited to Proto Zapotec and Proto Chatino horizons.

PZn Parent and Child Terms

Two Proto Zapotecan parent terms, both of them morphologically complex, distinguish father from mother, while a single term classifies together children of either sex. The mother term shares the same final element as ***gu-naʔa** *woman,* and the final element of the father term is a reflex of a POM form meaning *male.*

*š-yu-zi	Pm	*father*
*ši-naʔa	Pf	*mother*
*žiʔni	C	*child*

PZn Grandkinsman Terms

Competing patterns of reference for grandkinsmen existed during PZn times. First, senior and junior grandkinsmen were classified together reciprocally (by Rule I), distinguishing male grandkinsman from female grandkinsman but not directly distinguishing seniority apart from the addition of inflectional material to do so. These categories of grandkinsmen extended to all lineal kintypes more than one generation distant from ego as well as to all collateral kintypes other than those of ego's generation. Unfortunately, Chatino does not give witness to the terms for these categories preventing reconstruction at the PZn level, but Proto Zapotec forms are fairly strongly supported.

*pi-ši-yu	PPm(I,2)	male grandkinsman
*žusa	PPf(I,2)	female grandkinsman

The lack of Chatino reflexes for these terms and the competing system of reference to be introduced below give evidence that there was considerable instability during the PZn period in the naming of grandkinsmen. A probable factor in this instability is the shift from the POM self-reciprocal system of reference with reciprocal ranges best characterized by Rule R and terms which distinguished *sex of the senior member of the ego-alter dyad* to a system with reciprocal ranges best characterized by Rule I and terms which distinguished *sex of alter* regardless of seniority.

Another probable factor related to this instability is influence from nearby Proto Mixtecan populations as is witnessed by the introduction of a PMn grandmother term into the PZn vocabulary of some communities (including Chatino). Although the original term named a female grandkinsman in PMn, it settles into PZn as a term to name a male grandkinsman, due in part to the confusion which was present in the PZn shift from Rule R reciprocity to Rule I reciprocity. (Other factors are discussed below.) Modern Zapotecan sources do not make it clear how far the loan from PMn extended over lineal and collateral kintypes.

*ši-taʔa	PPm(I)	male grandkinsman

The second pattern of reference for grandkinsmen appears to have encompassed only lineal kinsmen and was based on modified parent and child terms without the reciprocal ranges which characterized the first pattern of reference.

*š-yu-zi gula	PPm(L)	grandfather
*ši-naʔa gula	PPf(L)	grandmother
*žiʔni suwa, *žiʔni žaga	CC(L)	grandchild

The modifier occurring with the parent terms is a form meaning *big, old*, but the sources of the two alternate modifiers of the grandchild term is unknown. The grandchild terms are not supported beyond the PZ horizon since Chatino reflects the term above borrowed from PMn in reference to grandchild (but see below for further detail).

PZn Sibling Terms

As in the case of grandkinsman terms, Proto Zapotecan evidences an unstable system of reference for collateral kinsmen, the instability having resulted in this case from the development of a separate set of sibling terms distinct from that which names collaterals other than those of ego's generation. In the first place, Proto Chatino does not support the same set of sibling terms that Proto Zapotec supports. In the second place, the Proto Zapotec terms, though very solidly supported at the PZ horizon, show radical lexical innovations from the POM horizon.

The PZ terms do, nevertheless, appear to represent the sort of system of reference which is likely to have been present in the earlier PZn system, namely, three Jivaran terms which extended to all kinsmen of ego's generation. If seniority was a parameter at the PZn horizon, it has been lost in Zapotecan with almost no trace. The three Proto Zapotec terms are as follows.

*bi-či?	mPCm(G)	*man's brother*
*bela, *žila	fPCf(G)	*woman's sister*
*bi-za?-na	aPCb(G)	*cross-sex sibling*

Proto Chatino shows a complete collapse of the earlier system of reference for siblings, retaining only a single, generic sibling term which extends to any collateral kinsman.

| ***i-ta?a** | PC(0) | *sibling* |

PZn Collateral Grandkinsman Terms

Two additional terms are weakly supported at the Proto Zapotec level to designate collateral kinsmen other than siblings. These two terms distinguish male and female kinsmen, and range over all collateral kintypes other than those of ego's generation. These ranges overlap with those of grandkinsman terms in such a way that these collaterals may be considered a subset of grandkinsmen, namely, *collateral grand-kinsmen.*

| ***šiči** | PPCm(I,1) | *male collateral kinsman* |
| ***š-ni-su** | PPCf(I,1) | *female collateral kinsman* |

PZn Affinal Terms

Once again, Chatino departs from Zapotec, preventing reconstruction at the PZn level. Proto Zapotec attests descriptive phrases to denote parents-in-law. The phrases consist of a parent term followed by ***ča?pa** *woman* or **gi? male.*

*šuzi ča?pa	mSPm	*man's father-in-law*
*šuzi gi?	fSPm	*woman's father-in-law*
*ši-na?a gi?	fSPf	*woman's mother-in-law*
*ši-na?a ča?pa	mSPf	*man's mother-in-law*

Chatino also bases parent-in-law terms on parent terms, but postposes ***la** *church* to form just two terms distinguishing only sex of alter. The same modifier also occurs in the son-in-law term, but the daughter-in-law term exhibits a unique modifier.

*suti la	SPm	*father-in-law*
*nya?a la	SPf	*mother-in-law*
*šinyV? la	CSm	*son-in-law*
*šinyV? šę	CSf	*daughter-in-law*

Proto Zapotec attests considerable instability in child-in-law terms, with various forms occurring, each with moderate support from several languages.

*žuʔ-dyV, *bi-guʔ-dyV	CSm	son-in-law
*žu-wa li-dyV, *žiʔ-žV	CSf	daughter-in-law

Curiously enough, although Chatino does not support PZ in the reconstruction of many PZn consanguineal terms or of other affinal terms, it does seem to provide cognates to support three Jivaran sibling-in-law terms which classify together sibling of spouse and spouse of sibling.

*gwVlaʔ	mPCSm(V,G)	man's brother-in-law
*sitya	fPCSf(V,G)	woman's sister-in-law
*si-luʔna	aPCSb(V,G)	cross-sex sibling-in-law

PZn Spouse Terms

Zapotecan languages appear to support the existence of a single spouse term, not distinguishing sex, at the PZn horizon although it is not completely clear that the PZ term is cognate with the PCh term. If such a term did exist at the PZn horizon, it competed with separate terms for husband and wife which were based on words meaning *male* and *female*, respectively.

*čaʔla, *kwilyoʔo	S	spouse
*giʔ-yu	Sm	husband
*gu-naʔa	Sf	wife

The Development of PZn Parent and Child Terms.

Lingua franca **tata** and **nana** seem to have become a part of Zapotec vocabularies by PZ times, but based on the available data do not seem to have had success in Chatino.

PZ 1. *tata *Pm.*
    At **tātá** *Pm(S-),* **Ct tát?** *Sir,* **Cx tad** *Sir,* **I ta** *Sir,* **Mt štadä** *Pm,* **Oz te-dad-doʔl-na** *PPm,* **Yg dad** *Pm.*
PZ 2. *nana *Pf.*
    At **nāná** *Pf(S-),* **Mt šnanä** *Pf,* **Oz te-mna-goʔl-na** *PPf.*

Otherwise, PZn exhibits only two parent terms from POM sources and, of these, the term for father requires a fairly innovative (and unconfirmed) derivational history to show that it is a POM reflex. The Zapotec cognates call for initial *š as probable source consonant; but Zapotecan shows preposed š to possessed forms of nouns. This permits the hypothesis that an underlying *y has been suppressed or fused with surrounding material in the sequence *š-yu. If this is indeed what happened, the PZn father term can result from **POM 361**, but replacing the final-syllable reflex of **POM 387 **wa** *male* with a reflex of **POM 254 **sehn** *male*. The PZn term for mother harks back to **POM 350 **nahn**.

POM 361. **kwin-yu-wa, **kin-yu-wa, **nwin-yu-wa *Pm, PPCm(R,G), male.*
PZn 1. *š-yu-zi *Pm.* < **POM **yu-sen.**
PZ 3. *bi-šuzi: Am **šuz** *Pm;* At **bēšudiā** *priest;* Cm **šuza?,** **šuzi** *Pm;* Ct **šuz** *Pm;* I **bi'šòzé?** *Pm,* **šùzé?** *CSP;* L **žu³ce³** *Pm;* Mx **pšoz** *Pm;* Oc **šùzìā** *Pm;* T **uzą** *Pm;* V **pi-šoze, pi-šoze-a** *Pm(1);* Yg **šúza?** *Pm,* **bišúz** *priest;* Yt **ṣa** *Pm,* **bšoz** *priest.*
PCh 34. *suti: Y **stị¹** *Pm,* T **sti** *Pm.*
POM 350. **ntaHn, **naHn, **yaHn *Pf(vocative), PPCf(R,G), female.*
PZn 2. *ši-na?a *Pf.* < **POM **nahn.**
PZ 4. *ši-na?a: Am **šna** *Pf;* Cm **žna?** *Pf;* Ct **šna?** *Pf;* Cx **šna?** *Pf;* I **hñàá?** *Pf;* L **ši³ña?³,** **na³** *Pf;* Mx **žni?a** *Pf;* Oc **šnī?āyà** *Pf;* T **ñaą** *Pf;* V **naa-ya, ñaa-ya** *Pf(1);* Yg **šiná?a** *Pf;* Yt **ẓna?** *Pf.*
PCh 35. *nya?a: Y **y?ǫ¹** *Pf.*
PZ 5. ži?ni ča?pa *Cf.* < ***ča?a-kwa** < **POM **ntahn.**
Am **ščap** *Cf,* Ct **šinezap** *Cf,* Cx **rsap** *Cf,* I **žiñi jaapa** *Cf,* L **šin²** **ču²ku³** *Cf,* Mx **šiNdzo?p** *Cf,* Oc **šcá?āpā** *Cf,* Oz **šin-dsa?p-na** *Cf,* V **šini čapa** *Cf(1).*
PZn 3. *gu-na?a *woman.* < **POM **kwi-nahn.**
PZ 6. *gu-na?a: Ct **goc** *female;* I **gu-na?a** *woman;* L **u³na³?a³** *Sf;* Mx **žiwna?** me **Sf(third);** Oz **wna?** *female,* te-**wna?-na** *Sf;* T **mñaą** *Sf,* V **gonna** *female.*
PCh 33. *kwe-?ną: T **kuna?ą** *woman,* Y **kwa?ǫ** *woman.*
PZ 7. *la *female.* < **POM **nya.**
At **ži?nī nīūlá** *Cf;* Cm **žgula?** *Sf;* I **nagola** *female;* Yg **nigúla** *female, Sf;* V **nagòla** *old woman.*

Zapotecan languages uniformly exhibit reflexes of **POM 258,** and modifiers harking back to **POM 387** and **350,** respectively, which are postposed to mark the children as male and female.

POM 258. **si? *youngster.*
PZn 4. *ši?ni *C.* < **POM **si?.**
PZ 8. *ži?ni: Am **šin?** *C;* At **ži?ní** *C;* Cm **ži?ina?,** **ži?i** *C;* Ct **šin?** *C;* Cs **šin?** *C;* I **žìíñé?** *C(G);* L **ši³ña³** *C;* Mt **ši?nä** *C;* Mx **žin** *C;* Oc **šìnìā** *C;* Oz **šin-gan-na** *Cm,* **šin-dza?p-na** *Cf;* T **ži?ña** *C;* V **šini, šini-a** *C(1);* Yg **ži?ina?** *C;* Yt **ẓi?inn** *C.*
PCh 36. *šinyV?: Y **snye?³²** *C,* T **sñi?** *C.*
POM 387. **kwa, **ka, **wa *male.*
PZ 9. *ži?ni ga?na *Cm.* < **POM **ka?n.**
Am **šgan?** *Cm,* Ct **šinegan** *Cm,* Cx **šgan?** *Cm,* I **žiñi gaana** *Cm,* L **žia¹na¹** *Cm,* Mx **šiNgan** *Cm,* Oc **šgá?ānā** *Cm,* Oz **šin-gan-na** *Cm,* V **šini gana** *Cm(1).*

Finally, a number of Zapotec languages exhibit child terms which are reflexes of **POM 428** and **POM 87.**

POM 87. **tun, **yun *child.*
POM 428. **nkwan, **nwan *(diminutive).*
PZ 10. *mba?du *C.* < **POM **nkwa?n-tun.**
Ct **mbäz** *C,* Mx **špä?d (mä?d)** *C,* Oz **te-mä?d-na** *C,* I **ba?du(?)** *C.*

The ranges of reference of parent and child terms have not changed by PZn times, but consist of *Pm, Pf,* and *C* with association of Rule L in the presence of modifiers as will be discussed below. Extension to collateral kinsmen is not important in Zapotecan as will be shown at the end of this chapter. Only Isthmus and Valley Zapotec show the child term extending collaterally, Isthmus by Rule G (because a fused grandchild term becomes discrete from it in Isthmus) and Valley by Rule 1 (where grandchild remains a subclass of child).

$\emptyset \rightarrow \quad G \ / C$ (I).

$\emptyset \rightarrow \quad 1 \ / C$ (V).

The Development of PZn Grandkinsman Terms

The POM grandkinsman terms find reflexes in PZ but not in PCh. Indirect evidence to be discussed below suggests, nevertheless, that the classification of grandkinsmen by self-reciprocal terms probably persisted into PZn times in both Zapotec and Chatino communities. The PZ forms of the POM terms for grandkinsmen show syntactic innovations in the form of preposed or postposed material not clearly attested at the POM horizon. There is also a semantic shift in reference to reciprocals from Rule R to Rule I; namely, the PZ terms mark sex of kinsman whereas POM had marked sex of the senior member of the dyad.

POM 429. ****seh, **hkeh** *PPm(R,2)*.
  PZ 11. ***pi-ši-yu** *PPm(1,2)*. < POM ****kwi-se-yu.**
    Am šey *PPm(1)*, **šey gol** *PPPm*, **šin šey** *CCCm;* **L še¹yu¹** *PPCm(L);* **Mx pšey** *PPCm(1,S)*, **pšey gol** *PPPCm(1);* **V pi-šio-ni, pi-šio-a** *xPPCm;* **Yg šitá?awa?** *PPm(?).*
POM 430. ****Ynsan, **Ynan** *PPf(R,2)*.
  PZ 12. ***žusa** *PPf(1,2)*. < POM ****Ysu-nsan.**
    Am šo?z *PPf(1);* **Ct šuz šoc** *PPm*, **sna šoc** *PPf*, **šin šoc** *CC;* **Cx šot** *PPf(L)*, *CC(L);* **L ni²su²** *PPCf(1);* **Mx žus** *PPCf(1,S);* **T šusą** *PPf(G);* **V šose, šosea** *PPf(L).*

Scattered evidence in Zapotec and Chatino witnesses influence from the PMn grandmother term during the period when Zapotecan grandkinsmen were still classified by self-reciprocal terms. Recall that PMn ***θe-ta?m** *PPf(1)* was a Mixtecan innovation based on the grandfather term (**PMn 304 *θeh** < POM **429 **seh**) with postposed **PMn 161 *ta?m** *companion* (< **POM 61 **ta?n**). This form was borrowed and can still be traced in Valley Zapotec, Yagallo Zapotec, and Chatino. The Yagallo data suggest that the association of the penult with the grandfather term was too strong to permit application of the term to female kinsmen. It was accordingly applied to male grandkinsman in its full form, and the penult was suppressed to provide a second matching term for corresponding female kinsmen. Only this latter truncated form survives in Valley Zapotec. Chatino, on the otherhand, retains a reflex of this borrowed term only in reference to junior grandkinsman, providing the evidence that the POM tradition of self-reciprocal terms for grandkinsman was still alive. Since Rule I has continued to be a viable rule of extension for grandkinsman terms even to the present time in some Zapotec languages, it is not necessary to assume that the Mixtecan term itself reflected the self-reciprocal tradition as long as Chatino remained in the Zapotecan tradition.

PZn 5. ****ši-taʔa** *PPm(1)*, ***taʔa** *PPf(1)*. < **PMn *ⴲe-taʔm** *PPf(1)*.
PZ: V taʔu *PPf(L)*; Yg šitáʔawaʔ *PPm(?)*, táʔawaʔ *PPf(?)*.
PCh 303. ***šinyVʔ** sitạʔ *CC(?)*.
Y snyeʔ³² stẹʔ¹ *CC(?)*, **T** sñiʔ steʔ *CC(?)*.

While the POM terms for grandkinsmen can still be traced in a number of Zapotec languages, the POM pattern of modified parent and child terms is a means of referring to lineal ancestors and descendents continues as an even stronger tradition in Zapotecan. Phrases for grandfather and grandmother with the augmentative modifier which harks back to **POM 189 **kweʔn²** *big, old* are strongly supported in both Zapotec and Chatino. The modifiers of grandchild terms, however, are more problematic. As mentioned, Chatino has borrowed the Mixtecan grandmother term in reference to grandchildren. Zapotec languages, on the other hand, show two forms which may be related, and which may even hark back to the PZ grandmother term with some sort of fused ending, but the details are obscure and the two terms are here presented separately.

PZn 6. ***š-yu-zi gula** *PPm(L)*. < **POM **yu-sen kwen-ya.**
PZ 13. ***šuzi gula:** At tá gūlá *PPm(L)*, Cm žuzi gulaʔ *PPm(?)*, I bỉ'šòzé bídà *PPm(1)*, L taʔ¹ u³la³ *PPm(L)*, Mt štadgolä *PPm(?,S-)*, Mx pšoz gol *PPm(L)*, Oz te-dad-goʔl-na *PPm(?)*, T gulạ *PPm(G)*, V pi-soze gola *PPm(L)*, Yg šúzaʔ gul *PPm(?)*, YT ṣa goⱡi *PPm(?)*.
PCh 30l. ***suti ku·la:** Y stⱼ²ʔǫ³ kula³ *PPm(?)*.
PZn 7. ***ši-naʔa gula** *PPf(L)*. < **POM **nsi-nahn kwen-ya.**
PZ 14. ***ši-naʔa gula:** At ná gūlá *PPf(L)*, Cm žnaʔ gulaʔ *PPf(?)*, I hñàá bídà *PPf(1)*, L na² u³la³ *PPf(L)*, Mx žniʔa gol *PPf(L)*, Oz te-mna-goʔl-na *PPf(?)*, V šose gola *PPf(L)*, Yg šináʔa gul *PPf(?)*, Yt ẓnaʔa goⱡi *PPf(?)*.
PCh 302. ***nyaʔa ku·la:** Y yʔǫ¹ʔǫ³ kula³ *PPf(?)*.
PZ 15. ***žiʔni suwa** *CC(L)*.
At žiⴲūä *CC(L)*, Cm žiʔi subaʔ *CC(?)*, Yg šíʔwaʔ *CC(?)*, Yt *ẓesoa *CC(?)*.
PZ 16. ***žiʔni žaga** *CC(L)*.
I žiàgáʔ *CC(1,S)*, L ši³ʔñi² a³ka⁴ *CC(L)*, Mt šagä *CC(?,-S)*, Mx žiag (miag) *CC(2)*, Oc sìnžàgā *CC(?)*, Oz te-mäʔd-biag-na *CC(?)*, T yaga *CC(G)*, V šiaga-ya, šini šiaga-ya *CC(2)*.

Zapotec languages show two other innovations in respect to grandparent reference. First, the following data show a term most likely from Spanish for grandmother or mother, with Oc showing it as referring both to grandfather and grandmother. Harvey (1963) also lists one or two additional towns which show this term for grandmother.

Mt šmamä *PPf(S-)*, **Mx žmama** *Pf*, **Oc šmámä** *PP*, **Oz te-mamaʔ-na** *Pf*.

Second, Ct and Mx have alternate grandparent terms which appear as far away as Otomian, indicating fairly wide diffusion. It seems clear that they are loans and not of POM origin.

Ct tatit *PPm*, **natit** *PPf*; **Mx štatit** *PPm*, **žnanit** *PPf*. Cf. **PO 503.** ***tita** *PPm(2)*; **PO 504.** ***nita** *PPf(2)*.

The data from Zapotecan languages seem to indicate a general breakdown of the old system of reference with many incursions of loan words (even more so in terms for collaterals and for affinals) and of limitations in older rules of extension. Many of the grandparent terms are reported as not having any extended ranges, leaving many kintypes for fairly near *kinsmen* outside the system. Apart from this apparent de-emphasis on kinship relations, a few trends in semantic change can be traced.

First of all, as was indicated above, the reciprocal relationship shifted in PZ to type I from type R; and except in those few languages where Rule I persists today (Am, Ct, Cx), the Zapotec languages retained POM grandkinsmen terms for senior grandkinsmen, while Chatino languages retained them for junior grandkinsmen. These shifts may be characterized as follows:

$R \rightarrow I / PP$ (PZn).

$PP(I) \rightarrow$ $\begin{cases} PP \\ CC \end{cases}$ (PZ).
(PCh).

The extension of POM terms by Rule 2 is only indirectly reflected in Zapotecan, except for a single direct reference in the grandchild term of Córdova's Valley Zapotec. Otherwise, the grandparent terms are seen to have reflexes which are divided into two groups: those which extend only to lineal kinsmen (Cx V) and those which extend only to collateral kinsmen (L Mx). The exception is Texmelucan where grandkinsman terms are reported to extend by Rule G.

$PP(2) \rightarrow$ $\begin{cases} PP(L) \\ PPC(1) \end{cases}$ (Cx V).
(L Mx).

$2 \rightarrow I / PP,CC$ (T).

$1 \rightarrow G / PP,CC$ (T).

The Development of PZn Sibling Terms

Zapotecan languages support and reflect the POM pattern of classifying siblings, but also show a good deal of lexical innovation and, in some languages, a general collapse of the early system. Only a small number of the languages which make up the sample upon which the study is based show traces of some of the earlier lexical material and patterns of classification.

The most stable part of the system is the set of three terms in Zapotec languages—excluding Chatino—which divides ego's generation in Jivaran fashion. This set is stable in the sense of showing internal phonological consistency throughout the fifteen Zapotec languages of the sample and in ranging over the same kintypes in each language (except for the distinguishing of cousins from siblings in some languages, probably under pressure from Spanish). The lexical association of these terms with POM sibling terms is, however, less sure. The following hypotheses are tentatively proposed.

In the preceding section, the PZ grandfather term was seen to have developed from **POM 429** **seh *PPm(R,2)* to **PZ 11** *pi-šu-yu *PPm(1,2)*, with the addition of final *yu particularly in those languages (L,V) where modern reflexes specifically denote senior collateral kinsman, that is *uncle*. In this context, *yu is considered to represent a Zapotec reflex of **POM 423** **tu ~ **nu ~ **yu *emPCm(0)*, which was conjoined with the reflex of **seh to narrow its focus from *PPm(2)* to *PPCm(1)*. The combination of the two terms, thus, meant something like *senior collateral grandfather*—not a lineal grandfather, but not an elder brother.

This possible reflex of **POM 423** is the only place it appears in Zapotecan, and its use in this connection may have motivated the shift to other lexical material for the man's term for brother in these languages. This latter role is an apparent reflex of the more generic sibling term, **POM 159**, in its diminutive form, but the association must be considered with reservation.

If the association with **POM 159** is in fact correct, it divides into two terms in PZn in the same manner as **POM 423** in PMn and PPn for the same kintypes, dividing collateral kinsmen into those of ego's generation as opposed to all others.

$$PC(0) \rightarrow \begin{cases} PPC(I,I) \\ PC(G). \end{cases}$$

In the case of **159**, its PZ reflexes combine with reflexes of **POM 429** ****seh** *PPm(R,2)* for nongeneration peers of ego, competing with **PZ 11** ***pi-ši-yu** *PPm(I,2)* when referring to collateral kintypes not of ego's generation.

POM 159. **nsi-kihn, **kihn-si *yPC(0)*.

> **PZ 17. *bi-či?** *mPCm(G)*. < POM ****kwi-nsi.**
> Am **weč** *mPCm(G)*; At **bēc-ị̃?** *mPCm(G)*; Cm **biča?**, **biči** *mPCm(0)*; Ct **wit** *mPCm(G)*; Cx **wes** *mPCm(G)*; I **bìčé?** *mPCm(G)*; L **bi³či³** *mPCm(G)*; Mt **becä** *mPCm(G)*; Mx **bec** *mPCm(G)*; Oc **bìčá** *mPCm*; Oz **bec-na** *mPCm(G)*; T **bikyą** *mPCm*; V **peče, peče-a, ta-peče-a** *mPCm(G)*; Yg **bíča?** *mPCm(G)*; Yt **bìši?** *mPCm(G)*.

> **PZ 18. *ši-či** *PPCm(I,I)*. < POM ****se-nsi.**
> Am **šič** *PPCm(I)*, Ct **šit** *PPC(I)*, Cx **šis** *PPCm(I)*.

Am, Ct, and Cx thus adopt a form of **POM 159** to specify senior and junior collaterals, whereas L and V adopt a form of **423**, in both cases by postposing them to the grandfather term.

Zapotec terms for *woman's sister* show two traditions only one of which can be considered to reflect the corresponding POM term (**236**). Both traditions appear to reflect **POM 350** ****yaHn** *female* in their final syllables, one penultimate syllable reflecting **POM 236** ****kwaHn** *efPCf(0)*, the other perhaps reflecting the same diminutive **POM 258** ****si?** *youngster* exhibited by **POM 159** ****nsi-kihn** *yPC(0)*.

POM 350. **ntaHn, **naHn, **yaHn *Pf(vocative), PPCf(R,G), female.*

> **PZ 19. *bela, *žila** *fPCf(G)*. < POM ****kwan-yan, **nsin-yan.**
> Am **bal** *fPCf(G)*; At **žilá** *fPCf(G)*; Cm **žila?**, **žila** *fPCf(0)*; Ct **bäl** *fPCf(G)*; Cx **bel** *fPCf(G)*; I **bèndá?** *fPCf(G)*; L **be³la³** *fPCf(G)*; Mt **bälä** *fPCf(G)*; Mx **beL** *fPCf(G)*; Oc **bèldä** *fPCf*; Oz **baL-na** *fPCf(G)*; T **bilyą** *fPCf*; V **pela, peLa** *fPCf(G)*; Yg **žíila?** *fPCf(G)*; Yt **bìłi** *fPCf(G)*.

Whereas the *man's brother* term appeared to split by inflection and by combining with the grandfather term to separately denote *mPCm* and *PPCm*, the sister's term does not show a corresponding pattern. The PZ term for *PPCf* (as opposed to *fPCf*) can be the result of the combining of two POM terms for mother (or female): either ****yaHn** is

reflected in pretonic position showing *nya < *ni, or (more probably) POM 255 **niHn
female is directly reflected, the final syllable resulting in either case from POM 340
**suhn *female*.

POM 255. **siHn, **niHn *Pf, PPCf(R,G), female*.
POM 340. **suhn, **nuhn *Pf, PPCf(R,G), female*.
PZ 20. *š-ni-su *PPCf(I,1)*. < POM **ni-su.
Am šnis *PPCf(I)*, L ni²su² *PPCf(I)*, Cx šit *PPCf(I)*.

The PZ cross-sex sibling term also presents a problem and can be associated with the
corresponding POM sibling term only by proposing innovations which have not been well
substantiated by other data. The association is, nevertheless, tentatively proposed here in
the absence of a better hypothesis.

POM 431. **nsi-ʔya *eaPCb(0)*.
PZ 21. *bi-zaʔ-na *aPCb(G)*. < *ku-zi-aʔ < POM **kuhn-si-ʔya.
Am bzan *aPCb(G)*; At dānà *aPCb(G)*; Cm zanaʔ, zan *aPCb(0)*; Ct bzan *aPCb(G)*;
Cx ptaʔn *aPCb(G)*; I bìʼzàná? *aPCb(G)*; L za³na³ *aPCb(G)*; Mt bisianä *aPCb(G)*;
Mx bzian *aPCb(G)*; Oc zànä *aPCb*; Oz psan-na *aPCb(G)*; T zaną *aPCb*; V zaana,
ta-zaana, pi-zaana *aPCb(G)*; Yg záana? *aPCb(G)*; Yt zan *aPCb(G)*.

Chatino reflects none of the foregoing terms but rather classifies all collaterals under a
single term which results from POM 61.

POM 61. **taʔn *PC(0)*.
PCh 304. *i-taʔa *PC(0)*. < POM **taʔn.
Y taʔǫ⁴³ *PC(0)*, T tyaʔa *PC(0)*.

In summary, Chatino shows a complete collapse of the POM system of reference for
siblings, retaining only one single generic term without changing its range of reference.
Zapotec languages, on the otherhand, retain a Jivaran pattern of reference, but divide
collaterals into generation peers of ego vs. all others. The new categories of nongeneration peers of ego are named by a composite form based on the grandfather
term—in the case of males—and by a composite form of uncertain origin—probably
terms for mother—in the case of females.
These composite forms, however, are not well supported across all Zapotec languages.
We cannot be sure that they were ever well established for all of Zapotec since most
northern and central Zapotec languages utilize either modified parent and child terms for
senior and junior colaterals or resort to loans from Spanish. In Isthmus Zapotec, for
example, the father term and a personal name combine to denote uncle. Thus, *father
John* denotes a senior collateral kinsman named John. In Yatzachi, the personal name or
benni? *person* are preposed to the parent term. Atepec postposes kwāná to the father
term for males and tíá from Spanish to the mother term for females. kwāná may be the
result of borrowing from another Otomanguean language since it appears uniquely in
Atepec to denote uncle, but it can also perhaps have its source in POM 189 **kweʔn² *big,
old,* or even POM 428 **kwan *(diminutive)*. These same languages classify junior

collaterals by the child terms directly (I), the child term with modifier (Yt), or by Spanish loans (At).

Zapotecan languages show very little trace of the POM pattern of distinguishing seniority in terms of relative age, but there are two exceptions, both found in published materials. In Mitla, Parsons (1936:547, fn. 14) noted a case where a male second cousin (*PPPCCCm*) was referred to by the uncle term because he was a good deal older than ego. In Juquila, Nader (1967) reports that sibling terms extend to all collateral kinsmen with modifiers marking relative age further designating them as older males, older females, or younger persons of either sex.

The Development of PZn Affinal Terms

No elementary term for parent-in-law reconstructs for Proto Zapotecan. Rather, descriptive phrases appear to have been used in Proto Zapotec, combining a term denoting the spouse by reference to his or her sex with a parent term. For example, *šuzi* *father* combines with *ča?pa* *female* to designate a man's father-in-law, the *father of his woman*, while *ši-na?a* *mother* combines with *gi?* *male* to designate a woman's mother-in-law, the *mother of her man*. The evidence for such phrases is as follows:

PZ 22. **šuzi ča?pa *mSPm*.**
Am šuz žap *mSPm*, Ct šuz žap *mSPm*, Cx šudzap *SPm*, I šùzé? *CSP*, Mx pšoz ʒo?p *mSPm*, Tx us gudą *SPm*.

PZ 23. *šuzi gi? *fSPm*.
Am šuz ye? *fSPm*, Ct šuz gi? *fSPm*, I šùzé? *CSP*, Mx pšoz bgi *fSPm*, Yg što? ži?ina? *SPm*, Yt ʒtaobi?in *SPm*.

PZ 24. *ši-na?a gi? *fSPf*.
Am šna ye? *fSPf*, Ct šna? gi? *fSPf*, Mx žni?a bgi *fSPf*, Yg to? ží?ina? *SPf*, Yt taobi?in *SPf*.

PZ 25. *ši-na?a ča?pa *mSPf*.
Am šna žap *mSPf*, Ct šna? žap *mSPf*, Cx šna?zap *SPf*, Mx žni?a ʒo?p *mSPf*, Tx ñaa gudą *SPf*.

Of the seven Zapotec languages represented above, only three exhibit all four phrases. Four languages do not distinguish sex of speaker, and three of these appear to exhibit different modifiers from those here reconstructed. Cuixtla is alone in retaining a reflex of *ča?pa* in what must be now considered a lexicalized form which no longer reflects the original meaning *male*.

Yagallo and Yatzachi also show different forms in the first position of the phrase, where we expect parent terms. The source of these terms, distinguishing sex of kinsman as they do by the presence or absence of š- or ʒ-, is unclear.

Chatino also exhibits phrases to designate parents-in-law, but in this case reference is apparently made to the marriage ceremony since the modifier appears to be based on the word for *church*.

PCh 305. *la *church, in-law*.
Y stilyǫ⁴³ *SPm(L)*, y?ǫ¹lǫ⁴³ *SPf(L)*, snyę?³ lǫ⁴³ *CSm(L)*, la³ *church;* T sti laa *SPm*, šta?ǫ laa *SPf*, sñi? laa *CSm*, laa *church*.

In the case of terms for son-in-law and daughter-in-law, it is unfortunate that we do not have access to a thoroughgoing reconstruction of Proto Zapotec phonology. In the absence of such a study, the best that can be done here is to make a very loose hypothesis, particularly so because of the morphological complexity of the modern terms. No attempt is made to associate any of these with POM sources since no strong argument can be supported.

It does seem clear that children-in-law were classified into two groups, defined by sex of kinsman, and that there were at least two variants of the term for each of the two groups.

PZ 26. *žuʔ-dyV *CSm.*

Am šuž *CSm;* At žūīcī *CS;* Cm žuʔuẓaʔ, žuʔuẕi *CSm(L);* Ct šin yuž *CSm,* wit yuž *mSPCSm;* Cx šuuz *CSm;* L u³či³ *CSm;* Mx bec yuẕ *mSPCSm;* Oc žúʔūdčā *CSm;* V yo-či-a *CSm(L), mPCSm(V,G);* Yg žá ójaʔ *CSm;* Yt ẓoʔož *CSm.*

PZ 27. *bi-guʔ-dyV *CSm.*

I špíʹgúʔjè? *CSm;* Mt špagozä *CSm;* Mx žimguẕ, žniʔuẕ *CSm;* Oz ši-bguẕ-na *CSm;* T ngujạ *CSm;* V pi-yo-ko-či-a *CSm(L).*

PZ 28. *žu-wa li-dyV *CSf.*

Cm žualiẕaʔ, žualiẕi *CSf(L);* I žúáá lîjèʔ *CSf;* Mt škulizä *CSf;* V šini wa-lihči-a *CSf(L);* Yg žóaʔ lîjaʔ *CSf;* Yt ẓoʔoliž *CSf.*

PZ 29. *žiʔ-žV *CSf.*

Am šiš *CSf;* Ct šin šiš *CSf,* bäl šiš *fSPCSf;* Cx šiiš *CSf;* L ži²ši⁴ *CSf;* Mx šiNžiž (wngužiž) *CSf,* beL wžiž *fSPCSf;* Oc žíʔīžā *CSf;* Oz šin-šiž-na *CSf;* T šisạ *CSf, fPCSf(V);* V šisa-ya *fPCSf(V,G,S-).*

The final vowel is not recoverable for any of these terms, and the value of the final consonantism is clearly open to further definition. This being the case, no serious consideration can be given to associating these terms with POM sources. Nevertheless, the sketchy picture we have does not rule out the possibility that they hark back to the proposed terms **POM 432 **kah** *CSm(R,0)* and **POM 433 **nsan** *CSf(R,0).*

Modern sources indicate that the final element of **PZ 28** should be associated with words for *home.*

The Chatino son-in-law term patterns with the parent-in-law terms formed on a word for *church,* as mentioned above. The corresponding daughter-in-law term, however, does not. It may be cognate with the Zapotec terms above (**PZ 29**), but we cannot be sure. Superficially, it resembles the Amuzgo parent-in-law term šę³, but the latter probaby has POM **an as its source rather than the **i which the Chatino term implies. If an association could be established between the two terms, it would strengthen the hypothesis presented above that POM 433 ranged over *CSf(R).*

PCh 306. *sę *CSf.*

Y snyę?³ šę⁴³ *CSf,* T šñiʔ sịị *CSf.*

The majority of Zapotecan languages have borrowed Spanish terminology for siblings-in-law, but a few languages show what appear to be native terms. In any case, they appear to be Zapotecan innovations if we can judge from the lack of cognates in other Otomanguean languages. Only Otopamean shows a comparable set of terms in this area of reference, but the POP terms are not cognate with these. As in the case of POP, the sibling-in-law terms match the sibling terms. In POP it is a set of four Quechuan terms; here it is a set of three Jivaran terms.

PZn 7. *gwVla? *mPCSm(V,G)*.
    PZ 30. *bVle? *mPCSm(V,G)*.
    Ct blä? *mPCSm(V)*, **Cx ble?** *mPCSm(V,G)*.
    PCh 307. *kulya *mPCSm(V,0)*.
    Y kulyǫ[43] *mPCSm(V,0)*, **T kulyaa** *PCSm(V)*.
PZn 8. *sitya *fPCSf(V,G)*.
    PZ 31. *bi-šiča *fPCSf(V,G)*.
    Ct bšic *fPCSf(V)*; **Cx fšit** *fPCSf(V,G)*; **Mt bišisä** *fPCSf(V,G)*; **T šisą** *CSf, fPCSf(V,G)*; **V pi-šisa-ya, ši(h)sa-ya** *fPCSf(V,G,S-)*.
    PCh 308. *šitya *fPCSf(V,0)*.
    Y štyǫ[43] *fPCSf(V,0)*, **T štya** *PCSf(V)*.
PZn 9. *si-lu?na *aPCSb(V,G)* .
    PZ 32. *ši-lo?na *aPCSb(V,G)*.
    Ct šlon? *aPCSb(V)*; **Cx slon** *aPCSb(V,G)*; **T šnuną** *aPCSb(V)*; **V ši-lona-ya, či-lona-ya, či-Lona-ya** *aPCSb(V,G)*.
    PCh: Y hynǫ?[43] *aPCSb(V,0)*.

There is an interesting question of relative chronology which could tie **PZn 7** to Spanish **cuñado**, but it is highly unlikely that the term could have been taken into Zapotec in time for all of the sound shifts to occur. Given the correct time frame, the following derivation is possible: **cuñado → *kwVnya-? → *gwVnya-? → *gwVle-? → *bVle-? → ble?.**

The disjunctive definition of the Texmelucan reflex of **PZn 8** is either the product of normal sound change and the coalescing of **PZ 29** and **PZ 31** in that language or evidence that the two terms are but variants of an earlier form with at least a range of *CSf(2)* and perhaps *CSf(0)*. The latter alternative is consistent with the hypothesis that Zapotec affinal terms do hark back to the proposed POM affinal terms. The corresponding term in this instance would be **POM 433 **nsan** *CSf(R,0)*.

Affinal kintypes have been incorporated into the ranges of reference of consanguineal terms in several of the contemporary Zapotec systems. These are undoubtedly shifts patterned on the Spanish model of relatively recent times. The semantic shifts can be characterized in summary fashion by the following statements.

$\emptyset \to S-$ /	P	(At)
	C	(I)
	PP	(Mt)
	CC	(I)
	PPC	(I Mt Mx)
	PCC	(Mt).
$\emptyset \to -S$ /	C	(I)
	CC	(I Mt)
	PPC	(I Mt Mx)
	PCC	(Mt).

The Development of PZn Spouse Terms

A variety of terms are used for spouse in Zapotecan languages. A single term which does not distinguish sex is found in several languages, but possessed forms of terms meaning *man* or *woman* are also common. The generic spouse terms are not known to have cognates in other Otomanguean languages, but the terms for *man* and *woman* are clearly of POM origin.

PZ 30. *ča?la *S.*

Am sa *S;* At cèla *S;* Ct čal? *S;* Cx sa?len *S;* I šèélá? *S;* L še²?la³ *S;* Mt čälä *S;* Mx ci?el *S;* Oc cé?ēlā *S;* V le-čela-ya *S.*

PCh 310. *kwilyo?o *S.*

Y kwilyo?y³ *S,* T kwilyo?o *S.*

POM 361. **kin-yu-wa *Pm,* ****kin** *PPCm(R,G).*

POM 421. **yu *person.*

PZn 8. *gi?-yu *male, Sm.* < POM ***ki?n-yu.*

PZ 31. *gi?-yu *male, Sm.*

Cm škiuwa?, škiu *Sm;* Ct bgi? *male;* I ngi?iu *man;* Mx bgi *male,* žimgi me *Sm(third);* Oz bgi *male,* te-mgi-na *Sm;* V nigio, nigi?o *male;* Yt byo *man,* ẓyogwa? *Sm.*

PCh 32. *ki-?yu *man.*

Y ki?yu *man,* T ki?yu *man.*

POM 350. **ntaHn, **naHn, **yaHn *Pf(vocative), PPCf(R,G), female.*

PZn 3. *gu-na?a *woman, Sf.* < POM ***kwi-nahn.*

L u³na³?a³ *Sf,* Oz te-wna?-na *Sf,* T mñaạ *Sf.*

PZ 7. *la *female, Sf.* < POM ***nyan.*

Cm žgula? *Sf,* Yg nigúla *Sf,* Yt ẓo?oɬ *Sf.*

CHAPTER 6
PROTO CHINANTECAN
KINSHIP TERMS

This chapter proposes a set of Proto Chinantecan kinship terms with corresponding ranges of reference, presents and discusses the evidence upon which the proposal is made, and summarizes a possible sequence of development to contemporary Chinantec languages.

PCn KINSHIP TERMS

The Chinantecan data provide sufficient information for a relatively firm reconstruction of most of the PCn terminology and system of kinship reference. Apart from the naming of parent and child, age relative to ego plays a primary role in the classification of kinsman, as well as the marking of sex of senior kinsman.

PCn Parent and Child Terms

Parents are distinguished by sex, while a generic child term may occur alone or be modified by forms meaning *male* and *female* to distinguish son from daughter. First person and third person parent terms are listed below (in that order), with the father term showing suppletive forms. Vocative terms for parents are also listed.

*ŋiu?, *hmi·[1]	Pm	*father*
*tiá[2]	Pm(vocative)	*father*
*sia, *siá·[2]	Pf	*mother*
*mï·, *ma; *ni·	Pf(vocative)	*mother*
*hạ·	C	*child*
*ha-ŋiu?	Cm	*son*
*ha-mï·	Cf	*daughter*

119

PCn Grandkinsman Terms

Grandparent terms also distinguish sex only for senior kinsman. The grandchild term is an elementary term, but the grandparent terms are based on parent terms to which modifiers are postposed. The modifier for the grandfather term is *yu·ʔ old(male); that for the grandmother term is *ʔya· woman. In spite of the fact that most modern Chinantec languages show both forms of the father and mother terms, depending only upon inflection for person, their corresponding reflexes in grandparent terms are distributed differently, each daughter language choosing one or another of the variants, regardless of person inflection, and postposing the modifier to it. The terms extend to all kinsmen two degrees of seniority distant from ego, in terms of relative age.

*tiá²yu·ʔ²,*ŋiu?-yu·ʔ²,*hmi·¹yu·ʔ²	$PPm(e^20)$	grandfather
*ma-·ʔya·²,*sia-ʔya·²,*siá·²ʔya·²	$PPf(e^20)$	grandmother
*zia·²¹²	$CC(y^20)$	grandchild

The penultimate syllables of grandparent terms are unstressed in modern languages and very likely were unstressed at the PCn horizon as well. The reconstruction of unstressed material is not as well understood as that of stressed material, however, so that the presentation above—which presents penults as though fully stressed—does not claim to be a completely accurate phonological representation, but rather serves to identify the lexical material which makes up each term.

PCn Sibling Terms

Three terms classify all collateral kinsmen older than ego in Jivaran fashion while a fourth generic term is at the same time a reciprocal to the three but, more generally, a term for any collateral without regard to seniority.

*ŋiu	emPCm(0)	man's elder brother
*nï	efPCf(0)	woman's elder sister
*ʔiạ·³¹³	eaPCb(0)	cross-sex elder sibling
*ru·ʔn	PC(0)	sibling

The range of the category elder in the PCn sibling terms is from ego's age, at the lower threshhold, to roughly one generation of distance, at the upper threshhold, where it passes over to the two degrees of seniority (e^2) category of grandparent terms. The boundary between these two categories of seniority is not fixed but, of necessity, is variable.

PCn Affinal Terms

There are four categories of affinals, distinguishing sex of kinsman and seniority. Two compound terms, based on *zá·²¹ male and *mï̃¹ female with postposed parent terms, denote parents-in-law and more remote lineal ancestors of spouse. Two elementary terms, on the otherhand, denote the spouse of son or daughter, but extend to the spouse of any of ego's younger collateral kinsmen.

*zá·²¹ŋiu?, *zá·²¹hmi·¹	SPm(L)	father-in-law
*mí¹sia·	SPf(L)	mother-in-law
*ŋá·	CSm(y0)	son-in-law
*lá·	CSf(y0)	daughter-in-law

None of spouse's collateral kinsmen or the spouses of ego's senior collaterals are accounted for within the ranges of the above terms since such affinals are invariably named by loan words from Spanish based on **cuñado** or **cuñada** in modern Chinantec languages, making it difficult to discern the nature of the earlier system. The parent-in-law terms are restricted to lineal affinals, presumably, because of the morphological association of the parent terms which name only lineals when used independently. It is probable that the parent-in-law terms are a lexical innovation at the PCn horizon.

PCn Spouse Terms

Spouses can be referred to in a variety of ways, but a single term makes reference to the joining of hands (*gwa·¹ *hand*) in the marriage ceremony, and names a spouse without regard to sex.

*hį-gwa·¹	S	spouse

The Development of PCn Parent and Child Terms

There was no significant shift in the range of reference of parent and child terms from POM to PCn times. At the PCn horizon there is, because of sound change, a suppletive father term with *Pm* as its full range of reference, a mother term with the range *Pf*, a child term with the range *C*, and a pattern of modifying the child term by postposed forms (related to the parent terms) denoting sex to narrow the reference of the child term to *Cm* or *Cf*.

Both POM terms for father continue in Chinantec languages. **POM 49** is directly reflected as a vocative term in most modern languages, but is also used in reference. Some languages appear to form a father term of reference on reflexes of **POM 361** with this vocative term preposed, but the reduction of phonological contrasts in pretonic position makes it difficult to be sure that the modern pretonic material is a true result of **POM 49.**

The PCn regular term of reference for father—here associated with **POM 361**—appears in many of the contemporary languages to consist of two suppletive forms, one form occurring with first singular and second person inflection, the other occurring with first plural and third person inflection. The proposed derivation of the form upon which the first singular term is based was discussed in the POM chapter as being exploratory and tentative. The proposal is based upon the occurrence of **POM 361** with **POM 421 **yu** *person* in three other branches of Otomanguean—PMn, PZn, and PCM—but remains innovative and open to further phonological analysis.

As in other families of Otomanguean, the PCn term for father shows a close association with terms for certain collateral kinsmen and, more generally, to any male. Comment upon the connection to collateral kinsmen will be reserved until the end of this chapter, when all the PCn terms have been introduced.

POM 49. **Ytah *Pm(vocative)*.
PCn 76. *tiá² *Pm(vocative)*. < POM **Ytah.
A tä³¹ *Pm;* L ta³¹hmi·³ *Pm(vocative);* O ta³¹ *Pm(vocative);* P tiá³ *Pm(vocative),*
ti³ŋie?¹ *Pm(first),* ti³hmi² *Pm(third);* U tia²³ *Pm(vocative).*
POM 361. **kwin-yu-wa, **kin-yu-wa, **nwin-yu-wa *Pm, PPCm(R,G), male.*
PCn 359. *hmi·¹ *Pm(third).* < POM **hnwi.
A hmi·² *Pm,* C hmi·r¹ *Pm,* L hmi·³ *Pm(S),* O hmi²a² *Pm,* P ti³hmi² *Pm,* Q hmi·²
Pm, U hmai³ *Pm.*
PCn 563. *ŋiu? *Pm(first).* < POM **nkin-yu-?.
C ŋyé?²e *Pm,* Ch ŋiu? *Pm,* L ŋyu?n²³ *Pm(S),* M ŋiu? *Pm,* O ñi²⁴ *Pm,* P ti³ŋie?¹ *Pm,*
Q ñú?³ü *Pm,* S ŋiu?³² *Pm,* T ŋe?³ *Pm,* Tl niu? *Pm,* U nei?³ *Pm,* VN noi? *Pm,* Y ŋiu?
Pm.
PCn 810. *ŋiu *emPCm(0).* < POM **nkin-yu.
A ŋió¹ *ePCm(0),* P ŋiu¹ *ePC(0).*
PCn 801. *ŋiu? *male.* < POM **nkin-yu.
A ŋiǘn?² *m,* C ŋyü?¹ *m,* L hǫ²³ŋyö·?³¹ *Cm,* O ñi?² *m,* P ŋio?¹² *m,* Q ñü?¹ *m,* T
ha¹ŋi?³¹ *Cm,* VN hoŋiü? *Cm.*
PCn 804. ha-ŋiu? *Cm.* < POM **hya-nkin-yu.
A hǫ·² ŋiǘn?² *Cm,* L hǫ²³ŋyö·?³¹ *Cm(third)(S),* O ca² ñi?² hǫ² *Cm,* P ha³ŋiu?¹ *Cm,* Q
ha³ñú?³ü *Cm,* T ha¹ŋi?³¹ *Cm,* VN hoŋiü? *Cm.*

The forms above marked as first person forms are actually first person singular forms.
The third person forms stand for third singular or plural. Closely related second person
forms could be included with the first singular forms, and closely related first plural
forms could be associated with the third person forms, but the two forms presented will
suffice to show the general pattern. The third person form shows no phonological
problems within Chinantecan, but the first person form, though strong, does. ñ or ny is
expected from Usila and Valle Nacional, rather than n, and Palantla e is unaccounted for.
Mugele (1976:5) accounts for Lalana u, where we might expect ö, as a regular shift in the
context of palatal consonant and postvocalic n.
All four POM terms for mother are reflected in Chinantec, but **POM 340** is the source
of the standard referential term for mother in most Chinantec languages.

POM 340. **suhn, **nuhn *Pf, PPCf(R,G), female.*
PCn 651. *siá·² *Pf(third).* < POM **Ysuhn.
A čó·i¹ *Pf,* L šó·² *Pf(S),* O se¹a² *Pf,* P mi³ciéw³ *Pf,* Q sá·²³à *Pf,* U sie²³ *Pf.*
PCn 802. *sia *Pf(first).* < POM **Ysun.
C sé·¹e *Pf,* Ch Θiạ *Pf,* L šen²³ *Pf(S),* M Θia²¹ *Pf,* O se²⁴ *Pf,* P mi²cie¹ *Pf,* Q sá³a *Pf,*
S mí²Θia³² *Pf,* T cya³ *Pf,* Tl Θia *Pf,* U sia³⁴ *Pf,* VN cia *Pf,* Y sia *Pf.*

What appears to be a fairly standard vocative term for mother in Chinantecan can
result from either **POM 350** or **POM 148** since PCn *m may have either **nn or **nw as
its source. Both possible derivations are presented below. **POM 255**, a probable
inflectional variant of **POM 340**, is only marginally represented in Chinantecan by
Comaltepec and Lalana mother terms.

POM 148. **kwin, **kin, **win *Pf, PPCf(R,G), female.*
PCn 280. *mí¹*female.* < POM **n?kwihn.

A mę̂³ *f*, C mî¹ *f*, L mɨ̇³ *f*, O mî³ *f*, P mî² *f*, Q mî² *f*, U a³ṳ⁴ *f*, Y mî *Sf*.
PCn 287. *mɨ̇·, *ma *Pf(vocative)*. < POM **nwin, **nwen.
A ma·¹ *Pf;* O ma³¹ *Pf(vocative);* P mai¹³ *Pf(vocative)*, mi²cie¹ *Pf(first)*, mi³ciéw³
Pf(third); U ma⁴³ *PPf(vocative);* S mî²Θia³² *Pf*, VN ma *Pf(vocative)*.
PCn 805. *ha-mɨ̇· *Cf*. < POM **hya-nwin.
A họ·² mɨ̇³² *Cf*, L họ²³mɨ̇³¹ *Cf(third)(S)*, O ca² mɨ̇³ họ² *Cf*, P ha²mái¹³ *Cf*, Q ha²mî³ɨ̇
Cf, T ha¹mî̇g²¹ *Cf*, VN homag *Cf*.
POM 350. **ntaHn, **naHn, **yaHn *Pf(vocative)*, *PPCf(R,G)*, *female*.
PCn 280. *mî¹ *female*. < POM **nnahn.
(See immediately above for data listing.)
PCn 287. *mɨ̇·, *ma *Pf(vocative)*. < POM **nnan, **nna.
(See immediately above for data listing.)
PCn 805. *ha-mɨ̇· *Cf*. < POM **hyan-nan.
(See immediately above for data listing.)
PCn 808. *ʔya· *woman*. < POM **ʔya.
L tu³ ʔyo·² *turkey pullet;* O kwa¹ hwɨ̇² ʔye³¹ *cow;* P ʔio¹³ *woman*, ʔio³ *woman (post-menopause)*, cieʔ³ ʔiéw³ *pullet;* Q hóʔ²¹ ʔyia·² *cow*.
PCn 809. *sia-ʔya·² *PPf(e²0)*. < POM **Ysun-ʔya.
(See below for data listing.)
PCn 811. *nɨ̇· *efPCf(0)*, < POM **ntan.
A nɨ̇·¹ *ePCf(0)*, C nɨ̇¹²ɨ̇ *PPCf(1,-S)*, P nïy¹ *ePCf(0)*, Q nɨ̇·³ɨ̇ *PPCf(1)*.
POM 255. **siHn, **niHn *Pf*, *PPCf(R,G) female*.
PCn 807. *ni· *Pf(vocative)*. < POM **nin.
C ni²¹ kié²e *Pf*, L ni·²³² *Pf(vocative)*.

POM 308 comes down into Chinantecan as the child term most used in kinship reference. POM 87 is reflected as a term meaning child also, but is generally used of any infant and does not show the type of possession characteristic of other kinship terms. Similarly, POM 258, is reflected as a general term for a young person, being paired in at least some Chinantec languages with an inanimate form meaning *tender*.

POM 308. **Yhnsan, **hyan *C*.
PCn 803. *họ· *C*. < POM **hyan.
A họn³ *C;* C hǫ̇·¹o *C;* Ch họ *C;* L họ·n²³ *C(first)(S)*, họ·³¹ *C(third)(S);* M họ¹² *C;* O yj²họ² *C;* P họw¹² *C;* Q họ·⁴³ *C(third);* S họ³² *C;* T hǫ̇³ *C(vocative);* Tl họ²¹ *C;* U a³họ³⁴ *C;* VN họa *C;* Y hạ *C*.
POM 87. **tun, **yun *child*.
PCn 764. **yṳ·n *infant, baby*. < POM **yuHn.
L ši³yṳ·³; O yj²; P gyéw¹, gyjw²; Q yü·²; U dyei³.
POM 258. **siʔ *youngster*.
PCn 806. *si·ʔ² *youngster*. < POM **siʔ³.
L ši·ʔ³, O si?² yj², P ciʔ², T cyiʔ² kyą́³ *C*, U si³maiʔ².

The Development of PCn Grandkinsman Terms

The self-reciprocal POM grandkinsman terms are not retained in PCn to refer to grandparents, but the female term does persist as the grandchild term for ego of either sex. The grandfather term apparently lost out altogether in competition with the POM phrases based on parent terms, while the grandmother term was replaced only in reference to senior grandkinsmen, its use by female ego for junior grandkinsmen of either sex spreading to men's usage as well with the demise of the grandfather term.

POM 430. **Ynsan, **Ynan $PPf(R,2)$.
  PCn 452. *zia·²¹² $CC(y^20)$. < POM **Ynsa.
    A žon³² $CC;$ C gyé·¹³e $CC;$ Ch ciǫ $CC;$ L ja·n³² $CC(first)(2,S),$ jo·²³² CC(third)(2,S); M cie¹² $CC;$ O yi̧² cye²⁴ $CC;$ P ziew¹ $CC(S);$ Q tyiá·³a $CC;$ S ciau³² $CC;$ T syo³² $CC(1,S);$ Tl ciǫ² $CC;$ U a³tyie³⁴ $CC;$ VN zoi $CC;$ Y zia· $PPf,CC(2).$

Conversely, the POM modified child term to designate lineal descendents did not survive into Chinantecan times, being replaced entirely by the above reflex of the grandmother term. The POM modified parent terms, on the other hand, did survive as the means for designating grandparents in PCn, with some lexical reshaping. Unlike the modifiers in some of the other OM families, Chinantecan shows different modifiers in each of the two modified terms.

The modifier of the father term is probably a reflex of the **y-initial alternant of the same modifier found in PMn and PZn, namely, POM 423 **nu, **yu *big, old*. As indicated in the POM chapter, it is not clear how this form might be related to POM 189 **kwe?n², **ke?n *big, old* which shows up as the modifier in other of the OM families, such as PPn, PZn (penultimate syllable), A, and PTl (for great-grandparents). Rensch's original PCn 765 is here divided into what appear to be two closely related sets. PCn 807 does not figure directly in the formation of the grandfather term, but is presented here as a minor clarification of the earlier material.

POM 423. **nu, **yu *big, old*.
  PCn 765. *yu·? *old(male)*. < POM **yu?.
    A gyü?, M yi?, P giu?¹³, Q yú?¹³, S ye?, U dyi?³², VN ni-giü? $PPCm(G).$
  PCn 807. *yu·?n *old(female)*. < POM **yu?n.
    A ma-gyų?, C ni¹yúŋ?¹² $PPf,$ P giuw?² *post-menopause*.

The modifier occurring with the mother term harks back to **POM 350 **yaHn**, itself a term with reflexes referring to *mother* in some languages or more generally to any woman. It may be that **PCn 808** should also be divided into more than one set based on minor inflectional differences also.

POM 350. **ntaHn, **naHn, **yaHn $Pf(vocative),$ $PPCf(R,G),$ *female*.
  PCn 808. *?ya·³ *woman*. < POM **?ya.
    L tu³ ?yo·² *turkey pullet;* O kwa¹ hwɨ² ?ye³¹ *cow;* P ?io¹³ *woman,* ?io³ *woman(post-menopause),* cie?³ ?iéw³ *pullet;* Q hó?²¹ ?yia·² *cow.*

At least three underlying forms of the father term are found in various Chinantec languages as the basis of the grandfather phrase. Several langauges reflect **POM 49 **Ytah**, several reflect the first person form of the reference term **PCn 563 *ŋiu? *Pm*, and several the third person form **PCn 359 *hmi·¹ *Pm*. Similarly, both vocative and reference forms of the mother term are found in the modified mother term, reflecting **PCn 287 *ma· $Pf(vocative),$ **PCn 802 *sia $Pf(first),$ or **PCn 651 *siá·² $Pf(third).$

PCn 766. *tiá²yu·?², *ŋiu?-yu·?², *hmi·¹yu·?² *PPm(e²0)*. < POM **Ytah-yu?, **nkin-yu?, **hnwi-yu?.

A tä²giü·?¹ *PPm;* C ti¹yü?¹³ *PPm;* Ch ŋi-dạu *PPm(1);* L yi²³u·?n²³² *PPm(first)(S),* yi²³u·?² *PPm(third)(S);* M ŋi¹dau?¹² *PPm;* O hmi²?yi?²⁴ *PPm;* P hi̧²giu?³ *PPm(e²0,S),* ti³giu?¹³ *Sir;* Q yü̋?¹³ü *PPm;* S ŋiú²de?³ *PPm;* T i²gi?³¹ *PPm(2,S);* Tl ?i²dạu?¹ *PPm;* U ni³dyei?³² *PPm;* VN hmi-giü? *PPm(1);* Y zyu? *PPm.*

PCn 809. *ma·-?ya·², *sia-?ya·², *siá·²?ya·² *PPf(e²0)*. < POM **nwen-?ya, **Ysun-?ya, **Ysuhn-?ya.

A ma²?ia·¹ *PPf;* Ch di-?io *PPf(1);* L ši²?ya·n²³ *PPf(first)(S),* ši²?yo·² *PPf(third)(S);* M ndi¹gyi³ *PPf;* O si¹?ye²⁴ *PPf;* P ci³?io¹³ *PPf(e²0,S);* Q si̋³?yiá³a *PPf;* S dí²?io³ *PPf;* T cyi¹?yo³¹ *PPf(2,S);* Tl ti²io¹ *PPf;* U si²?dyie³² *PPf;* VN ci-?ie *PPf(1);* Y ?ia· *PPf.*

While the modified parent terms have replaced the lexical forms of the POM grand-kinsman terms they have not replaced them semantically. Rather, they have in at least some Chinantec languages been applied to the full ranges of the lexical material they have replaced. Specifically, in Palantla Rule e²0 survives which is the equivalent of Rule 2 except that it is based on the relative age principle of seniority as opposed to that of genealogical generation. Rule e²0 may, in fact, more adequately express the POM definition of seniority than does Rule 2. Tepetotutla exhibits Rule 2 for senior kinsmen and Rule 1 for junior kinsmen (Palantla shows y²0 for junior kinsmen), but while Lalana and Yolox show Rule 2 for juniors; most Chinantec reports show no extension rules of any sort for grandkinsmen terms. This paucity of rules of extension is considered more a function of incomplete data than of semantic shift. Without, therefore, attempting to formalize the semantic shifts which have taken place in every detail, the following statements characterize the change that is implied in the above discussion from POM times to the PCn horizon.

$2 \rightarrow e^2 0 \ / \ PP$ (PCn).

$2 \rightarrow y^2 0 \ / \ CC$ (PCn).

The Development of PCn Sibling Terms

Proto Chinantec continues a Jivaran pattern of refernce for elder siblings, but shows some lexical innovation in the process. Only the cross-sex sibling term continues directly into Chinantecan. The PCn terms used between siblings of the same sex appear to result from POM parent terms, though the male term can be partially from the corresponding POM sibling term since it shares **yu̇ with the father term.

POM 361 **kwin-yu-wa, **kin-yu-wa, **nwin-yu-wa *Pm, PPCm(R,G), male.*
POM 423. **tu, **nu, **yu *emPCm(0).*
   PCn 810. *ŋiu *emPCm(0)*, < POM **nkin-yu.
      A ŋió¹ *ePCm(0),* P ŋiu¹ *ePCm(0).*
POM 350. **ntaHn, *naHn, **yaHn *Pf(vocative), PPCf(R,G), female.*
   PCn 811. *nï· *efPCf(0).* < POM **ntan.
      A ní·¹ *ePCf(0),* C nï̋¹²ï *PPCf(1,-S),* P nïy¹ *ePCf(0),* Q nï·³ï *PPCf(1).*
POM 431. **nsi-?ya *eaPCb(0).*
   PCn 231. *?iạ·³¹³ *eaPCb(0).* < POM **?yahn.

C ?ę́¹²e *PPCm(1,-S);* L ?ę·n³² *PPCm(first)(L,S),* ?ę·²³² *PPCm(third)(L,S),* ki²³?ę·n³² *PPCSf(L,V);* Q ?ą·³a *PPCm(1);* VN ?iąg *PPCf(G);* Y ?ią·a *PPC.*

The proposed derivation of **PCn 810** is subject to the same considerations discussed above of **PCn 563** *ɲiu? Pm(first).*

PCn also continues the pattern of a generic sibling term which marks neither sex nor seniority but which serves as the reciprocal of senior sibling terms. As was indicated in the discussion of POM sibling terms, the source of PCn *r is unknown. **PCn 758** is, therefore, tentatively considered the result either of **POM 61** or **POM 159.**

POM 61. **ta?n *PC(0).*
POM 159. **kuHn *PC(0);* ****nsi-kihn, **kihn-si** *yPC(0).*
PCn 758. *ru·?n *PC(0).* < POM ****Yta?n** or ****nsi-ku?n.**

A ön? *yPC(0);* C rú?²n *PC(1);* Ch rų? *PC(0);* L u·?n² *companion, spouse;* M ru?² *PC(0);* O rǫ?²⁴ *PC(0);* P ro?¹² *yPC(0);* Q ru?²¹na *PC(0);* S rę?² *ePC(0);* T rį̃?³ *PC(0,S);* Tl rų? *PC(0);* U ręu?³ *PC(0),* VN iu?¹³ *PC(1),* Y ru?n *PC(G).*

There are a few modern terms which are left unaccounted for by the reconstruction of the above four terms. In Lalana, the sibling term hą·n³² is a tone pair with the child term hą·n²³. Sochiapan dá²hąu³² *younger sibling* does not appear to be cognate with the Lalana term. The Lalana aunt term tʌn²³ *PPCf(L)* is completely unaccounted for, and the cousin term za·n³¹na¹ *PPCC* is clearly a borrowing from Zapotec—cf. Yagallo Zapotec záana? *aPCb(G).*

In the discussion above of terms for grandkinsmen, a commitment was made to the interpretation, based mostly on data from Palantla, that relative age was a primary feature in distinguishing categories of collateral kinsmen. The grandparent terms are considered to have extended to collateral kinsmen who were age peers of grandparents, and the grandchild term is considered to have extended to collateral kinsmen who were age peers of grandchildren.

This same commitment to the importance of relative age is made in regard to the four terms reconstructed above for collateral kinsmen. They divide such kinsmen into two further age groups—those older than ego but not age peers of grandparents, and those younger than ego but not age peers of grandchildren. Three terms further categorize the senior group while a single term designates the junior group.

In the case of a single term for the junior group *(PCn 758),* it is quite likely that it had at least two senses—a narrow sense in which it was the primary and most direct way to refer to a member of the *younger sibling* group, and a more generic sense in which it referred to any collateral kinsman (or perhaps any consanguineal kinsman whether lineal or collateral). The modern Palantla means for expressing a consanguineal relationship employs this form in the phrase hu³rǫ?¹² and, as the cognates in many of the other contemporary Chinantec languages show, many of the modern forms of ***ru·?n** extend to all collateral kinsmen. It is probable that this latter usage does not represent a semantic shift in the use of ***ru·?n,** but merely the loss of the other terms which specifically had reference to senior collaterals.

The three terms for senior collaterals are considered to have continued the Jivaran pattern of reference of POM even though no modern Chinantec system employs a relative sex as a criterion for distinguishing collateral kinsmen as do Zapotecan and Mixtecan languages. One of the Chinantecan sets **(231),** however, includes cognates which refer to males in some languages and to females in others. The Jivaran hypothesis cares for this nicely.

Semantic shifts occurring in the development of modern ranges of reference for these terms may be illustrated by a series of graphs, one for each modern language which retains a reflex of one or more of the three terms in question and one for the source language (See Figure 5). Each graph represents a semantic field of all senior collaterals for one language, with the field being divided according to the specific denotations of the terms of each system. The proposed PCn system is taken as underlying the others, with arrows indicating the direction of semantic change in the latter. Arrows originating within a semantic field indicate the extension of the range of denotation of a modern reflex of one or another of the three source terms. Arrows originating at the outside margin of a field indicate an encroachment into the system by a term from outside the PCn system.

The proposed semantic shifts represented graphically in Figure 5 may be formalized in the following rules:

$$
\begin{aligned}
m &\to \quad \emptyset \quad / \_PCm \qquad &\text{(A P VN).} \\
f &\to \quad \emptyset \quad / \_PCf \qquad &\text{(A C L P Q).} \\
a &\to \quad \emptyset \quad / \_PCb \qquad &\text{(C L Q VN Y).} \\
b &\to \begin{cases} f & / PC\_ \\ m & / PC\_ \\ \emptyset & / PC\_ \end{cases} \qquad &\begin{array}{l} \text{(VN)} \\ \text{(C L Q)} \\ \text{(Y).} \end{array}
\end{aligned}
$$

The utter simplicity of the systems of reference for collaterals in a majority of modern Chinantec systems—with a single term that not only often classifies all collaterals, but also doubles as a generic term for all kinsmen—is the result of the collapse of the earlier system and loss of previous terminological distinctions. It is unlikely that so simple a system could have been adequate to the social needs of the people, before they settled into more or less permanent communities, whether those settlements were congregated or dispersed.

One possible cause of this collapse was pressure from a foreign system of kinship reference (perhaps the Spanish system from the time of the conquest, or perhaps the dominant Nahuatl-speaking peoples had some influence before that), but it is also conceivable that a shift to a more sedentary life at least twice that long ago (1000 years?) had an influence on the function of collateral kinsmen in the society and on related kinship classification. Either of these forces, but especially the former, could have contributed to the obsolescence of a system based on relative age of a sort still found in Palantla.

The interpretation of the current Palantla system as a direct reflection of PCn is much easier than attempting to account for it from a system which lacked relative age as an essential component. There is also other support for the relative age hypothesis found outside of the Chinantec data. Weitlaner and Hoogshagen (1960) discuss the importance of age ranks in the social organization of a number of Oaxacan groups, and relative age does show itself as a factor in the kinship systems of other related Otomanguean families included in this study, as well as in nearby non-Otomanguean areas (Merrifield 1965, Waterhouse and Merrifield 1968).

Finally, as in the case of lineal kinsmen, there has been a shift to include affinals within the ranges of terms for collateral kinsmen. Specifically, this is the case in Comaltepec and Lalana.

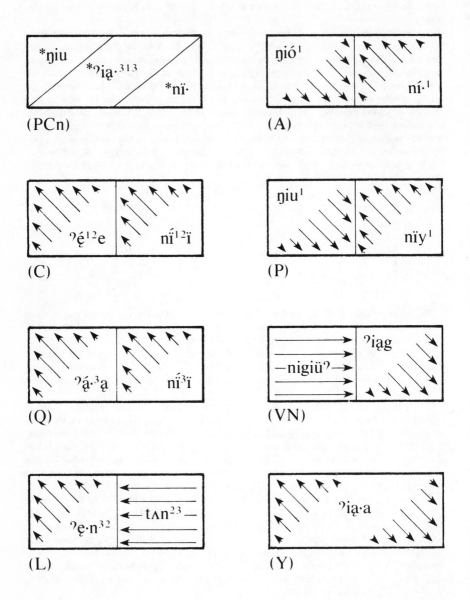

Figure 5. PCn Semantic Shifts — senior collateral kinsmen.

In Lalana, the situation is quite complex, suggesting a series of semantic and lexical shifts of the following sort. Beginning with the three PCn elder sibling terms which have been proposed, the shift from relative age to generation probably took place as follows:

*ŋiu	$emPCm(0)$	→ $mPPCm(L)$
*nï·	$efPCf(0)$	→ $fPPCf(L)$
*ʔiạ·³¹³	$eaPCb(0)$	→ $aPPCb(L)$

Perhaps at the same time, the concept *sex of ego* was suppressed, triggering the loss of two of these lexical items, leaving the third to distinguish *sex of alter* by the addition of pretonic material:

*ŋiu	$mPPCm(L)$	→ LOSS	
*nï·	$fPPCf(L)$ →	LOSS	
*ʔiạ·³¹³	$aPPCb(L)$	→ { *ʔiạ·³¹³	$PPCm(L)$
		*ki-ʔiạ·³¹³	$PPCf(L)$

It may or may not have been the same forces putting pressure on Lalana Chinantec to adjust the filial ranges of these terms which also caused the development of Lalana's present system of affinal reference; but, in any case, these filial terms were extended to affinal kinsmen:

*ʔiạ·³¹³	$PPCm(L)$	→ $PPCm(L,S)$
*ki-ʔiạ·³¹³	$PPCf(L)$	→ $PPCf(L,S)$

This represents the current system for male senior collateral kinsmen. In the case of females, filial kinsmen are now once again distinguished from affinals through the intrusion of an additional term of unknown origin into the system:

*ki-ʔiạ·³¹³	$PPCf(L,S)$ →	$tʌn^{23}$	$PPCf(L)$
		$ki^{23}ʔ\text{ẹ·}n^{32}$	$PPCSf(L,V)$

The Comaltepec situation is not nearly so complex, but it is nevertheless important due to the fact that spouse of collateral is not classified together with collateral of spouse. Specifically, two terms extend to spouses of collateral filial kinsmen, but not to collateral filial kinsmen of spouse. Perhaps the following series of shifts took place in Comaltepec:

*ŋiu	$emPCm(0)$	→ $mPPCm(1)$	→ LOSS		
*nï·	$efPCf(0)$	→ $fPPCf(1)$	→ $PPCf(1)$	→ $nï̈^{12}ï$	$PPCf(1,-S)$
*ʔiạ·³¹³	$eaPCb(0)$	→ $aPPCb(1)$	→ $PPCm(1)$	→ $ʔẹ^{12}e$	$PPCm(1,-S)$

The Development of PCn Affinal Terms

Four affinal terms find wide support at the Proto Chinantec horizon, but it is unlikely that more than two of them hark back to POM as true kinship terms. The Chinantec forms for children-in-law are among those which motivate the tentative proposal for two POM child-in-law terms. The lack of parent-in-law terms in PCn which are obvious

reflexes of POM forms is an argument from silence for the self-reciprocal analysis of the
POM child-in-law term.

POM 432. **kah CSm(R,0).
PCn 814. *ŋá· CSm(y0). < POM **nkahn.
A ŋo³¹ CSm, C zya¹ŋó·¹³ CSm(2), Ch ŋo CSm, O yi²ŋo³¹ CSm, P ŋo¹³ CSm(L), Q
ŋó·¹³ CSm, S ŋó³² CSm, T ŋo³¹ CSm, U a³ŋo³² CSm(L), VN ŋoa CSm, Y ŋa· SPm
[sic].
POM 433. **nsan, **nyan CSf(R,0).
PCn 815. *lá· CSf(y0). < POM **nyah.
C zya¹ma¹ló·¹³o CSf(2), Ch lo CSf, O yi²lo² CSf, P lo¹³ CSf(L), Q cá² y³ló·¹³ CSf, S
ló³² CSf, T lo³¹ CSf, U a³lo⁴ CSf(L).

It is tempting to argue for Chinantecan evidence of self-reciprocity in the son-in-law
term from the early eighteenth-century Yolox form which is glossed by Barreda as father-
in-law (rather than son-in-law). But this is more likely due to a printing error and not to
be taken as supporting such an analysis. If the Barreda list were more complete,
including forms for children-in-law as well as parent-in-law, or at least some indication of
how both senior and junior in-laws were classified, we would be in a better position to
evaluate his data.
    In the presentation of POM affinal terms above, the father-in-law term was suggested
as a possible reflex of **POM 433**; but, as was also indicated, it is more likely that the two
PCn parent-in-law terms are innovations which developed simultaneously since they
share morphological and semantic make-up. The initial syllables of the two terms are
reflexes of POM forms meaning *male* and *female,* respectively, while the second syllables are forms of the respective parent terms. Since terms for *male* and *female* are
known to have been used in reference to spouse throughout Otomanguean with considerable antiquity, it is likely that this has influenced the development and lexicalization of
these phrases which can be considered to have been interpretable earlier as *father-type
male* and *mother-type female,* respectively.

POM 254. **sehn, **yehn *male.*
PCn 812. *zá·²¹ŋiu?, *zá·²¹hmi·¹ SPm(L).** < POM **nsehn-kin-yu-?, **nsehn-wi.
A zó² hmin³ SPm, C zya²¹ ŋyé?²e SPm(L), Ch caŋiu? SPm, O co⁴ñi?²⁴ SPm, P
zu²ŋie?¹ SPm, Q cá·²³ñü?³ü SPm, S ca³ŋiu?³² SPm, T zï²ŋe?³ SPm, U a⁵nei?²
SPm(L), VN zonoi? SPm.
POM 148. **kwin, **kin, **win *female.*
PCn 813. *mí·sia· SPf(L). < POM **n?kwihn-sun.
A ma²čon³ SPf, C ?yé·¹³ mi¹sé·¹e SP(L), Ch mïϴia SPf, O ?ye³¹ mï³se²⁴ SPf, P
mï²cie¹ SPf, Q ?yiá·¹³ y³sa¹³a SPf, S mï³ϴia³² SPf, T mï²cya³ SPf, U a¹sia³⁴ SPf(L),
VN mïcia SPf, Y mïsia SPf.

A few idiosyncracies are reported in modern reflexes of these terms. Usila utilizes the
common a- formative, meaning *person,* as the first element of the terms, rather than the
male and female formatives. The word for woman (**PCn 808 *?ya·**) is commonly used in
C, O, Q, and P, preceding the mother-in-law term. In P, at least, the use is optional and
adds a note of respect to the reference. Ayotzintepec apparently uses the third person

suppletive form of the father term (**PCn 359** *hmi·[1]) for the father-in-law term regardless of person inflection of the latter.

There is little to be said about the phonological structure of the child-in-law terms except to note that they do occur with a variety of formatives in some of the contemporary languages. C and Q show forms of **440** *za·[1] *person* (Rensch 1963:179, 1977:282) which is phonologically close to **PCn 445** above, and probably related morphologically to the U formative a- which is also present in child-in-law terms. The O formative is from **PCn 764** *yụ·n[1] *infant, baby*. Its use here parallels that of the O child term introduced above. C and Q not only use the term for person, but also the term for female as presyllables to the daughter-in-law term. Alternatively, rather than the daughter-in-law term itself, A and VN use the form for female in a descriptive phrase with the child term to mean, literally, *child's woman*.

A fifth term is widely used for Chinantec affinals today, but it is based on a loanword from Spanish rather than a PCn form.

cuñado, cuñada *sibling-in-law*.

A kọ·[2]ŋia[3] *SPC(V,0)*, C ku[1]ŋyaa[2] *SPC(0)*, Ch kuŋia *SPC(V,0)*, P ku[2]ŋi[13] *SPC(V,0)*, Q ñá·[23] *SPC(V,G)*, S ku[2]ŋia[21] *SPC(V,0)*, T ko[2]ŋya[31] g*SPC(V,G)*, U ku[3]ña[23] *SPC(V,0)*.

The reconstruction of the system of reference for Proto Chinantecan affinal terms must remain a good deal more conjectural than that of the consanguineal system. The primary reference of the parent-in-law terms was undoubtedly *Sm* and *Sf*, respectively, and the primary range of child-in-law terms *Sm* and *Sf;* but the extended ranges are not at all clear. The morphological structure of the parent-in-law terms—with such close relationship to the terms for consanguineal parents—would argue for these two terms not being extended to the collateral kinsmen of spouse; but in the case of child-in-law terms, no such morphological tie seems to exist and at least one modern language (C) extends the terms both to lineals and to all collaterals of generations below that of ego.

The borrowing of Spanish **cuñado**, with Chinantec forms ranging in most cases over all of spouse's collaterals as well as the spouses of all of ego's collaterals, provides very little evidence for reconstructing the nature of the affinal system of reference. The designation *SPC(V,0)* is all we have to work with as the most common range of sibling-in-law terms.

The situation in Lalana, however, does bear some discussion in that it is the only modern Chinantec language for which we have a full set of data on sibling-in-law terms and their ranges of reference which does not borrow **cuñado**. Specifically, there are three terms for affinals of ego's generation. I repeat them here from Rensch's article in this volume:

tu[3]ñu?n[23]	m*PCSm(V)*	*man's brother-in-law*
ki[23]u·?n[32]na[23]	f*PCSf(V)*	*woman's sister-in-law*
lʌ?n[32]	a*PCSb(V)*	*cross-sex sibling-in-law*

The first term in this set is clearly based on **PCn 801** *ŋiu? *male*, the source of the presyllable being unclear.

The second term is based on the sibling term **PCn 758** *ru·?n *PC(0)* with preposed **ki[23]** which marks the form as having specific reference to a female. This female marker is not to my knowledge a common phenomenon in Chinantec, but it does occur in three Lalana pairs, as follows:

$ki^{23}?\varrho\cdot n^{32}$	$PPCSf(V,L)$	vs.	$?\varrho\cdot n^{32}$	$PPCm(L,S)$
$ki^{23}h\varrho\cdot n^{23}$	CSf	vs.	$h\varrho\cdot n^{23}$	$C(S)$
$ki^{23}u\cdot?n^{23}n\varrho^{23}$	$fPCSf(V)$	vs.	$u\cdot?n^2na^{23}$	companion

The third term is borrowed from nearby Zapotec. As mentioned above, the southeastern Chinantecs have been heavily influenced by neighboring Zapotec, both in their kinship terms and otherwise. This term reflects **PZn 9** **si-lu?na* $aPCSb(V,G)$. It was noted above that the Lalana cousin term was borrowed from Zapotec. It is also very likely that the Lalana system of reference for affinals of ego's generation is of Zapotec origin, though perhaps not a very recent borrowing.

Comaltepec data may provide a better clue concerning the PCn affinal system than other contemporary languages. Specifically, the filial kinsmen of spouse are never classified with the spouses of ego's own filial kinsmen. The first of these groups is divided into lineals and collaterals by parent-in-law terms—$SPm(L)$ and $SPf(L)$—and a sibling-in-law term—$SPC(0)$. The second group is divided into junior and senior kinsmen by extension of filial terms for senior collateral kinsmen to affinals—$PPCm(1,S)$ and $PPCf(1,-S)$—and by extension of child-in-law terms to all spouses of junior filial kinsmen—$CSm(2)$ and $CSf(2)$.

Unfortunately, since the sibling-in-law term is obviously of Spanish origin and since the extension of senior collateral filial terms to include their spouses is also most likely of post-PCn origin, we are left with probable PCn lexical material for only two of the four sub-groups of affinals in this configuration, namely, the parent-in-law terms for lineal ascendents of spouse and child-in-law terms for spouses of junior filial kinsmen. This is, nevertheless, the strongest hypothesis available to us, with one minor revision.

It seems unlikely that the Chinantec of PCn times would be classifying spouses of junior filial kinsmen on the basis of generation, as extension Rule 2 would imply, while at the same time classifying filial kinsmen on the basis of relative age. Having already determined that relative age was most likely in focus in distinguishing junior and senior filial kinsmen, the probable corresponding ranges of reference for the spouses of the junior filial kinsmen were $CSm(y0)$ and $CSf(y0)$, respectively.

We thus have accounted for PCn reference to $SP(L)$ and $CS(y0)$ by four PCn lexical forms: but we are left in the dark regarding the lexical means through which reference may have been made to $SPC(0)$ or $ePCS(0)$.

The Development of PCn Spouse Terms

There are a variety of ways to refer to spouse in modern Chinantec. At least five languages, and probably more than that, utilize phrases which literally translated mean something like *my male person* and *my female person*, respectively. At least five languages, however, also exhibit a term for spouse of either sex which is formed of a presyllable and a word for *hand*, viz. **PCn 609** **gwa·¹* (Rensch 1963:206, 1978:252).

PCn 816. *hi-gwa·¹ S.

O hi^1kwo^{24} S, P hi^2guw^1 S, S ηi^2 $u\acute{o}^{32}$ S, T i^2gu^3 S, U i^3kue^{34} S.

The source of the presyllable is not certain, but evidence from Ch, O, and P points to a verb meaning *to bring two objects into contact with each other,* the reference being to the joining of the spouses' hands in the wedding ceremony. The Palantla expression referring to marriage is based on this verb, as in **ma²hé?²dsa guw²** *he is married* (literally, has-joined-he hand). The Proto Chinantecan form of the presyllable of the spouse term may be an unstressed form of this verb. It may also be that the concept of joining hands in marriage ceremonially is a Christian innovation introduced into Chinantec life in relatively recent times, so that the significance of this expression for the Proto Chinantec horizon may be nil.

CHAPTER 7
OTHER OTOMANGUEAN
KINSHIP TERMS

This chapter summarizes a possible sequence of development from Proto Otomanguean kinship terms and ranges of reference to contemporary Amuzgo, Huave, Tlapanec and to the extinct Chiapanec and Mangue languages, including preliminary evidence for terms and corresponding ranges of reference at Proto Tlapanecan and Proto Chiapanec-Mangue horizons.

OTHER OTOMANGUEAN
KINSHIP TERMS

Amuzgo, Huave, Tlapanec, and Chiapanec-Mangue are discussed together in this section since relatively limited data from each group does not merit separate treatment for each.

The Development of Amuzgo Parent and Child Terms

Amuzgo parent terms reflect POM vocative terms for parent, although the source of Amuzgo ɔ in the mother term is not clear. It is more likely the result of **an,** and therefore of **POM 350,** but the possibility remains that it is from **un** and **POM 340.** If the correct sources of the parent terms are the POM vocative terms, that may indicate that the source of the Amuzgo child term, **POM 57** or **87,** was also vocative.

POM 49. **Ytah *Pm(vocative).*
A co¹tyǎ¹ *Pm,* co¹tyé² *Pm(third);* tá¹² *Pm;* tyé?³ *Pm(vocative).* < POM **Ytah, **tah,
**Ytah?.
**POM 350. **ntaHn, **naHn, **yaHn *Pf(vocative), PPCf(R,G), female.*
A ná¹² *Pf.* < POM **nahn.
A co¹ñtɔ́³ *Pf.* < *co-ti-nɔ́ < POM **nahn (**nuhn?).

137

POM 57. **ʔntan C.
A **hnta²¹**, **hntá²** C(L). < POM ****hntan.**
A **ʔnta¹** *very young person (vocative).* < POM ****ʔntan.**
A **tyhɔ́¹²** *young person (vocative).* < POM ****Yhtahn (**Yhtuhn?).**

There has been no change in range of reference for Amuzgo parent and child terms from POM times to the present.

The Development of Amuzgo Grandkinsman Terms

No trace of the POM self-reciprocal grandkinsman terms is found in Amuzgo which classifies grandkinsmen by reflexes of the POM modified parent and child terms in the same fashion (extension by Rule L) as in POM times. The POM sources of the Amuzgo terms are **POM 49 **Ytah** *PM(vocative),* **POM 350 **ntaHn, **naHn, **yaHn** *Pf(vocative),* **POM 189 **kweʔn, **keʔn** *big, old,* and **POM 50 **ʔntan³ Yhntah³** CC(L).

co¹tyá̃¹ cą¹tkie² *PPm(L).* < POM ****Ytah Yken.**
co¹ñtɔ́³ cą¹tkie² *PPf(L).* < POM ****nahn Yken.**
hntá² ka²ñthɔ́² CC(L). < POM ****hntan Yhntan³.**

The Development of Amuzgo Sibling Terms

The POM cross-sex sibling term is lost in Amuzgo along with the principle *sex of ego* as a distinguishing feature in the classification of siblings. The man's term for brother becomes the term for brother for ego of either sex, and the woman's term for sister, correspondingly, the sister term for any ego. As in Chinantecan, the Amuzgo generic term for sibling can result from either **POM 61** or **POM 159**.

POM 423. **tu, **nu, **yu *emPCm(0).*
A **šiɔ²¹**, **šió²** *ePCm(0).* < POM ****si-yu.**
POM 236. **kwaHn, **kaHn *efPCf(0).*
A **šhɔ²¹** *ePCf(0).* < **šuhɔ* < POM ****kwaHn.**
POM 61. **taʔn *PC(0).*
POM 159. **kuHn *PC(0);* ****nsi-kihn, **kihn-si** *yPC(0).*
A **tyhɔ́¹²**, **tyhe³²** *yPC(0).* < POM ****Yhta** or < **ci-hku* < POM ****nsi-kuhn.**

The loss of *sex of ego* as a semantic parameter of these terms may be expressed as follows:

$$e \rightarrow \emptyset \ / \_\_ PC \qquad\qquad\qquad (A).$$

The Development of Amuzgo Affinal Terms

Amuzgo has just three elementary terms for affinals. The two child-in-law terms, distinguishing son-in-law from daughter-in-law but including within their ranges spouses of all descendents and collateral kinsmen, appear to be direct reflexes of the corresponding POM terms, retaining an extended range characterized by Rule 0 but losing the self-reciprocity feature of the proposed earlier terms.

POM 432. **kah $CSm(R,0)$.
A **lko²** $CSm(0)$. < POM ****Ykan.**
POM 433. **nsan, **nyan $CSf(R,0)$.
A **n¹nca²** $CSf(0)$. < POM ****n-nsa.**

The single Amuzgo term **šę³** $SP(0)$, for any ancestor or collateral of spouse, may result either from POM ****Y?kahn** or POM ****Ysahn.** It may thus be a reflex of either **POM 432** or **POM 433**, or it may be the result of coalescence and have its source in both of those earlier forms. If this is so, we can see that the earlier self-reciprocal terms probably first occurred with preposed material to specify differences in seniority when the terms were used, respectively, by senior or junior in-laws. This preposed material may have then affected the results of sound change upon the consonantisms of the underlying forms, resulting in a split (and perhaps also merging) of the two terms to three.

The Development of Amuzgo Spouse terms

Amuzgo terms for husband and wife are possessed forms of more general terms meaning *male* and *female*, respectively, which hark back to POM forms with these same ranges of meaning.

POM 254. **sehn, **yehn *male*.
A **s?á³** *Sm*. < POM ****?sehn.**
POM 148. **kwin, **kin, **win *female*.
A **skú³** *Sf*. < ***kuh** < POM ****kwihn.**

The Development of Huave Parent and Child Terms

Not a great deal is known of the phonological development of Otomanguean in Huave, but it would appear that the Huave parent and child terms do directly reflect POM forms, as well as ranges of reference. The Huave father term appears to be a reflex of **POM 49**—the vocative term—with influence of lingua franca **tata**. The Huave mother term appears to descend from **POM 148** without difficulty. The child term, however, can be only very tentatively associated with **POM 308**, with preposed **POM 428 **nkwan** (*diminutive*), on the analogy of similar terms from POP and PCM, since it is not possible to securely reconstruct the value of the final POM vowel from the Huave data.

POM 49. **Ytah *Pm(vocative)*.
H **téàt** *Pm*. < POM ****Ytah.**
POM 148. **kwin, **kin, **win *Pf, PPCf(R,G)*, *female*.
H **mím** *Pf*. < POM ****nwin.**
POM 308. **Yhnsan, **yan *C*.
H **kwál** *C(L)*. < POM ****kwan-yV** (****kwan-yan?**).

As will be seen in the next section, POM grandkinsman terms are reduced in range in Huave to include only senior grandkinsmen. In their place, the range of the child term is extended to lineal descendents by Rule L.

$\emptyset \to L \ / \ C$ (H).

The Development of Huave Grandkinsman Terms

The two POM self-reciprocal grandkinsman terms continue in Huave as terms for grandfather and grandmother, but their ranges no longer include grandchildren which are designated within the extended range of the modern Huave term for child.

POM 429. **seh, **hkeh *PPm(R,2)*.
H šéèč *PPm(e₂0)*. **< POM **sinseh.**
POM 430. **Ynsan, **Ynan *PPf(R,2)*.
H nčéy *PPf(e₂0)*. **< POM **Ynsa.**

The extension Rule e²0 does not necessarily imply a semantic shift in the extension of these terms to collateral kinsmen from POM times, as has been mentioned above.

Interestingly, in addition to the rule of extention given in the foregoing statement, data from Diebold recapped in Warkentin's article of this volume indicate alternate rules of extension for grandparent terms, namely, Rule L or Rule 1, depending upon the situation. This may be a direct reflex of the POM situation where the self-reciprocal terms appear to have had one sort of extension (Rule 2 or e²0) while phrases based on parent terms had another (Rule L). The phrases apparently no longer find reflexes in Huave as lexical items, but perhaps the underlying semantic distinction does in usage which accomodates to particular contexts.

The Development of Huave Sibling Terms

The Jivaran terms of POM are lost in Huave, but the generic sibling term is retained in its unmodified form to designate elder sibling and in its modified form to designate younger sibling.

POM 159. **kuHn *PC(0);* **nsi-kihn, **kihn-si** *yPC(0)*.
H kóh *ePC(0)*. **< POM **kuh.**
H čîig *yPC(0)*. **< *ši-gi < POM **nsin-ki.**

The semantic shift of the unmodified term, narrowing its reference to senior kinsman may be stated as follows:

$\emptyset \to e \ / \ PC$ (H).

The Development of Huave Affinal Terms

Huave has just two affinal terms which directly reflect the corresponding POM terms which have been proposed, except that the introduction into the Huave system of the

Spanish loan **kùñádà** *PCS(V,0)* has reduced their ranges to lineal affinals—ancestors of spouse and spouses of descendents.

POM 432. **kah *CSm(R,0)*.
  H òkwáàc *CSm(R,L)*. < POM ****kahnsa.**
POM 433. **nsan, **nyan *CSf(R,0)*.
  H ápïw *CSf(R,L)*. < POM ****kwan.**

Huave **kw** in the son-in-law term could represent a ****kw**-initial variant of ****kah,** but it is here taken to be the result of influence from preposed material of which **ò-** is the partial reflex. The Huave daughter-in-law term is included as a reflex of **POM 433** on the basis of the POM alternation between ****kw** and ****s** (Rensch 1976:33). Its membership in this set is, of course, open to considerable question; but it is by no means impossible. There seems to be no better hypothesis available, given the present data.

The Development of Huave Spouse Terms

Huave shares the widely attested POM pattern of two terms for husband and wife with at least the latter being a reflex of a general term for *female;* but the source of Huave **nóh** *Sm* is unknown.

POM 350. **ntaHn, **naHn, **yaHn *female.*
  H ntáh *Sf.* < POM ****ntah.**

Proto Tlapanec Kinship Terms

A careful comparison of Tlapanec languages and reconstruction of a parent language is not available for use in this study. A tentative statement is therefore proposed here of possible Proto Tlapanec terms. The reconstruction is tentative, being based solely upon the data included in this volume from Lemley and from Wheathers, but is nevertheless dependable enough for the purposes of this study because of the close similarities which exist between the two languages compared.

As is true in other Otomanguean languages, first person inflection apparently takes several forms in Tlapanec, thereby complicating the phonological realization of kinship terms. The assumption is made here that, apart from tone (which is ignored in the reconstruction), first person inflection is marked by an ending of varying forms: **iʔ, uʔ,** and **Vʔ** (where **V** stands for a vowel, sequence of vowels, or perhaps represents different vowel sources for the two languages of the corpus). These endings are set off by hyphen in the reconstruction.

There is remarkable agreement between the two languages of the sample in kinship terminology. Only the elder sibling term fails to show clear phonological affinity in the two languages. The proposed cognate sets are:

PTl 1. *a-na-uʔ *Pm.* < POM ****na.**
  M ānù?, T a²nu?³.
PTl 2. *ru-du-uʔ *Pf.* < POM ****nyan-sun.**
  M rūdú?, T ru³du?¹.

PTl 3. *a-ʔda-Vʔ C. < POM **ʔntan.
 M àʔdéʔ, T aʔ³dyoʔ¹.

PTl 4. *ši-ʔnu-uʔ $PPm(1)$. < POM **seʔnu.
 M šìʔyų́ʔ $PPm(1,S)$ or $PPCm(1,S)$, tátá šìʔyų́ʔ $PPm(L,S)$; T šiʔ³ñuʔ¹ PPm.

PTl 5. *ši-nu-uʔ $PPf(1)$. < POM **si-nan.
 M šíyų̀ʔ $PPf(1,S)$ or $PPCf(1,S)$, nánà šíyų̀ʔ $PPf(L,S)$; T ši¹ñuʔ¹ PPf.

PTl 6. *a-ʔda ši-nu-Vʔ $CC(1)$. < POM **ʔntan si-nan.
 M àʔdá šíyų̀ʔ $CC(L,S)$, T aʔ³da¹ ši¹ñuʔ²yoʔ³ CC.

PTl 7. *agaʔ big. < POM **nkeʔn.
 M ígòʔ, T a²gaʔ².

PTl 8. *ji-yo-uʔ $mPCm$. < POM **si-yu.
 M jíyòʔ, T ji²³yuʔ³.

PTl 9. *di-ya-Vʔ $fPCm$. < POM **nsi-ʔya.
 M díyêʔ, T dyaʔ¹²yoʔ³.

PTl 10. *j-weʔ-gu-uʔ $fPCf$. < POM **nsi-kwaʔn-kuhn.
 M jwíʔgúʔ, T jweʔ³¹guʔ¹.

PTl 11. *ja-gu-iʔ $mPCf$. < POM **nteHn-kwin.
 M jágwíʔ, T ja¹dyuʔ¹.

PTl 12. *giʔta-Vʔ $yPC(G)$. < POM **kihn-ta.
 M gèʔtéʔ $yPC(G,S)$, T giʔ³tyoʔ³ yPC.

PTl 13. *a-ma-uʔ $PPCm(G)$. < POM **nwin.
 M àmúʔ $PPCm(G,S)$, T a³muʔ² $PPCm(1,S)$.

PTl 14. *ni-yų-iʔ $PPCf(G)$. < *ndi-yų < POM **nsi-nuhn.
 M nìyų́ʔ $PPCf(G,S)$, T ni³ñuʔ¹ $PPCf(1,S)$.

PTl 15. *a-ʔda riša-Vʔ $PCC(G)$.
 M dríšêʔ $PCC(1,S)$, T aʔ³da¹ ri¹šyoʔ¹ $PCC(1,S)$.

PTl 16. *aʔda riša gahma-uʔ $PPCC(G)$.
 M àʔdá ršāhmūʔ, T aʔ³da¹ ri¹ša¹ ga³hmuʔ³.

PTl 17. *hmegu-iʔ SPm. < POM **hnwin-kan.
 M hmégwìʔ, T hme¹³dyuʔ³.

PTl 18. *jagu-iʔ SPf. < POM **Y-ntan-kan.
 M jàgwìʔ, T ja³dyuʔ³.

PTl 19. *nigų-iʔ CSm.
 M nìgwî̜ʔ $CSm(G2)$, nìgų́ šíyî̜ʔ $CCSm(L)$; T ni³dyųʔ¹ CSm.

PTl 20. *guʔgų-iʔ CSf.
 M gùʔgwî̜ʔ $CSf(G2)$, gùʔgų́ šíyî̜ʔ $CCf(L)$; T guʔ³dyųʔ¹ CSf.

PTl 21. *ahmba-Vʔ Sm. < POM **hnkwa.
 M àhmbéʔ Sm, āhmbā $male$; T a³hmbaʔ²³yoʔ³ Sm.

PTl 22. *aʔgu-iʔ Sf. < POM **nʔkwi.
 M àʔgwìʔ Sf, àʔgò $human$ $female$; T aʔ³dyuʔ³ Sf.

PTl 23. *aʔda hmegu-iʔ SPC. < POM **ʔntan hnwin-kan.
 M àʔdá mègwìʔ, T aʔ³da¹ me³dyuʔ³.

PTl 24. *nigų gahma-uʔ $SPCSm$.
 M nīgwáhmùʔ, T ni³gų¹ ga³hmuʔ³.

PTl 25. *guʔgų gahma-uʔ $SPCSf$.
 M gūʔgwáhmùʔ, T guʔ³gų¹ ga³hmuʔ³.

The Development of PTl Parent and Child Terms

As in the case of Huave, relatively little is known of the phonological history of Tlapanec within Otomanguean, so that the proposals made here must be understood as being only tentative suggestions to guide future detailed analysis of that history.

The father term can reflect **POM 49** only if an ****n**-initial alternant of that stem existed. Since no other OM father term reflects such a form, the hypothesis is extremely weak. There does appear to be an uncle term, however, that can easily be a result of **POM 361**. Two terms—for mother and for aunt—can also descend from **POM 340**, the two terms differing by preposed **350** and **255**, respectively. The PTl child term reflects **POM 57**.

POM 49. **Ytah *Pm(vocative)*.
  PTl 1. *a-na-u? *Pm.* < POM ****na.**
POM 361. **kwin, **kin, **win *Pm, PPCm(R,G), male*.
  PTl 13. *a-ma-u? *PPCm(G).* < POM ****nwin.**
POM 340. **suhn, **nuhn *Pf, PPCf(R,G), female*.
POM 350. **ntaHn, **naHn, **yaHn *Pf, PPCf(R,G), female*.
POM 255. **siHn, **niHn *Pf, PPCf(R,G), female*.
  PTl 2. *ru-du-u? *Pf.* < POM ****nyan-sun.**
  PTl 14. *ni-yу-i? *PPCf(G).* < *ndi-yу < POM ****nsi-nuhn.**
POM 57. **?ntan³ *C*.
  PTl 3. *a-?da-V? *C.* < POM ****?ntan.**

The POM ranges of reference of parent and child terms continue into PTl and the contemporary languages without change. Discussion of the terms in reference to collateral kinsmen is taken up at the end of the chapter, after all the PTl terms have been introduced.

The Development of PTl Grandkinsman Terms

The two POM self-reciprocal grandkinsman terms continue into Proto Tlapanec and to the contemporary languages with only minor changes. In particular, sex of senior kinsman in the grandparent-grandchild dyad is no longer marked, the distinction having been shifted to sex of alter *in the case of* senior kinsman. The grandfather term thus continues, designating senior male grandkinsman, but loses out to the grandmother term in designating junior grandkinsman. This latter term designates both senior female grandkinsman and all junior grandkinsmen, male and female.

POM 429. **seh, **hkeh *PPm(R,2)*.
  PTl 4. *ši-?nu-u? *PPm(1).* < POM ****se?nu.**
POM 430. **Ynsan, **Ynan *PPf(R,2)*.
  PTl 5. *ši-nu-u? *PPf(1).* < POM ****si-nan.**
  PTl 6. *a-?da ši-nu-V? *CC(1).* < POM ****?ntan si-nan.**

The semantic shifts from POM times to PTl may be summarized as follows: Rule 2 was reduced to Rule 1. Rule R was lost as the indirect result of shifting reference from sex of senior member of dyad to sex of alter in the case of senior kinsmen. These facts may be characterized as follows (*a* stands for *m* or *f*).

$2 \rightarrow 1 \ / \ PP,CC$ (PTl).
$a \rightarrow \emptyset \ / \ \_\_CC$ (PTl).
$R \rightarrow \emptyset \ / \ PP$ (PTl).

The shift to not mark sex in reference to grandchildren placed the two grandchild terms in competition since they now ranged over exactly the same kintypes. The term formerly used by grandmothers won out over that used by the men.

The Development of PTl Sibling Terms

All POM sibling terms appear to be retained by Tlapanecan which, if anything, expands the inventory of kinship terms over the earlier number. Along with POP, Tlapanecan attests a Quechuan system of four terms which mark a full set of contrasts of sex of both ego and alter. The three POM Jivaran terms carry directly into PTl with the cross-sex term becoming a woman's term for brother as in POP. The man's term for sister, here considered an innovation, also follows POP in harking back to **POM 148**.

POM 423. **tu, **nu, **yu $emPCm(0)$.
   PTl 8. *ji-yo-u? $mPCm$. < POM **si-yu.
POM 431. **nsi-?ya $eaPCb(0)$.
   PTl 9. *diya-V? $fPCm$. < POM **nsi-?ya.
POM 236. **kwaHn, **kaHn $efPCf(0)$.
   PTl 10. *j-we?ǧu-u? $fPCf$. < POM **nsi-kwa?n-kuhn.
POM 148. **kwin, **kin, **win $Pf, PPCf(R,G)$, female.
   PTl 11. *ja-gu-i? $mPCf$. < POM **nteHn-kwin.

These terms are apparently used only for true siblings and not for cousins, indicating a loss of extension Rule 0 in this context and also the loss of the principle of seniority, which becomes a key principle in a second set of sibling terms.

$e,0 \rightarrow \emptyset \ / \ PCm, \ PCf$ (PTl).

Both POM generic sibling terms, **POM 61** and **POM 159**, continue in PTl, developing as a second set of sibling terms to mark seniority as opposed to sex of ego and alter. **POM 159** appears to have occurred with **POM 423** to denote elder sibling (supported only by T) and with **POM 61** to denote younger sibling (supported by M and T). The Malinaltepec elder sibling term appears to be based directly upon **POM 159** with the same preposed material as occurs with the man's sister term.

POM 159. **kuHn $PC(0)$; **nsi-kihn, **kihn-si** $yPC(0)$.
   PTl: T gi?³ñu?² ePC. < POM **kihn-yu.
   PTl: M žáhù? $ePC(G,S)$. < POM **ntehn-kuhn.
   PTl 12. *gi?ta-V? $yPC(G)$. < POM **kihn-ta.

The semantic shift of the generic term to specify only senior siblings may be stated as follows:

$ø → e / PC$ (PTl).

These terms also narrow reference to true siblings in T and to generation peers of ego in M.

$0 → \begin{cases} ø & / PC \\ G & / PC \end{cases}$ (T)

(M).

The Development of PTl Affinal Terms

The two Tlapanec languages in the corpus both support the reconstruction of four affinal terms, two for parents-in-law and two for children-in-law, a male and female term in each set. It is not clear from the data just how these terms extend beyond their primary ranges if they do at all. Moreover, although a number of hypotheses are possible, the PTl terms do not fit well with the proposed POM affinal terms.

The parent-in-law terms appear to reflect terms for *male* and *female* in their respective penultimate syllables, but not without some phonological problems. They share the same ultima which can perhaps have **POM 432 **kah** *CSm(R,0)* as its source.

POM 361. **kwin, **kin, **win *male.*
PTl 17. *hmegu-i? *SPm.* < **POM **hnwin-kan.**
PTl 23. *a?da hmegu-i? *SPC.* < **POM **?ntan hnwin kan.**
POM 350. **ntaHn, **naHn, **yaHn *female.*
PTl 18. *jagu-i? *SPf.* < **POM **Y-ntan-kan.**

The expected source of PTl ***a** in the penult of **PTl 18** is POM ****en** rather than POM ****an** which ordinarily yields PTl ***u.** In **PTl 17**, the source of PTl ***e** is uncertain.

It may be that these difficulties can be overcome, but the son-in-law and daughter-in-law terms are even more difficult. They would be less so if they were reversed, since the penult of the son-in-law term resembles forms for *female* while that of the daughter-in-law term can have its source in **POM 432 **kah** *CSm(R,0).* To be specific, **POM 350 **naHn** *female* has known palatal reflexes which could provide a source compatible with the initial syllable of ***nigu-i?** *CSm,* while the first syllable of ***gu?gu-i?** *CSf* can conceivably have derived from ****nka?n,** a possible variant of **POM 432.** Alternatively, the initial syllable of this latter term can have been the result of a variant of **POM 148 **kwin** *female.*

Equally as troublesome is the second syllable of these terms. While this ultima could perhaps be interpreted to be the result of **POM 428 **kwan** *(diminutive)* with an additional laryngeal as context for the development of PTl ***u,** we do not particularly expect a diminutive in this context. The long and short of the matter is that a good deal remains unclear as to how the Tlapanec affinal terms fit into the POM picture.

The Development of PTl Spouse Terms

PTl terms for husband and wife, which are possessed forms of general words for *male* and *female,* respectively, derive from POM terms of the same general range of meaning.

POM 387. **kwa, **ka, **wa *male.*
PTl 21. *ahmba-V? *Sm.* < **POM **hnkwa.**

POM 148. **kwin, **kin, **win *female.*
PTl 22. *a?gu-i? *Sf.* < POM **n?kwin.

Proto Chiapanec-Mangue Kinship Terms

Detailed kinship materials are not available for this family of Otomanguean languages, but the following terms and possibly-related words from Chiapanec (Ch), Proto Chiapanec (PCh), and Proto Chiapanec-Mangue (PCM) have been taken from Fernández de Miranda and Weitlaner (1961), with a few adjustments by the present author.

PCM 34. *ngu-tá?	Pm	father
PCM 221. *pu-yu-wa(?)	Pm	father
PCM 221 *nu-wa	m	man, male
PCM 158. *hwe, *nu-hwe	m	man, male
PCM 158. *mbu-hwe, *nu-hwi	Sm	husband
PCM 179. *ngu-má?, *ngi-má?	Pf	mother
PCM 197. *mba-hwi, *nu-hmi	Sf	wife
PCM 159. *na-hwí	f	woman, female
PCM 37. *na-tu-me, *na-ru-me	C	child
PCM 206. *mba-ña	C	child
PCh 87. *na-ču-ndi		small
PCM 182. *ña-mu		small
PCM 188. *na-mu-mu		seed
PCM 110. *ma-ngu, *ma-mba	PC(G)	sibling
Ch 181. ni-mà-hi		family
PCM 277. *aka		big

The Development of PCM Parent and Child Terms

Only a limited picture of the PCM kinship system can be deduced from the few sets made available to us through the work of Fernández de Miranda and Weitlaner. Nevertheless, we are fortunate to have good evidence for parent and child terms which directly reflect POM antecedents. One father term reflects **POM 361**; another reflects the antepenult of **361** proposed to **POM 49**—perhaps a PCM vocative term. The PCM term for mother is also a compound, reflecting **POM 148** proposed to **POM 350**. POM is also reflected in PCM words for *female* and *wife*. One child term can be the result of **POM 57**; another of **POM 428 **kwan** (*diminutive*) and **POM 308**.

POM 361. **kwin-yu-wa, **kin-yu-wa, **nwin-yu-wa *Pm, PPCm(R,G), male.*
POM 49. *Ytah *Pm(vocative).*
  PCM 221. *pu-yu-wa *Pm.* < POM **kwi-yu-wa.
  PCM 34. *ngu-tá? *Pm.* < POM **nkwi-tah?.
POM 148. **kwin, **kin, **win *Pf, PPCf(R,G), female.*
POM 350 **ntaHn, **naHn, **yaHn *Pf(vocative), PPCf(R,G), female.*
  PCM 179. *ngu-má?, *ngi-má? *Pf.* < POM **nkwin-nah?, **nkin-nah?.
POM 57. **?ntan³ *C.*
  PCM 37. *na-tu-me, *na-ru-me *C.* < POM **tan.

POM 308. ****Yhnsan, **hyan** *C*.
PCM 206. ***mba-ña** *C*. < POM ****nkwan-ya.**

No information is available regarding whether these terms had extended ranges of reference.

Unfortunately, Fernández de Miranda and Weitlaner do not provide us with data pertaining to grandkinsman terms in PCM.

The Development of PCM Sibling Terms

Two PCM sibling terms, apparently of very general reference, are provided by Fernández de Miranda and Weitlaner. They both presumably hark back to **POM 159.**

POM 159. ****kuHn** *PC(0)*; ****nsi-kihn, **kihn-si** *yPC(0)*.
PCM 110. ***ma-ngu, *ma-mba** *PC(G)*. < POM ***nku, **nkwen.**

The Development of PCM Spouse Terms

As in other Otomanguean languages, PCM attests terms for husband and wife which are variants of terms meaning *male* and *female,* respectively. In this case, we get the curious situation which was first addressed above in the examination of POM terms for father and mother; namely, that PCM reflects two very similar POM terms for these kinsmen. PCM husband terms and related PCM terms for *male* hark back to **POM 361,** while PCM spouse terms and related PCM terms for *female* hark back to **POM 148.**

POM 361. ****kwin, **kin, **win** *Pm, PPCm(R,G), male.*
PCM 158. ***mbu-hwe, *nu-hwi** *Sm*. < POM ****hwin, **hwi.**
PCM 158. ***hwe, *nu-hwe** *male.* < POM ****hwin.**
POM 148. ****kwin, **kin, **win** *Pf, PPCf(R,G), female.*
PCM 197. ***mba-hwi, *nu-hmi** *Sf*. < POM ****hwi, **hnwi.**
PCM 159. ***na-hwí** *female.* < POM ****hkwi.**

PART TWO

DATA

CHAPTER 8
MIXTECAN KINSHIP TERMS

This chapter reports Mixtec, Trique, and Cuicatec kinship terms as well as an earlier analysis of Proto Mixtec terms.

CHAPTER

MATERIAL PROPERTIES

ATATLAHUCA MIXTEC KINSHIP TERMS
Ruth Mary Alexander

This kinship schedule is closely related to that of Ocotepec Mixtec, and is merely presented in summary fashion below. The rules of extension of in-law terms are not known, nor are those for junior and senior collateral consanguines of ego except that the latter do extend collaterally without limitation.

tátá	*Pm*	*father*
náná	*Pf*	*mother*
sèʔē	*C*	*child*
tátá xěʔnū	*PPm(1,S)*	*grandfather*
náná xěʔnū	*PPf(1,S)*	*grandmother*
sèʔē čání	*CC(1,S)*	*grandchild*
ñānī	*mPCm(G)*	*man's brother*
kūʔù	*fPCf(G)*	*woman's sister*
kwàʔā	*aPCb(G)*	*cross-sex sibling*
stōō	*PPCm(?)*	*uncle*
šīšī	*PPCf(?)*	*aunt*
sāxį̀	*PCCm(?)*	*nephew*
šīkù	*PCCf(?)*	*niece*

čìsō	SP(?)	spouse's consanguine
kàsá	CSm(?)	consanguine's husband
xènū	CSf (?)	consanguine's wife
žᵫ̃	Sm	husband
ñàsᵻ̃ʔᵻ̃	Sf	wife

AYUTLA MIXTEC KINSHIP TERMS
Leo Pankratz

These data were collected by the author in field trips to Tepango, Ayutla, Guerrero, Mexico between 1959-1962 under the auspices of the Summer Institute of Linguistics. The speakers of this dialect reside in the Municipio of Ayutla and number approximately 5000. The main informant used for securing these data was Artemio Alvarez (c. 55 years old).

Ayutla Mixtec terms of reference very nicely complement those of certain other modern systems in that parent and grandparent terms appear which are probably more typical of early Mixtec than the reflexes of the tata/nana variety which occur both in linguistically related and unrelated languages of southern Mexico.

Though **tātā** and **nānā** do occur in Ayutla as alternates for *father* and *mother*, respectively, the main terms for lineal consanguines are apparently those presented below. The terms for lineals of the second generation removed from that of ego extend to more distant generations as well and collaterally without limit; they also extend to corresponding affinals—to both spouses of consanguineals and to consanguineals of spouse.

yùvā?	*Pm*	*father*
sìʔīʔ	*Pf*	*mother*
sīʔè	*C*	*child*

š̃ĩ	*PPm(l,S)*	*grandfather*
šìt̪ạ̀?	*PPf(l,S)*	*grandmother*
sīyànī	*CC(l,S)*	*grandchild*

Ayutla terminology and usage differs from that of other Mixtec groups in two respects. First, there has evidently been a semantic shift in the denotation of the Ayutla sibling terms: **kū?và** *woman's sister* is a cognate of terms in other dialects which mean *cross-sex sibling*, while another term **tạ̃?ạ̃?** (which in San Miguel means *companion*) has taken over this latter denotation.

Second, whereas Mixtec sibling terms are often exceptional among those which extend to include collateral relatives in that they do not also include the spouses of such relatives, in Ayutla the spouses of those referred to by sibling terms are also included under sibling terminology.

ñàni	*mPCm(G,-S)*	*man's brother*
kū?và	*fPCf(G,-S)*	*woman's sister*
tạ̃?ạ̃?	*aPCb(G,-S)*	*cross-sex sibling*

Terms for collaterals of the first ascending and first descending generations extend collaterally without limit and to all corresponding affinals—to both spouses of consanguineals and to consanguineals of spouse.

šìtò	*PPCm(G,S)*	*uncle*
šìšì	*PPCf(G,S)*	*aunt*
sāšị̀	*PCCm(G,S)*	*nephew*
šīkù	*PCCf(G,S)*	*niece*

A feature of Ayutla consanguineal terms which is typical of the language as a whole is that some of the terms occur also in a more abbreviated form, *viz.* **št̪ạ̀?** *grandmother*, **štò** *uncle* and **šĩ** *aunt*.

Step-relatives are referred to by consanguineal terms.

The Affinal Terminology

The classification together of the spouses of ego's siblings with children-in-law and of siblings of ego's spouse with parents-in-law which is so symmetrically displayed in certain other Mixtec systems has evidently been broken down in Ayutla under pressure of Spanish usage. As mentioned above, the spouses of ego's siblings are referred to by consanguineal sibling terms thus limiting the use of 'in-law' terms to lineal affinals, while siblings of ego's spouse are referred to by variations of terms borrowed from Spanish. Terms for spouse are typically Mixtecan, and a single term for 'co-parent-in-law' denotes the parent of a child's spouse.

tìsò	*SP*	*parent-in-law*
kàsā?	*CSm*	*son-in-law*
šànù	*CSf*	*daughter-in-law*
kuñero	*SPCm(G)*	*brother-in-law*

kuñada	SPCf(G)	sister-in-law
vēšī	CSP	co-parent-in-law
ìi	Sm	husband
ñāsì7ī	Sf	wife

Ritual-relationship Terminology

Relations established through the Christian rite of water baptism utilize the parent and child terminology with the postposed element -ñú7ù. The relationship between parents and godparents is referred to by terms from Spanish *compadre* and *comadre*.

yùvāñú7ù	godfather
sì7īñú7ù	godmother
sī7èñú7ù	godchild
kompari	co-godfather
komari	co-godmother

The Vocative Terminology

The vocative terminology comprises a few of the reference terms, a few borrowings from Spanish, and an additional term or two which do not particularly denote relatives. Parents are addressed as **tātā** *father* or **nānā** *mother*. Spanish **papa** and **mama** are also heard. Any child may be addressed as **pé7é** whether related or not. An older sister may use this for a younger sibling. **tàā** for males and **nàā** for females are used between persons of approximately the same age whether related or not. **ñànì** *man's brother* is also extended in vocative usage as an alternate form for **tàā**. Persons of father's age related or not are referred to by reference terms **štò** and **šìī**. Very old people are addressed as **vélō** (Sp. *abuelo*) or **vélā** (Sp. *abuela*) with more respectful usage demanding **tàkwī7è** to an old man and **nàkwī7è** to an old woman. Co-parents also use the term **kwī7è** in greeting and conversing: **kōmpárī kwī7è** and **kōmárī kwī7è**. Personal names are rarely used in greeting unless a specific person is being called. Because of witchcraft certain individuals will not divulge their names under any circumstances.

COATZOSPAN MIXTEC KINSHIP TERMS
Janet Turner
Priscilla Small

These data were obtained in 1969 from Agripina Arellano, age 25, and Perfecta Díaz, age 55, natives of San Juan Coatzospan, Oaxaca, Mexico.

Two parent and one child term classify together all lineal consanguines of ego.

ùbǎ	Pm(L)	father
dìʔì	Pf(L)	mother
íʔšá	C(L)	child

Grandparents may be specified by adding either **àtǎ** *back, old* or **kwìʔì** *sickly* to the parent terms. The latter term implies more respect or endearment than the former. An alternate term **dyòkó** is used for direct descendants, showing less endearment than the child term.

Collateral consanguines are classified into three groups on the basis of seniority—those of ego's own generation, those of ascending generations, and those of descending generations. Sex of these kinsmen is specified by elementary kinship terms only for those of ascending generations except that, in the case of ego's generation, there is a specific term used between males in addition to a generic sibling term.

159

éní	mpPCm(G)	man's brother
tặʔặ	PC(G)	sibling
dító	PPCm(1)	uncle
dídí	PPCf(1)	aunt
ákwécï	PCC(1)	junior collateral

The term for junior collateral kinsman is derived from the nonkinship term **kwècì** *small* and the prefix **à-** *(diminutive)* from **ĩʔsá** *child*. The sex of consanguines of descending generations, both lineal and collateral, is indicated by use of three forms preposed to the child term.

čéʔnù ĩʔšá	fCm(1)	woman's male junior consanguine
nà ĩʔšá	mCm(1)	man's male junior consanguine
táʔnù ĩʔšá	Cf(1)	female junior consanguine

The form **mìì** is added to sibling terms to indicate they have the same parents as ego, while the term **ìkà** *far*, when postposed, indicates cousins as distinct from siblings. **ìkà** is also added to aunt, uncle, and junior collateral terms to indicate more distantly related consanguines such as cousins of parents and children of cousins. Socially proximal aunts and uncles may be referred to alternatively by **nàná** and **tàtá**, respectively.

Words meaning *man* and *woman* are possessed to refer to husbands and wives, respectively.

šñ	Sm	husband
ñàdɨʔɨ	Sf	wife

A single term classifies all consanguineals of spouse who are of spouse's or ascending generations, and two terms distinguish the sex of spouses of consanguineals of ego's or descending generations. Consanguineals of spouse of descending generations and spouses of collateral consanguineals of ascending generations do not figure in the Coatzospan terminological system of kinship reference. The three affinal terms, then, map precisely that semantic area corresponding to Lounsbury's (1965:163) use of the term *relative-in-law*, while *stepkinsmen*, in his sense (ibid.), fall outside the Coatzospan domain of kinship.

ñùndɨ	SP(2)	spouse's consanguine
kàdá	CSm(2)	consanguine's husband
ènú	CSf(2)	consanguine's wife

Finally, the term **nìʔì** is postposed to in-law terms to designate *co-in-laws*. When appended to the term for *spouse's consanguine*, it designates a generation peer of ego who is a senior consanguine of an individual who marries a junior consanguine of ego.

ñùndɨ nìʔì	CSP(G2)	co-senior consanguine-in-law

EXTENSION RULE (G2):
> *A may be applied to the left side of S only once more than B is applied to the left side of S; further, B must be applied to the right side of S as many times as A is*

applied to the left side of S, *and* A *must be applied to the right side of* S *as many times as* B *is applied to the left side of* S.

When appended to the terms for a consanguine's spouse, **nìʔì** designates an individual of the same sex as ego who marries a consanguine of ego's spouse of the same generation as spouse.

kàdá nìʔì	*mSPCSm(G)*	*co-brother-in-law*
ènú nìʔì	*fSPCSf(G)*	*co-sister-in-law*

DIUXI MIXTEC KINSHIP TERMS

Joy Oram

The following data were obtained from Román Pablo Reyes, of San Juan Diuxi, Nochixtlán, Oaxaca, México.

Terms for mother, father, and child extend lineally to include all direct consanguines.

'tá	*Pm(L)*	*father*
dí'ʔí	*Pf(L)*	*mother*
dá'ʔyá	*C(L)*	*child*

Siblings are best treated as collaterals in that the three sibling terms encompass all collaterals of ego's generation, while collaterals of other generations than ego's are referred to by terms that distinguish them from lineal kinsmen.

'ñànì	*mPCm(G)*	*man's brother*
kú'ʔú	*fPCf(G)*	*woman's sister*
kú'ʔá	*aPCb(G)*	*cross-sex sibling*

Four terms accomplish this latter end, marking the collateral kinsman as being either male or female, and as being either older or younger than ego. The fact that relative age is a factor in classifying collateral kinsmen not of ego's generation while relative age seems not to be a factor in classifying kinsmen of his generation is curious enough to merit further investigation. Being a peer, in the sense of generation, must have more importance for ego than relative age. The latter criterion comes into play when classifying those outside the generation-peer group. (The affinial extension of these terms is discussed below.)

'dìtò	*ePPCm(I,1,-S)*	*uncle*
'dìdí	*ePPCf(I,1,-S)*	*aunt*
dà'ší	*yPCCm(I,1,S-)*	*nephew*
dí'kú	*yPCCf(I,1,S-)*	*niece*

This conflict is resolved partially for cousins. That is, it is possible to indicate that a cousin is older or younger than ego by joining the sibling term with an aunt/uncle, niece/nephew term. Although the same mechanism would theoretically work as well for older and younger full siblings, it is reserved only for cousins.

kú'ʔá dà'ší	*yfPPCCm(G)*	*woman's younger male cousin*
'dìdí kú'ʔú	*efPPCCf(G)*	*woman's elder female cousin*
dí'kú kú'ʔú	*yfPPCCf(G)*	*woman's younger female cousin*

The form **šą́'tnú** *great* is added to terms for senior kinsman to indicate second ascending generation lineals and very old collaterals: **'tà šą́'tnų́** (*PPm, PPPm, PPPPm, PPPPCm,* etc.), **'dì šą́'tnų́** (*PPf, PPPf, PPPPf, PPPPCf,* etc.), **'dìtó šą́'tnų́** (very old: *PPCm, PPPCm, PPPCCm,* etc.), and similarly for **'dìdí šą́'tnų́.** The term **dá'ʔyá 'ñànì** specifies lineals beyond the first descending generation.

The terms *primu* and *prima* can be added to sibling terms to distinguish cousins from true siblings.

There are only three basic affinal terms, two which distinguish the sex of a consanguineal's spouse, and one for consanguineals of spouse. The full extension of these terms is not known at the time of writing. While it is clear that they extend to all *relatives-in-law*, in the Lounsbury (1965:163) sense, it has not been verified that they do not also include *steprelatives (ibid.)*. On the other hand, although it is known that terms for collateral kinsman of other than ego's generation may extend to *steprelatives,* there is some evidence of overlap with affinal term usage that needs to be clarified by further investigation. This presentation of the definition of the terms does not show any such overlap.

dì'dó	*SP(2)*	*spouse's consanguine*
kà'dá	*CSm(2)*	*consanguine's husband*
šà'nú	*CSf(2)*	*consanguine's wife*

Parent terms are modified by the generic term for spouse's consanguine to specify the parents of spouse.

'tàdídó	*SPm*	*father-in-law*
'dìdídó	*SPf*	*mother-in-law*

Two spouse terms complete the inventory of kinship terms.

| 'ží̱i̱ | Sm | husband |
| 'ñàdí̱ʔi̱ | Sf | wife |

METLATONOC MIXTEC KINSHIP TERMS
†Wm. Edward Overholt

All consanguineals of ego's generation are denoted by three terms which specify male kinsman of a male, female kinsman of a female, or opposite sex kinsman.

yānī	mPCm(G)	man's brother
kū?vī	fPCf(G)	woman's sister
kū?vā	aPCb(G)	cross-sex sibling

The form **kwàčī** *small* is postposed to sibling terms to specify cousins. Relative age within ego's generation is indicated by adding **čéè** *older, greater* or **lõ?õ** *younger, little*.

yānī čéè	emPCm	man's older brother

The term **ndīšá?nū** is postposed to sibling terms to specify an older sibling who, in certain respects, takes the place of a deceased parent. For example, **yānī ndīšá?nū** refers to an older brother of a male who has taken some or all of the responsibilities and authority of the deceased father. If the mother is living, her authority supercedes that of the son acting in the father's stead. If both parents are deceased and the children are in the care of the older sibling, he or she bears full authority and responsibility. The term **ndīšáʔnū** is further discussed below in connection with its use for certain affinals.

Tata/nana terms are used in direct address with parents, but are also used in reference as alternants of what we might term the *regular* parent terms of reference. These latter combine to form **yūvásîʔī** which specifies *parents* or *governmental officials* of ego's native town, county, district, state, or nation.

yūvá	*Pm*	*father*
sîʔī	*Pf*	*mother*

The grandparent terms class together all lineal and collateral consanguines beyond ego's first ascending generation and may also be applied to such kinsmen of spouse.

šīī	*PPm(1,S-)*	*grandfather*
šītà	*PPf(1,S-)*	*grandmother*

The third ascending generation may be specified by the postposed term **šíkwā** *great* and the fourth by adding after **šíkwā** the form **kwîī** *great, long time*. These terms also designate third and fourth descending generations when joined with the child term.

sēʔē šíkwā	*CCC(G)*	*great-grandchild*
sēʔē šíkwā kwîī	*CCCC(G)*	*great-great-grandchild*

The grandfather term with postposed **ñų̄ʔų̀** *fire* is the name of a spirit still honored among the Mixtecs. *Grandfather Fire* is fed by putting pieces of tortilla or corn gruel into the fire. In return, he cooks their food, guards the members of the household, and reports to one or another marriage partner any infidelity on the part of the other partner.

The unmodified child term is used to refer to any consanguine of ego of descending generations, whether lineal or collateral. Sex may be distinguished for any kinsman referred to by this term by postposing either **rālōʔō** *he-little* or **ñálōʔō** *she-little*.

sēʔē	*C(1)*	*child*

The form **yání** is a tone pair with the form used between male siblings. When modifying the child term, it designates consanguines of the second descending generation. It is also used alone as a vocative term of endearment by spouses, to one another and to their children.

sēʔē yání	*CC(1)*	*grandchild*

Collateral kinsmen of first ascending and descending generations are classified by four terms which distinguish them by their sex and seniority.

šītò	*PPCm(G)*	*uncle*
šīšī	*PPCf(G)*	*aunt*
sāšį̄	*PCCm(G)*	*nephew*
šīkū	*PCCf(G)*	*niece*

Affines

[Editor's note: Ed Overholt is now deceased, the eventual result of a broken leg sustained while travelling in the Mixtec area away from immediate medical attention. In the process of reworking his materials for presentation here, I find that I cannot tell how step kinsmen are classified. I have, therefore, had to tentatively treat them as outside the system.]

The wife is referred to as **ñásíʔi**, the husband as **ȋi**. A second wife is referred to as **ñásíʔi ùvì** *wife two*, whether the union is polygynous or not. The second wife of a polygynous union may be referred to by an outsider as **tǎčìndīvàʔā** *evil wind*. The term **tānī** refers to a paramour.

A single generic term classifies together all spouse's consanguines of spouse's own and ascending generations, while descriptive phrases are required to specify more specific relationships to spouse.

sīsó	*SP(2)*	*spouse's consanguine*
kūʔvā ñásíʔi-yū	*mSPCm(G)*	*my wife's brother*
yānī ȋi-yū	*ʃSPCm(G)*	*my husband's brother*

As mentioned above, grandparent terms extend to include all consanguineal kinsmen of spouse of beyond the first ascending generation. Although such kinsmen may be referred to as in-laws, the consanguineal terms seem to be preferred. [Whether this is reciprocally true for the grandchild term and spouse's of consanguines of beyond the first descending generation is not clear.]

Two terms distinguish the sex of spouses of consanguine's of ego's own or descending generations.

kāsā	*CSm(2)*	*consanguine's husband*
šānù	*CSʃ(2)*	*consanguine's wife*

The term **šíʔȋ** *(accompaniment)* is appended to the above terms to designate same-sex co-siblings-in-law.

kāsā šíʔȋ	*mSPCSm(G)*	*co-brother-in-law*
šānù šíʔȋ	*ʃSPCSʃ(G)*	*co-sister-in-law*

There is a generic term which may be used alone to designate the parent of any person referred to as consanguine's spouse, and which serves as a modifier to three other terms, at least two of which are from Spanish *compadre* and *comadre*, to specify a parent of one's own child's spouse.

ndīšáʔnū	*CSP(2)*	*co-in-law*
mbáá ndīšáʔnū	*CSP*	*co-parent-in-law*
cōmpárī ndīšáʔnū	*CSPm*	*co-father-in-law*
cōmárī ndīšáʔnū	*CSPʃ*	*co-mother-in-law*

Vocative Usage

As previously mentioned, certain of the terms of reference are also vocative terms. Thus, in ego's generation the terms referring to siblings are also the vocative terms. These may be modified by the terms čéè *older, great* or lõʔõ *little, younger*. One case has been observed of a man one year older than his paternal uncle who refers to the uncle as šĩtõ *uncle* but addresses him as yānĩ *man's brother*.

Persons who may be addressed as yānĩ čéè or kũʔvā čéè *older brother* are often (particularly after their marriage) addressed as tã lõʔõ *little father*. One man has been observed to refer to the tenth younger brother of his maternal grandfather who is three years his senior as šĩ but to address him as tã lõʔõ.

The vocative term tõʔó *dear* is used to address a husband or male child. čĩʔí or sĩʔí *dear* is used to address a husband or female child. tõʔó is extended in reference and direct address to members of the community who are particularly respected.

The vocative terms for the first ascending generation are tātā *father* and nānā *mother*. The term tātā and sometimes tã lõʔõ is extended to include all male relatives of the parent's generation. It is further extended to include all males of the parent's generation or older who are not relatives. In its broadest extension it means *sir*, and is sometimes used interchangeably with the Spanish *Señor*. It is also used in addressing the saints and God.

The terms tātā and nānā in extended usage referring to nonfamily persons are modified by the postposed term čéè *great* when a person older than ego's generation is addressed.

The vocative terms for second (and succeeding) ascending generations are those of the first generation plus the term pēʔé *dear*. This term is used by itself for second and succeeding generations. The terms tātā péʔē and nānā péʔē are extended to include respected members of the community outside the family group.

Spouses of consanguineals are addressed as kāsā or šānù, while consanguineals of spouse are addressed as one's own consanguineals.

OCOTEPEC MIXTEC KINSHIP TERMS

Ruth Mary Alexander

Approximately 200,000 Mixtecs live in the states of Oaxaca, Guerrero, and Puebla in southern Mexico. Between two and three thousand live in Santo Tomás Ocotepec, where these data were gathered in 1961. The informant from whom the data were obtained was Ireneo Avendaño, age 31. All terms occur with first person pronominal enclitics -sá (polite) and -nì (familiar).

Three terms denote parents or child in reference.

žūbá	Pm	father
sĩʔí	Pf	mother
sèʔē	C	child

The sex of a child may be specified by adding žií male or sĩʔí female to the child term. A grandkinsman is specified by the use of the modifier ñáʔnú old, appended to a parent or child term, though in the case of grandparents, the basic parent terms used are tātá and nāná, which also occur alone as alternate terms for parents. Grandkin terms extend both lineally and collaterally without limit, and to corresponding affinals as well—to both consanguineal's of spouse and to spouses of consanguineals.

171

tātá ñá?nú	PPm(1,S)	grandfather
nāná ñá?nú	PPf(1,S)	grandmother
sè?ē ñá?nú	CC(1,S)	grandchild

The term **súkwá** (Cf. **súkwà** *eyebrow*) is postposed to grandparent terms to specify great-grandparents, and to either the child or the grandchild term to specify great-grandchildren.

Three sibling terms classify siblings according to their sex and that of ego. They also extend collaterally to all cousins of ego's generations, the relationship being further defined as not that of true sibling when the need arises by the addition **prímò** *male cousin* or **prímà** *female cousin*, from Spanish. These latter terms may be used alone without the sibling terms, with the same meanings.

ñānì	mPCm(G)	man's brother
kù?ù	fPCf(G)	woman's sister
kwà?ā	aPCb(G)	cross-sex sibling

There are four terms for collateral consanguines not of ego's generation, distinguishing the sex of both junior and senior kinsmen. In addition to kinsmen of the first generation removed from that of ego, they extend to more remote generations as well, thus providing an alternative to grandkinsman terms for such relatives to make their collaterality explicit. The four terms also include spouses of senior collaterals and junior collaterals of spouse; that is, *stepkinsmen* in the Lounsbury (1965:163) sense.

šītò	PPCm(1,-S)	uncle
šīšì	PPCf(1,-S)	aunt
sà̰xḭ̀	PCCm(1,S-)	nephew
šìkù	PCCf(1,S-)	niece

The **tātá** and **nāná** terms followed by **véló**, from Spanish **abuelo**, may also be used for senior collaterals of two or more generations' distance. These **tātá** and **nāná** terms may also be used vocatively in respect to parents, and with following modifier **súčí** *young* are used vocatively of collaterals of any senior generation.

Three terms classify all in-laws, in the Lounsbury (1965:163) sense. A single term classes all consanguineal's of spouse, and two terms distinguish only the sex of spouses of consanguineals. Because of the extension of grandkinsman terms to all affinals, in-laws of two or more generations' distance may be referred to by either set of terms.

čìsō	SP(2)	spouse's non-junior consanguine
kàsá	CSm(2)	non-senior consanguine's husband
xànū	CSf(2)	non-senior consanguine's wife

Parent and child terms join with in-law terms to specify a parent-in-law or child-in-law.

tātá čìsō	SPm	father-in-law
nāná čìsō	SPf	mother-in-law
sè?ē kàsá	CSm	son-in-law
sè?ē xànú	CSf	daughter-in-law

A man refers to a fellow brother-in-law (a man who marries a sister of ego's wife) and a woman to a fellow sister-in-law (a woman who marries a brother of ego's husband) by preposing the morpheme **tā** to terms for *nonsenior consanguine's husband* and *nonsenior consanguine's wife*, respectively.

tākàsá	*mSPCSm(G)*	co-brother-in-law
tāxànú	*fSPCSf(G)*	co-sister-in-law

The term for *spouse's nonjunior consanguine* is extended to a co-sibling-in-law of the opposite sex, namely *aSPCSb(G)*.

Co-parents, the relationship between the parents of a man and the parents of his wife, refer to each other by partially assimilated forms of the Spanish terms **compadre** and **comadre**.

mpáà	*CSPm*	co-father
márì	*CSPf*	co-mother

There are two spouse terms, based on words meaning *male* and *female*.

žíí	*Sm*	husband
ñasî?í	*Sf*	wife

Ritual relationships are established by water baptism. The terminology used to specify these relationships is formed by the use of consanguineal terminology followed by **ntúté** derived from **ntūtē** *water*.

tātá ntúté	*godfather*
nāná ntúté	*godmother*
sè?ē ntūté	*godchild*

A godparent and a parent refer to each other by co-parent terms.

General terms for all consanguines are **tá?á** *relative* and **tātà bē?ē-sá** *descendants of my house*. The term **kē̯ē̯** is added to parent, child, and sibling terms to indicate a step relationship. Half siblings may also use this term.

PEÑOLES MIXTEC KINSHIP TERMS
John P. Daly

Six lineal terms distinguish two ascending and two descending generations, with sex of alter marked in ascending generations only, all but the *child* term extending to lineal affinals as well.

tǎtá	*Pm(S-)*	*father*
nǎná	*Pf(S-)*	*mother*
dé?e	*C*	*child*
šíí	*PPm(S-)*	*grandfather*
šitą́	*PPf(S-)*	*grandmother*
dé?e ñani	*CC(-S)*	*grandchild*

Parents-in-law are distinguished from parents by postposing forms borrowed from Spanish—**suěgrú** to the father term and **suěgrá** to the mother term.

The sex of a child may be specified by modifying the basic child term. Postposed **tée** *man* or **dúkų́** (phonologically identical to **dúkų́** *tall*) indicate a male child. Postposed **dɨ?ɨ́** *female* or **žoko** (phonologically identical to **žoko** *corn tassel*) indicate a daughter. The grandchild term is a compound of a child term followed by what is at least a tone pair with the man's term for brother if not a special form of that term found in this context

175

only. The sex of a grandchild may be specified by an appositional phrase such as **dé?e ñani dé?e dì?í**, literally *grandchild child female*.

Three sibling terms merge all collaterals of ego's generation, distinguishing brothers of males, sisters of females, and siblings of the sex opposite that of ego.

ñaní	*mPCm(G)*	*man's brother*
kú?ú	*fPCf(G)*	*woman's sister*
kú?a	*aPCb(G)*	*cross-sex sibling*

Cousins may be distinguished from siblings by postposing forms borrowed from Spanish to the sibling terms, **prïmá** for female cousins and **prïmú** for male cousins.

No distinction is made between full and halfsiblings, but stepsiblings, stepfathers, stepmothers, and stepchildren are specified by postposing **čà?á** to the appropriate consanguineal terms.

Remaining collateral kinsmen are classified by four terms which denote sex of alter and distinguish ascending generations from descending without further specifying generation levels. These terms, unlike sibling terms, extend to all corresponding affinals—to both spouse of collateral kinsman and to collateral kinsman of spouse.

dïtó	*PPCm(1,S)*	*uncle*
dïdí	*PPCf(1,S)*	*aunt*
dášį́	*PCCm(1,S)*	*nephew*
díkú	*PCCf(1,S)*	*niece*

Spanish bilingualism has influenced the system of reference for in-laws. As indicated above, senior kinsmen of spouse (and for that matter, junior kinsmen as well), are generally referred to by consanguineal terms. Similarly, there are four terms for generation peers of spouse, two of which are from Spanish.

Since a Mixtec man typically learns more Spanish than a Mixtec woman, it is not surprising to see that it is he who uses the Spanish terms while she uses a Mixtec term for male in-law and a Mixtec phrase which has had to be granted status as a kinship term to fill out the system as modified by the differential influence from Spanish.

kùñádú	*mSPCm(G)*	*wife's brother*
kùñádá	*mSPCf(G)*	*wife's sister*
šído	*fSPCm(G)*	*husband's brother*
kú?a žíí	*fSPCf(G)*	*husband's sister*

For in-laws who have married a consanguineal kinsman of ego, two Mixtec terms distinguish the sex of in-laws but merge spouses of children with spouses of siblings.

kada	*CSm(G2)*	*male junior in-law*
sánu	*CSf(G2)*	*female junior in-law*

Differential ability in Spanish also applies in respect to junior in-laws, in that male ego optionally may (and does so especially if he is bilingual) specify a sibling's spouse by a form of the corresponding Spanish term which he uses for spouse's sibling. For such an individual, definitions are revised as follows:

kùñádú	mSPCm(V,G)	brother-in-law
kùñádá	mSPCf(V,G)	sister-in-law
kada	mCSm	son-in-law
sánu	mCSf	daughter-in-law

The term for husband is **žì** *male* and the term for wife is the morpheme **ña** *mature* plus **dì?í** *female*. Another term for wife is **famìlíá** from Spanish *familia*. The term **tḁsa?nu** specifies the relationship between the parents of children married to each other, and is composed of two morphemes **tḁ**, apparently from **tà?ḁ** *together* and **sa?nu** *old*.

Men married to sisters refer to one another as **kònkúñú** *co-brother-in-law* from Spanish *concuño*. Women married to brothers specify their relationship by the term **kú?ú sǎnu** which is composed of two morphemes **kú?ú** *sister* and **sánu** *female in-law*.

There is no term of reference for the relationship of male and female married to sister and brother. Male ego would describe his relationship to such a woman as **ñadì?í kú?a ñadì?íí**, literally *wife-brother-wife-my*. Female ego would describe her relationship to such a man as **žì kú?a žíí**, literally *husband-sister-husband-my*.

The use of **kada** and **sánu** to denote both child-in-law and sibling-in-law probably arises from father and son sharing the work in the fields with their son-in-law and brother-in-law, respectively, who lives and works with his in-laws for the first year or two of his married life. Likewise, the mother and daughter share the work of the house with their daughter-in-law and sister-in-law when she lives with her husband in her in-laws' house for a few years or for the lifetime of his parents. On occasions, this custom would bring together women married to brothers, which would account for the two outsiders referring to each other as **kú?ú sǎnu**.

By the sponsoring of a child for Roman Catholic baptism, a number of ritual relationships are established. The term **mbǎá** (Spanish *compadre*) refers to the relationship between the father and godfather of the child. The term **mbàlí** (Spanish *comadre*) refers to the relationship between the mother and godmother, and also each one's relationship to the other's husband. The father and godfather each refer to the other's wife as **kùmáří** (Spanish *comadre*).

Parent, child, and sibling terms occur with **mání** to designate ritual relationships. (The parent terms are shortened in this context.)

támǎní	godfather
námǎní	godmother
dé?e mání	godchild
ñaní mání	man's godbrother
kú?ú mání	woman's godsister
kú?a mání	cross-sex godsibling

SILACAYOAPAN MIXTEC KINSHIP TERMS

Joanne North
Jäna Shields

These data were obtained from Fidencio Ramírez Alvarado, 31-year-old native of San Jerónimo Progreso, Silacayoapan, Oaxaca, México. The terms are presented with inflection for first person singular possession, usually in the form of a suffix -ì. Certain morphophonemic changes accompany the suffixation of this personal pronoun. They are: (1) Stem-final **a** is suppressed in the terms for parents, sibling of the opposite sex, son-in-law, and sister-in-law. (2) Stem-final **o** is neutralized to **u** in the terms for uncle, brother-in-law, and co-sibling-in-law. (3) The suffix itself undergoes reduction in the terms for child, niece, grandparents, man's brother, woman's sister, and aunt, though the tone remains.

Lineal kinsmen are distinguished from collateral in all generations, for both consanguineals and affinals. Two parent terms and a child term designate lineal consanguineals one generation removed from that of ego, while additional modifiers designate lineals of two generations' distance.

tátì, tátáì	*Pm*	*father*
nánì, nánáì	*Pf*	*mother*
xà?ži	*C*	*child*
táčé?ê	*PPm(L)*	*grandfather*

| náčéʔê | PPf(L) | grandmother |
| xàʔžĩ ñánî | CC(L) | grandchild |

Alternate grandparent terms use the adjective **sáʔnū** *old*, and **xíkó** is postposed to grandkin terms to designate lineals of three generations' distance. (Note that the u versus o distinction is neutralized stem finally before the ending -ì and that either sequence may be pronounced [oi] or [ui].

| tásáʔnūì | PPm(L) | grandfather |
| náčéʔé xíkóì | PPPf | great-grandmother |

For lineal affinals, sex is not regularly distinguished for parent of spouse, but is for spouse of a child.

šòxòì	SP	parent-in-law
kàxî, kàxáì	CSm	son-in-law
sànùì	CSf	daughter-in-law

The above terms, combine with grandkin terms to designate grandparents of spouse and spouse of grandchildren.

táčéʔé šòxòì	SPPm	grandfather-in-law
tásáʔnū šòxòì	SPPm	grandfather-in-law
náčéʔé šòxòì	SPPf	grandmother-in-law
násáʔnū šòxòì	SPPf	grandmother-in-law
kàxá ñánî	CCSm	grandson-in-law
sànù ñánî	CCSf	granddaughter-in-law

Possessed forms of words meaning *man* and *woman*, respectively, are used to designate spouses.

| žî | Sm | husband |
| ñāxíʔî | Sf | wife |

Three terms designate ego's siblings, marking both sex of ego and of alter in a Jivaran pattern (Murdock 1970:175), and also all more distantly related collaterals of ego's generation when modified by **kwàčí**.

ñánî	mPCm	man's brother
kĩʔvî	fPCf	woman's sister
kyàʔvì, kyàʔvàì	aPCb	cross-sex sibling
ñánī kwàčí	mPPCCm(G)	man's male cousin
kĩʔvì kwàčí	fPPCCf(G)	woman's female cousin
kyàʔvà kwàčî	aPPCCb(G)	cross-sex cousin

The spouses of siblings (but not of cousins) and siblings (but not cousins) of spouse are classified by terms based on Spanish *cuñado* and *cuñada*.

| **kũñádóì** | *SPCm(V)* | *brother-in-law* |
| **kúñádì, kùñádáì** | *SPCf(V)* | *sister-in-law* |

Four terms, most if not all from Spanish, designate the relationship between co-parents-in-law and co-siblings-in-law.

mbáì	*mCSPm*	*man's co-father-in-law*
mbálî	*fCSPm*	*woman's co-father-in-law*
málî	*CSPf*	*co-mother-in-law*
kũkúñóì	*SPCS*	*co-sibling-in-law*

Collaterals not of ego's generation are classified by four terms which distinguish sex of kinsman and ascending versus descending generation. All four terms extend collaterally and to more distant generations without limit, and in the case of kinsmen of senior generations, also to corresponding affinals—to senior consanguine's spouse and to spouse's senior consanguine. This courtesy is not extended reciprocally to younger collateral affines who must be referred to by circumlocutions that designate them as junior kinsman of spouse or spouse of a junior kinsman, as in **kàxá ñànì** *son-in-law of my brother* (for husband of a niece). The system is thus somewhat top-heavy in the sense that it extends farther in ascending generations than in descending ones.

xìtòì	*PPCm(1,S)*	*uncle*
xìxì	*PPCf(1,S)*	*uncle*
xàšì	*PCCm(1)*	*nephew*
xũkũ	*PCCf(1)*	*niece*

The above assymetry may be considered a function of the importance given in Silacayoapan society to seniority. This is reflected elsewhere in the system by optional adjustments which can be made on the basis of relative age. It is the case, for example, that a cousin as few as 10 or 12 years older than ego may be referred to as *uncle* or *aunt* to indicate respect and a closer social relationship between kinsmen than genealogy alone would dictate. This is an optional rule for the *uncle* and *aunt* terms which may be characterized as follows:

EXTENSION RULE 2A:
   In the case of a kinsman 10 or more years ego's senior: B may apply once more than A.

The older kinsman in this dyad does not, however, demote his younger kinsman to a more remote relationship than is genealogically his due; that is, he does not use the expected reciprocal nephew or niece terms unless it is genealogically appropriate. An older cousin may be referred to as *aunt* or *uncle,* but uses the appropriate cousin term for his younger alter ego.
   A second case of optional skewing of the system relates to the sibling terms. Ego may extend a sibling term to a collateral kinsman of a junior generation who is, in terms of age, his senior or his peer. In this case the usage is reciprocal and the junior kinsman (by genealogical reckoning) would also use a sibling term. This may be characterized as follows:

EXTENSION RULE 2B:

    In the case of a nephew or niece who is older than ego, B may apply once more
than A; and in the case of an aunt or uncle who is younger than ego, A may apply
once more than B.

SAN MIGUEL MIXTEC KINSHIP TERMS

William R. Merrifield

This presentation is based on data collected in Mexico City in February, 1962, during a brief interview with Miss Cirila Pérez (age 25). My SIL colleagues Helen Ashdown and Betty Stoudt later corrected my transcription of the tone and checked the manuscript for errors. All terms cited are terms of reference and occur with the first person singular possessive form **-ná** *my*.

The San Miguel system of consanguineal kinship reference encompasses at least five generations, with lineal and collateral consanguines merged in even-numbered generations (0, +2, -2) but distinguished in odd-numbered generations (+1, -1).

The parent terms designate father and mother, respectively, and are not extended to other more distantly related kinsmen.

táã	*Pm*	*father*
náã	*Pf*	*mother*

A single term is the reciprocal of these parent terms to designate ego's child, to which modifiers **ǯìì** *male* and **síʔí** *female* may be added to distinguish sons from daughter.

sè?ē	C	*child*
sè?ē žíí	Cm	*son*
sè?ē sî?í	Cf	*daughter*

Relations established by a second marriage are designated by postposing ?ūù to a parent or child term.

táā ?ūù	PSm	*step-father*
náā ?ūù	PSf	*step-mother*
sè?ē ?ūù	SC	*step-child*

These parent and child terms form the basis for grandparent and grandchild terms by the use of modifiers, but the latter differ from the former in extending beyond primary consanguines to all collateral consanguines of the second ascending and second descending generations, respectively, as well as to those affines of these generations who are *step kinsmen* in the Lounsbury (1965:163) sense; namely, to the spouse of any consanguine referred to by a grandparent term, and to any consanguine of spouse to whom he (or she) refers by the grandchild term.

(Study of other Mixtecan systems since 1962 has caused me to suspect that these terms for grandkinsmen probably also extend to kinsmen of more than two generations' distance from that of ego. Although neither my memory nor my field notes provide sure confirmation of this, I here indicate extension of these terms by Rule 1, with the understanding that Rule G may in fact be correct.)

tātá ñúù	PPm(1,-S)	*grandfather*
nāná ñúù	PPf(1,-S)	*grandmother*
sè?ē tíhání	CC(1,S-)	*grandchild*

Collateral consanguines of the first ascending and first descending generations are designated by four terms which denote generation and sex of kinsman. Like grandkin terms, they extend to all degrees of collaterality and to corresponding step kinsmen.

stóō	PPCm(G,-S)	*uncle*
šíī	PPCf(G,-S)	*aunt*
sāhį̀	PCCm(G,S-)	*nephew*
šíkù	PCCf(G,S-)	*niece*

All consanguines of ego's own generation are classified as siblings by three terms of Jivaran pattern (Murdock 1970:175) as man's brother, woman's sister, and opposite sex sibling.

ñānì	mPCm(G)	*man's brother*
kūʔà	fPCf(G)	*woman's sister*
kwàʔá	aPCb(G)	*cross-sex sibling*

Half siblings are terminologically considered as full siblings, while children of a step-parent are not considered to be kinsmen.

The two terms for *husband* and *wife* are possessed forms of words meaning *male* and *female*, respectively.

| žīī | Sm | husband |
| ñàsí?ɨ | Sf | wife |

The phrase ñą̄?ą̄ úù, literally *woman two*, designates the second wife in a polygynous union.
There are three elementary terms for relatives-in-law (Lounsbury 1965:163). A single term designates any consanguine of spouse of his or her own generation.

| čìsó | SPC(G) | spouse's sibling |

Two terms distinguishing the sex of alter are reciprocal to čìsó, designating the spouse of any consanguine of ego of his or her own generation.

| kāsá | PCSm(G) | sibling's husband |
| hànū | PCSf(G) | sibling's wife |

These three terms for relatives-in-law also occur as modifiers of parent or child terms to designate the parents of a spouse or the spouse of a child, respectively.

táā čìsó	SPm	spouse's father
náā čìsó	SPf	spouse's mother
sè?ē kàsá	CSm	daughter's husband
sè?ē hànū	CSf	son's wife

As defined, the seven forms above map only a portion of the kinship space corresponding to the category *relative-in-law* in the sense used here. Unfortunately, because of the brevity of the interview in which the kinship data were gathered and of my own lack of experience at the time, a few questions remain unanswered. In particular, it is not clear which terms are used to refer to (a) spouse's ascending-generation collateral kinsmen, (b) descending-generation collateral kinsmen's spouses, (c) grandchildren's spouses, and (d) spouse's grandparents.

Comparison with certain other Mixtecan systems would lead me to expect further investigation to show that the three elementary in-law terms extend over all of these uninvestigated areas and that the last four modified forms are merely ways to be specific regarding a spouse's parent or a child's offspring. Without further data, the status of this guess remains in doubt; but, for the record, the definition of the elementary terms would then be as follows:

čìsó	SP(2)	spouse's nonjunior consanguine
kāsá	CSm(2)	nonsenior consanguine's husband
hànū	CSf(2)	nonsenior consanguine's wife

A preposed element **ta-** is added to the terms for sibling's spouse to designate a co-sibling-in-law.

| **tákásá** | *SPCSm(G)* | *co-brother-in-law* |
| **táhánú** | *SPCSf(G)* | *co-sister-in-law* |

Two co-parent terms refer to the parents-in-law of ego's child.

| **mbáà** | *CSPm* | *co-father-in-law* |
| **kwàlyá** | *CSPf* | *co-mother-in-law* |

Relationships established through the Christian rite of water baptism utilize modified forms of parent and child terms.

táà līnú	*godfather*
náà līná	*godmother*
sè?ē ndúčá	*godchild*

The terms **līnú** and **līná** are undoubtedly from Spanish *padrino* and *padrina*, respectively. **ndúčá** is the San Miguel word for *water*. The reference terms used between the parents of the child baptized and its godparents are the same as those used between co-parents-in-law.

SOUTH PUEBLA MIXTEC
KINSHIP TERMS
Kent Wistrand

Influences of change from Spanish have affected the system of kinship reference among the South Puebla Mixtec with the result that terminology and usage shift from village to village and between generations. These data reflect the usage of Renato Sosa Mejía, age 33, a native of Gabino Barreda, *municipio* of San Gerónimo Xayacatlán, Acatlán, Puebla (hereafter **GB**).

A main feature of the system is a clear distinction between lineal and nonlineal kinsmen, both consanguineals and affinals, and five distinct generations centered in that of ego.

There are two parent terms, a child term, a grandchild term based on the child term, a grandmother term, and (unexpectedly) a single term for grandparents that has no cognate in other Mixtec systems.

žūā	Pm	*father*
dīʔī	Pf	*mother*
dèʔē	C	*child*
nītá	PPf	*grandmother*
lántè	PP	*grandparent*
dèʔē ñānī	CC	*grandchild*

līkwā, a diminutive form of dīkwà *eyebrow*, may be added to a grandparent or grand-child term in Xayacatlán de Bravo, Acatlán, Puebla (hereafter **XB**) to designate third generation lineals. Sex of offspring or a step-relationship may be indicated by postpositionals.

dè?ē ?ī	*Cm*	*son*
dè?ē žōkō	*Cf*	*daughter*
dī?ī kį̄į̄	*PSf*	*stepmother*

The expected three terms for siblings occur but because of the extension of other terms for collaterals, they seem to be best treated as terms for co-lineals rather than for collaterals.

ñānī	*mPCm*	*man's brother*
kù?ì	*fPCf*	*woman's sister*
kù?ā	*aPCb*	*cross-sex sibling*

For affinal lineals, sex is distinguished for junior kinsmen rather than for seniors, with kinsmen of two generations' distance being referred to by compounds including consanguineal elements.

dìdō	*SP*	*parent-in-law*
kādà	*CSm*	*son-in-law*
sànū	*CSf*	*daughter-in-law*
lántè sà?nų́	*SPP*	*grandparent-in-law*
kādà ñànì	*CCSm*	*grandson-in-law*
sànū ñānī	*CCSf*	*granddaughter-in-law*

There are four terms of Mixtecan origin for collaterals of the first ascending and first descending generations. They extend to all degrees of collaterality and to all corresponding affinals—to both spouse of collaterals and to collaterals of spouse.

dītō	*PPCm(G,S)*	*uncle*
dīdī	*PPCf(G,S)*	*aunt*
dášì	*PCCm(G,S)*	*nephew*
dīkū	*PCCf(G,S)*	*niece*

Though these native Mixtec terms for collateral kinsmen do exist, they have been replaced almost completely in everyday usage by terms of Spanish origin: tìù and tìà for the first ascending generation, sōbrīnú and sōbrīná for first descending generation.

There are, in addition, four terms for collaterals of ego's own generation and of the second ascending generation, three of which are of Spanish origin. These all extend collaterally and to affinals, and it is this extension that gives rise to the statement above that the sibling terms are in this sense best treated as other than terms for collaterals.

prīmú	*PPCCm(G,S)*	*male cousin*
prīmá	*PPCCf(G,S)*	*female cousin*

| bēlú | PPPCm(G,S) | great-uncle |
| nītá | PPPCf(G,S) | great-aunt |

Spanish terms name co-lineal affinals.

| kūñãdú | SPCm(V) | brother-in-law |
| kūñãdá | SPCf(V) | sister-in-law |

The 33-year-old informant from **GB** was not able to give a term for collateral consanguines of the second descending generation.

The first word of the phrase that designates *co-parent* literally means *head*, and the phrase as a whole is used in a wider context within the community to mean *boss*. The co-sibling-in-law terms are from **XB**; the informant from **GB** did not know them.

dìnì sà?n**ų**	CSP	co-parent
sànū šū?ã	SPCSm	co-brother-in-law
kādà šū?ã	SPCSf	co-sister-in-law

There are two terms for spouse.

| ?ìi | Sm | husband |
| ñã?à dì?í | Sf | wife |

A variety of terms for lineal grandparents and collaterals of their generation suggest that the lineal/collateral contrast is recent. The **GB** grandparent term is a term of affection in **XB** where the main terms are **bēlú** and **bēlá**, from Spanish *abuelo* and *abuela*. As indicated above, **bēlú** is the **GB** term for male collateral consanguines of the second ascending generation.

The use of **bēlú** for a collateral kinsman, where the Spanish counterpart *abuelo* is normally considered to denote lineal kinsman, would seem to be evidence for an earlier Mixtec system in which lineal grandparents and their collateral generation peers were merged, a suggestion that receives support from some other Mixtec systems (e.g., Ayutla). Counter to this, however, is the practice in **XB**, where collaterals of the second ascending generation are referred to by aunt and uncle terms modified by **sã?nų** *big*, as in **dītō sà?nų** and **dīdī sā?nų**. Spouse's grandparents are also handled differently in the two towns. In **GB**, **sã?nų** is postposed to the parent-in-law term. In **XB**, both grandparent and grandchild terms extend to grandparents of spouse and spouse of grandchild, respectively.

WESTERN JAMILTEPEC MIXTEC KINSHIP TERMS

C. Henry Bradley

The kinship map, apart from spouses, is divided into five tripartite areas in Western Jamiltepec. First, three terms designate parents and child, marking only the sex of the former.

sutu	*Pm*	*father*
siʔi	*Pf*	*mother*
seʔe	*C*	*child*

Second, the above terms are modified to form idioms for designating kinsmen of two generations' distance. The modifier for grandparents means *old*; that for grandchild appears related to the term for a man's brother. The modifier *old*, when added a second time to the grandparent terms, specifically marks kinsmen of (at least) the third ascending generation.

sutu čaʔnu	*PPm(L)*	*grandfather*
siʔi čaʔnu	*PPf(L)*	*grandmother*
se yani	*CC*	*grandchild*

191

Third, three terms designate sibling, marking both sex of alter and relative sex of ego and alter.

yani	mpCm	man's brother
kuʔwi	fPCf	woman's sister
kuʔwa	aPCb	cross-sex sibling

Fourth, collateral kinsmen are designated by two terms for kinsmen of ascending generations, while kinsmen of ego's own and all descending generations are classified by a single third term. These three terms extend to kinsmen of all degrees of collaterality and generational distance, although the modifier meaning *old* in grandparent terms may in fact be applied to the terms for senior kinsmen to designate them as of more than one generation removed from that of ego.

šito	PPCm(1)	uncle
čiši	PPCf(1)	aunt
sačį	PCC(2)	junior collateral

Fifth, in-laws are designated by three terms: one term classes together spouse's parents with spouse's siblings, while two terms distinguish the sex of spouses of any consanguineal kinsman.

čiso	SP(C)	spouse's parent or sibling
kasa	CSm(0)	consanguineal's husband
čanu	CSf(0)	consanguineal's wife

Finally, two terms designate husband and wife, respectively.

ii	Sm	husband
ña siʔi	Sf	wife

The modifier **kįį** is postposed to parent, child, and sibling terms to designate relationships established through second marriages.

YOSONDUA MIXTEC KINSHIP TERMS

Ed Farris

The following data were obtained from Juventino Martínez Cruz, age 26, of the *ranchería* Atalaya, in the Municipio of Yosondúa, Tlaxiaco, Oaxaca.

Parents and children are designated by three terms with sex terminologically marked only for the former.

tātà	*Pm*	*father*
nānà	*Pf*	*mother*
sē̃ʔē̃	*C*	*child*

Lineal consanguineal kinsmen and corresponding lineal affinal kinsmen are terminologically merged in second ascending and descending generations, the grandparent terms being from Spanish *abuelo* and *abuela*.

bēlù	*PPm(L,S)*	*grandfather*
bēlà	*PPf(L,S)*	*grandmother*
sē̃ʔē̃ čání	*CC(L,S)*	*grandchild*

Five generations distinguished for lineals (including ego) are coalesced to three for collateral kinsmen: senior generations, ego's, and junior generations. Except for ego's generation, collaterals of spouse and spouses of collaterals are all terminologically merged with corresponding collateral consanguines.

Four terms distinguish such collateral kinsmen by seniority and sex.

šītō	PPCm(1,S)	uncle
šišī	PPCf(1,S)	aunt
sāxį̀	PCCm(1,S)	nephew
šīkù	PCCf(1,S)	niece

In ego's generation, consanguines are distinguished from relatives by marriage. Three sibling terms extend to all consanguines of ego's generation in a Jivaran pattern (Murdock 1970:175), while two terms for affinals distinguish only the sex of kinsmen, merging spouse of sibling, sibling of spouse, and spouse of sibling of spouse.

ñānī	mPCm(G)	man's brother
kū?à	fPCf(G)	woman's sister
kwã?ā	aPCb(G)	cross-sex sibling
kàsà	PCSm(V,G,S-)	brother-in-law
xānū	PCSf(V,G,S-)	sister-in-law

Words for man and woman are the probable historical sources of the terms for husband and wife , respectively, but the current term for man is čàà and the wife term is only very occasionally heard for woman. Sibling-in-law terms and čìsò (discussed below) serve as modifiers to parent and child terms to designate parents of spouse and spouse of child.

žī̃	Sm	husband
ñàsí?í	Sf	wife
tātā čìsò	SPm	father-in-law
nānà čìsò	SPf	mother-in-law
sē?ē kásá	CSm	son-in-law
sē?ē xánú	CSf	daughter-in-law

Evidence from related Mixtec languages indicates that the earlier Mixtecan source of Yosondúa čìsò designated siblings and senior consanguineal kinsmen of spouse, and that current Yosondúa sibling-in-law terms designated only spouses of ego's siblings and junior consanguineal kinsmen. In the present system, the use of čìsò has been reduced to that of modifier for parent-in-law terms, and as an alternate for kàsà in the primary sense of the latter; namely, to designate spouse's male collateral kinsman of spouse's own generation.

čìsò	SPCm(G)	spouse's brother

Two co-parent terms refer to the parents-in-law of ego's child.

| mbāà | CSPm | co-father-in-law |
| kwālīā | CSPf | co-mother-in-law |

Social proximity is a factor which, on occasion, is allowed to override the genealogically-based system described above. A case in point is described below in which a collateral kinsman is regarded as lineal, and generation distinctions are ignored or adjusted to meet socially-based (rather than genealogical) conditions.

Figure 6. represents genealogical relationships which exist between seven living and one deceased individual. The families of A and B are made up of twenty-seven living persons, excluding spouses, all of whom occupy one of the seven positions of the figure. The number given each position is the age of a representative individual who occupies that genealogical position.

When B was still a young child, his father deserted the family, leaving A as the guardian of his sister and her child. This situation resulted in A eventually treating the children of B as his own family. He refers to B as his nephew (saxį̀), but to D as child (sē?ē) and to E and G as grandchildren (sē?ē čání). The informant explained this in terms of A treating D (and his siblings) as orphans, in spite of the fact that both of D's parents are living and that it was B who lost a parent.

On occasion, A might refer to B as his *child* and to D as his *grandchild*, but he much more regularly recognizes them as *nephew* and *child*, respectively. This usage is recognized as genealogically aberrant and based on affection.

B usually refers to A as his uncle (šītò); but, as above, occasionally might use the parent term (tātà). On the other hand, D, who is almost always referred to by A as child (sē?ē), returns reference to A by the grandfather term (bēlù), thus violating what we would expect as a reciprocal term. The explanation for this cannot be that a grandchild is just a kind of child, since the informant would not accept the possibility of A using the child term to refer to his true grandchild F. Rather, it seems to be sufficient to note that D would not refer to A as *father* when he has had a 'true' father all of his life.

E and G also refer to A as grandfather.

In summary, A refers to B's descendants as lineal descendants of his own, and they reciprocate by referring to him as their lineal ancestor; nevertheless, A and B normally refer to each other by collateral terminology. A refers to D as though he were of the first descending generation from his own, although he is in fact of the second. This is apparently a key to further genealogical skewing between the descendants of A and those of B, as is indicated in some detail below.

D (with his siblings) refers to C (and his siblings) by sibling terms—that is, as collaterals of the same generation—in spite of the fact that he (D) refers to C's parent as grandfather. This derives from A considering D as his own child. In line with this, D refers to F as his nephew (sāxį̀).

E refers to F as sibling (kwā?ā) and to C as uncle (šītò). Genealogically they are of course both *uncles*, as is A. E is a twenty-year-old mother and F only a nine-year-old boy. Presumably on the basis of the differences in their ages, the informant on one occasion stated firmly that E would refer to F as nephew, but later he said the sibling term was more appropriate.

This confusion, even for the informant, results from the anomaly of referring to members of two different generations as though they were of the same one. That is, F refers to (and is referred to by) both E and G as sibling; and, similarly, C refers to both B and D and is referred to by them as sibling. In the latter case, it is genealogically

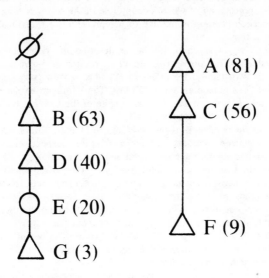

Figure 6. Kinship term usage of a Yosondúa family.

'correct' for B and C to use sibling terms. The use of sibling terms between D and C results from A's 'adoption' of D and his siblings as children.

The case of F is more difficult to explain. E, F, and G are all classed as grandchildren by A, and this may be the key; but one may well wonder at the power of this influence at so far a distance from the original adoption of D by A that it should allow F to refer to both mother (E) and son (G) as his siblings. It seems likely that proximity in age must also be an influence on F for him to refer to G as his sibling. Note that genealogically he is G's senior by two generations.

The only individual represented in Figure 6 who consistently refers to all members of the two families strictly according to genealogy is B. His own line includes children (D) and grandchildren (E and G); that of A includes his uncle (A), his classificatory siblings (C), and his nephew (F). For the rest of the family, values of social proximity override cold genealogy.

THE PROTO MIXTEC KINSHIP SYSTEM

C. Henry Bradley

Permanent records lasting generations, centuries, and millenia are seldom, if ever, kept by nonliterate people. Because of this fact, anyone who is interested in the history of culture change is seriously handicapped. But this handicap can be overcome to some extent in certain areas. Sapir (1916) has very ably shown that in spite of the lack of documentary evidence valid inferences about earlier periods can be drawn from vestigial remains found in the life-ways and speech of any group of people. Prior to the time in which Sapir wrote, certain European scholars had suggested that some aspects of a previous stage of culture could be inferred from reconstructed linguistic forms. Thus the *Wörter-und-Sachen* technique was applied by Delbrück (1889) in the reconstruction of the Proto Indoeuropean kinship system. Since that time our knowledge of the methods of linguistic reconstruction and our experience in reconstructing proto kinship systems have increased. Kroeber (1937) was one of the first to apply this method to the problem of reconstructing the kinship system of an American Indian group. He has since been followed by Shimkin (1941), Hoijer (1956), and Matthews (1959).

Kroeber realized the importance of basing this kind of a study on linguistic evidence when he said, "To be sure, philologists mainly reconstruct the forms or sounds of words, and only secondarily their meanings; and we have in culture relatively little material so sharply formalized as to lend itself to comparisons as exact as that of language forms" (1937:607). His attempt to reconstruct the Proto Athapaskan kinship system was really only a pilot study. It has since been modified and elaborated by Hoijer. Shimkin's study also was experimental in the sense that he reconstructed the lexical and conceptual categories of the Proto Utoaztecan kinship system by building on the basic linguistic work of Sapir and Whorf. With Hoijer's elaboration of Kroeber's work and Matthew's Proto Siouan reconstruction a method has become fairly well delineated by which proto kinship systems can be reconstructed.

Recently Murdock (1949) has developed another theory which leads to reconstructing earlier stages in the history of a given kinship system by means of a theory of social change. He has traced the development of a number of kinship systems and found them to follow certain lines of development according to their type. This procedure was tested with Southern Athapaskan material by Charles B. White (1957). His conclusions differed from those of Kroeber and Hoijer, and suggested that the application of the Murdock method yielded results that were more in line with the social facts. However, this position has been refuted by Hymes and Driver who believe that "the role of culture contact greatly reduces the probability of any long-range internal reconstruction of kinship systems, apart from linguistic and other ethnological evidence" (1958:153).

In order to avoid the serious pitfall observed by Hymes and Driver, I have here attempted to reconstruct the Proto Mixtec (PM) kinship system by using the first of these two methods, viz., the comparative method of linguistic reconstruction. This study, however, involves not only a reconstruction of the linguistic forms of the kinship system but also a reconstruction of the kintypes which they represent. The procedures for attacking the problem are two: first, cognate terms from each of the daughter languages are brought together in order to determine the form and meaning of the original PM word for each set of cognates; second, a comparison of the kinship categories represented by each reconstructed term in the daughter languages is made. Each comparison suggests one or more hypotheses about the pattern of kin groups characteristic for PM. In this way somewhat more precise information is given on the PM kinship system than could be gained from the cognate sets alone (Hoijer 1956:308). The major criterion used for determining the extent of the kinship categories represented by each reconstructed form is the distribution of the form and the kinship category or categories associated with the form in the daughter languages. A restricted distribution suggests that the term is local and the result of later developments.

The procedure adopted here is to divide the kinship terms into two sets, first, on the basis of the distinction between consanguineal and affinal terms and, then, on the basis of generation distinctions (which is the most important single dimension of the system within the consanguineal set); to present charts within each section, along with discussion, showing the distribution of the reconstructed terms from the four dialects and the kintypes signified by each of these terms; to reconstruct the proto terms along with their meanings for each set; to trace the changes which have taken place between the proto system and the four contemporary daughter systems; to describe briefly the kinds of changes which have taken place; and to discuss briefly some possible cause of these changes.

Linguistic and Social Structure

Today Mixtec languages are spoken by approximately 250,000 people, most of whom live in the State of Oaxaca, Mexico. The outlying edges of the territory occupied by the Mixtecs reach into the neighboring states of Puebla and Guerrero. Although my data do not give as wide a cross section of Mixtec kinship systems as I would like, four mutually unintelligible languages from different parts of the area are represented. San Miguel (SM) is located in the middle of the Mixtec area in the district of Tlaxiaco, Metlatonoc (M) on the western fringe in Guerrero, Ayutla (Ay)in the southwestern corner of the area in Guerrero, and Western Jamiltepec (WJ) on the southern extremity just across the Guerrero border in Oaxaca. Ay is separated from J by the area occupied by the Amuzgo. [Mixtec, Cuicatec, and Trique (the latter two also located in Oaxaca) form the Mixtecan language family (McQuown 1955:531); at an earlier horizon Amuzgo split away from the common source to form a separate branch of Macro Mixtecan parallel with Mixtecan (Longacre 1957:1-3).] Unfortunately, data from three other important languages are not available and until they are, the conclusions drawn in this paper are extremely tentative. The missing languages are: Peñoles on the eastern edge of the Mixtec region in Oaxaca, Tonahuixtla on the northern fringe in Puebla, and San Juan Coatzospan-Cuyamecalco isolated and completely surrounded by Mazatec speakers in the northeastern corner of Oaxaca. (This last mentioned language is extremely important since it has been isolated from the rest of the Mixtec-speaking people since before the time of the Spanish conquest. It could very well preserve evidence which has been lost in the other languages since it has been unaffected by changes which have taken place in the Mixtec region itself. Of course, it is possible that other changes have obliterated any witness that this language could give.)

Mak and Longacre (1960) have worked out the sound correspondences in Proto Mixtec ultimate syllables and I have based this study on their work. For the most part, information which they give about the reconstruction of ultimate syllables is valid also for a large number of penultimate and pretonic syllables and some of these syllables are reconstructed here. In a few cases, some doubt remains concerning the shape which these forms are to take, but in no case is the reconstruction of the form itself questionable. Since the Mak-Longacre study does not include the reconstruction of tone, it is not marked here. Although all Mixtec kinship terms are obligatorily marked for possession in the daughter languages, usually by a postposed possessive pronoun, I will cite the forms without their possessive marker. I have made no attempt to reconstruct terms of address, or ritual terms (which have been introduced through the influence of the Roman Catholic church since the time of the conquest).

Today the Mixtecs are organized into at least two kinds of territorial grouping—the village and the ranch. These two types are distinguished by the fact that the village is a compact sociopolitical and territorial unit (not part of any other larger indigenous unit) whereas the ranch is a relatively isolated territorial unit dependent on a sociopolitical center. The ranch type organization is found largely in the area from which groups showing the village type reputedly emigrated some six or seven centuries ago (Holland 1959:31).

On the ranch the play group is limited to the child, his siblings, and the children of his paternal uncle (since residence is patrilocal). Only seldom does the child, then, come into contact with other children or adults not of his own ranch. On the other hand, in the village the play group has a somewhat broader base. The child plays principally with his own siblings and the children of any paternal uncle who happens to be living in patrilocal residence. Little difficulty is found in maintaining patrilocal residence on the ranch where there is a lot of room, but in the compact village younger brothers and now sons are often forced into neolocal residence, since there is no more room for new buildings around the father's house. The village child, as a result, plays first with his own relatives, but quickly includes in his play group children of his nearest neighbors; he also has contact with a wider range of adults than does a ranch child. The difference in the socialization of the child may have been part of the cause for a difference in cousin terminology between the two areas (cf. *Change in Mixtec Kinship Systems*, below).

The kinship terms reconstructed here hark back to roughly 1000 A.D. Undoubtedly the Mixtecs of that period shared some of the Mesoamerican traits elaborated by Steward (1955) for the incipient stages of the period of regional development and florescence, such as, the rise of multicommunity states, the development of a class-structured society, etc. But there are no kinship data available for that early period and what is available for later periods is random and scanty. Dahlgren's collation (1953) of the historical sources contains as much material as is found in them. Apparently very little information on the kin group aspects of the social life of the Mixtecs was recorded by the friars and early Spanish historians. Therefore, we know very little about the previous social organization of these people into family or other larger kin groups. At any rate a complement of kinship terms are reconstructed which are not too different in form or kintype designation from some contemporary daughter systems even though during the intervening period a great number of social changes have taken place.

Terms in the Grandparent Generation

Two terms are reconstructed in the grandparent generation as attested by Ay and M.

PM III. *Өii *PPm(G,-S)*
    Ay šii *PPm, PPPCm, PPPCSm;* M šii *PPm, PPPCm, PPPPCCm.*
PM 112 *Өitą *PPf(G,-S).*
    Ay šitą? ~ štą? *PPf, PPPCf, PPPCSf;* M šitą *PPf, PPPCf, PPPCSf, PPPPCCf.*

SM has borrowed terms, possibly from Nahuatl (**tata ñuu** and **nana ñuu**, respectively). They cover the same area of semantic space as the Ay terms. The attribute **ñuu** is of Mixtec origin. J, on the other hand, has coined a completely new expression, **sutu čaʔnu**. Both terms reconstruct on the same early horizon as do the other reconstructed kinship terms. They represent, therefore, either the use of two dialectal variants in the early period or a subsequent coinage using two words which date back to that early horizon. In addition, the range of kintype designation is more restricted than in the other languages. **sutu čaʔnu** and **siʔi čaʔnu** mean only *PPm* and *PPf*, respectively; they are not extended to include siblings and cousins of grandparents.

Figure 7 indicates the ranges of reference of each term in the four languages. From it the meanings of the two reconstructed terms are inferred. (A blank space in a table indicates that the description of the particular daughter system is uncertain, cf. SM for *PPPPCCm*. Silence on the part of the investigator seems to indicate that the meaning of the term does not extend beyond that given in the description.)

Figure 7. Mixtec Grandparent Term Ranges of Reference.

	PPm	*PPPCm*	*PPPPCCm*	*PPf*	*PPPCf*	*PPPPCCf*
Ay	šii	šii		šitą?	šitą?	
M	šii	šii	šii	šitą	šitą	šitą
SM	tata ñuu	tata ñuu		nana ñuu	nana ñuu	
J	sutu čaʔnu	šito	šito	siʔi čaʔnu	čiši	čiši

The figure shows that two inferences for the reconstruction of meaning of the terms are possible. Either proto terms *Өii and *Өitą meant only *PPm* and *PPf* , respectively, while siblings and cousins of grandparents were indicated by other terms as in J, or *Өii and *Өitą had wider ranges of meaning including siblings and cousins of grandparents, as M suggests. (The intermediate possibility, limiting the range of these terms to *PPPC*, excluding *PPPPCC*, would be tenuous since it would be based on silence—the reports of those languages do not tell us.) Since the differences shown by J are restricted to this language alone and it is on the southern fringe of the area, I assume that the differences are innovations. In contrast M, (and possibly Ay) are extremely conservative, maintaining the PM system here without change.

Terms in the Parent Generation

Four terms are reconstructed in the parent generation as attested by M and Ay for *yuva, M, Ay, and J for *Өiʔi, and all four languages for *Өito and *ӨiӨi.

PM 102. *yuva *Pm*.
Ay yubaʔ (~ tata) *Pm*; M yuba (~ tata) *Pm*.
PM 108. *Өiʔi *Pf*.
Ay siʔiʔ (~ nana) *Pf*; M siʔi (~ nana) *Pf*; J siʔi *Pf*.
PM 118. Өito *PPCm(G,-S)*.
Ay šito (~ što) *PPCm, PPPCCm, PPCSm, PPPCCSm*; M šito *PPCm, PPPCCm*; SM stoo *PPCm, PPPCCm, PPCSm, PPPCCSm*; J šito *PPCm, PPPCCm, PPPCm*.
PM 107. *ӨiӨi *PPCf(G,-S)*.
Ay šiši (~ šii) *PPCf, PPPCCf, PPCSf, PPPCCSf*; M šiši *PPCf, PPPCCf*; SM šii *PPCf, PPPCCf, PPCSf, PPPCCSf*; J čiši *PPCf, PPPCCf, PPPCf*.

In addition to the dimension of sex which was the characteristic distinguishing the two terms found in the grandparent generation, a second dimension distinguishing lineal and nonlineal relatives is found here. Again SM has borrowed, possibly from Nahuatl, but this time without modification. Apparently the borrowed **naa** and **taa** of SM are being extended to M and Ay but not to J, cf. the variants cited in etymologies **PM 102** and **PM 108**. **sutu**, the unmodified dialectal variant of *yuva, occurs in J.

Figure 8 shows the distribution of these four terms with their kintypes in each of the 9 languages. In this case the reconstruction of kintypes is relatively straightforward, since there is no conflict in any of the daughter languages.

Figure 8. Ranges of Reference of Mixtec Terms in the Parent Generation.

	Pm	*PPCm(G)*	*Pf*	*PPCf(G)*
Ay	yuba?, tata	šito	si?i?, nana	šiši
M	yuba, tata	šito	si?i, nana	šiši
SM	taa	stoo	naa	šii
J	sutu	šito	si?i	čiši

Only one inference is possible for the meaning of each of the four terms reconstructed in the parent generation; *yuva means *Pm*, *Өi?i means *Pf*, *Өito means *PPCm(G)*, and *ӨiӨi means *PPCf(G)*. (The last two terms designate other kintypes as well, but these are not demonstrated until affinal terminology is discussed.) Therefore, except for the SM and J form for *Pm* and the SM form for *Pf*, the daughter systems show no change from the parent PM system.

Terms in Ego's Generation

Three terms are reconstructed for ego's generation as attested by all four dialects for *yani and *kwa?a and by three for *ku?vi. A fourth term *ta?ą *companion* is reconstructed for PM, but not within the universe of kinship terminology as present-day SM and J indicate. Two dimensions—distinct from the two which were found in the parent generation—operate on this level, viz., sex of ego and sex of referent.

PM 117 *yani *mPCm(G)*.
   Ay ñani *mPCm, mPPCCm, mPCSm, mPPCCSm*; M yani *mPCm, mPPCCm*; SM ñani *mPCm, mPPCCm*; J yani *mPCm*.
PM 106. *ku?vi *fPCf(G)*.
   M ku?vi *fPCf, fPPCCf*; SM ku?u *fPCf, fPPCCf*; J ku?vi *fPCf*.
PM 119. *kwa?a *aPCb(G)*.
   Ay ku?va *fPCf, fPPCCf, fPCSf, fPPCCSf*; M ku?va *aPCb, aPPCCb*; SM kwa?a *aPCb, aPPCCb*; J ku?va *aPCb*.
PM 120 *ta?ą *companion*.
   Ay ta?ą *aPCb, aPPCCb, aPCSb, aPPCCSb*; SM ta?ą *companion*; J ta?ą *companion*.

The kintypes to which these three terms refer are established by a different configuration of the witnesses in all three cases. First, that *yani means *mPCm(G)* is established by Ay, M, and SM. Second, M, SM, and J witness to the establishment of **kwaʔa** as *aPCb* and ***kuʔvi** as *ʃPCʃ*. Third, M and SM (with only the slightest inference from Ay, show that the reference of these terms is extended by *Rule G* as well. Therefore, M and SM directly reflect the proto system at this point without change. In Ay, ***kuʔvi** was lost and replaced by a reflex of ***kwaʔa**, and **tą̀ʔą̀** replaced ***kwaʔa**. In J, the three terms were restricted to their respective sibling referents alone and ***Θahį** extended to all other collaterals of ego's generation. These developments are catalogued in Figure 9.

Figure 9. Ranges of Reference of Mixtec Terms in Ego's Generation.

	mPCm	*mPPCCm*	*ʃPCʃ*	*ʃPPCCʃ*	*aPCb*	*aPPCCb*
Ay	ñani	ñani	kuʔva	kuʔva	tą̀ʔą̀	tą̀ʔą̀
M	yani	yani	kuʔvi	kuʔvi	kuʔva	kuʔva
SM	ñani	ñani	kuʔu	kuʔu	kwaʔa	kwaʔa
J	yani	sačį	kuʔvi	sačį	kuʔva	sačį

Catholic missionaries writing in the sixteenth century give brief but corroborative documentary evidence that the system described for PM, SM, and M was the system in use during their contacts with the Mixtecs. Fray Antonio de los Reyes observed that "pocas veces vsan los naturales de estos términos de primos o primas segundas, su más común modo es llamarse todos hermanos aunque sean primos" (1593:87). On the other hand, the recent comment made by Dahlgren seems to be without basis. Although she says that "para algunos de los grados de parientes más cercanos como hermano, hermana, primo y prima hay distintos términos, según el sexo del que habla. De los hermanos se distinguía, además, entre primogénitos, mayores, menores, y benjamines" (1954:157), no report shows that present-day languages make such distinctions in ego's generation. Of course, what Dahlgren was aiming at in her first statement here is the sex of ego and the sex of referent described earlier in this section. Her second statement is not true for the languages represented in this paper nor is there any inference of its being true for an earlier period. This is not to say that such a discrimination cannot be made, but if made, it is not with elementary kinship terms but rather by a construction whose 'total equals the sum of its parts'.

Terms in the Child Generation

Again, three terms are reconstructed in the child generation, but they are distinguished along different dimensions.

PM 110. *Θaʔyu *C*.

Ay **siʔe** *C*; M **seʔe** *C*; SM **seʔe** *C*; J **seʔe** *C*; (Tonahuixtla **deʔe** *C*; Estetla **daʔyu** *C*; Tidaa **daʔa** *C*; Santiago Mitlatongo **laʔa** *Cm*, **laʔ** *Cf*; San Juan Tamazola **daʔya** *Cm*; Tilantongo **da** *Cf* (Mak and Longacre 1960:39).)

PM 105. *Θahį *PCCm(G)*.
  Ay **sašį** *PCCm, PPCCCm*; M **sašį** *PCCm, PPCCCm*; SM **sahį** *PCCm, PPCCCm*; J
  sačį *PCC, PCCC, PPCC, PPCCC, PPCCCC*.
PM 103. *Θiku *PCCf(G)*.
  Ay **šiku** *PCCf, PPCCCf*; M **šiku** *PCCf, PPCCCf*; SM **šiku** *PCCf, PPCCCf*.

***Θa?yu** is lineal and makes no sex distinction whereas ***Θahį** refers to a male collateral
and ***Θiku** to a female collateral. All four languages testify to ***Θa?yu** and ***Θahį** but only
Ay, M, and SM to ***Θiku**. Figure 10 shows that ***Θahį** is consistently *PCCm(G)* in Ay, M,
and SM. It is paralleled by the corresponding feminine kintype referents for ***Θiku** giving
a consistent reconstruction of the kintypes of these two terms.

Figure 10. Ranges of Reference of Mixtec Terms in the Child Generation.

	C	PCCm(G)	PCCf(G)
Ay	si?e	sašį	šiku
M	se?e	sašį	šiku
SM	se?e	sahį	šiku
J	se?e	sačį	sačį

Without a doubt, Ay, M, and SM have come down from the PM system without a
change. J, as before, contains the innovation. ***Θiku** disappeared and ***Θahį** developed the
kintype referents of ***Θiku**. In this way the dimension of sex was lost in J in the collateral
dimension.

Terms in the Grandchild Generation

In the grandchild generation only one term is reconstructed or, more precisely, the
phrase ***Θa?yu hani**.

PM 114. Θa?yu hani *CC(G)*.
  Ay **si yani** *CC, PCCC, PPCCCC*; M **se?e yani** *CC, PCCC, PPCCCC*; SM **se?e ti-
  hani** *CC, PCCC, PPCCCC*; J **se(?e) yani** *CC*.

All four languages attest this reconstruction. There is some disagreement, however, as
to what kintypes are designated by it. Again, it is a question of J in disagreement with
Ay, M, and SM. It is assumed, therefore, that the three languages in agreement reflect
the original meaning of the term. To look at the coin from the other side, those three are
conservative and show no change from the PM system at this point and J represents
another innovation. Figure 11 shows the distribution of the terms over kintypes.

Figure 11. Ranges of Reference of Mixtec Terms in the Grandchild Generation.

	CC	PCCC	PPCCCC
Ay	si yani	si yani	si yani
M	se?e yani	se?e yani	se?e yani
SM	se?e tɨ-hani	se?e tɨ-hani	se?e tɨ-hani
J	se(?e) yani	sačɨ	sačɨ

Spouses of Kinsmen

Only two terms are reconstructed for spouses of kinsmen, *kaΘa and *hanu, both of which are attested in all four languages.

PM 122. *kaΘa *CSm(2), mSPCSm(G)*.
Ay kasa? *CSm*; M kasa *CSm, PCSm*; M kasa šɨ?ɨ *mSPCSm, mSPPCCSm*; SM kasa *PCSm, PPCCSm*; SM se?e kasa *CSm, PCCSm*; SM ta-kasa *SPCSm, SPPCCSm*; J kasa *CSm, CCSm, PCSm, PPCCSm, PPCSm, PPPCSm*.
PM 123. *hanu *CSf(2), fSPCSf(G)*.
Ay šanu *CSf*; M šanu *CSf, PCSf*; M šanu šɨ?ɨ *fSPCSf, fSPPCCSf*; SM hanu *PCSf, PPCCSf*; SM se?e hanu *CSf, PCCSf*; SM ta-hanu *fSPCSf, fSPPCCSf*; J čanu *CSf, CCSf, PCSf, PPCCSf, PPCSf, PPPCSf*.

Consanguineal terms are used in some languages to designate some affines of this class. The reconstruction of the ranges of reference of these two complementary terms, distinguished only by the dimension of sex of the referent, is one of the most difficult and most tentative reconstructions of the paper. Figure 12 shows how the two affinal terms belonging to this class are distributed among the languages and how other terms are used to designate some of the affinal kintypes of this class.

Figure 12. Ranges of Reference of Mixtec Terms for Spouses of Kinsmen.

	PPPCSm	PPCSm(G)	PCSm(G)	CSm(G)	CCSm(G)
Ay	šii	šito ~ što	ñani, tạ?ạ	kasa?	
M			kasa	kasa	
SM	tata ñuu	stoo	kasa	se?e kasa	
J	kasa	kasa	kasa	kasa	kasa

Figure 12 (Continued).

PPPCSf	PPCSf(G)	PCSf(G)	CSf(G)	CCSf(G)

	PPPCSf	PPCSf(G)	PCSf(G)	CSf(G)	CCSf(G)
Ay	šitạ?	šiši ~ šii	kuʔva, tạ?ạ	šanu	
M			šanu	šanu	
SM	nana ñuu	šii	hanu	seʔe hanu	
J	čanu	čanu	čanu	čanu	čanu

In ego's and child's generation the picture for reconstructing kintypes seems fairly clear. M, SM, and J agree in allocating the kintypes *PCSm(G)* to *kaⴲa and *PCSf(G)* to *hanu. Ay, M, and J agree in allocating *CSm(G)* to *kaⴲa and *CSf(G)* to *hanu. SM differs only in preposing the word seʔe. Affinal relatives in the grandparent generation and the parent generation are designated by the same terms as are consanguineals in Ay and SM. M is silent at this point and J is in contrast. As in the preceding cases, the testimony of Ay and SM is given priority over that of J so that these kintypes are designated by *ⴲii, *ⴲitạ, *yuva, *ⴲiʔi, *ⴲito, and *ⴲiⴲi, respectively. If this is the case, then Ay and SM are conservative and reflect the PM system without change, while J extends the ranges of *kaⴲa and *hanu to include affinals of ascending generations. This type of innovation is also found in Ay in ego's generation; the sibling/cousin terms are extended to include the spouses of these with the resultant loss of these kintypes from the ranges of *kaⴲa and *hanu. Further, J extends the ranges of these two terms to affinal relatives of the second descending generation, whereas the other three dialects do not discriminate these kintypes. Thus, again J proves to be the most innovating member of the four languages. A unique feature of both M and SM is the discrimination of *mSPCSm* and *fSPCSf* by the formation of specialized constructions with *kaⴲa and *hanu, respectively, as the base, e.g. ta-kasa, kasa šjʔj, and ta-hanu, šanu šjʔj.

Terms for Spouse and Kinsmen of Spouse

Three terms are reconstructed in PM which indicate husband, wife, or any consanguineal relative of spouse.

PM 124. *yⱨ *Sm.*
  Ay ii *Sm*, M ii *Sm*, SM žii *Sm*, J ii *Sm*.
PM 109. *ña ⴲiʔɨ *Sf.*
  Ay ña-siʔi *Sf*, M ña-siʔi ~ ya-siʔi *Sf*, SM ña-siʔɨ *Sf*, J ña-siʔi *Sf*.
PM 121. *tiⴲo *SP(2).*
  Ay tiso *SP*; M siso *SP, SPC, SPPCC*; SM čiso *SP, SPC*; SM taa čiso *SPm*; SM naa čiso *SPf*; J čiso *SP, SPC, SPPCC*.

Both the term and the kintype designation are reconstructed systematically without question for *yɨɨ *Sm* and *ña Θɨʔɨ *Sf* in all four languages. They also attest to the form *tiΘo, and the kintypes of *tiΘo reconstruct with relatively little difficulty as well—M, SM, and J giving a consistent witness to the reconstruction of *SP(2)*.

Figure 13. Ranges of Reference of Mixtec Terms for Kinsmen of Spouse.

	SPm	*SPf*	*SPC*	*SPPCC*	*mSPCSm(G)*	*fSPCSf(G)*
Ay	tiso	tiso	kuñero/kuñada		ta kasaʔ	ta šanu
M	siso	siso	siso	siso	kasa šįʔį	šanu šįʔį
SM	taa čiso	naa čiso	čiso		ta-kasa	ta-hanu
J	čiso	čiso	čiso	čiso		

*tiΘo is preserved relatively unaltered in all four languages. SM specializes it by preposing **taa** and **naa** to distinguish *SPm* and *SPf*, respectively. In Ay, the kintype designation for *SPC* was lost, very likely under the influence of Spanish since today the kintype has split into **kuñero** *SPCm* and **kuñada** *SPCf*. Reports are silent as to whether SM and Ay have these terms for *SPPCC*; the usage is clearly preserved in M and J, however.

Ay, M, and SM have developed special constructions with *kaΘa and *hanu as base to indicate affinal relatives of the spouse who are related to ego through the spouse, e.g. *mSPCSm(G)* and *fSPCSf(G)*. These kintypes are not reconstructed for their respective terms even though attested by three languages because two different constructions are used, e.g., **kasa šįʔį** and **šanu šįʔį** in M and **ta-kasa** and **ta-hanu** in the other two.

Change in Mixtec Kinship Systems

Changes in kinship systems can be classified in at least three different ways, i.e., according to their kind, degree, or cause. In these data, several *kinds* of change occur which are classified along three dimensions. The most important dimension distinguishes form and meaning (or kintype designation); the next—which cuts across the first—distinguishes replacement, gain, or loss of an element. Finally, borrowing (the source of the new element is outside of the indigenous system) and coining (the source of the new element is within the same system) operate as subdivisions of replacement and gain but not loss. Eggan recognized two of these dimensions some time ago when he said, "Kinship terminology and the kinship pattern may vary independently: the terms may change without affecting the pattern, as when a simple substitution occurs, or the pattern may change without affecting the terminology, or both" (1937:49). Figure 14 tabulates these types of change shown in the daughter systems of PM.

Figure 14. Types of Change in Mixtec Kinship Systems.

	FORM	MEANING
Replacement—borrowing	tata ñuu (SM)	PPPC (J)
Replacement—coining	sutu ča?nu (J)	
Gain—borrowing	kuñero (Ay)	SPCS (Ay)
Gain—coining	ta?a (Ay)	PPCC (J)
Loss	kwa?a (Ay)	PPCm (J)

As Figure 14 indicates, kintype replacements are not coined.

Change can be classified according to *degree* of change as well. Figure 15 shows the amount of agreement (marked by x) between PM and the four languages in the forms of the kinterms and the percentage of their divergence from PM (scored in the last column of the figure). The PM terms are arbitrarily represented by letters *a* through *s*, in the order presented in this paper.

Figure 15. Degree of Mixtec Divergence from PM Kinship Terms.

	a	b	c	d	e	f	g	h	i	(j)	k	l	m	n	o	p	q	r	s	percent
Ay	x	x	x	x	x	x	x				x	x	x	x	x	x	x	x	x	x	05
M	x	x	x	x	x	x	x	x	x			x	x	x	x	x	x	x	x	x	00
SM				x	x	x	x	x	(x)	x	x	x	x	x	x	x	x		21
J			x	x	x	x	x	x	(x)	x	x		x	x	x	x	x	x		21

Figure 16 shows the amount of agreement between the kintype designations of PM terms and those of the four contemporary languages, and the percentage of divergence from PM.

Figure 16. Degree of Mixtec Divergence from PM Kintypes.

	a	b	c	d	e	f	g	h	i	j	k	l	m	n	o	p	q	r	s	percent
Ay	(x)	(x)	x	x	x	x				-	x	x	x	x		x	x			33
M			x	x		x	x	x	-	x	x	x	x		x	x	x			33
SM	(x)	(x)	x	x	x	x	x	x	x	-	x	x	x	x		x	x			17
J			x	x					-	x					x	x	x			67

In form M reflects PM completely; Ay has only one change (**h** → **j**); SM and J show the most change. In kintype designation, SM modified the PM system in only three places; M and Ay modified it in six places; J modified it in twelve places. (The computation of percentage of divergence for kintype designation gives only a gross measurement since the change of several kintypes for a given term is given the same value as the change of a single kintype. A more refined measure needs to be used here.) Taken as a whole Ay, M, and SM cluster together with relatively few changes in form and meaning from PM; J, on the other hand, proves to be quite innovative.

The reason for J's flexibility may lie in two different directions. First, the area in which J is located was the most recently settled (still in pre-Conquest times) by emigrants probably from somewhere in the mountain area which is now the district of Tlaxiaco (Holland, Longacre). A number of changes took place in this move from the mountains to the coast, including the development of a new pattern of residence—village rather than ranch—which, in turn, may have been the *cause* for the change in sibling and cousin terminology observed in J. As I mentioned earlier, the constituency of the play group in the village very likely changed to include more than the child's siblings and cousins. It probably included the children of neighbors as well. But more importantly, the village child probably played with fewer of his cousins who, with their father, lived in neolocal residence.

Second, not only did these Mixtec emigrants develop new social patterns in a new environment but they also had new neighbors to the south and east, the Zapotecs. From them they may have learned to distinguish lineal from collateral relatives in second ascending and descending generations. This distinction, found only in J, is also a characteristic of the kinship system of Cuixtla Zapotec, the closest Zapotec language for which I have data.

In both cases of change in J, the distinction between lineal and collateral relative was extended to new levels—either ego's generation or second ascending and descending generations. Although these two changes were likely from different sources, they were mutually reinforcing and yielded a system making this distinction in all generations rather than merely in alternate ones as in other Mixtec languages.

Summary

    The PM kinship system consisted of eighteen terms; thirteen indicated consanguineal kinsmen and five affinal kinsmen. The consanguineal terms were distributed unequally through five generations with alternate generations showing first Hawaiian and then Eskimo characteristics. That is to say, lineal kinsmen were not distinguished from collateral kinsmen in the second ascending and descending generations and ego's generation whereas in the first ascending and descending generations they were so distinguished. The affinal terms fell into two classes, one consisting of terms for affinal relatives related to ego through a consanguineal kinsman and the other of terms for affinal relatives related to ego through a spouse. Other relevant dimensions in the PM system were sex of referent, sex of referent relative to ego, affiliation of mediator, and degree of affinity.

CHICAHUAXTLA TRIQUE
KINSHIP TERMS
Robert E. Longacre

Trique, which is linguistically related to and geographically surrounded by the Mixtec, displays a typical Mixtecan consanguineal kinship structure with elements of Hawaiian and Eskimo type systems in alternate generations. The data presented here were gathered by the author from a variety of informants during field trips to San Andrés Chicahuaxtla over a period of fifteen years (1947-1962).

The two grandparent terms which distinguish sex of referent extend bilaterally to include all four grandparents, their same-generation collaterals, and their spouses. Reciprocally, members of the second descending generation, both lineal and collateral of ego and spouse, are classed together under a single term for grandchild.

ži³	*PPm(1,-S)*	*grandfather*
žu³gwą?³ąh³⁴	*PPf(1,-S)*	*grandmother*
da³?ni⁴⁵ zi⁵?ni⁵	*CC(1,S-)*	*grandchild*

In parents' generation, lineal relatives are distinguished from collateral by the four terms for father, mother, uncle, and aunt. The two latter terms extend to include all same-generation collaterals of parents, but contrary to usage in the second ascending generation, spouses of these relatives are designated by affinal terms (see below).

213

As in parents' generation, lineal relatives are distinguished from collateral relatives in the first descending generation from ego. A single term for child may be modified to indicate sex as in **da³ʔni⁴⁵ zna³ʔu⁴** *son* and **da³ʔni⁴⁵ ža⁵na⁵** *daughter*. Two additional nephew and niece terms distinguish sex of the children of all relatives referred to by sibling terms.

dreh³	Pm	father
n·i³	Pf	mother
da³ʔni²¹	C	child
da³ʔni?⁴⁵	PPCm(G)	uncle
du³ʔwi³	PPCf(G)	aunt
du³kų?⁴⁵	PCCm(G)	nephew
du³gwa³či?³⁴	PCCf(G)	niece

In ego's generation the criterion of sex is the important factor in differentiating three terms—one used between males, one used between females, and one used between individuals of the opposite sex. These terms class together siblings of ego and children of those referred to by aunt and uncle terms.

di³nɨ²¹	mPCm(G)	man's brother
žu³gwih³⁴	fPCf(G)	woman's sister
žu³gweh³⁴	aPCb(G)	cross-sex sibling

Relatives of the third ascending generation are denoted by postposing **zi³ gi⁵ʔnų?⁵** to the grandparent terms. Great-grandchildren are referred to merely as children of grandchildren as in **da³ʔni²¹ da³ʔni⁴⁵ zi⁵ʔni⁵**.

Steprelationships are denoted by the addition of **gą?⁵ą⁵** to consanguineal terms. Stepsiblings, whose parents are living together as spouses, but who were born by previous marriages and share no consanguineal parent, are not considered related and employ no kinship term to refer to one another.

The Affinal Terminology

Trique affinal nomenclature is also characteristically Mixtecan in distinguishing relatives of spouse from spouses of consanguineal relatives.

Two terms distinguish the sex of persons who marry consanguineal relatives of ego. They include spouses of all collateral relatives of generations below the second ascending generation.

zi³ga³tah³⁴	CSm(3)	consanguineal's husband
ža⁵ko?⁵	CSf(3)	consanguineals's wife

Spouses of descendants may also be referred to by these terms in conjunction with consanguineal terms.

da³ʔni⁴⁵ ža⁵ko?⁵	CSf	daughter-in-law
da³ʔni⁴⁵ zi³ga³tah³⁴ zi⁵ʔnɨ⁵	CCSm	grandson-in-law

Etymologically it is likely that these terms are related to ža³ko?² *we take, we marry* and zi²¹ ga³tah³⁴ *the young man who spoke*; i.e., the young man who asked for the girl in marriage (Cf. Longacre 1959, fn 15).

Consanguineal relatives of spouse, other than collaterals below the first descending generation, are all classed together under a single term which does not distinguish their sex.

ži³če²¹   *SP(3)*   *spouse's consanguineals*

Parents-in-law are denoted by postposing this term to consanguineal parent terminology, as in n·i³ ži⁵čeh⁵ *mother-in-law*. Grand-parent-in-law terms further postpose the morpheme a³čih³⁴ *elderly*.

There is a single term for spouse.

ni³ka⁴   *S*   *spouse*

The Ritual-relationship Terminology

Ritual relationships are established through sponsorship of a child for infant baptism. Typical of Mesoamerica, the co-parent relationship established is of more immediate importance than the godparent/godchild relationship. Godparents furnish their new godchild with a new suit of clothing and take special interest in him as he grows up. Parents treat their co-parents to a feast where it is notable that their interrelationships are quite informal. Food and drink are served and the co-parents get drunk together. Whereas in Mesoamerica in general it is reported that co-parents must maintain a formal relationship which involves never drinking together lest they should get drunk and quarrel, Trique co-parents do drink together and even murder of a co-parent is known in the area.

The godparent/godchild terms utilize consanguineal parent/child terms with a postposed morpheme **ma³ne²** which has not been identified elsewhere in the language. The co-parent terms are three in number and distinguish sex of ego and of the referent. Two of the three terms seem to have been assimilated from Spanish *compadre* and *comadre*. The co-parent terms are also used vocatively.

dreh³ ma³ne²   *godfather*
n·i³ ma³ne²   *godmother*
da³?ni⁴⁵ ma³ne²   *godchild*
go³ba³reh³   *man's co-father*
gwa³neh³   *woman's co-mother*
ma²   *cross-sex co-parent*

The Vocative Terminology

Vocative terms are used extensively in greetings with one of four typical intonation contours which indicate respectively: casualness, attention calling, assertion, and respect. Most of the terms are taken from the consanguineal kinship nomenclature, but a few additional terms also appear.

tah²³	*father*
n·ǝh²³	*mother*
tu?³	*son*
ti?³	*daughter*
da³tah³	*very old man*
na³nah³	*very old woman*
da³?ni²	*older man*
du³?wi²	*older woman*
di³ni²	*man's male contemporary*
žu³gwe²	*contemporary of the opposite sex*
l·e?⁵	*woman's female contemporary*
(z)du³kɥ²	*younger man (man speaking)*
l·u?⁵	*younger man (woman speaking)*
du³gwa⁴ži²	*younger woman (man speaking)*
l·e?⁵	*younger woman (woman speaking)*

Parent and child terms are the only vocative terms which are limited in use to consanguineal relatives. All other vocative terms extend to unrelated members of the community and occur in a greeting form following the morpheme ma³⁴ *hello*.

Assimilated forms of the familiar tata/nana are used to address very elderly people. Uncle and aunt terms are extended to include all members of the community older than ego. Two sibling terms are used between contemporary males and contemporaries of the opposite sex, but contemporary women address one another and also younger women by a term not found in the kinship nomenclature. There are four terms used for addressing younger persons; men employ consanguineal nephew and niece terms, while women employ nonkinship terms.

COPALA TRIQUE KINSHIP TERMS

Barbara E. Hollenbach

The following is a brief restatement of Hollenbach 1973, incorporating a few corrections by the author.

Five generations of consanguineals are distinguished. In the second ascending generation from that of ego, two terms distinguish the sex of lineals, collaterals, and their spouses.

ži⁵³	*PPm(1,-S)*	*grandfather*
žu³gwaʔə̧h⁵³	*PPf(1,-S)*	*grandmother*

In the first ascending generation two pairs of terms distinguish lineals from collaterals.

reh³	*Pm*	*father*
ni³	*Pf*	*mother*
daʔnuʔ³	*PPCm(G)*	*uncle*
duʔwę³	*PPCf(G)*	*aunt*

In ego's generation, siblings are merged with collaterals by three terms which distinguish male collaterals of males, female collaterals of females, and collaterals of the opposite sex.

dinu[21]	mPCm(G)	man's brother
žuʔwih[34]	fPCf(G)	woman's sister
raʔwih[34]	aPCb(G)	cross-sex sibling

In the first descending generation, a single term designates lineals, while two terms distinguish the sex of collaterals.

daʔni[21]	C	child
židukụ?[3]	PCCm(G)	nephew
dagwači?[3]	PCCf(G)	niece

In the second descending generation, a single term designates lineals, collaterals, and collaterals of spouse.

| daʔnih[3] ziʔnọ[5] | CC(1,S-) | grandchild |

A single term is used reciprocally between spouses.

| ni[3]kạ[4] | S | spouse |

Two terms distinguishing sex merge spouses of junior lineals, spouses of collaterals, and spouse's younger collateral's spouses, except for spouses of second ascending collaterals and spouses of second descending collaterals of spouse.

| zigatah[34] | CSm(3,yS-) | consanguineal's husband |
| žo[3]ko?[5] | CSf(3,yS-) | consanguineal's wife |

One term designates spouse's younger collaterals, while the same term with preposed father and mother terms designates spouse's older consanguines, merging lineals and collaterals of spouse and spouses of elder consanguines of spouse.

reh[3] čeh[5]	eSPm(3,-S)	father-in-law
ni[3] čeh[5]	eSPf(3,-S)	mother-in-law
žiče[21]	ySP(3)	younger-in-law

TEPEUXILA CUICATEC KINSHIP TERMS

Marjorie Davis

Lineal kinsmen are generally distinguished from collaterals, if siblings are counted with the latter. (An exception will be mentioned below.) Six terms designate lineals, specifying one or two generations' distance from ego, and specifying sex of ancestors (but not of descendants).

čiidá	Pm	father
čääkú	Pf	mother
daiyá	C	child
č'ęę́	PPm(L)	grandfather
čikųʔų́	PPf(L)	grandmother
daiyíínú	CC(L)	grandchild

Elementary terms designate three generations of collaterals, ego's generation and adjacent descending and ascending generations. Siblings are merged terminologically with all consanguineals of ego's generation. Terms differ at a few points for collateral consanguines (and also for some affines) depending upon the sex of ego, males having special terms for uncle and brother. In typical Mixtecan fashion, sex of collateral consanguines is marked (at least in part) regardless of whether they are older or younger than ego.

ʔdiinú	mpCm(G)	man's brother
viʔí	PC(G)	sibling
duunū	mPPCm(G)	man's uncle
diiʔyá	fPPCm(G)	woman's uncle
duudí	PPCf(G)	aunt
daakú	PCCm(G)	nephew
nguučí	PCCf(G)	niece

The exception alluded to above, refers to usage of older Cuicatecs; namely, that collaterals of the second ascending and second descending generations were apparently formerly merged with third generation lineals. The term **dääkwä** designated collaterals of the second descending generation and was also postposed to the grandchild term to designate third descending generation lineals. Similarly, **ndiikú** old was postposed to grandparent terms to designate both lineal great-grandparents and collaterals of the second ascending generation.

The term **ngwäädí** is postposed to a parent or child term to indicate a steprelationship.

The affinal system divides naturally into three sections, terms for spouses (of which there are two), terms for consanguineals of spouse, and terms for spouses of consanguineals. In the latter two sections there are three terms each with somewhat skewed reference which may be the result of change in the system through contact with Spanish kinship terms and concepts.

There is a pair of terms for parents-in-law which disregards the sex of ego, and a term borrowed from Spanish (from *cuñado, -a*) to designate all siblings of spouse. This simple division is skewed by some speakers in that the mother-in-law term also designates brothers of spouse, thus overlapping half the semantic range of the term borrowed from Spanish. Father-in-law would thus seem to have a special place among spouse's kinsmen in having a term which specifies him alone.

In referring to a consanguine's spouse, the wife of a sibling is distinguished from the wife of a son, but the husband of a sister and a daughter are classified together by a single term.

inčą ndiikú	SPm	father-in-law
indáʔą́	SPf,(SPCm)	mother-in-law
kunyáà	SPC(G)	spouse's sibling
daadá	CSm(G2)	consanguineal's husband
adakųų̀nú	CSf	son's wife
čäänú	PCSf(G)	collateral's wife
isáʔà	Sm	husband
nʔdaatá	Sf	wife

A final triad of terms designates the parents of a child's spouse. Women use a single term, while men have two terms which distinguish the sex of their co-parents.

kumbaa	*mCSPm*	*man's co-father*
čudaiyá	*mCSPf*	*man's co-mother*
staiyá	*fCSP*	*woman's co-parent*

Neither lineal affinals of second ascending and descending generations, nor collateral affinals of ascending and descending generations—spouses of consanguineals or consanguineals of spouse—are referred to by Cuicatec kinship terms, although corresponding Spanish terms may be used for them .

TEUTILA CUICATEC KINSHIP TERMS
E. Richard Anderson

The data as presented here were obtained from Fidel Cabrera Torres, a 47-year-old native of Teutila, and were checked with various speakers from San Andrés Teotilalpam. The Teutila dialect of Cuicatec is spoken in the municipios of San Pedro Teutila, San Andrés Teotilalpam, and Santa María Tlalixtac, all of the district of Cuicatlán, Oaxaca. Two terms for parents distinguish their sex, while a single term merges all children.

či³da³	Pm	father
čä³ko³	Pf	mother
da³ya³	C	child

A grandfather term utilizes the father term modified by č?än² old man, and a grand-mother term is the possessed form of če²ku²?un² old woman. The grandchild term utilizes the child term modified by i²no² seat of the emotions.

či³da³ č?än²	PPm(L)	grandfather
če²ku²?un²	PPf(L)	grandmother
da³ya³ i²no²	CC(L)	grandchild

223

Both of the great-grandparent terms are stereotyped noun phrases in which the grandparent terms are modified by a morphophonemic form of **ndi³¹ko⁴** *old* on which the tones of a fossilized tone sandhi pattern occur. The great-grandchild term similarly utilizes the grandchild term modified by the unique morpheme **b?ä⁴to⁴**.

či³da³ č?än² ndi²ko²	*PPPm*	*great-grandfather*
če²ku²?un² ndi²ko²	*PPPf*	*great-grandmother*
da³ya³ i²no² b?ä⁴to⁴	*CCC*	*great-grandchild*

There are three sibling terms differentiated on the basis of sex; one term used between males, one term used between females, and one term used between persons of the opposite sex. These terms extend bilaterally to include ego's cousins (when the social relationship is close) thus disturbing the otherwise typically lineal-type terminological system.

d?i²no⁴	*mPCm(G)*	*man's brother*
ko³?o⁴	*fPCf(G)*	*woman's sister*
k?ä²be²	*aPCb(G)*	*cross-sex sibling*

The term **bi³?i⁴**, however, is more often used in a specific sense to refer to cousins being modified by either of the two sex-distinguishing prepositives **s?an²³** *man* or **t?an¹** *woman*. The general term *kinsman* is distinguished from these cousin terms by the prepositive **?i⁴yan⁴** *people* which is part of the respect system. The terms **pri²mo⁴** and **pri²ma⁴** of Spanish origin are also heard in present-day usage to denote cousins.

s?an²³ bi³?i⁴	*PPCCm(G)*	*male cousin*
t?an¹ bi³?i⁴	*PPCCf(G)*	*female cousin*
?i⁴yan⁴ bi³?i⁴		*kinsman*

Three aunt and uncle terms extend bilaterally to include all collaterals of ascending generations, and their spouses. Similarly, all collateral consanguines of descending generations are classified together with their spouses under two terms which distinguish their sex.

du³no⁴	*mPPCm(1,-S)*	*man's uncle*
d?i³ya³	*fPPCm(1,-S)*	*woman's uncle*
du³de²	*PPCf(1,-S)*	*aunt*
da³kwa⁴	*PCCm(1,-S)*	*nephew*
r?u³če⁴	*PCCf(1,-S)*	*niece*

There are three terms for denoting relationships established by second marriages. The stepfather and stepchild terms utilize the consanguineal term modified by a unique morpheme **be³¹de⁴ ~ be³de⁴**. Consanguineal terms extend to include half siblings, while stepsiblings are not considered relatives.

či³da³ be³¹de⁴	*PSm*	*stepfather*
če²ku³¹ma⁴	*PSf*	*stepmother*
da³ya³ be³de⁴	*SC*	*stepchild*

The term for husband is the resultant form of ča³ʔan³ *man* with a fused element of the respect system. The term for wife literally means *woman*.

| ʔi⁴nča³ʔan³ | Sm | husband |
| ndʔa³ta³ | Sf | wife |

Parents, grandparents, and siblings of spouse are classified together under two terms which distinguish sex. These terms occur in phrases with elements of the respect system. Since the respect system is based primarily on relative age, in practical usage spouse's parent is often distinguished from spouse's sibling by respect elements.

| nča³ʔan³ ndi⁴ko⁴ | SPm(L,G2) | spouse's male consanguine |
| ʔi⁴nda²ʔan² | SPf(L,G2) | spouse's female consanguine |

Spouses of consanguines are denoted by three terms. Husbands of siblings and descendants are merged, while their wives are usually distinguished. Certain women speakers, however, utilize a simpler system in which čä³no³ denotes wives of both siblings and descendants. For such individuals, de⁴ku³¹no⁴ is limited to a man's term for wives of descendants.

da³da³	CSm(L,G2)	consanguineals's husband
de⁴ku³¹no⁴	CSf(L)	descendant's wife
čä³no³	PCSf(G)	sibling's wife

There are three co-parent terms used to denote parents of descendants' spouses. The man's term for co-father is of Spanish origin. The woman's term for co-father literally means *of my child*. The co-mother term literally means *child's mother*.

ko³mba²⁴	mCSPm	man's co-father-in-law
če³da³ya³	fCSPm	woman's co-father-in-law
čä³ko³ da³ya³	CSPf	co-mother-in-law

Five Christian rites are currently practised by which ritual relationships are established. These include baptism, matrimony, ecclesiastical blessing, ceremonial prayer, and burial. The relationships established in such rites are denoted by three terms which utilize consanguineal terms or variants thereof modified by the postpositive na³ʔan³ *important*.

či¹na³ʔan³		godfather
če²ku¹ na³ʔan³		godmother
da³ya³ na³ʔan³		godchild

Persons may sponsor more than one such rite for a given person. This is usually the case in matrimony and burial if the baptismal sponsor is still living. In addition, the co-parent-in-law terms described above extend to include the relationship between such sponsors and those who solicit their sponsorship. The godparents of children-in-law are also considered co-parents.

Referential consanguineal terminology is also used vocatively with relatives and non-relatives. There are a few vocative terms which do not occur in the referential system. Some of which are of non-Cuicatec origin. Cf. ta^2ta^4, $bwe^3li^2to^4$, na^2na^4, $bwe^3li^2ta^4$ used in addressing grandparents and elderly nonrelatives; pa^3pa^{24}, ma^2ma^{24} used in addressing parents, $l?in^1$ *little one*, da^{24} *child (vocative form)*, used in addressing children. However, the most common vocative terms in current usage are those resulting from the ritual relationships described above.

CHAPTER 9
POPOLOCAN KINSHIP TERMS

This chapter reports Mazatec, Ixcatec, and Popoloca kinship terms.

HUAUTLA MAZATEC KINSHIP TERMS
Florence Cowan

A more complete statement concerning Huautla Kinship may be found in Cowan, 1947.

The sex of lineal kinsman is normally only marked in senior generations, though special terms for *son* and *daughter* do exist in addition to the more generic term. Grandparent terms embrace all direct forbears beyond parents, and a grandchild term embraces all direct descendants beyond ego's own children.

n?ai³	*Pm*	*father*
na⁴	*Pf*	*mother*
?nti¹	*C*	*child*
ti³	*Cm*	*son*
co²ti³	*Cf*	*daughter*
n?ai³hča¹	*PPm(L)*	*grandfather*
na⁴hča¹	*PPf(L)*	*grandmother*
?nti¹ntai⁴	*CC(L)*	*grandchild*

Siblings are classified together with all collateral kinsmen of ego's generation. When there is need for further clarification between a sibling or cousin, the phrase **to⁴hnko³**

229

n?ai³-le⁴, to⁴hnko³ na⁴-le⁴, *only one father, only one mother,* may be used to clarify that siblings are meant. The term **nco¹** *younger sibling* has no corresponding term to express the relationship of older sibling.

nc?e⁴	*PCm(G)*	*brother*
nti³čha³	*PCf(G)*	*sister*
nco¹	*yPC(G)*	*younger sibling*

The aunt and uncle terms classify together (distinguishing only sex) all persons referred to by parents and grandparents as siblings. Nephew and niece terms refer to all descendants of persons referred to by ego as siblings.

ci³ni³	*PPCm(1)*	*uncle*
nčo³khǫa³	*PPCf(1)*	*aunt*
ti³kha⁴?me³	*PCCm(1)*	*nephew*
co²ti³kha⁴?me³	*PCCf(1)*	*niece*

Relationships established when a person marries a second time or takes a second wife (polygyny is common practice in Mazatec culture) are specified by use of consanguineal terminology plus the morpheme **-hǫ** *on the surface of,* as in **n?ai³hǫ³** *stepfather;* **ti³hǫ³** *stepson;* **nc?e⁴hǫ³** *stepbrother, half brother,* etc. Both stepsiblings and half siblings are classified together in this manner.

The terms for parents-in-law are those of the consanguineal terminology with the morpheme **-ča¹** postposed. While unique terms refer to siblings of spouse, spouses of siblings and of children are merged under two terms which distinguish only sex.

n?ai³ča¹	*SPm*	*father-in-law*
na⁴ča¹	*SPf*	*mother-in-law*
čha⁴	*SPCm(G)*	*spouse's brother*
šo⁴nko¹	*SPCf(G)*	*spouse's sister*
ška⁴?nta³	*CSm(G2)*	*consanguineal's husband*
ha⁴?nta³	*CSf(G2)*	*consanguineal's wife*

-kao⁴ is postposed to these latter terms to refer to a spouse of spouse's collateral and the parents of a married couple refer to one another by Mazatec forms of the Spanish terms *compadre* and *comadre* to which the morphemes **-ča¹** and **-kao⁴** have been postposed. Two terms designate spouses.

ška⁴?nta³kao⁴	*SPCSm(G)*	*spouse's sister's husband*
ha⁴?nta³kao⁴	*SPCSf(G)*	*spouse's brother's wife*
mpa²⁺ča¹kao⁴	*CSPm*	*co-father*
ko²rre⁴ča¹kao⁴	*CSPf*	*co-mother*
š?į⁴	*Sm*	*husband*
čhǫ⁴²	*Sf*	*wife*

JALAPA DE DIAZ MAZATEC
KINSHIP TERMS

Paul L. Kirk
California State University, Northridge

Jalapa de Díaz Mazatec is spoken by approximately 8000 people in the District of Tuxtepec, Oaxaca, Mexico. Data for this paper were gathered on field trips during 1954 to 1966 under the auspices of the Summer Institute of Linguistics. Earlier studies of Mazatec kinship appear in Cowan (1947) which discusses Huautla de Jiménez Mazatec reference terms; Kirk (1962) gives a componential analysis of Jalapa de Díaz Mazatec address terms; Kirk (1966a) describes many of the basic features of both the address and reference terminology of Jalapa de Díaz Mazatec as they apply to social structure.

For a discussion of Mazatec phonology see Pike and Pike's (1947) seminal article that discusses Huautla de Jiménez syllable structure (similiar features occur in most of the Mazatec dialects); Jamieson (1977a, 1977b) describes the phonology of Chiquihuitlán Mazatec; a few general features of Jalapa de Díaz Mazatec are discussed in Kirk (1966b), but a detailed presentation of the vowels is found in Schram and Pike (1978) and I presented a similiar analysis at the 1972 annual meeting of the American Anthropological Association. This paper utilizes the Schram and Pike analysis except that, for orthographic purposes, I use *e* for the low front vowel.

A few general remarks about Jalapa Mazatec morphology need to be made before turning to the kinship terms themselves. First, the only class of nouns which are obligatorily possessed, occurring with a pronominal enclitic, are kinship terms of refer-

231

ence. When a kinship term occurs without such an enclitic, its meaning is vocative or is generalized in such a way that it no longer specifies a kinship relationship. For example, the word for husband, when unpossessed, may refer to any male person, the word for wife to any female, and the word for daughter to any young girl. Nevertheless, in the interest of economy and clarity, the kinship terms are cited in this paper without their pronominal endings.

Second, Mazatec nominals do not ordinarily differentiate number, although a very small class of nouns do. Most of the members of this class are kinship terms and only a few of these terms obligatorily indicate number. The following forms are among those which are specifically singular or plural. All except **ča²** and **hmi²** can occur with possessive enclitic to designate kinsmen, all of them can occur alone in general reference with the meanings specified and, more importantly for the purposes of this paper, all may be compounded with certain kinship terms (or personal names) to narrow reference by number, age, sex of referent, and sex of speaker.

nda³	*singular, male referent, male speaker*
ha¹	*plural, male referent, male speaker*
ča²	*singular, adult male referent, female speaker*
hmi²	*plural, adult male referent, female speaker*
ti²	*singular, young male referent, female speaker*
na³	*singular, female referent*
hmi²	*plural, female referent*

Consanguineal Kinsmen

Consanguineal kinsmen form an important unit in Mazatec society since exogamous marriage is the ideal (Kirk 1966a:477-78). There are two terms for father, the first one listed being the more basic since it occurs in compounds with other forms to indicate step or affinal relationships (discussed below). A single term designates mother.

na³ʔmi², **ʔei¹te¹**	*Pm*	*father*
na³	*Pf*	*mother*

A large number of generic and specific terms may be used in reference to a child, distinguishing singular from plural, male from female, younger child from adult child, and in some cases sex of the speaker.

First of all, there are four basic terms for child—a generic term, two terms for sons differing by sex of ego, and one for daughters.

nti¹, ti¹	*C*	*child*
nda³	*mCm*	*man's son*
ti²	*fCm*	*woman's son*
ca³khi¹, ʔi³khi¹	*Cf*	*daughter*

These terms generally make reference to adult children, and occur regularly with **-či¹** *little* when referring to younger children. Tone changes occur in the presence of the diminutive ending (i.e., the final stem tone glides to low tone).

nti¹³či¹, ti¹³či¹	C(young)	younger child
nda³či¹	mCm(young)	man's younger son
ti²³či¹	fCm(young)	woman's younger son
ca³khį¹³či¹, ʔi³khį¹³či¹	Cf(young)	younger daughter

The four terms also occur in plural form, both in regular and diminutive form. The diminutive ending in the plural is -nti¹. In the case of the most generic child term, this plural ending may be added directly to the singular term, or it may be added to a special plural form of the term.

nti¹nti¹, ti¹nti¹	C(young,plural)	younger children
ʔi³sti²	C(plural)	children
ʔi³sti²nti¹	C(young,plural)	younger children

The first of the above terms is used in its entirety as the diminutive of the plural term for a man's son when postposed to ha¹.

| ha¹ | mCm(plural) | man's sons |
| ha¹ti¹nti¹ | mCm(young,plural) | man's younger sons |

The woman's plural term for sons occurs in two forms in reference to adults, all ending in nčha¹, only one of which occurs with the diminutive ending.

hmi²nčha¹	fCm(plural)	woman's sons
ti²³sti²nčha¹, ʔi³sti²nčha¹	fCm(plural)	woman's sons
ti²³sti²nčha¹nti¹, ʔi³sti²nčha¹nti¹	fCm(young, plural)	woman's younger sons

The plural terms for daughters are based on the plural form of the generic child term and a form which also appears in a plural word for women: mi³nčhį¹.

| ʔi³sti²nčhį¹ | Cf(plural) | daughters |
| ʔi³si²nčhį¹nti¹ | Cf(young,plural) | younger daughters |

Two final terms refer to infants, distinguishing sex of ego. Both are based on the generic child term in its singular form, with male speakers postposing čhy³¹ wife and female speakers postposing nta² soft.

| nti¹³čhy³¹, ti¹³čhy³¹ | | baby, male speaker |
| nti¹nta², ti¹nta² | | baby, female speaker |

Grandparents are designated by postposing ča¹ old to a parent term, and great-grandparents by further postposing khi² far (of the two father terms, only na³ʔmi² occurs when khi² is postposed). Grandchildren are designated by a phrase of two child terms. The first word of the phrase designates the category of the grandchild while the second word indicates the category of ego's child, e.g., daughter of my son.

There are two sibling terms—one for brother and one for sister. The sister term occurs in a constant two-syllable form, but the brother term consists of a final syllable to which is preposed one of the five forms introduced at the beginning of this paper which denote a male referent but which also specify number, age, and sex of speaker, namely, **nda³**, **ha¹**, **ča²**, **hmi²**, or **ti²**. The first of these is used below as a citation form.

nda³nc?e¹	*PCm(singular)*	*brother*
ni²čha²	*PCf*	*sister*

Although the sister term is fixed in form and does not occur without the penultimate syllable cited above, it too may be narrowed in reference by compounding with parent and child terms introduced above.

na³ni²čha²	*eʃPCf*	*woman's elder sister*
ca³khį¹ni²čha²	*yʃPCf*	*woman's younger sister*
?i³sti²ni²čha²	*ʃPCf(plural)*	*woman's sisters*

A female speaker may also prepose **?i³sti²** to the brother term rather than **hmi²** to denote a plural referent.

Two unique terms designate uncle and aunt while modified sibling terms designate nephew and niece. The modifier of the latter two terms is possibly from the plural form of the generic term for child.

ci²ni²	*PPCm*	*uncle*
ču²kwhą²	*PPCf*	*aunt*
nc?e²sti²	*PCCm*	*nephew*
ni²čha²sti²	*PCCf*	*niece*

Cousins are most frequently designated as **ši²nkhį̇ą¹**, a term which may also be used to designate any distant consanguineal kinsman, but some speakers extend the nephew and niece terms to cousins while others simply identify them with a phrase *child of uncle* or *child of aunt*.

Affinal Kinsmen

A bound morpheme postposed to parent terms distinguishes father and mother of spouse. (Of the two father terms, only **na³?mi²** occurs in this construction.)

na³?mi²nči¹?ya²	*SPm*	*father-in-law*
na³nči¹?ya²	*SPf*	*mother-in-law*

All other kinsmen of ego's spouse are designated by descriptive phrases, such as *uncle of my wife*, or *spouse of the uncle of my wife*.

Three forms designate the spouse of a consanguineal kinsman, all but one occurring obligatorily with the forms introduced at the beginning of the paper which specify number, sex of referent, and sex of ego. (The form **ti²**, which specifies a junior kinsman, does not occur with these affinal terms.) The full set of compounds is presented below, as is the third (daughter-in-law) term which does not occur with the preposed morphemes.

nda³čhe³	mPCSm(singular)	man's brother-in-law
ha¹čhe³	mPCSm(plural)	man's brothers-in-law
ča²čhe³	fPCSm(singular)	woman's brother-in-law
hmi²čhe³	fPCSm(plural)	woman's brothers-in-law
na³čhe³	PCSf(singular)	sister-in-law
hmi²čhe³	PCSf(plural)	sisters-in-law
nda³ška²nta²	mCSm(singular)	man's son-in-law
ha¹ška²nta²	mCSm(plural)	man's sons-in-law
ča²ška²nta²	fCSm(singular)	woman's son-in-law
hmi²ška²nta²	fCSm(plural)	woman's sons-in-law
n³ta²	CSf	daughter(s)-in-law

There are two elementary terms for husband and wife.

| š?i³ | Sm | husband |
| čhụ³¹ | Sf | wife |

Stepkinsmen

The morpheme **-hụ²** *on the surface* is compounded with parent or grandparent terms to indicate a stepkinsman (of the two father terms, only **na³?mi²** occurs in this construction). In the case of stepchildren, the ending **-š?ạ³** *poor* occurs with any child term. (Half siblings are not distinguished terminologically from full siblings.)

na³?mi²ča¹hụ²	PPSm	stepgrandfather
na³ča¹hụ²	PPSf	stepgrandmother
na³?mi²hụ²	PSm	stepfather
na³hụ²	PSf	stepmother
nti¹š?ạ³,...	SC	stepchild

Ritual Kinsmen

The morpheme **-ča²kụ²** *baptize, holy* is compounded with parent and child terms (only **na³?mi²** of the two father terms) to designate ritual relationships between generations, while forms based on Spanish *compadre* and *comadre* designate such relationships between generation peers.

na³?mi²ča²kụ²		godfather
na³ča²kụ²		godmother
nti¹ča²kụ²,...		godchild
mba²³		ritual co-father
ma²ra³		ritual co-mother

Deceased Kinsmen

The morpheme **nte²-** *dead* is compounded with kinship terms to specify a deceased kinsman, as in **nte²na³?mi²** *deceased father*.

CHIQUIHUITLAN MAZATEC KINSHIP TERMS

Allan R. Jamieson
Carole Jamieson

Three elementary terms denote parents and child; three additional terms grandparents and grandchild, the latter extending lineally to all kinsmen beyond the first ascending and first descending generations.

na⁴ʔmi³⁴	Pm	*father*
na·³⁴	Pf	*mother*
ki³ʔnti², ni⁴šti³⁴ *(pl.)*	C	*child*
nča³wa¹⁴	PPm(L)	*grandfather*
či³kụʔ³¹⁴	PPf(L)	*grandmother*
ki³ʔnti²ntai²⁴	CC(L)	*grandchild*

Attributive **ča³nka¹⁴** is postposed to grandparent and aunt and uncle terms to designate extended generational ranges.

Four terms distinguish the sex of collaterals of ego's generation (including siblings) and of the first ascending generation, while two terms, which do not mark sex of kinsman, designate any collateral or a junior collateral.

ʔncä⁴	PCm(G)	brother
ti³čha³	PCf(G)	sister
ši²khį²	PC(0)	collateral kinsman
ci³ni³⁴	PPCm(1)	uncle
nču³khyą³⁴	PPCf(1)	aunt
ki³ʔnti² nču²⁴ʔme²	PCC(1)	junior collateral

Terms for affinals designate sex of parents of spouse, of siblings of spouse, of spouse of child or sibling, and of spouse.

na⁴ʔmi³⁴ nča³ʔya³⁴	SPm	father-in-law
na⁴ʔya³⁴	SPf	mother-in-law
čha⁴	SPCm(G)	brother-in-law
šu⁴nkу²	SPCf(G)	sister-in-law
ška³ʔnta³⁴	CSm(G2)	consanguineal's husband
ha⁴ʔnta³⁴	CSf(G2)	consanguineal's wife
šį?³⁴	Sm	husband
čhу⁴²	Sf	wife

The morpheme **-hñu³⁴** *dark* may be added to consanguineal terms to indicate relationships established through secondary marriage, as in **na⁴ʔmi³⁴hñu¹⁴** *stepfather*. In one case, however, there is a special phonologically fused, single-syllable form, namely, **nuh³⁴** *stepmother*.

IXCATEC KINSHIP TERMS
†María Teresa Fernández de Miranda

The following data have been extracted from Fernández de Miranda (1961), and present only basic denotata of terms without extensions. They are presented without comment.

ta¹ta¹	*Pm*	*father*
na²ʔa¹	*Pf*	*mother*
ʔnje¹	*C*	*child*
na²ʔmi¹ci¹	*PPm*	*grandfather*
na²ci¹	*PPf*	*grandmother*
ʔnje¹ye¹	*CC*	*grandchild*
ʔnje¹ ša²šku²	*CCC*	*great-grandchild*
ki²či¹	*PCm*	*brother*
kwa²ki²či¹	*PCf*	*sister*
ci²ña¹	*PPCm*	*uncle*
kwa²ʔa¹	*PPCf*	*aunt*
na²ʔmi¹čʔa¹	*SPm*	*father-in-law*
na²čʔa¹	*SPf*	*mother-in-law*

239

ška¹ʔnda¹	CS	child's spouse
nda²ba¹	Sm	husband
kʔwa¹-	Sf	wife

EASTERN POPOLOCA KINSHIP TERMS

Alice Beebe
Marjorie Kalstrom

Six terms suffice to refer to any consanguine, three terms for lineals, and three for collaterals (considering siblings as other than lineals). Parent terms merge all ascending lineals, and the child term all descending lineals. Three sibling terms merge the remaining consanguines and corresponding affinals, distinguishing sex of those older than ego.

t?a²na¹³	*Pm(L)*	*father*
na⁴na¹³	*Pf(L)*	*mother*
šhạ⁴na²³	*C(L)*	*child*
sa⁴na¹³	*ePCm(0,S)*	*elder brother*
kha³na¹³	*ePCf(0,S)*	*elder sister*
ki¹či²na¹³	*yPC(0,S)*	*younger sibling*

These terms are presented with first person singular possession for comparative purposes, but such usage would in fact be disrespectful in designating parents. To indicate proper respect for grandparents, first plural possession **-ni²** is used and **tata/nana** forms are postposed. (The form of the pronoun also results in vowel fronting of the parent terms.)

241

i³t?e¹ni² ta¹²da² $PPm(L)$ *my (respected) grandfather*
i²⁴ne¹ni² na¹²na² $PPf(L)$ *my (respected) grandmother*

Three additional terms may be used to specifically designate lineal consanguines as being more than one generation distant from ego. The či⁴ of grandparent terms means *old*.

t?a¹či⁴na²³ $PPm(L)$ *grandfather*
na¹či⁴na²³ $PPf(L)$ *grandmother*
šha⁴nti²na¹³ $CC(L)$ *grandchild*

Two final terms specify that older collaterals are not siblings, merging consanguineals and affinals. Sibling terms used for such older collaterals indicate social proximity and endearment, as when such collaterals live in the same residence with ego.

ši⁴ni²na¹³ $ePPCm(I,0,S)$ *elder male collateral*
khoa⁴na³ $ePPCf(I,0,S)$ *elder female collateral*

Although sex of alter is not indicated in the basic terms for younger consanguines, it may be marked by additional prefixes or endings. The suffix -čhi indicates females and ndo³wa³ indicates males when postposed to the child term. tha- indicates females and č?i- males when prefixed to the younger sibling term.

There is a single term for senior lineals of spouse, and another for the spouses of junior lineals. The terms for spouse are possessed forms of the words for *man* and *woman*.

č?a⁴ $SP(L)$ *parent-in-law*
ki¹nta⁴ $CSm(L)$ *son-in-law*
ti¹ki²nta⁴ $CSf(L)$ *daughter-in-law*
ši¹⁴ Sm *husband*
čhi² Sf *wife*

Third person possessed forms of several of the above terms are presented below as possibly being of interest for comparative purposes.

sa⁴we¹ni² $ePCm(0,S)$ *elder brother*
kha⁴we¹ni² $ePCf(0,S)$ *elder sister*
ki¹čo¹ni² $yPC(0,S)$ *younger sibling*
ši⁴ne¹ni² $ePPCm(I,0,S)$ *elder male collateral*
khoe⁴e²ni² $ePPCf(I,0,S)$ *elder female collateral*

WESTERN POPOLOCA KINSHIP TERMS
Ann F. Williams

Western Popoloca kinsmen of Otlaltepec, Puebla, Mexico are divided into three classes: lineals, colineals, and ablineals. Lineal consanguineals are divided by generation, elementary terms serving to denote those of the first ascending and descending generations. Second generation terms are built on those of the first, and third generation may be specified by adding šà̧ȟ ̧ to the second generation terms.

t?ánâ	Pm	*father*
n?ánâ	Pf	*mother*
čhà̧?nà	C	*child*
t?áčí̧nà	PPm(L,S)	*grandfather*
n?áčí̧nà	PPf(L,S)	*grandmother*
čhá̧ndínâ	CC(L,S)	*grandchild*

Colloquial Spanish *apá* and *amá* are used alternatively as parent terms, and with postposed elements to denote grandparents.

āpá sīnō?nâ	PPm(L,S)	*grandfather*
āmá sítá?nâ	PPf(L,S)	*grandmother*

243

Colineals (siblings) and ablineals (collaterals other than siblings) are classified according to age relative to that of ego, with sex being distinguished for older relatives only. A
colineal or ablineal of spouse, or spouse of ego's colineal or ablineal, is referred to by a
colineal or ablineal term, using the first plural (exclusive of addressee) possessive
pronoun.

s?ónâ	ePCm(S)	elder brother
khǒnâ	ePCf(S)	elder sister
?ìčą̂	yPC(S)	younger sibling
čî?nínâ	ePPCm(I,0,S)	distant elder brother
khoã?nà	ePPCf(I,0,S)	distant elder sister
čãw?ę̀	yPCC(I,0,S)	distant younger sibling

The terms for ablineals are all but disappearing, being replaced by three forms
modified from Spanish.

tiú?nâ	ePPCm (I,0,S)	distant elder brother
tiá?nâ	ePPCf(I,0,S)	distant elder sister
prímú?nâ	yPCC(I,0,S)	distant younger sibling

Sex of alter is marked in basic terms only for older kinsman. Special additional forms
may be postposed to terms for younger kinsmen to indicate their sex: šą̂šî *male* and šą̀čî
female. There is also a series of prefixes which indicates sex of alter with varying
degrees of respect: čʔî- and thą̀- refer to male and female, respectively, with highest
respect; šî- and rî- refer to male and female, respectively, with moderate respect; and
čhą̀- is used to refer to youngsters of either sex.

A single term merges both parents of spouse, but spouses of children are distinguished
as to their sex by a basic term **gīndā** for males which is modified by **tà-** to designate
females. This same term **gīndā** also occurs with postposed term for colineal or ablineal to
designate the spouse of a colineal or ablineal (as well as the spouse of a colineal or
ablineal of spouse).

čʔánâ	SP	parent-in-law
gīndā?nà	CSm(G2)	son-in-law
tàgīndā?nà	CSf(G2)	daughter-in-law

The sex-marking forms mentioned above also function as terms for spouse. A third
term merges parents of a child's spouse.

šî?nà	Sm	husband
čî?nà	Sf	wife

There are a few archaic kinship terms known by older members of the community, but
which are not commonly heard.

sã?wê	ePCm	his elder brother
gíčú	yPC	his younger sibling
yátā	SPm	father-in-law

NORTHERN POPOLOCA
KINSHIP TERMS

Polly Machin
Sharon Stark

The following data were obtained from Juan Salvador, age 27, a native of San Marcos Tlacoyalco, Puebla, Mexico. The system of kinship reference distinguishes lineal consanguines, lineal affinals, and collateral kinsmen (merging consanguines and affinals) in the three central generations—first ascending, ego's, and first descending—if siblings are considered lineal (or co-lineal) as opposed to collateral. The collateral terms extend indefinitely to all degrees of collaterality in each generation.

Three terms denote parents and child. The second parent terms are unique unpossessed forms. All other terms are obligatorily possessed.

n̯odana, n̯oda?a	Pm	*father*
hạnana, hạna?a	Pf	*mother*
šạ?na	C	*child*

A single sibling term does not distinguish sex of sibling, but alternate terms that do may be used to indicate respect for older brother or sister. The latter terms are very formal and seldom heard.

šǫčiǫ	PC	sibling
saona	ePCm	elder brother
haona	ePCf	elder sister

Parent-in-law terms are based on parent terms and nča; children-in-law terms on the child terms and kįnṭa (for males) or ḍąinṭa (for females).

ntǫnčana	SPm	father-in-law
hąnčana	SPf	mother-in-law
šąkįnṭaʔna	CSm	son-in-law
šąḍąinṭaʔna	CSf	daughter-in-law

Parent terms occur with oešį to designate the parent of child's spouse.

| ntǫoešįna | CSPm | co-father-in-law |
| hąoešįna | CSPf | co-mother-in-law |

Two terms designate male and female collaterals of the first ascending generation, and a third all collaterals of the first descending generation.

činina	PPCm(G,S)	uncle
hoaʔna	PPCf(G,S)	aunt
šąkǫęʔę	PCC(G,S)	junior collateral

In ego's generation, sex of kinsman is distinguished for cousin, sibling-in-law, and spouse.

šiprimona	PPCCm(G,S)	male cousin
nčiprimana	PPCCf(G,S)	female cousin
šikoňadona	PCSm(V)	brother-in-law
nčikoňadana	PCSf(V)	sister-in-law
šišiʔna	Sm	husband
čiʔna	Sf	wife

Beyond the first ascending and first descending generations, lineals, collaterals, consanguines, and affinals are all merged. Three terms based on parent and child terms classify all kinsmen of two or more generations' distance from ego.

ntǫoelitona	PPm(1,S)	grandfather
hąoelitana	PPf(1,S)	grandmother
šąntina	CC(1,S)	grandchild

The third ascending generation is specified by postposing šaçhę to grandparent terms, and the fourth by postposing iča šaçhę. The spouse of a lineal grandchild can be distinguished from a true grandchild by apposing the child-in-law term to the grandchild term with both terms being possessed.

šikįnṭaʔna šąntina   *my grandson-in-law*
                                                              (lit. my son-in-law, my grandchild)

With few exceptions, the terms are made up of three elements. The root element, in most cases, is preceded by a form which indicates sex or rank of the kinsman. For example, a number of the terms, particularly those for kinsmen of ego's generation, may occur with **ši** *man* or **nči** *woman* to designate an adult kinsman—typically, a married adult with children. The diminutive ending **-čhą** is added to this preposed element when the kinsman is not yet fully adult. The child term may also be preposed in this way when the designated kinsman does not yet have children.

šičhą čią   *(young) brother*
nčičhą čią   *(young) sister*
šąprimona   *(young) male cousin*

The two elements which distinguish sex and which are preposed to parent, parent-in-law and grandparent terms, **nṭo** and **hą**, occur elsewhere in the language suffixed to pronouns to designate kinship reference. Thus, **heʔe-nṭo** *he (father or grandfather)* and **heʔe-hą** *she (mother or grandmother)*.

The terms for older siblings, uncle, aunt, spouse, and child are the only ones which do not occur with these preposed elements, but the child term itself is one of the elements that may be preposed to other terms.

The diminutive terms for man and woman presented above may also be possessed directly to designate an offspring of a particular sex.

sičhąʔna   *my son*
nčičhąʔna   *my daughter*

The root of each term follows this preposed element. The roots of the parent terms are presumably from *tata* and *nana*, though this is not certain. The roots for grandparent, cousin, and sibling-in-law terms are from their Spanish counterparts.

The final element of each kinship term is a possessive pronoun. In most instances it has the form **-na** or **-ʔna** in the first person. The exceptions are the term for sibling and junior collateral where the pronominal element cannot be easily segmented from the root. The forms of these two terms with possession marked for either second or third person are **šąčo** *your/his sibling* and **šąkoę** *your/his junior collateral*.

With the exception of two terms which distinguish the sex of children-in-law, the pattern seems to be to distinguish sex of kinsmen of ascending generations but to ignore it for kinsmen of descending generations.

CHAPTER 10
OTOPAMEAN KINSHIP TERMS

This chapter reports Otomí, Mazahua, Pame, and Chichimeca kinship
terms.

1640 OTOMI KINSHIP TERMS

The following terms have been extracted from Ecker (1930), an unpublished manuscript which includes an appendix listing Otomí kinship terminology which Ecker collected from an anonymous unpublished dictionary bearing the date 30 January, 1640. This latter manuscript is said to bear evidence of emendations made in January, 1669, and is stated to be located in the *Biblioteca Nacional de México*.

Ecker extracted all the kinship terms he could find in the dictionary. Starting with a section which apparently deals particularly with kinship terms, he then lists all other data in the numerical order of the pages upon which they appear. He lists the terms making only those changes "imposed by the limitations of modern printing," indicating in footnotes (1) that the 1669 editor changed some t's to d's in several words (among them **idą** *woman's elder brother*) and (2) that the dictionary uses ö for "open o" and ę for "what we usually write as ö." He then states his intention of transcribing the latter as ǫ, but note that ę does occur in his list.

The data taken from Ecker's appendix are listed here in Appendix I, in English translation (from Spanish). They have been rearranged to facilitate comparison of different spellings and statements regarding the ranges of reference of each term. There is a good deal of variation in the transcription of vowels, in particular, especially as to the presence or choice of diacritics.

A number of ambiguities in the Spanish also present some problems for the English translation (and for our analysis). First, certain masculine nouns (e.g., *hijos*) may have reference to males only (i.e., *sons*) or they may have been meant to refer more generically to children, without sex differentiation. Second, the phrase "sean mayores o menores" has been interpreted as referring to relative age (whether older or younger), whereas in at least some cases there is reason to believe the intent must have been *whether an adult or a minor.*

This paper presents an interpretation of the data found in the appendix of Ecker's paper without, however, engaging in a full-scale discussion of the exegetical process that has given the present result. The reader can assess the validity of this interpretation by reference to the data appended to this paper. The orthography used in the body of this paper has been chosen to conform more closely to those of related modern systems reported in this volume.

Three terms designated parents and child, distinguishing the sex of the former only, with two additional terms serving to distinguish the sex of the latter.

htä	*Pm*	*father*
mé	*Pf*	*mother*
bącį	*C*	*child*
t?ï	*Cm*	*son*
t?įšų	*Cf*	*daughter*

A set of three grandkin terms similarly distinguished only the sex of seniors, but a fourth term was used by female ego for her grandchildren. In the case of grandfather, two forms of the term are apparently based on the father term. The terms seem to have extended to collaterals and ascending generations beyond the second from ego, especially when modified. Specifically, terms with **bo-** designated kinsmen of beyond the second ascending and descending generations.

dąhta, šihta	*PPm(1)*	*grandfather*
dącu	*PPf(1)*	*grandmother*
bähią	*CC(1)*	*grandchild*
bähto	*fCC(1)*	*woman's grandchild*
bošihta	*PPPm(1)*	*great-grandfather*
bocu	*PPPf(1)*	*great-grandmother*
boabähią	*CCC(1)*	*great-grandchild*

Four terms for elder siblings marked the sex of both ego and alter. A fifth term for younger siblings did not mark sex of either.

khuądą	*emPCm*	*man's elder brother*
įdą	*efPCm*	*woman's elder brother*
khųhuä	*efPCf*	*woman's elder sister*
nkhų	*emPCf*	*man's elder sister*
hkų	*yPC*	*younger sibling*

Three terms (at least) existed for collaterals of the first ascending generation, and four existed for the first descending generation.

mo, ue	PPCm	uncle
hi	xPPCf, PPCf	aunt
bämo	=mPCC	man's brother's child
bäue	xmPCC, PCCm	man's sister's child
bäzici	=fPCC	woman's sister's child
bähi	xfPCC	woman's brother's child

The evidence for the denotation of terms for senior and junior collaterals is also inconsistent through the manuscript. **mo** and **hi** are stated to be the terms for *uncle* and *aunt*, respectively. Later, **ue** is offered as an *uncle* term, and **hi** is presented as though it were limited to *sister of father*, but no corresponding *sister of mother* term is given. Similarly, the terms for junior collateral are presented in various ways.

Sex of both ego and alter again came into play in four separate elementary terms for parents-in-law, although only sex of alter was marked in child-in-law terms.

hią	mSPm	man's father-in-law
cä	fSPm	woman's father-in-law
hkɔ	fSPf	woman's mother-in-law
hto	mSPf	man's mother-in-law
bäąhą	CSm	son-in-law
c?įhuä	CSf	daughter-in-law

Sibling-in-law terms tended to a pattern of four terms distinguishing sex of both ego and alter, denoting both spouse of sibling and sibling of spouse. One of the terms, however, is clearly stated to have designated brothers-in-law of ego of either sex. A fifth term was used between siblings-in-law of the same sex.

hkó	PCSm(V)	brother-in-law
mɔ	fPCSm(V)	woman's brother-in-law
mųdų	fPCSf(V)	woman's sister-in-law
bähpo	mPCSf(V)	man's sister-in-law
bäcä	aPCSa(V)	same-sex sibling-in-law

There were also special terms for men who married sisters, for women who married brothers, and for parents whose respective children married each other.

mihki	mSPCSm	man's co-brother-in-law
minmakhɔ	fSPCSf	woman's co-sister-in-law
chɔni	CSP	co-parent-in-law

Finally, there was a term for *husband*, but a clear term for *wife* does not appear in the manuscript.

dąmé	Sm	husband

Appendix I

nóhtä, anhtä *Father, male or female ego.*
nóhǫhtä *Stepfather.*
nónmé, anmé *Mother, male or female ego.*
nohǫnmé, nóhǫtçu *Stepmother.*
nóbëü, ambëü *Parent or ancestor.*
ambãtçĩ, anttü, anttübãtçĩ, nomé bãtçĩ *Child.*
andabãtçĩ *Only child.*
nãdäyonbãtçĩ, bëttónbãtçĩ *First-born or older child.*
nanyohobãtçĩ, ninëhtënnaui noccómãdã, noyãtziui noccómãdã *Second child.*
anomëgui, nonzünxĩyã *Last-born child.*
no xũbãtçĩ, anttinxũ *Daughter.*
nãdayonttĩnxũ, mãdãttinnxũ *First-born or older daughter.*
yogo, yocquёnyã, yogocqũnyã [sic], dangandögui eyohó *Twins.*

no xĩhtá, no dãhtá *Grandfather, male or female ego.*
mabó-xihta, madatehta *Grandfather's brother.*
madahta, bódahta *Grandmother's brother.*
nodãhtä *Brother of grandfather or grandmother.*
andãtçu, madãtçu, andãçũ *Grandmother.*
ãndãtçu. mabódatçu *Sister of grandfather or grandmother.*
nebёhtó *Grandson or granddaughter, female ego.*
nabёhiã *Grandson or granddaughter.*
emabó a hiã, bёphä *Descending grandchildren.*

bóxihtä *Great-grandfather, male or female ego.*
nobóhtähtä, no bósihtä *Great-grandfather.*
bótçu *Great-grandmother, male or female ego.*
nobódatçu, nobótçu *Great-grandmother.*
nonbó abёhiã *Great-grandchild.*
nohcũ a bóabёhiã *Great-great-grandchild.*

yo chuãdã *Elder brother, male ego.*
anqhuãdã, madaqhuada *Elder brother.*
mãchuãdabodahta *Great-grandfather's brother.*
yódichuada *Brother of mother or father, male ego.*
mahǫ qhuãdã *Step-brother.*
yó idã, mi ĩdã, *Elder brother, female ego.*
mi ĩdã bódahta *Great-grandfather's brother, female ego.*
omada *Elder brother, or elder brother of female ego.*
o madã *Elder sister of male ego.*
obǫttö *Elder brother.*
yó chũhhuё, michũhuё *Elder sister, female ego.*
michũhuё bódatçu *Great-grandfather's sister, female ego.*
yódihuihuё *Sister of father or mother, female ego.*
ma hǫ chũnhhuё *Step-sister.*

yónchu, machū, omadā manchū, omadādenchū *Elder sister, male ego.*
mimanchū bódatçu *Great-grandfather's sister.*
yó hcu *Younger brother or sister, male ego.*
mahcū, denchū, mimanchū, mitzühcanchū *Younger sister, male ego.*
mihcū *Younger sister, [?] ego.*
mihcu, mihcuîdā, mi ŷdāhcū *Younger brother.*
nohcu, anz[?]xîyā, obëphä *Younger brother.*

anuë *Brother of father or mother.*
maué *Father's brother, "common to all."*
na bëuë *Son of brother or sister, daughter of sister of male ego.*
an dä bëué *Son of sister of female ego.*
nabëué *Brother's son.*
mā mó *Uncle, older or younger, male or female ego.*
an dä bëmó *Brother's son, older or younger, male ego.*
mahi *Aunt, older or younger, male or female ego.*
ānhi *Sister of father or mother.*
mihi, dehi *Father's sister.*
mahi, mi nabëhi *sister's daughter, female ego.*
mi na bëhi *Brother's son, older or younger, female ego.*
mi na bëzitçi *Sister's son, older or younger, female ego.*

māhiā, mahîa, nohiā *Father-in-law, male ego.*
mitçä *Father-in-law, older or younger, female ego.*
andäbetçä *Sibling's husband or spouse's brother, male ego.*
mi nabëtçä *Sibling's wife or spouse's sister, female ego.*
mahtó, nohtó *Mother-in-law, older or younger, male ego.*
mihcö *Mother-in-law, older or younger, female ego.*
manbëaha, nonbëāhā *Son-in-law, older or younger, male or female ego.*
Also means *sleepy head* (Cf. **āhā** *to sleep*).
nonbëāhā a bëhiā *Grandson-in-law.*
mātzîhhuë *Daughter-in-law, older or younger, male or female ego.*

mahco, nihco, nohco *Brother-in-law, male ego.*
mihco *Brother-in-law, older or younger, female ego.*
misco *Sister's husband, female ego.*
mi mūdū *Brother's wife or husband's sister, older or younger, female ego.*
mi mö *Husband's brother, female ego.*
nabëhpo, ān dabëhpo, mi cuñada *Sister-in-law, male ego.*
andäbëhpó *Brother's wife, older or younger, male ego, whether or not she is wife's sister.*

tçhönî *Parent of child's spouse, older or younger, male or female.*
mi mîhqui, mamîhqui, adinuiçem *Wife's sister's husband, male ego, if not his brother.*
mimimachö, mi mînmāchö *Husband's brother's wife, female ego, if not her sister.*

andānmé, mamendanxū *Husband.*
nó mënthāhtî, ma nodinthahti *Husband or married woman*
mamendāmé, mamë enthāhtî, no nenthāhtiui *Husband's woman.*

EASTERN OTOMI KINSHIP TERMS
Katherine Voigtlander

Eastern Otomí is here represented by data from San Gregorio, Huehuetla. There are minor differences in just about every town. The kinship terminology classifies consanguineal relatives bilaterally with lineal-type terminology in all generations except ego's.

There are two parent terms, and one child term, plus separate terms for son and daughter.

The term for mother is homophonous with the word for weaver. The terms for child and son may occur unpossessed in which case they are not kinship terms. The latter consists of c?ɨ *little* (adverb), -n- connective, and t?ɨ ~ t?i *little* (adjective). t?ɨ ~ t?i also occurs in the child and daughter terms. The morpheme šy in the daughter term means *female*.

hta	*Pm*	*father*
mbe	*Pf*	*mother*
t?ɨhni	*C*	*child*
c?int?ɨ	*Cm*	*son*
t?įšy	*Cf*	*daughter*

257

Grandparent terms are compound forms with prefix **pë-**. This prefix is quite productive in regard to kinship terms and elsewhere in the language. It has a wide range of meanings. In certain environments it seems to emphasize a difference, as in **pëkhą̈ʔi** *other person* (i.e., a nonrelative). In other environments it seems to emphasize a similarity, as in **pëcna** *round-like* (i.e., a bullet). The second half of the grandchild term, viz. **hto**, is identical with the second half of the man's mother-in-law term. The implications of this, if any, are not apparent to the author.

pëhta	*PPm(L)*	*grandfather*
pëna	*PPf(L)*	*grandmother*
ʔbähto	*CC(L)*	*grandchild*

The morpheme **mpom ~ mpon** from **mpòni** *substitute, another* or possibly **mpo** *inside, further over* is preposed to the grandparent and grandchild terms to designate relatives of (at least) the third ascending and descending generations.

mpòmpëhta	*PPPm*	*great-grandfather*
mpòmpëna	*PPPf*	*great-grandmother*
mpòmʔbähto	*CCC*	*great-grandchild*

There are four terms for sibling which mark the sex of both ego and alter, and a fifth term which does not mark sex at all. All five terms extend to all kinsmen of ego's generation.

nʔyöhï	*mPCm(G)*	*man's brother*
khụhwä	*fPCf(G)*	*woman's sister*
nkhụ	*mPCf(G)*	*man's sister*
ʔįta	*fPCm(G)*	*woman's brother*
hkụ	*PC(G)*	*sibling*

The term for a man's brother literally means *companion*, cf. **n-** *(nominalizer)*, **ʔyo** *walk*, **hï** *(plural inclusive)*. **nʔyöhï** is also the common word for *man*.

It is possible that the two sister terms are derived from the sibling term. Note the following as an example of such derivational phenomena: **ì hkụ̈tʔi** *he closes it*, **ì khụ̈tʔi** *it is closed*, **nkhụ̈ʔtʔi** *closed*.

Two terms distinguish the sex of collateral kinsmen of ascending generations, while one designates collateral kinsmen of descending generations, irrespective of sex.

ntë̈ʔwe	*PPCm(1,S)*	*uncle*
cìhci	*PPCf(1,S)*	*aunt*
ʔbä̈ʔwe	*PCC(1,S)*	*junior collateral*

The uncle term is reciprocal with the junior collateral term, to which may be preposed a sex-designating morpheme: **ntë-** *male* as in **ntëmbìši** *male cat*. **ʔbä-** also occurs in the grandchild term and means *afterwards*. An alternate term for *aunt* is **nàna**.

Compounding of terms is sometimes done to indicate more specific relationship.

ʔbǎʔwentě̌hko	mPCfCm	man's sister's son
(Cf. ntě̌hko *man's sister's husband*)		
ʔbǎʔwenkhu̧	mPCfCf	man's sister's daughter
ʔbǎʔwenʔyóhï	mPCmCm	man's brother's son
ʔbǎʔweʔbǎhpo	mPCmCf	man's brother's daughter
ʔbǎhtoʔbǎʔwe	PCCC(1)	grand-junior collateral

Relationship established by a second marriage is designated by the use of the consanguineal terminology plus the prefix hë-. The stepgrandfather term is also used for a comic character in fiestas.

hě̌mbe	PSf	stepmother
hě̌tʔi̧šu̧	SCf	stepdaughter
hě̌pě̌hta	PPSm	stepgrandfather
hě̌hku̧	PSC	stepsibling

There are two special vocative terms which are not however specifically kinship terms.

nʔyë	sir *(male speaker)*
kwë	friend

Use of the latter implies mild rebuke. Consanguineal relatives address each other by the consanguineal terms or by their proper names.

Child-talk terminology used to or by children either as vocative terms or in reference are as follows:

tàta	father
mbèmbe	mother
pïpi	daughter
tǔhku	son
nàna	any older female relative other than mother

There are two aspects from which the consanguineal terminology may be viewed. The first aspect takes into consideration the terms as they occur in their basic forms described above.

Seven generations of lineal relatives are distinguished. Sex of alter is distinguished in all except the second and third descending generations. In ego's generation four terms distinguish both the sex of the relative and the sex of ego, and one term does not distinguish sex at all. All five terms extend to include all collateral relatives of ego's generation. Collateral relatives other than those of ego's generation are classified as of ascending or descending generations. The sex of the relative is distinguished for the former but not for the latter.

The second point of view from which the consanguineal terminology can be viewed takes into consideration elementary terms and their modifications. This point of view recognizes *distance* (Grimes and Grimes, 1962) as a factor in grouping kintypes and may be presented graphically as in Figure 17.

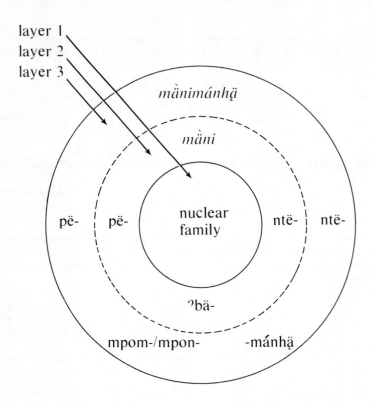

layer 1
layer 2
layer 3

mǎnimánhậ

mǎni

nuclear
family

pë-   pë-   ntë-   ntë-

ʔbä-

mpom-/mpon-   -mánhậ

Figure 17. Eastern Otomí
Consanguinial Distance.

The kintypes in the innermost circle of the figure are ego's primary relatives as defined by Murdock (1949). There is no cover term for this group, nor are the terms modified in any way.

Terms of the second group refer to relatives once removed from the nuclear family: grandparents, grandchildren, uncles, aunts, nephews, and nieces. These correspond to secondary relatives as defined by Murdock (ibid.). Relatives of this second group are classified under the cover term **mäni**. Prefixes which distinguish terms for this group are **pë-**, **ʔbä-**, and **ntë-**. These are an integral part of all terms but that for aunt which is apparently already a reduplicated form. **pë-** and **ntë-** are commonly added to the sibling terms to specify this layer of relationship in ego's generation, *viz.* cousins.

pëʔįta	*woman's male cousin*
ntĕnʔyóhï	*man's male cousin*

The term *prìmu* from Spanish is also often added to sibling terms to indicate the cousin relationship.

prìmunkhụ	*man's female cousin*
prìmunʔyóhï	*man's male cousin*

In the nearby town of San Lorenzo Achiotepec, **mäni** occurs in the word **tòmäni** *family plot* (**to** *rock*) which indicates a piece of property used for housesites of the family. Each such plot may accommodate several houses and households, members of which stand to each other in the relation of **mäni**. Each family group may have more than one such plot, and moving back and forth between different plots and even exchanging houses between **mäni** is not uncommon.

The morpheme **mä** means *resident, native of*, as in **mänʔïštèhe** *resident or native of San Gregorio* (**nʔïštèhe** *San Gregorio*).

The third group of relatives is not always so clearly distinguished from the second group as this latter is from the nuclear family, and is therefore separated in Figure 17 from the second group only by a dotted line.

These relatives include great-grandparents, great-uncles and great-aunts, and their children and grandchildren, cousins, children of cousins and of nieces and nephews, and great-grandchildren. These may all be called **mäni**, but more specifically are referred to as **mänimánhạ** (**mánhạ** *stand apart from*).

The prefix **mpom-** ~ **mpon-** distinguishes certain members of this group.

mpòmʔbäʔwe	*grand-nephew/niece*
mpòntëʔwe	*great-uncle*

Other members of this group are distinguished by the suffix **-mánhạ**.

nʔyŏhïmánhạ	*mPPPCCCm*	*man's second male cousin*

This suffix in the form **ʔbäʔwemánhạ** is equivalent to **mpòmʔbäʔwe** (and **bähtoʔbäʔwe**). Since no prefix occurs on the aunt term for a secondary relative, the form **pĕcîhci** is used to designate a *great-aunt*.

Both sex of ego and of alter are distinguished in parent-in-law terms. The morpheme
hcu in the mother-in-law (and one of the wife terms) means *female*. The morpheme ntë
occurring in both the father-in-law terms has been discussed, as has been the morpheme
pë in the woman's term for mother-in-law.

ntëhyą	mSPm	*man's father-in-law*
ntëhca	fSPm	*woman's father-in-law*
hcùhto	mSPf	*man's mother-in-law*
pĕhkɔ	fSPf	*woman's mother-in-law*

Sex of ego is not important in the two child-in-law terms, but sex of alter is
distinguished. The morpheme hwä is common to the terms for a woman's sister and
daughter-in-law. The morpheme mʔbä occurring in the son-in-law term is possibly related
to the first morpheme of the words mʔbätʔo *first, foremost*, and mʔbäkhwa *last, least*.

mʔbähą	CSm	*son-in-law*
cʔįhwä	CSf	*daughter-in-law*

There are also four sibling-in-law terms. The morpheme mbe in the woman's brother-
in-law term may be the same as the term for *mother*, and the same as in the term tą̀mbe
husband used in nearby Texcatepec, Veracruz. The morpheme ʔbä in the man's sister-in-
law term may be the same as in the consanguineal terms for grandchild and
niece/nephew.

ntëhko	mPCSm(V,G)	*man's brother-in-law*
mbèke	fPCSm(V,G)	*woman's brother-in-law*
ʔbähpo	mPCSf(V,G)	*man's sister-in-law*
mǔtu	fPCSf(V,G)	*woman's sister-in-law*

There are two co-sibling-in-law terms, which refer to relatives of the same sex as ego.
The morpheme mi ~ mmi in the co-sibling-in-law terms, means *fellow*, i.e., another of
the same kind, as in rą́ míphani wi *his fellow horse (dual)*. Spouses of siblings of the
opposite sex to ego's spouse recognize no relationship.

mmìhki	mSPCSm	*man's co-brother-in-law*
mìnkhɔ	fSPCSf	*woman's co-sister-in-law*

Siblings of parents-in-law and children and grandchildren of siblings-in-law are referred
to by the corresponding consanguineal terms. But a more specific terminology may be
achieved by compounding the consanguineal term with the affinal term.

ntëʔwentëhca	*woman's sibling of father-in-law*
ʔbäʔwemmìhki	*man's son of co-brother-in-law*
ʔbähtomʔbähą	*husband of granddaughter*

Terms for parents of parents-in-law are either compounds of the consanguineal term or
the affinal term.

pĕnapĕhkɔ   *woman's mother of parent-in-law*
căntéhca   *woman's father of parent-in-law*
   prefixed by **cä-** (**cănté** *old man*)
mpŏmpĕhkɔ   *woman's mother of parent-in-law*
   prefixed by second layer of relationship marker **mpom ~ mpon**.

A sample of great-grandparent-in-law terminology is **mpŏmpĕhtantĕhyą**, or such a distant relative may be called **ʔyàpĕhta**, meaning a grandfather but not particularly related.

Two wife terms may occur unpossessed meaning *woman*. Other words which may be used to mean wife when possessed are **kĭni** *grinder*, **mbàphi** *worker*, **nʔyŏʔbe** *companion (dual exclusive)*, **mànkyʔbe** *fellow householder (dual exclusive)*. Besides the regular husband term, a woman may refer to her husband by any of the last three words cited above. In case of dual marriage, the term for first wife is **nyŏmpĕmbe** *old woman*, and for second wife **ʔwăhci**.

ntë	*Sm*	*husband*
sĭhcu, pĕmbe	*Sf*	*wife*

Neither the sex of the parent or of the parent-in-law is distinguished by the single term for co-parent.

chèhni	*CSP*	*co-parent-in-law*

Ritual-relationship Terminology

There are two types of ritual in which ritual-relationship teminology is used, that having to do with the native Otomí religion and that having to do with Roman Catholic ceremony. Two terms are common to both types of ritual.

htàkhą	*godfather*
mbèkhą	*godmother*

These are composed of the consanguineal parent terms plus **khą**, which is a morpheme occurring in such words as **òkhą** *God*, **nĭkhą** *church*, **mbɔkhą** *priest*, and **tĕkhą** *ocean*, and seems to mean *sacred* or *holy*.

In the Roman Catholic baptism ceremony these terms mean *godfather* and *godmother*. In Catholic processional ceremonies these terms refer to those who carry the images. In both these ceremonies the collective word for the two offices is **ntăšte** *carrier (in one's arms)*. The godchild in the baptism ceremony is called **thăcʔi** *the one carried*. The actual parents of the child and the godparents refer to each other as co-parents by terms borrowed and adapted from Spanish *compadre* and *comadre*.

mpăre	*co-father*
măndä	*co-mother*

In the Otomí religious ceremonies the **htakhạ** and **mbekhạ** are the ones in charge of the offerings to the powers being honored. They are chosen each year. The **htàkhạtêni** *ceremonial guardian of the flowers* (marijuana) and the **mbèkhạt?ëhë** *ceremonial guardian of the mountain* are two such terms.

STATE OF MEXICO OTOMI KINSHIP TERMS

Henrietta Andrews

These data were gathered primarily from the town of San Felipe Santiago in the State of Mexico.

Otomí consanguineal kinship nomenclature classifies relatives with generation-type terminology in grandparents and ego's generation, and with lineal-type terminology in the first ascending and first and second descending generations.

Four terms classify lineal males and females of first and second ascending generations, while two terms classify first and second descending generation lineals without regard to sex. The two terms for lineals of the second ascending generation extend also to collateral kinsmen, and in a more general sense may denote any elderly person.

tá	Pm	father
mé	Pf	mother
bậhcí	C	child
tìtá	PPm(1)	grandfather
čùhčú	PPf(1)	grandmother
ʔbậhtó	CC(L)	grandchild

The child term may denote any child, including the adult offspring of a person, and is also used in the sense of offspring of animals and plants. Though it does not distinguish sex, there are two additional terms which do.

t?í	*Cm*	*son*
t?ǐšú̧	*Cf*	*daughter*

Relatives of the third ascending and descending generations are specified by the word mböší *great* preposed to the appropriate term.

mböšítìtá	*PPPm*	*great-grandfather*
mböšíčùhčú	*PPPf*	*great-grandmother*
mböší?bà̧htó	*CCC*	*great-grandchild*

The criterion of sex is fully exploited in the sibling terminology. Four terms distinguish both the sex of ego and of his relative. These terms are extended to include cousins, though the more sophisticated speaker may add the phrase gá primo after the Otomí term, borrowing the Spanish word for cousin; and some younger speakers use only the Spanish terms *primo/a*. Neighboring Temoayan Otomí has a slightly different form of the woman's sister term.

khwà̧dá̧	*mPCm(G)*	*man's brother*
?ì̧dá	*fPCm(G)*	*woman's brother*
khù̧hwá̧, Tm: khwá̧	*fPCf(G)*	*woman's sister*
nkhú̧	*mPCf(G)*	*man's sister*

A fifth term for sibling does not distinguish sex at all, and is used in a more extended sense to mean one's fellow. It may also be used of animals or inanimate objects as of a fellow dog or the mate of a shoe.

?ñò̧wí	*PC(G)*	*sibling*

Relationships established by a second marriage are specified by the use of consanguineal terminology plus the preposed morpheme hě.

jětá	*PSm*	*stepfather*
hěkhù̧hwá̧	*fPSCf*	*stepsister of a woman*

These terms, however, are not used to refer to half siblings. Persons who share one parent refer to each other by full sibling terminology. Aunt and uncle terms are used for all siblings of parents and for the children of grandparents' siblings. The uncle term (which is from Spanish) also denotes the spouse of a relative referred to by the aunt term. This is not true of spouses of those referred to by the uncle term; these are referred to by the Spanish term *tía*.

tio	*PPCm(G,-S)*	*uncle*
zìhcí	*PPCf(G)*	*aunt*
tia	*PPCSf(G)*	*aunt-in-law*

The nephew and niece terms, which are extended to include children of cousins, are Spanish in origin. Neighboring Temoayan Otomi has a native word ʔbädìcí for these junior collaterals.

sobrino	*PCCm(G)*	*nephew*
sobrina	*PCCf(G)*	*niece*

Collateral relatives of the second descending generation are referred to by the grand-child term qualified by the Spanish nephew and niece terms.

The criterion of sex is again important in the affinal terminology. Both sex of ego and of his relative are distinguished in parent-in-law and sibling-in-law terms, there being four of each.

nděhñą́	*mSPm*	*man's father-in-law*
cǎ	*fSPm*	*woman's father-in-law*
kɔ̀	*fSPf*	*woman's mother-in-law*
tǒ	*mSPf*	*man's mother-in-law*
kǒ	*mPCSm(G,V),fPCSm(G)*	*brother-in-law*
mó	*fSPCm(G)*	*husband's brother*
mų́dų́	*fPCSf(G,V)*	*woman's sister-in-law*
ʔbähpó	*mPCSf(G,V)*	*man's sister-in-law*

The sibling-in-law terms exhibit an assymetric classification. Male and female ego each have a separate term for sisters-in-law, but female ego designates a sister's husband by the term male ego applies to either a sister's husband or to his wife's brother, and designates her husband's brother by another term.

Special terms are used between men who marry sisters and women who marry brothers.

mį̀hkí	*mSPCSm(G)*	*man's co-brother-in-law*
mìmìnkhɔ́, mìnkhɔ́	*fSPCSf(G)*	*woman's co-sister-in-law*

Sex of ego is not relevant in the child-in-law terms; and in the single term used between parents and parents-in-law, neither does it distinguish the sex of the referent.

ʔmähą́	*CSm*	*son-in-law*
cʔìhwǎ	*CSf*	*daughter-in-law*
chěhní	*CSP*	*co-parent-in-law*

The word for wife is the word regularly used to mean woman. The husband term, however, is restricted to the affinal relationship, except as it appears in the compound dą̀méʔění *turkey gobbler* or lit. *husband turkey*.

dą̀mé	*Sm*	*husband*
ʔbähñą́	*Sf*	*wife*

There are five terms of ritual-relationship terminology. Two of these are borrowed from Spanish and adapted slightly to Otomí. The other three are descriptive compounds, doubtless of post-Conquest origin. The five terms refer to the persons involved in the christening of a child according to Roman Catholic practice.

tăkhą́	*godfather*
mĕkhą́	*godmother*
thăšyàkhą́	*godchild*
mbăré	*co-father*
măré	*co-mother*

The terms for godparents are derived from the words for father and mother, with the postposed morpheme **-khą́**. This morpheme appears in the words for God, church, priest, and bless, and seems to mean *sacred* or *holy* . The term for godchild is composed of the verb stem **thăcí** *to carry in one's arms* plus postposed **-khą́**. The actual parents of the baptized child and the godparents refer to each other as co-parents by terms borrowed and adapted from Spanish.

MESQUITAL OTOMI KINSHIP TERMS

Hugh Steven
Norma Steven

Lineal and collateral relatives are distinguished in both consanguineal and affinal terminology, with siblings classified as collateral relatives. Three generations of direct ancestors and two generations of direct descendants are distinguished by elementary terms. There are three terms for child, one which does not specify the child's sex and two which do.

dǎdá	*Pm*	*father*
nǎná	*Pf*	*mother*
bàcí	*C*	*child*
tʔǐ	*Cm*	*son*
tʔìšú	*Cf*	*daughter*
títá	*PPm(L)*	*grandfather*
nítá	*PPf(L)*	*grandmother*
ʔbàtó	*CC(L)*	*grandchild*
šítá	*PPPm(L)*	*great-grandfather*
čúčú	*PPPf(L)*	*great-grandmother*

269

There are five sibling terms which class together all siblings and collaterals of ego's generation. Four terms designate older relatives and specify both sex of ego and of alter. The fifth term designates younger relatives without specifying sex.

xwą̀dą́	empCm(G)	man's elder brother
ìdą́	efPCm(G)	woman's elder brother
xúxwä̀	efPCf(G)	woman's elder sister
nkhų́	empCf(G)	man's elder sister
kų́	yPC(G)	younger sibling

All senior collaterals (i.e., of ascending generations) are classified together under two terms distinguishing their sex. Native Otomí terms have been replaced by loan-words from Spanish. The terms extend to include spouses of senior collaterals and senior collaterals of spouse. All collaterals of the first descending generation are classified together under a single term. This term extends to affinals in the same way as the terms for senior collaterals.

tìó	PPCm(1,S)	uncle
tìá	PPCf(1,S)	aunt
ʔbä̀dà̀ʔcí	PCC(1,S)	junior collateral

The forms **mbŏm** or **mbóngá** may be preposed to the grandchild and junior collateral terms to specify lineals beyond the second descending generation and collaterals beyond the first descending generation, respectively.

Steprelatives are specified by use of the form **hë**.

hĕtá	stepfather
hĕmé	stepmother
hĕtʔí	stepson
hĕnšú	stepdaughter
hĕkų́	stepsibling

Male and female ego have separate terms for parents-in-law. The terms used by female ego are borrowed from Spanish. This is an interesting departure from the more common practice in rural communities of Mexico where it is the men who more frequently add Spanish words to their vocabulary than the women. In this case, these terms may well have been introduced in a church and marriage context in which women participated more than men.

ndèhñą́	mSPm	man's father-in-law
suégró	fSPm	woman's father-in-law
suégrá	fSPf	woman's mother-in-law
tŏ	mSPf	man's mother-in-law

Two terms for spouses of children distinguish only the sex of alter.

ʔmà̀ʔhą́	CSm	son-in-law
cʔìhwä̀	CSf	daughter-in-law

There are only three sibling-in-law terms, one for males and two for females which distinguish the sex of ego. Judging from related Otomí systems, the absence of two terms for brother-in-law distinguishing the sex of ego represents the loss of one term in the Mesquital system. The sibling-in-law terms denote both collaterals of spouse and spouses of ego's collaterals (of ego's generation).

kǒ	*PCSm(V,G)*	*brother-in-law*
múdú	*fPCSf(V,G)*	*woman's sister-in-law*
ʔbǎpó	*mPCSf(V,G)*	*man's sister-in-law*

There is a single term for the person who marries sibling of spouse, regardless of sex of alter or ego.

mìkí	*SPCS(G)*	*co-sibling-in-law*

Similarly, a single term designates a parent-in-law of one's child.

sèhní	*CSP*	*co-parent-in-law*

Two terms designate spouse.

dàmé	*Sm*	*husband*
ʔbǎhñą	*Sf*	*wife*

As mentioned, collateral affinals of generations other than that of ego are generally classed with consanguineals. It is possible to distinguish them, however, by modifying the consanguineal term by a phrase which includes a lineal affinal term, as in **ʔbǎdàcí gá cʔìhwǎ** *niece-in-law*.

TENANGO OTOMI KINSHIP TERMS
Richard Blight

The general term **mäni** *relative* includes all consanguines and affines.

There are elementary terms for ego's grandparents and all their descendants to the fourth generation (ego's grandchild generation). The form **mbo(n)-** is prefixed to grandparent and grandchild terms to designate lineal relatives of the third ascending and descending generations from ego.

ta	*Pm*	*father*
me	*Pf*	*mother*
bąsį	*C*	*child*
ts?int?ï	*Cm*	*son*
t?įšų	*Cf*	*daughter*
šita	*PPm(L)*	*grandfather*
su	*PPf(L)*	*grandmother*
?bähto	*CC(L)*	*grandchild*

Most speakers use **mamá** and **papá** to refer to parents, but in a nearby town **me** and **ta** are used. These forms also occur in the compounds **mexą** *godmother* and **taxą** *godfather*, and when talking about the parents of animals.

273

Only in ego's generation is there a distinction between male and female speakers. Spanish borrowing has made it possible to distinguish cousins from siblings by adding **primo** before the various sibling terms, but otherwise the sibling terms do extend to all collateral kinsmen of ego's generation.

n?yohï	*mPCm(G)*	*man's brother*
?įdą	*fPCm(G)*	*woman's brother*
xųhwä	*fPCf(G)*	*woman's sister*
nkhų	*mPCf(G)*	*man's sister*
kų	*PC(G)*	*sibling*

Two terms distinguish the sex of all collateral kinsmen of ascending generations, while one term, used alone, denotes collaterals of the first descending generation and, coupled with the grandchild terms, all collaterals beyond the first descending generation.

?we	*PPCm(1)*	*uncle*
zisi	*PPCf(1)*	*aunt*
?bä?we	*PCC(G)*	*sibling's child*
?bähto ?bä?we	*PCCC(1)*	*sibling's grandchild*

Four terms, distinguishing sex of ego and alter, denote parents of spouse, while two terms for child's spouse distinguish only sex of alter.

ndëhyą	*mSPm*	*man's father-in-law*
ndësa	*fSPm*	*woman's father-in-law*
kɔ	*fSPf*	*woman's mother-in-law*
to	*mSPf*	*man's mother-in-law*
m?bähą	*CSm*	*son-in-law*
c?įhwä	*CSf*	*daughter-in-law*

Lineal affinal terms of the first generation combine with consanguineal terms of the second generation to designate lineal affinals of the second generation.

šita ndëhyą	*mSPPm(L)*	*wife's grandfather*
sukɔ	*fSPPf(L)*	*husband's grandmother*
?bähtoc?įhwä	*CCSf(L)*	*granddaughter-in-law*

The senior collaterals of spouse and the spouses of senior collaterals are designated by compounding senior collateral terms with parent-in-law terms.

?wehyą	*mSPPCm(V,1)*	*man's uncle-in-law*
?wesa	*fSPPCm(V,1)*	*woman's uncle-in-law*
zisikɔ	*fSPPCf(V,1)*	*woman's aunt-in-law*
zisito	*mSPPCf(V,1)*	*man's aunt-in-law*

As in the case of parent-in-law terms, both sex of ego and of alter are specified for spouses of siblings and siblings of spouse.

ko	*mPCSm(V,G)*	*man's brother-in-law*
mege	*ʃPCSm(V,G)*	*woman's brother-in-law*
mʉtʉ	*ʃPCSf(V,G)*	*woman's sister-in-law*
ʔbähpo	*mPCSf(V,G)*	*man's sister-in-law*

There are also special terms for men who marry sisters and women who marry brothers.

| mjkj | *mSPCSm(G)* | *man's co-brother-in-law* |
| miŋkhɔ | *ʃSPCSf(G)* | *woman's co-sister-in-law* |

A final term denotes the parent of one's child-in-law.

| hsëhni | *CSP* | *co-parent-in-law* |

Terms for spouse are the words for man and woman.

| ndë | *Sm* | *husband* |
| šisu | *Sf* | *wife* |

MAZAHUA KINSHIP TERMS

Hazel Spotts
Don Stewart

There are a variety of terms for senior lineal kinsmen and two for junior lineals. The parent terms and the grandchild term are restricted to lineals, while grandparent and child terms extend to collaterals of ascending and descending generations, respectively. (When palatal and nonpalatal variants of a term are listed, the first (palatal) form is first person, the other third person.)

tata, hyo	*Pm*	*father*
nana;ʔñï, ʔnï	*Pf*	*mother*
čʔi, tʔi	*C(1)*	*child*
títa, pále	*PPm(2)*	*grandfather*
níta, mále	*PPf(2)*	*grandmother*
ande, lande	*PP(?)*	*grandparent*
bʔäče	*CC(L,-S)*	*grandchild*

The ending -hwä may be added to the child term to designate a daughter. The term šuntʔi is also commonly heard for daughter, but may mean any young girl.

čʔihwä, tʔihwä, šuntʔi	*Cf(1)*	*daughter*

277

The first child of parents is called the **šokoyote**, the last **cjʔj**.
Terms of Spanish origin compete with the grandparent and child terms for collateral kinsmen of ascending and descending generations, also extending to corresponding affinals, as in Spanish.

tio	*PPCm(1,S)*	uncle
tia	*PPCf(1,S)*	*aunt*
sobrenu	*PCCm(1,S)*	*nephew*
sobrena	*PCCf(1,S)*	*niece*

These aunt and uncle terms are also used both in reference and direct address for any man or woman. A few speakers have been heard to use **tio** and **tia** for father's brother and sister, respectively, while using distinct terms, as follows, for mother's brother and sister; but this distinction is nonexistent for most speakers.

ʔwe	*xPPCm*	*mother's brother*
zizi	*=PPCf*	*mother's sister*

In the town of San Juanico (*Municipio* of Temascalcingo), there are bifurcate collateral aunt and uncle terms which include **tio** as one of the four.

tio	*PmPCm*	*father's brother*
ʔwe	*PfPCm*	*mother's brother*
zizi	*PfPCf*	*mother's sister*
ndahi	*PmPCf*	*father's sister*

Ancestors and descendants beyond the second generation are specified by adding **mboš(a)** to grandparent and grandchild terms, and a variant of **ta ~ nda ~ ča** *big* is added to specify fourth generation grandparents.

mbošpale, mbošatita	*PPPm(L)*	*great-grandfather*
mbošmale, mbošanita	*PPPf(L)*	*great-grandmother*
mbošbʔáče	*CCC(L)*	*great-grandchild*
čatita	*PPPPm(L)*	*great-great-grandfather*
čanita	*PPPPf(L)*	*great-great-grandmother*

There are six terms for siblings. Four of these specify the sex of both ego and alter, and extend bilaterally to all consanguines of ego's generation. The remaining two are respect terms applied to the eldest brother and sister who serve as parent substitutes in the event of the decease of father or mother. These terms continue to be used, and the authority of the eldest brother and sister is accordingly continued to be recognized, even when all the siblings are grown and have established their own households. They are also used generally, in reference and direct address to mean young man and young woman, respectively.

khwąrhmą; čʔï, tʔï	*mPCm(G)*	*man's brother*
ʔñinžǫmį, ʔinžǫmį	*fPCm(G)*	*woman's brother*
chįhhwä; khųhhwä	*fPCf(G)*	*woman's sister*

khụ	mPCf(G)	man's sister
sę?ę; nžasę?ę, ndasę?ę	ePCm	eldest brother
sïngï; nžasïngï, ndasïngï	ePCf	eldest sister

True siblings are distinguished from cousins by the expression ?natho in tata, ?natho in nana one my father, one my mother (?natho ~ d?atho).

Three terms distinguish parents of spouse by sex of ego and of parent, and two distinguish spouses of children by their sex, but not of ego.

nžą?ą, ndą?ą	SPm(L)	father-in-law
cɔ?ɔ, kɔ?ɔ	fSPf(L)	woman's mother-in-law
čo?o, to?o	mSPf(L)	man's mother-in-law
?męñ?ę	CSm(L)	son-in-law
chɔ?ɔ, khɔ?ɔ	CSf(L)	daughter-in-law

Both sex of ego and alter are distinguished in terms for siblings-in-law which denote both spouses of siblings and siblings of spouse. The second term for a man's sister-in-law, chorišu ~ khorišu, appears to be a compound based on the man's term cho?o ~ kho?o and a combining form of ndišụ woman.

cho?o, kho?o	mPCSm(V,G),fPCSm(G)	brother-in-law
me?e	fSPCm(G)	husband's brother
mụrį	fPCSf(V,G)	woman's sister-in-law
b?ähpe	mPCSf(G)	man's sister-in-law
chorišụ, khorišụ	mSPCf(G)	wife's sister

The spouse of a spouse's sibling is designated by one of two terms distinguishing sex of kinsman.

| mic?męñ?ę | SPCSm(G) | co-brother-in-law |
| minkhɔ | SPCSf(G) | co-sister-in-law |

Finally, there are two terms for spouse, and one for the parent-in-law of child.

šįra	Sm	husband
su?u	Sf	wife
shëhnë	CSP	co-parent-in-law

Mazahua tone carries a minimal functional load in distinguishing meaning, and is usually unmarked. The grandfather and grandmother terms títa, pále, níta, and mále, however, carry high tone on the first syllable in reference to grandparents, but falling tone on the first syllable in general reference to old man or old woman: tîta, pâle, nîta, and mâle. In this latter form, they are used by a spouse in reference to husband or wife.

The prefix hë- is added to consanguineal terms to denote step-relationships established through a second marriage.

CENTRAL PAME KINSHIP TERMS

Lorna F. Gibson

The following is a brief recapitulation of Gibson (1954). Where prefixes affect the form of terms, they are presented as inflected for first, second, and third person, respectively.

The terminology for consanguineals seems to represent a system with basic similarities to those of the Cheyenne and Arapaho. Father's brother is classified with father and mother's sister with mother, while separate terms exist for mother's brother and father's sister. That is, bifurcate merging terms distinguish parallel kinsmen from cross kinsmen in the first ascending generation.

These terms extend collaterally to cousins of parents as described for Seneca by Lounsbury (1964) in women's speech which is here taken as representative of traditional Central Pame usage. The men, who have been influenced more by Spanish usage, tend to treat all collateral kinsmen of the parent generation as uncles and aunts without respect to bifurcation, and in some cases may even use the corresponding Spanish terms **tío** and **tía.** The extended senses of a kinship term are often made explicit by the use of preposed modifiers **tochào** or **tónho** in their various inflected forms (see Gibson, 1954, for details).

The aunt and uncle terms also extend to spouse of parent's sibling, and to sibling of spouse's parents (whether parallel or cross).

281

rawé?, wíyɛo?, wómmɛo?	=Pm(G)	*father*
rawí, ác?ọ, wac?ọ̀	=Pf(G)	*mother*
rabbéo?, ábbɛo?, wobbéo?	xPm(G,S)	*uncle*
nc?ọ̀k, nc?ọ̀k?, nc?ọ̀p	xPf(G,S)	*aunt*

There is a single term for child, which may be modified to designate sex. This term extends to the children of siblings except that a man refers to his sister's children by preposing či to the uncle term.

na?í, ŋgodwì, ŋgodwí	=C(G),xfC(G)	*child*
či rabbéo?, etc.	xmC(G)	*man's sister's child*

Two terms for grandparents are used reciprocally for grandchildren, each term marking only the sex of the senior kinsman of the dyad. Although supplementary words may be added to make the distinction, the grandchildren of siblings are also referred to by these same two terms. [By analogy, the siblings of grandparent, apparently are also referred to by these terms. Ed.]

rahę́ŋ, wahę̀ŋ, wanhę́ŋ	PPm(R,G)	*grandfather*
rattòi, attòi, watòi	PPf(R,G)	*grandmother*

A single term for sibling extends to all cousins [apparently of ego's generation], as well as reciprocally for great-grandkinsmen.

hwèo, nhô, nhèo	PC(G),PPP(R)	*sibling*

There are additional sibling terms used primarily in direct address, but also in reference toward close kinsmen. Their vocative use extends to close friends not genealogically related.

lái?, lyài, wanái	ePCm(G),PPPm	*elder brother*
ttôi? or kyôi?	yPCm(G),CCCm,PCCm	*younger brother*
kǫ́e, ŋgǫ́e *(third)*	emPCf(G),mPPPf	*man's elder sister*
hóc	efPCf(G),fPPPf	*woman's elder sister*
wí	yPCf(G),CCCf	*younger sister*

A single term designates either parent of spouse, while two terms designate the spouse of son and daughter, respectively.

légŋ, lyègŋ, wanégŋ	SP(G)	*parent-in-law*
wat?ę̀, ma?ę̂, ma?ę̀	CSm(G)	*son-in-law*
waŋkháo, makâo, ŋgwáo	CSf(G)	*daughter-in-law*

There are two sibling-in-law terms. One term designates the male kinsman of a male speaker—his sister's husband or his wife's brother. The other term designates a brother-in-law for a female speaker or a sister-in-law for ego of either sex.

akkwá?, ákkwa?, wakwá?	*mPCSm(V,G)*	*man's brother-in-law*
kommǫ̀, kimyǫ̀, kamǫ̀	*ʃPCSm(V,G)*	*woman's brother-in-law*
	PCSʃ(V,G)	*sister-in-law*

Finally, there is one term for husband and one for wife.

?ywą́ŋ, n?wą̀ŋ, wan?wą́ŋ	*Sm*	*husband*
?já?ai, n?ʃa?a, wán?ja?a	*Sf*	*wife*

CHICHIMECA-JONAZ
KINSHIP TERMS

The following data come from Table 40, of Driver and Romero Castillo (1963). First, second, and third person singular forms are presented, in that order. Kintypes are listed for each term, as presented by Driver and Romero Castillo, followed by an interpretation of the range of reference by the present author.

1.	tátá, únkwǽʔ, émǽʔ	*Pm*	*Pm(L)*
2.	náná, úcʔy̨, ecʔý̨	*Pf*	*Pf(L)*
3.	ny̨khý̨, núkhy̨, nükhý̨	*C*	*C*
4.	tátálé?, únkwǽʔelé?, énhę́elé?	*PPm*	
5.	nánâlé?, utűelé?, erűelé?	*PPf*	
6.	nǫ́hę́, umhę́, énhę́	*PPm,PPCm,PPCSm,PCC,mCC*	*PPm(R,2,S)*

285

7.	natữ, utữ, erữ	*PPCf,PPCSf,fCC*	*PPf(R,2,S)*
8.	úrắ, urắ, énắ	*ePCm,ePPCCm*	*ePCm(G)*
9.	úkữ, ukữ, égữ	*yPCm,yPPCCm,PCCm*	*yPCm(G),PCCm(G)*
10.	mánthü, manthữ, énkữ	*mPCf,mPPCCf*	*mPCf(G)*
11.	nahí, únho, ẹnhí	*fPCf,fPPCCf,fPCCf*	*fPCf(G),fPCCf(G)*
12.	ná?ú, un?ý, ún?ý	*Sm*	*Sm*
13.	masý, uní?í, úní?i	*Sf*	*Sf*
14.	úkú?, úku?, égú?	*SPCm,PCSm*	*SPCm(V)*
15.	kamý, kámụ, ínó kamý	*SPCf,PCSf*	*SPCf(V)*
16.	úrí, urí, éní	*SP,CS*	*SP(R)*

No separate interpretation is given for terms 4 and 5 since they are merely parent terms (1,2) or grandparent terms (6,7) with affective suffix. It seems best to treat the extension of sibling terms to collateral kinsmen of the first descending generation as disjunctive, rather than through a special rule of extension from kintypes of ego's generation. This use of sibling terms competes with the extension of grandkinsman terms to these same kintypes.

A special term for sibling is presented by Driver and Romero Castillo in the phrase for cousin **mánó mísógum?** *nearly sibling*, but apparently does not occur alone as a sibling term. **ní** is the dimunitive form of **nahí** which may be used to affectionately address a sister or sibling's daughter (probably by a woman only). Words for male and female are **írý** and **mání**, respectively.

CHAPTER 11
ZAPOTECAN KINSHIP TERMS

This chapter reports Zapotec and
Chatino kinship terms as well as an
earlier analysis of Proto Zapotec
terms.

AMATLAN ZAPOTEC KINSHIP TERMS
Roger Reeck

San Cristóbal Amatlán, along with San Francisco Logueche, is somewhat related to the language of Cuixtla. Both towns are very monolingual and very conservative in many ways. Since a complete phonological analysis remains to be done, the data here presented are tentative. They were obtained from Ismael Martínez, a 50-year-old man who could speak very little Spanish.

Four terms distinguish the sex of parents and child and a fifth term classes sons and daughters together.

šuz	Pm	*father*
šna	Pf	*mother*
šgan?	Cm	*son*
ščap	Cf	*daughter*
šin?	C	*child*

Two self-reciprocal terms, with inverse ranges, distinguish only the sex of grand-kinsmen, ignoring seniority.

šey	PPm(I)	male grandkinsman
šoʔz	PPf(I)	female grandkinsman

Three sibling terms mark the sex of both ego and alter. Postposed **yeʔn** specifies cousins.

weč	mPCm(G)	man's brother
bal	fPCf(G)	woman's sister
bzan	aPCb(G)	cross-sex sibling

As in the case of grandkinsman terms, two self-reciprocal terms distinguish only the sex of senior and junior collateral kinsmen, not seniority.

šič	PPCm(I)	male collateral kinsman
šnis	PPCf(I)	female collateral kinsman

The grandkin terms combine with **gol** *old* to specify great-grandparents and with the child term to specify great-grandchildren.

šey gol	PPPm	great-grandfather
šoʔz gol	PPPf	great-grandmother
šin šey	CCCm	great-grandson
šin šolʔz	CCCf	great-granddaughter

Four phrases based on parent terms distinguish sex of both ego and alter in parent-in-law terms while two terms distinguish the sex of children-in-law.

šuz žap	mSPm	man's father-in-law
šuz yeʔ	fSPm	woman's father-in-law
šna žap	mSPf	man's mother-in-law
šna yeʔ	fSPf	woman's mother-in-law
šuž	CSm	son-in-law
šiš	CSf	daughter-in-law

Four terms distinguish affinal kinsmen of ego's generation; two of the terms are Spanish borrowings, one of which overlaps the co-brother-in-law term as used by some speakers.

škunyad	PCS(V),aSPCSb	sibling-in-law
weč mguž	mSPCSm	man's co-brother-in-law
škonkuin	fSPCSf,SPCS	co-sibling-in-law
liol	CSP	co-parent

A single term designates spouse of either sex.

sa	S	spouse

SIERRA JUAREZ ZAPOTEC KINSHIP TERMS

Neil Nellis

Three terms designate father, mother, and child. The child term is of Zapotecan origin, but parent terms are of the *nana/tata* variety so common in languages throughout Mexico. The latter extend to the parents of spouse.

tátá	*Pm(S-)*	*father*
nāná	*Pf(S-)*	*mother*
žíʔní	*C*	*child*

A grandchild term appears to be related morphologically to the child term, and grandparent terms add **gūlá** *old* to shortened forms of parent terms.

tá gūlá	*PPm(L)*	*grandfather*
ná gūlá	*PPf(L)*	*grandmother*
žīɵūā	*CC(L)*	*grandchild*

The sex of children may be specified by adding the words for man or woman to the child term; viz. **žíʔní bēžùū?** *son* and **žíʔní nīūlá** *daughter*. The sex of a grandchild is indicated by adding the personal name to the grandchild term. Great-grandparents may be specified by the addition of the form **bēcīgú?** to grandparent terms.

Three terms classify siblings together with cousins, though the latter are often designated by the Spanish cousin terms *prima* and *primo*.

bēc·ī?	*mPCm(G)*	*man's brother*
žīlá	*fPCf(G)*	*woman's sister*
dānà	*aPCb(G)*	*cross-sex sibling*

The parent terms also appear in the two aunt and uncle terms which designate all collateral kinsmen of senior generations. The nephew and niece terms are straight from Spanish. They classify all collaterals of descending generations.

tá kwāná	*PPCm(1)*	*uncle*
ná tíá	*PPCf(1)*	*aunt*
sōbrínó	*PCCm(1)*	*nephew*
sōbrína	*PCCf(1)*	*niece*

Parents of spouse and spouses of children are classed together by single terms which do not distinguish their sex. Spouses of siblings and siblings of spouse are referred to by Spanish terms. There is a single term for spouse of either sex, as well as separate terms for man and woman which serve as husband and wife terms when possessed.

kūlá	*SP*	*parent-in-law*
žūīcī	*CS*	*child-in-law*
kūñádó	*PCSm(V,G)*	*brother-in-law*
kūñádá	*PCSf(V,G)*	*sister-in-law*
cèlà	*S*	*spouse*
nùbēzùù?	*Sm*	*husband*
nīūlá	*Sf*	*wife*

The parents of a child-in-law are referred to by two terms from Spanish *compadre* and *comadre*.

ūmpálí	*CSPm*	*co-father*
kūmárí	*CSPf*	*co-mother*

CHOAPAN ZAPOTEC KINSHIP TERMS
Larry Lyman

Six terms define four generations of lineal kinsmen, two ascending generations in which the sex of the kinsman is marked, and two descending generations where sex is unmarked. (Each term is presented as inflected for first person singular possessor, followed by the unpossessed form.)

šuza?, šuzi	*Pm*	*father*
žna?, žna?	*Pf*	*mother*
ži?ina?, ži?i	*C*	*child*
šuzi gula?, šuzi gula	*PPm*	*grandfather*
žna? gula?, žna? gula	*PPf*	*grandmother*
ži?i suba?, ži?i suba	*CC*	*grandchild*

Three additional terms suffice to identify all collateral consanguines (including siblings) specifying only that ego and alter are both males, both females, or of opposite sex.

biča?, biči	*mPCm(0)*	*man's brother*
žila?, žila	*fPCf(0)*	*woman's sister*
zana?, zan	*aPCb(0)*	*cross-sex sibling*

Other Zapotec terms that in times past further classified collaterals have disappeared apparently under the pressure of differences in the Spanish system of kinship reference. Further precision in defining cousins, aunts, uncles, etc., distinguishing them from full siblings, requires a descriptive phrase; e.g., **žiʔi suba zan šuza?** *father's sister's grandchild* or **žiʔi zan žna? gula?** *grandmother's brother's child*.

Half siblings are referred to by the same terms as full siblings, whereas -**zi** is suffixed to the appropriate parent, child, or sibling term to indicate a steprelationship established through a second marriage.

As in the case of consanguineals, lineal affinals and collateral affinals are distinguished, with the latter all being merged under two terms from Spanish which distinguish only sex of alter. A single term merges all senior lineal affinals, and two terms distinguish only the sex of junior lineal affinals. The husband term is based on the word for man, while that for wife is literally *my old one*.

ben gula?, ben gula	*SP(L)*	*parent-in-law*
žuʔuᶎa?, žuʔuᶎi	*CSm(L)*	*son-in-law*
žualiᶎa?, žualiᶎi	*CSf(L)*	*daughter-in-law*
kuñado, kuñado	*PCSm(V,0)*	*brother-in-law*
kuñada, kuñada	*PCSf(V,0)*	*sister-in-law*
škiuwa?, škiu	*Sm*	*husband*
žgula?, žgula	*Sf*	*wife*

COATLAN ZAPOTEC KINSHIP TERMS

Roger Reeck

Santa María Coatlán is an extremely bilingual town with very few people under 40 who habitually use the language. Some people under 40 speak the language well but use it only to speak to older people. They switch to Spanish when talking to people their own age or younger. Although data were gathered at several households, the best and most reliable came from Isabel Jiménez, a lady of about 65 years of age. There were two terms—for nephew/niece and co-sister-in-law—concerning which speakers were uncertain. It would be good to visit other Coatlán towns where the language is still used by everyone, to see what terms they use there.

Three terms designate father, mother, and child, but more specific phrases for son and daughter also are heard. **bgi?** is a word for *man*, **goc** for *woman*. **mbäz** is a generic word for *child*.

šuz	*Pm*	*father*
šna?	*Pf*	*mother*
šin?	*C*	*child*
šinegan, mbäz bgi?	*Cm*	*son*
šinezap, mbäz goc	*Cf*	*daughter*

There are special vocative terms for parents.

pa	Pm	father
na?	Pf	mother

Grandkinsmen are also distinguished by three terms, the parent and child terms and a modifier.

šuz šoc	PPm	grandfather
šna šoc	PPf	grandmother
šin šoc	CC	grandchild

Alternate grandparent terms which appear to be loans from Spanish are used by younger speakers.

tatit	PPm	grandfather
nanit	PPf	grandmother

nja is postposed to any grandkin term to designate a kinsman of the third generation from ego.

Three sibling terms mark the sex of ego and alter, and may occur with postposed yen to specify cousins.

wit	mPCm(G)	man's brother
bäl	fPCf(G)	woman's sister
bzan	aPCb(G)	cross-sex sibling

A single term classes together, in reciprocal fashion, all senior and junior collaterals, according to at least one speaker. Most speakers, however, use a Spanish loan for junior collaterals, and some use a Spanish loan for senior collaterals as well.

šit	PPC(I)	collateral
ti	PPC	senior collateral
sobrin	PCC	junior collateral

Phrases based on parent terms mark the sex of both ego and of parents-in-law, while phrases based on the child term mark only the sex of child-in-law.

šuz žap	mSPm	man's father-in-law
šuz gi?	fSPm	woman's father-in-law
šna? žap	mSPf	man's mother-in-law
šna? gi?	fSPf	woman's mother-in-law
šin yuž	CSm	son-in-law
šin šiš	CSf	daughter-in-law

Six terms designate affinals of ego's own generation.

blä?	mPCSm(V)	man's brother-in-law
bšic	fPCSf(V)	woman's sister-in-law
šlon?	aPCSb(V)	cross-sex sibling-in-law
wit yuž	mSPCSm	co-brother-in-law
bäl šiš	fSPCSf	co-sister-in-law
lzan?	CSP	co-parent-in-law

There was uncertainty concerning the co-sister-in-law term, some offering **bäl yuž** as the correct form.

A single term stands for spouse, though **mgi?** *man* and **ngoc** *woman* are also used for husband and wife.

| čal? | S | spouse |

MIAHUATLAN ZAPOTEC KINSHIP TERMS
Manis Ruegsegger

Three elementary terms designate father, mother, and child, while two designate grandkinsmen—one for grandfather and one for both grandmother and grandchild.

šud	*Pm*	*father*
šna?	*Pf*	*mother*
šin?	*C*	*child*
tee	*PPm(L)*	*grandfather*
šot	*PPf(L),CC(L)*	*grandmother, grandchild*

Though a single term classifies all children without regard to their sex, two additional terms make this distinction.

šgan?	*Cm*	*son*
rsap	*Cf*	*daughter*

All kinsmen of ego's generation are denoted by three terms which specify kinship between males, between females, and between persons of opposite sex. When the need arises to distinguish siblings from cousins, the latter may be designated by suffixation of **yen?** to these terms, as in **wesyen?** *man's male cousin.*

wes	*mPCm(G)*	*man's brother*
bel	*fPCf(G)*	*woman's sister*
pta?n	*aPCb(G)*	*cross-sex sibling*

Relationships established when a person marries a second time are specified by use of consanguineal terminology, joining with them the morpheme **-byan?**, as in **šudbyan?** *stepfather*, **rsapbyan?** *stepdaughter*, and **pta?nbyan?** *stepsibling of opposite sex.* Stepsiblings and half siblings are classified together in this manner.

Two terms classify together all collateral kinsmen of ascending generations. The form **gol** may be added to aunt-uncle and grandparent terms to specify kinsmen of the third ascending generation. The single form **sobrin,** borrowed from Spanish, specifies descendants of siblings and cousins.

šis	*PPCm(1)*	*uncle*
šit	*PPCf(1)*	*aunt*
sobrin	*PCC(1)*	*junior collateral*

The terms for parents-in-law are those of the consanguineal terminology with the morpheme **-zap** postposed. This is not the case for the son- and daughter-in-law relationships, however, where distinct elementary terms are used.

šudzap	*SPm*	*father-in-law*
šna?zap	*SPf*	*mother-in-law*
šuuz	*CSm*	*son-in-law*
šiiš	*CSf*	*daughter-in-law*

Sibling-in-law terms include both collaterals of spouse and spouses of collaterals, and are three in number matching the sibling terms.

ble?	*mPCSm(V,G)*	*man's brother-in-law*
fšit	*fPCSf(V,G)*	*woman's sister-in-law*
slon	*aPCSb(V,G)*	*cross-sex sibling-in-law*

There are also three terms to designate the relationship established between persons who marry siblings. These terms are based on sibling terms with a postposed modifier. The modifier is the woman's sister-in-law term if alter and ego are both female. If either alter or ego (or both) are male, the modifier is **buuz.** The difference in terminology when a male is involved reflects the fact that a man lives in his father-in-law's house for a year after marrying.

wes buuz	*mSPCSm(G)*	*man's co-brother-in-law*
bel fšit	*fSPCSf(G)*	*woman's co-sister-in-law*
pta?n buuz	*aSPCSb(G)*	*co-cross-sex-sibling-in-law*

A single term is used for spouse of either sex.

sa?len   *S*   *spouse*

Co-parents, the relationship between the parents of a man and the parents of his wife, refer to each other by native forms of the Spanish terms *compadre* and *comadre*.

mbal   *CSPm*   *co-father*
mal   *CSPf*   *co-mother*

What remains of pre-Colonial Zapotec ritual practice is deeply embedded in the form of Christianity which is found widespread throughout Mesoamerica. Water baptism and related Zapotec-Christian practices are those by which ritual relationships are established. The terminology used to specify these relationships is formed by the use of consanguineal terminology and the Zapotec form of the Spanish term *compadre*.

šudmbal   *godfather*
šna?mbal   *godmother*
šin?mbal   *godchild*

The same terms, **mbal** and **mal**, that are used in the affinal nomenclature, also specify the relationship between the parent of a child and its godparent.

ISTHMUS ZAPOTEC KINSHIP TERMS
Virginia Embrey

Spanish terminology has made inroads into the Zapotec system of kinship reference to the extent that while a very few Zapotec terms are used in conversation to refer to kinsmen, these same kinsmen are often referred to by Spanish terminology when directly inquiring about kinship relations.

There are seven basic terms for consanguineals. The two parent terms, alone or modified, are the basis for classifying all consanguineal kinsmen of ascending generations. The form **bídà** (or **bíídà**) is postposed to parent terms to indicate consanguineals and affinals beyond the first ascending generation. Personal names are added to parent terms to designate collateral consanguineal and affinal ascending generation kinsmen, thus partially overlapping the range of terms with **bídà**.

bì'šòzé?	*Pm*	*father*
hñàá?	*Pf*	*mother*
bì'šòzé bídà	*PPm(1,S)*	*grandfather*
hñàá bídà	*PPf(1,S)*	*grandmother*
bì'šòzé (+ name)	*PPCm(1,S)*	*uncle*
hñàá (+ name)	*PPCf(1,S)*	*aunt*

There is a single term for child, and another for grandchild which classify all relatives of descending generations, both lineal and collateral, as well as corresponding affinals.

žìíñé?	*C(G,S)*	*child*
žìàgá?	*CC(1,S)*	*grandchild*

Three sibling terms classify all kinsmen of ego's generation—his siblings, children of parents' siblings, grandchildren of grandparents' siblings, etc.

bìčé?	*mPCm(G)*	*man's brother*
bèndá?	*fPCf(G)*	*woman's sister*
bì'zàná?	*aPCb(G)*	*cross-sex sibling*

Spanish terms may be used to designate collaterals beyond first cousins. Cf. **šprìmúá?** *my male cousin* and **sò'brìná?** *my niece.* Full siblings may be specified by phrases such as **bìčé gúlé níá?** *brother I was born with,* or **tòbì sí hñà*à*dǔ, tòbì sì bí'šòzèdǔ** *same mother, same father.* The phrase **bì'nìté síá? ñàlé ñíá lààbě** *I just missed being born with him/her* means the kinsman is a cousin.

Native Zapotec terms occur for parents of spouse and spouses of children, but terms of Spanish origin merge affinals of ego's generation—both spouses of siblings and siblings of spouse.

sùègrúá?	*SPm*	*father-in-law*
sùègrá?	*SPf*	*mother-in-law*
špí'gú?jè?	*CSm*	*son-in-law*
žúáá líjè?	*CSf*	*daughter-in-law*
škù'ñàdúá?	*PCSm(V,G)*	*brother-in-law*
škù'ñàdá?	*PCSf(V,G)*	*sister-in-law*

There is a single term for spouse that does not indicate sex.

šèélá?	S	**spouse**

The spouse term is seldom heard in the first person in conversation. Euphemisms of the following kind are more frequently heard: **bìnnì lìjé?** *person of my house* (for wife) and **bì'šòzé kà'žìíñé?** *father of my children.* First names are also used by some individuals.

A single term is used to refer to the parent of one's child-in-law.

šùzé?	*CSP*	*co-parent*

LACHIXIO ZAPOTEC KINSHIP TERMS
David Persons

There are a variety of parent and child terms, some of which mark sex of kinsmen and some of which do not. **pa³** and **na³** are terms of endearment often heard in direct address, while **žu³ce³** and **ši³ña³** are used in reference primarily by individuals of older generations. **e³ndu?⁴** is a very generic term, not limited to kinship reference.

u³za³na³	P	*parent*
žu³ce³, pa³	Pm	*father*
ši³ña?³, na³	Pf	*mother*
ži³?ñi², en³du?⁴	C	*child*
žia¹na¹	Cm	*son*
šin² ču²ku³	Cf	*daughter*

Grandkinsmen terms are found on parent and child terms by addition of **u³la³** *person from far away* or **a³ka⁴**.

u³za³na³ u³la³	PP(L)	*grandparent*
ta¹ u³la³, te¹ta¹	PPm(L)	*grandfather*
na² u³la³	PPf(L)	*grandmother*

305

ži³ʔñi² a³ka⁴	*CC(L)*	*grandchild*
žia¹na¹ a³ka⁴	*CCm(L)*	*grandson*
šin² ču²ku³ a³ka⁴	*CCf(L)*	*granddaughter*

Kinsmen of the third generation from ego are specified by further postposing a⁴kie¹ *beyond* to grandkin terms, while ma¹se¹ a⁴kie¹ (Spanish *más*) designates the fourth generation from ego.

Three terms for sibling mark sex of both ego and alter. e⁴ʔne?⁴ *young* is postposed to these sibling terms to specify cousins.

bi³či³	*mPCm(G)*	*man's brother*
be³la²	*fPCf(G)*	*woman's sister*
za³na³	*aPCb(G)*	*cross-sex sibling*

Zapotec terms designate senior collaterals, but a single term from Spanish (*sobrino*) designates junior collaterals.

še¹yu¹	*PPCm(1)*	*uncle*
ni²su²	*PPCf(1)*	*aunt*
su³bri¹ñu¹	*PCC(1)*	*junior collateral*

Conversely, Spanish terms (*suegro, suegra*) have been borrowed for senior in-laws, while local terms persist for junior in-laws.

sue¹gru¹	*SPm*	*father-in-law*
sue¹gra¹	*SPf*	*mother-in-law*
u³či³	*CSm*	*son-in-law*
ži²ši⁴	*CSf*	*daughter-in-law*

In ego's generation, Spanish terms prevail for siblings-in-law (*cuñada*) and co-siblings-in-law (*concuño*), although a Zapotec phrase designates co-parents. (sa¹ may be a short form of saʔa *like, another*, as in saʔa meša *similar table* or *another table*).

ku³ña¹da¹	*PCS(V,G)*	*sibling-in-law*
ku¹ñu¹	*SPCS(G)*	*co-sibling-in-law*
sa¹u¹la¹	*CSP*	*co-parent-in-law*

Terms meaning literally *my man* and *my woman* serve as husband and wife terms, although older members of the community use a single spouse term as well.

še²ʔla³	*S*	*spouse*
ni³yu³a⁴	*Sm*	*husband*
u³na³ʔa³	*Sf*	*wife*

ruku *second* is postposed to kinship terms to specify a step relationship.

MITLA ZAPOTEC KINSHIP TERMS
Carol Stubblefield

Three terms designate father, mother, and child; and three designate grandkinsmen. The latter extend to spouse of a senior grandkinsman and to the junior grandkinsmen of spouse.

štadä	Pm	*father*
šnanä	Pf	*mother*
ši?nä	C	*child*
štadgolä	PPm(S-)	*grandfather*
šmamä	PPf(S-)	*grandmother*
šagä	CC(-S)	*grandchild*

Three terms also designate siblings, indicating both sex of alter and relative sex of ego and alter. These terms extend collaterally in ego's generation without limit.

becä	mPCm(G)	*man's brother*
bälä	fPCf(G)	*woman's sister*
bisianä	aPCb(G)	*cross-sex sibling*

307

Terms for collateral kinsmen not of ego's generation are based on Spanish terms. They extend collaterally and to affines—both to spouse of consanguineal and to consanguineal of spouse—as well as vertically—terms for seniors to all ascending generations and terms for juniors to all descending generations.

štiwä	PPCm(1,S)	uncle
šnantiwä	PPCf(1,S)	aunt
šsobrinä	PCC(1,S)	junior collateral

Four terms distinguish the sex of parents of spouse and spouse of child. The latter are native to Zapotec, but the former employ parent terms with modifier from Spanish.

štad suegrä	SPm	father-in-law
šnan suegrä	SPf	mother-in-law
špagozä	CSm	son-in-law
škulizä	CSf	daughter-in-law

Two terms refer to siblings-in-law. A single term used between females is used reciprocally for *woman's brother's wife* and *woman's husband's sister*, using *brother* in the sense of any male kinsman of ego's generation. This term is of Zapotec origin as opposed to the other one from Spanish which has a disjunctive definition; namely, it is used both between males and between persons of the opposite sex. Presumably, it has replaced two early terms of Zapotec origin that functioned as part of a three-term system of reference with **bišisä** for siblings-in-law.

| škuniadä | mPCSm(V,G),aPCSb(V,G) | sibling-in-law |
| bišisä | fPCSf(V,G) | woman's sister-in-law |

A single term refers to spouse of either sex, and a second refers to co-parent of either sex—the parent-in-law of one's child.

| čälä | S | spouse |
| sagoolä | CSP | co-parent |

MIXTEPEC ZAPOTEC KINSHIP TERMS
Roger Reeck

Although San Juan Mixtepec is a very remote town, it has lost some of its indigenous kinship terms. The affinal terms, in particular, are fading out of the picture. The present data were collected over a period of seven years and are, therefore, quite dependable. The terms are presented as they would occur with postposed **me** to indicate third singular possession. In a few cases, where possession radically changes the initial consonantism of a term, the unpossessed form is also presented in parentheses. N and L represent fortis **n** and **l**; wn represents nasalized **w**.

In addition to indigenous parent terms, borrowed terms are also heard, but only infrequently. **mä?d** is a generic term for child, only marking a kinship relationship when possessed. **bgi** means *man*; **wna?** means *woman*.

pšoz, špapa	Pm	father
žni?a, žmama	Pf	mother
žin, špä?d (mä?d)	C	child
šiNgan	Cm	son
šiNozo?p	Cf	daughter

gol *old* is added to parent terms to designate grandparents while an elementary term designates grandchildren. This last term is reciprocal, however, both to the grandparent terms and to aunt and uncle terms which extend collaterally and lineally.

pšoz gol	*PPm(L)*	*grandfather*
žniʔa gol	*PPf(L)*	*grandmother*
pšey gol	*PPPCm(1)*	*grand uncle*
žus gol	*PPPCf(1)*	*grand aunt*
pšey	*PPCm(1,S)*	*uncle*
žus (žuz)	*PPCf(1,S)*	*aunt*
žiag (miag)	*CC(2)*	*grandchild*

With **pšoz** and **žniʔa, doʔ** *extremely, very, a god* is further postposed to **gol** to specify great grandparents, while loan words **štatit** and **žnanit** provide a means of specifying up to the fourth generation.

štatit	*PPm*	*grandfather*
žnanit	*PPf*	*grandmother*
štatit gol	*PPPm*	*great-grandfather*
žnanit gol	*PPPf*	*great-grandmother*
štatit gol doʔ	*PPPPm*	*great-great-grandfather*
žnanit gol doʔ	*PPPPf*	*great-great-grandmother*

Three terms designate siblings, distinguishing sex of both ego and alter. Postposed **yeʔN** specifies cousins.

bec	*mPCm(G)*	*man's brother*
beL	*fPCf(G)*	*woman's sister*
bzian	*aPCb(G)*	*cross-sex sibling*

Parent-in-law terms are descriptive phrases based on parent terms and words for man and woman, although a wife living with her in-laws may use parent terms for parents-in-law. There are two forms of the son-in-law term.

pšoz ẓoʔp	*mSPm*	*man's father-in-law*
pšoz bgi	*fSPm*	*woman's father-in-law*
žniʔa ẓoʔp	*mSPf*	*man's mother-in-law*
žniʔa bgi	*fSPf*	*woman's mother-in-law*
žimguẓ, žniʔuẓ	*CSm*	*son-in-law*
šiNžiž (wngužiž)	*CSf*	*daughter-in-law*

The oldest women in the community state that there were three indigenous terms for siblings-in-law, but only that used between females is remembered. A loan from Spanish is used generally for sibling-in-law or co-sibling-in-law of the opposite sex. Terms for same-sex co-siblings-in-law have been retained, as has a co-parent term.

bžis	*fSPCf(V)*	*woman's sister-in-law*
škunyad	*SPC(V),aSPCSb*	*sibling-in-law*
bec yuẓ	*mSPCSm*	*co-brother-in-law*
beL wžiž	*fSPCSf*	*co-sister-in-law*
žliol	*CSP*	*co-parent-in-law*

There is a single term for spouse, but **žimgi** me *his man* and **žiwna?** me *his woman* may also be used. These latter terms, however, are also used to make reference to an illicit relationship.

| **ci?el** | *S* | *spouse* |

OCOTLAN ZAPOTEC KINSHIP TERMS
Donald Olson

Five terms designate lineal kinsmen with sex being marked only for parents.

šùzìā	*Pm*	*father*
šnī́ʔāyà	*Pf*	*mother*
šìnìā	*C*	*child*
šmámā	*PP*	*grandparent*
šìnžàgā	*CC*	*grandchild*

There are, however, specific terms for son and daughter which may be employed to specify the sex of a child.

šgáʔānā	*Cm*	*son*
šcáʔāpā	*Cf*	*daughter*

Three terms designate siblings, one being used between males, one between females, and one between opposite sex sibling.

313

bìčá	*mPCm*	*man's brother*
bèldā	*fPCf*	*woman's sister*
zànā	*aPCb*	*cross-sex sibling*

Sibling terms are used for half siblings, but terms from Spanish are used for step-kinsmen: **špà′dràstā** (Sp. *padrastro*) **stepfather**, **šmà′dràstā** (Sp. *madrastra*) *stepmother*, and **sìntì′nàdā** (Sp. *entenado, -a*) *stepchild*.

If siblings are considered as other than collateral kinsmen, it may be said that all collateral relatives are indicated by terms from Spanish. The terms have been accommodated to Zapotec usage in that sex of alter is only marked for kinsmen of ascending generations.

šprímā	*PPCC(G)*	*cousin*
štíōā	*PPCm(1)*	*uncle*
štíāyā	*PPCf(1)*	*aunt*
sòbrínīā	*PCC(1)*	*junior collateral*

Of the affinal terms, only the child-in-law and spouse terms are Zapotec in origin.

swîgrā	*SP*	*parent-in-law*
žúʔùdčā	*CSm*	*son-in-law*
žíʔìžā	*CSf*	*daughter-in-law*
škúnyâdā	*PCS(V,G)*	*sibling-in-law*
céʔēlā	*S*	*spouse*

OZOLOTEPEC ZAPOTEC KINSHIP TERMS
Roger Reeck

These data were gathered in a few hours when travelling salesmen from San Francisco Ozolotepec passed through San Juan Mixtepec. The transcription is not phonologically accurate, but the system is nevertheless of interest, particularly in regard to descriptive nephew and niece terms which are of the same sort reported in the Fray Juan de Córdova (1578) dictionary and also in the Junta Colombina dictionary. Terms are presented with the first singular ending **-na**.

Loan-words designate parents, a general word for child does not specify sex of kinsman, and alternate phrases permit the distinguishing of sex of offspring.

te-wpaʔ-na	*Pm*	*father*
te-mamaʔ-na	*Pf*	*mother*
te-mäʔd-na	*C*	*child*
te-mäʔd-bgi-na, šin-gan-na	*Cm*	*son*
te-mäʔd-wnaʔ-na, šin-ʒaʔp-na	*Cf*	*daughter*

goʔl *old* is postposed to alternate parent terms, also borrowed, to designate grandparents, and a special term is postposed to the child term to designate grandchildren.

315

te-dad-go?l-na	PPm	grandfather
te-mna-go?l-na	PPf	grandmother
te-mä?d-biag-na	CC	grandchild

Three terms designate siblings, and postposed **ye?N** specifies cousins.

bec-na	mPCm(G)	man's brother
baL-na	fPCf(G)	woman's sister
psan-na	aPCb(G)	cross-sex sibling

Two nearly identical terms, probably from Sp. *tío* and *tía*, affect only the form of the pronominal ending and distinguish the sex of senior collateral kinsman, while descriptive phrases based on the child term and sibling terms distinguish the sex of ego and linking kinsman for junior collaterals.

te-ti?-no	PPCm	uncle
te-ti?-na	PPCf	aunt
šin-bec-na	mPCmC	man's brother's child
šin-baL-na	fPCfC	woman's sister's child
šin-psan-na	aPCbC	cross-sex sibling's child

Descriptive phrases were also offered for collateral kinsmen of the second ascending generation, in which sex of kinsman is not marked, but rather that of the first linking kinsman.

| še-ti te-wpa?-na | PmPPC | father's senior collateral |
| še-ti te-mama?-na | PfPPC | mother's senior collateral |

Parent-in-law terms were not obtained but two child-in-law terms distinguish sex of kinsman.

| ši-bguẓ-na | CSm | son-in-law |
| šin-šiž-na | CSf | daughter-in-law |

With the exception of a native co-parent term, affinals of ego's generation are classified by terms borrowed from Spanish.

te-kunya?d-no	SPCm(V),fSPCSm	brother-in-law
te-kunya?d-na	SPCf(V),mSPCSf	sister-in-law
te-konku?i-ño	mSPCSm	co-brother-in-law
te-konku?i-ña	fSPCSf	co-sister-in-law
lgol-na	CSP	co-parent-in-law

Possessed words for man and woman specify husband and wife.

| te-mgi-na | Sm | husband |
| te-wna?-na | Sf | wife |

TEXMELUCAN ZAPOTEC KINSHIP TERMS

Charles Speck
Jane Speck

San Lorenzo Texmelucan is a municipal center of the ex-District of Sola de Vega, Oaxaca. These data were elicited from Fernando Martínez Marcial, c. 18 years old, in October, 1972. Texmelucan Zapotec kinship terminology is of some interest because of its conservatism—it retains native terms for almost all kinship relationships even where most other Zapotec languages have borrowed Spanish terminology. First person singular possession is usually indicated by **-ạ**. Some terms, however, end in **-nę**, a contraction of **ni** *of* and **yạ** *me*. This latter form of possession occurs with optionally possessed nouns and is the regular pattern found with forms borrowed from Spanish.

Six terms define two ascending and two descending generations of lineal kinsmen, distinguishing sex of seniors only. Grandkin terms extend to second generation collaterals.

uzạ	*Pm*	*father*
ñaạ	*Pf*	*mother*
iʔñạ	*C*	*child*
gulạ	*PPm(G)*	*grandfather*
šusạ	*PPf(G)*	*grandmother*
yagạ	*CC(G)*	*grandchild*

A special term, homophonous with a form meaning *my eyelash*, designates third generation grandchildren.

gyič izą	CCC(G)	great-grandchild

Three sibling terms designate brother of a man, sister of a woman, and sibling of the opposite sex. Cousins are kept strictly apart from siblings terminologically by postposing **kweñą** to the terms for siblings.

bikyą	mPCm	man's brother
bilyą	fPCf	woman's sister
zaną	aPCb	cross-sex sibling
biky kweñą	mPPCCm(G)	man's male cousin
bily kweñą	fPPCCf(G)	woman's female cousin
zan kweñą	aPPCCb(G)	cross-sex cousin

Two terms distinguish the sex of aunt and uncle, and a third term nephews and nieces with sex unspecified. They extend bilaterally to all consanguineal collaterals of the first ascending and first descending generations.

šę	PPCm(G)	uncle
nisą	PPCf(G)	aunt
fen nę	PCC(G)	junior collateral

There are three terms for siblings-in-law; but it appears that there may have been an earlier system of just two terms since one is a loan from Spanish *cuñado*. Women use the daughter-in-law term to refer to sisters-in-law while men have a separate term. This is most likely a function of greater bilingualism among Zapotec men, and leads us to conjecture that the son-in-law term may have had similar reference to brothers-in-law at an earlier time.

uz gudą	SPm	father-in-law
ñaa gudą	SPf	mother-in-law
ngudžą	CSm	son-in-law
šisą	{ CSf	daughter-in-law
	{ fPCSf(V)	woman's sister-in-law
kuñad nę	mPCSm(V)	man's brother-in-law
šnuną	aPCSb(V)	cross-sex sibling-in-law

There are separate terms for husband and wife, and a single term from Spanish *concuño* which Zapotec men use to refer to the man who marries his wife's sister.

ngyeę	Sm	husband
mñaą	Sf	wife
kunkųy nę	mSPCSm	co-brother-in-law

VALLEY OF OAXACA ZAPOTEC (1578) KINSHIP TERMS

The following terms have been extracted from the vocabulary of Fray Juan de Córdova, originally published in 1578. The material taken from Córdova for this study is listed in Appendix I to facilitate an assessment by the reader of the present editor's interpretation of it. Córdova himself begins his work with several *avisos* which explain and justify the form of entries which follow. Some of these explanations are relevant to our study and may be summarized as follows:

The first person singular ending is **-ya** or **-a**; second person singular is **-loy** (lohui) or **-lo**; third person is **nicani** reduced to **-ni**. The possessive prefix is **xi-**. Adjacent entries may be related to each other so that the latin form *vede supra* (abbreviated to *vt sup̄*) indicates that such a relationship exists between an entry and those which precede. The form *assi* implies material in the preceding entry which Córdova does not repeat in full. Thus, in the second entry below *de mi abuela or visabuela* is implied:

Ermano de mi abuela o visabuela. **Pizàana xòcea.**
Ermana assi. **Pellaxócea.**

The form / indicates that the form which follows means the same as the form which precedes, sometimes not repeating a repetitious portion of a phrase. *s* is not explained. Note the following entry:

Tía hermana de padre. **Pizàanatìtia** /. **nàaya** *s. madre.*

This entry is unusually complex in that Córdova fails to make it clear that the abbreviated phrase designates a male, not a female. Nevertheless, we might rephrase the single entry as two in the following way:

Tía hermana de padre. **Pizàana tìtia** [cross-sex-sibling father-my]
Tío hermano de madre. **Pizàana nàaya** [cross-sex-sibling mother-my]

Córdova does not help us with the orthography, but we can assume the following equivalencies: **x → š, ch → č, ç → s, hu → w** preceding a vowel, **qu → k, c → s** before front vowels and **k** elsewhere. **ll → fortis L** [Córdova usually spaces **ll** as **l l**, presumably to distinguish it from the palatal **ll** of Spanish, but I have not preserved this spacing in the Appendix since, as it happens, it divides the morpheme **pella** *woman's sister*]. Treatment of laryngealization is difficult to interpret. Geminate vowels may indicate a long laryngeal, as in **ñaaya → ña·ʔ-ya** [**ñaʔaya**]. **j** before consonant, as in **xijci**, is probably also an attempt to recognize some sort of laryngeal treatment of the syllable preceding the consonant, but much of the laryngealization of Zapotec can be assumed to be overlooked in Córdova's orthography.

We may now proceed to an interpretation of the data. Reference is made to entries in Appendix 1 by numbers enclosed in parentheses, and the entries in the Appendix are numbered accordingly.

There are two grandparent terms, distinguishing sex. The grandfather term is based on the father term with following modifier indicating *old*. The grandmother term is elementary in form, but may also optionally be modified. Both terms extend to ancestors beyond the second ascending generation (3-5).

pi-šoze gola	*PPm(L)*	*grandfather*
šose(-a), šose gola	*PPf(L)*	*grandmother*

There is a second grandmother term which turns up in a phrase (42) which is also possibly of some interest for the reconstruction of POM terms, if we can interpret the h as a glottal catch. Extension is presumably the same.

taʔu-a	*PPf(L)*	*grandmother*

A single term, which may occur alone or postposed to the child term, designates grandchildren of either sex. It extends to lineal kinsmen beyond the second descending generation (9) and also to certain collateral kinsmen (51), even of the first descending generation. Since the child term also extends collaterally, it would appear that the grandchild term overlaps the range of the child term in designating collateral kinsmen of the first descending generation when reference to such kinsmen is intended to indicate that they are not true offspring of ego.

šiaga-ya, šini šiaga-ya	CC(2)	grandchild

While the grandchild term extends to more distantly-related descendants, there is another word, homophonous with the word for eyelash, for designating great-grandchildren and more distantly related descendants.

šihsi, sihsi, kiča ši(h)si	CCC(L)	great-grandchild

There are two forms for father, one for mother, and one for child of either sex. Modifiers specify the sex of a child (17,50,51). These terms all extend both lineally (13,18) and collaterally (31,32,44,49) in at least the parent and child generations, but probably to all senior and junior collaterals because of the lineal extension.

pi-šoze(-a), titi-a, tatiti-a	$Pm(1)$	father
naa-ya, ñaa-ya	$Pf(1)$	mother
šini(-a)	$C(1)$	child
šini gana	$Cm(1)$	son
šini čapa	$Cf(1)$	daughter

There are three sibling terms which extend to collaterals of ego's generation (25-29).

peče(-a), ta-peče-a	$mPCm(G)$	man's brother
pela, peLa	$fPCf(G)$	woman's sister
zaana, ta-zaana, pi-zaana	$aPCb(G)$	cross-sex sibling

Apart from the extension of the above terms, senior and junior collateral kinsmen are specified, according to Córdova, by the use of descriptive phrases such as (42) **pi-zaana šose-a** my grandmother's brother (lit. cross-sex-sibling (of) grandmother-my). There are, however, two unique terms, each of which was found twice in the vocabulary, that may have some significance for the reconstruction of POM kinship.

The first of these is found in a third person form (30) and a first person form (40) indicating, respectively, a woman's male cousin and a mother's brother. In both cases, the kinsman is male and a female figures as the generation peer of that kinsman. It is tempting to draw a conclusion from this that bifurcate categories were distinguished in a term that bridged more than one generation, perhaps marking relative age, perhaps not; but the data leave us in doubt.

pi-šio-ni, pi-šio-a	$xPPCm, fPPCCm$	uncle, woman's male cousin

The second term is probably not a kinship term at all, but a phrase indicating a deceased kinsman. The phrase, **šini ketao-a**, occurs three times in the corpus (26,48,59), appearing to mean variously male cousin, nephew, or brother-in-law; but in the last case, the full designation is, curiously enough, brother-in-law, husband of my sister, male speaker... if she is deceased. (The Spanish word muerta (deceased) is in its feminine form, but this is probably an error. It is certainly the brother-in-law who is indicated to be deceased, not the sister.) Córdova does, in fact, list **ketao** as meaning deceased (92), so that the phrase **šini ketao-a** apparently simply means my deceased child and is apparently extended to a variety of deceased kinsmen and affinals.

But it is surely underhanded for Córdova to include this phrase in entries 26 and 48 *as though* it truly represented a kinship term, failing to remark upon any such lamentable state of the kinsman in question, unless it truly did have reference to a relationship between living persons. While I tend to think Córdova has actually misled us here with a nonterm, it is perhaps best to explore its possible interpretation as a term, assuming it to be merely homophonous with the phrase of entry 92.

In such a case, the term would appear to designate cross kinsmen of more than one generation in a way similar to **pi-šio-a**; but whereas **pi-šio-a** may have designated a senior kinsman, this one would have designated a junior kinsman since it encompasses ego's (26) and the first descending (48) generation and since it includes the child term as its first element in both of its occurrences in the data.

šini ketao-a	$\begin{cases} PmPCfC \\ PCfC \end{cases}$	*father's sister's child* *sister's child*

Córdova does not indicate whether sex of ego figures in the use of this term, or whether it can occur without the child term as, for example, the grandchild term does. If **ketao-a** had the capability of occurring alone, without **šini** (as the grandchild term did), the phrase could be interpreted semantically in two distinct ways, namely, as meaning either *my child of* **ketao** *type* or *my* **ketao** *who is also a child*. The grandchild term in conjunction with the child term can presumably be interpreted correctly in both of these ways. If this term were open to this same kind of dual interpretation, then it would not mean *PmPCfC* and *PCfC*, as indicated above, but rather *PmPCf* (father's sister) and *PCf* (sister), and would not in itself mark a junior kinsman. It might even mark a senior kinsman, paralleling **šio** above, but there is no direct evidence one way or the other.

Córdova offers no elementary terms for parents-in-law but presents phrases such as **pi-šoze gonna-ya** *my woman's father*. There do, however, seem to be special forms for children-in-law and sibling-in-law. A term for sibling-in-law of the opposite sex is clearly distinct, as is a term used between females which is transcribed in several different ways. The latter also extends to co-sisters-in-law or women who marry brothers.

ši-lona-ya, či-lona-ya, či-Lona-ya	*aPCSb(V,G)*	*cross-sex sibling-in-law*
ši(h)sa-ya, lešisa-ya, pi-šisa-ya, ta-ši(h)sa-ya, le-šiši-a, le-šiša		
	fPCSf(V,G,S-)	*woman's sister-in-law*

A third term is used between brothers-in-law and for son-in-law, with an alternate also listed for son-in-law which may or may not serve for brother-in-law. This term unaccountably included the child term as first element.

šini yo-či-a	$\begin{cases} mPCSm(V,G) \\ CSm(L) \end{cases}$	*man's brother-in-law* *son-in-law*
pi-yo-ko-či-a	*CSm(L)*	*son-in-law*

The form **šose-a** is indicated to mean a man's co-brother-in-law *mSPCSm* (61,67). It may be a variant of the brother-in-law term, but note that it also appears to be homophonous with the grandmother term. Finally, a daughter-in-law term incorporates the word for home (93).

šini wa-lihči-a   CSf(L)   daughter-in-law

A single term is used for spouse of either sex, but numerous additional phrases are also used to refer to husband and wife, making use of the more general terms for man and woman or by reference to the parent of one's child.

le-čela-ya   S   spouse

Nonkinship terms which may figure in the POM reconstruction include the following:

peni, beni, penni, benni   *person*
nigio, nigi?o, gi?o, pešo   *male*
gonna, pinih   *female*
ni-gola, na-gola   *old*
si-roba, na-roba   *big*
na-wihni, na-wini, wa-wini   *small*
ketao, kietao   *deceased*
liči(-a)   *(my) home*

Appendix 1

Selected Data from Córdova's Vocabulario

Abuelo. **Pixòze gola.**
Abuela. **Xôce, xòce gòla.**
Abuelo abuela, o visabuelo. vt *sup̄.*

Bisaguelo, padre de aguelos o bisabuelo. **Pixòze gòlacoyòna tija.**
05   *Bisabuela assi.* **Xòcegòlani.**

Nieto or nieta mio. **Xiàgaya, xinixiàgaya.**
Nieto ò nieta dos vezes. **Quìcha xìci, quìcha xijzi.**
Nietos descendientes de alli. **Quìcha xìci, xijci.**

Bisnieto hijo de hijos. **Xiagaya còyotija, quìcha xìci. 1. cijci.**
10   *Bisnieta con todos los descendientes de alli abaxo.* **Quìcha xici.** *vel.* **xijci.**

Padre. **Pixóze.**
Padre mio mi padre. **Titia, tátítia, xizánaya.**
Padre y madre ascendientes todos. **Pixózetonó.**
Madre mia. Vide engendradora. **ñaaya, tàanàaya, xizànaya.**
15   *Engendradora que engendra o pare.* **Cozàana.**

Hijo o hija generalmente. **Xíni, xíni coxàna,** *si es engendrado.*
Hijo varon engendrado. **Xínigánacoxána, xizánaya,** *que yo engendre.*
Hijos hijos nietos bisnietos etc. **Xini,** *a todos los llaman hijos.*

Ermano o ermanos, ambos hombres. **Pèche, tápechea, pèchecoxána, còleñeea.**

20   *Ermano mayor.* **Pècheyóbi, pióbi, pèchecóla, hualào, huanici.**

Ermana de Pedro. **Záana, tazáana, pizáana.**

Ermanos o ermanas carnales mios. **Tàpechecoxana, pèllacoxána, tazána. 1. tazáana.**

Ermanos y hermanas todos los parientes al modo de los judios que se llamaban ermanos. **Péchea péchetonó.**

El ermano a ella. **Pizàanahueníchi.**

25   *Primos hijos de hermanos.* **Pécheènin, pèchelí hini, xínipéchetitia.**

Primo hijo de hermana de mi padre. **Xínipizáanatitia, xiniquetàoa.**

Primos y primas ellos a ellas y ellas a ellos. **Pizáana, tazàana.** *s. hermanos.*

Primos de qualquier manera. **Péche, pécheyèni.** *s. hermanos.*

Primas assi todas. **Pèla.**

30   *Prima llama al primo.* **Pixíyoni.**

Ermano de mi padre. **Pèchetítia, pixózea, pèchepixózeá.**

Ermana de mi padre. **Pizáanatítia. 1. pixózèa.**

Ermano de mi madre. **Pizáananàaya.**

Ermana de mi madre. **Péllanáaya.**

35   *Ermano de mi abuelo o visabuelo.* **Péchetítigólaya, pechepixózecólaya.**

Ermana de mi abuelo o bisabuelo. **Pizaanatitigòlaya. 1. pizáanapixòcecòlaya.**

Ermano de mi abuelo o visabuela. **Pizàana xòcea.**

Ermana assi. **Pellaxócea.**

Tio hermano de padre. **Pèchetìtia.**

40   *Tio hermano de madre.* **Pixìoa, pizàana ñàaya.**

Tio hermano de abuelo. **Pèchetìticòlaya.**

Tio hermano de abuela. **Pizàanaxòcea, pizàanatàhùa.**

Tia hermana de padre. **Pizàanatìtia. 1. nàaya.** *s. madre.*

Tia hermana de madre. **Pèla nàaya. 1. nàaya.**

45   *Tia hermana de abuelo.* **Vide madre. Pizàana tìti còlaya.**

Tia hermana de abuela. **Pèla xòcea.**

Sobrino hijo de mi hermano ambos hombres. **Xìni pèchea, xìnia.**

Sobrino assi hijo de mi hermana or sobrina. **Xìnitazànaya, xìniquètàoa.**

Sobrinos hijos de dos hermanas. **Xìni pèlaya. 1. xìnia.**

50   *Sobrina hija de mi hermano.* **Xìni chàpa pèchea.**

Sobrina hija de mi hermana. supra. **Xìni chàpa tazànaya, xiàgaya.**

Suegro padre de mi muger. **Pixòze gònnà, tìtia, pixòze gònnàya.**

Suegro padre del marido. **Pixòze niquijoya, pixòze niguijoa.**

Suegra assi. **Xiñàani guijoa. 1. ñàaya etc.**

55   *Suegra madre de mi muger.* **Xiñàa gònnàya.**

Yerno mio marido de mi hija o nieta. **Xìniòchia, pio còchia.**

Nuera muger de hijo. **Xini hualijchia, lechèlaxinia.**

Cuñado marido de hermana de la muger. **Chilònaya. xilònaya.**
Cuñado marido de mi hermana, dize el hombre. **Pèchea, xìniòchia xiniquetàoa,** *si es muerta.*
60 *Cuñadas una a otra.* **Lexìçaya, xiçaya, pixìçaya.**
Cuñadas muger de mi cuñado, o concuñas. **Lixìçaya, xòcea** *la llama el cuñado.*
Cuñada hermana de mi muger. **Chilònaya, xilònaya.**
Cuñada hermana de mi marido. **Taxìcia, pixìçaya, lixìçaya. 1. taxijcea, xijçaya.**
Cuñada muger de mi hermano. **Xiñaa pèchea, chilonaya.**
65 *Cuñados unos a otros se dizen.* **Xiniòchia.**
Cuñado hermano de mi marido. **Chillònaya.**
Cuñada muger del hermano de mi muger. **Xòcea**

Concuños casados con dos hermanas. **Pèche yóchini.**
Concuñas, vide cuñadas. **Lexíxa, lexíxia.**

70 *Esposo o esposa.* **Lèchelani, xilechàgañaani,**
leçàaninachèlanachàgatichaquelàhuechàgañaani. 1. *esposa.*
Marido de muger casada. **Xipèni niguìoni, lechèlaya,** *mio.*
Marido o muger casados. **Lechèlapèni, lachèla, lichèla, xicasado.**
Muger de marido o casada. **Lechèla, lichela, leçàaya, xihueyàanaya, xipènegònnaya,**
s. *mi muger.*
Macho en cada especie. **Niguio, niguijo, guijo.** 1. **pèxo.** *este* **pèxo** *es nombre antiguo. y especifico y no le alcançan todos.*
75 *Macho yrracional.* **Màni nigóla.**
Macho racional. **Nigòla.**
Persona. **Pèni, bèni, ...**
Ombre simpliciter. s. o muger absolute. **Pèni, bèni, peniáti, penni. 1. benni.**
Ombre varon. **Niguijo, pèniguijo.**

80 *Hembra en qualquier especie.* **Gónná, pinij, gónnàa.**
Hembra racional. **Pénigònnà, pènegónnà, pínij, pénigónná.**
Hembra yrracional. **Mánigónná, mànegónnà, pínij, gònnáa.**
Hembra pequeña. **Gónnáhujni, gónnàyyni.**
Muger generalmente. **Pènigònnà, pènegònnà.**

85 *Viejo generalmente.* **Nigòla.**
Vieja. **Nagòla.**
Viejo hombre de mucha edad. **Pècòxo, pènicòxotè, nigòla còxotète.**

Grande cosa. Vide gordo. pertotum. **Cirào, narào, ciròba, naròba.**
Grande de edad. **Huayàla, nagòla.**

90 *Pequeño o pequeña. Vide chico.* **Nahuijni, nalàhui, natòpati.**
Chica cosa pequeña. **Nahuini natòpa, naxija, huahuini.**

Muerto. **Pènicòti, nàti, yàti, quètào, quietào, piàba.**

Casa por la morada donde moramos. **Lìchi, lìchia mia.**

Pestaña. **Quichaxijzi, xijci.**

RINCON ZAPOTEC KINSHIP TERMS
Robert Earl

With the exception of sibling terms, Rincón Zapotec elementary terms of kinship reference denote only lineal kinsmen. Reference to collateral kinsmen—consanguineal or affinal—is accomplished through descriptive phrases which consist of combinations of the elementary terms. (All terms are presented as for first person singular possessor.)

Three such elementary terms classify parents and child.

šúza?	*Pm*	*father*
šiná?a	*Pf*	*mother*
ží?ina?	*C*	*child*

Three others similarly classify grandkinsmen, with the grandfather term being morphemically complex, based on the grandmother term.

šitá?awa?	*PPm*	*grandfather*
tá?awa?	*PPf*	*grandmother*
ši? sa?	*CC*	*grandchild*

Two alternate grandparent terms are formed of parent terms and the adjective *old*.

| šúza? gul | PPm | grandfather |
| šiná?a gul | PPf | grandmother |

Sibling terms complete the list of elementary terms for consanguineal kinsmen.

bŕča?	mPCm(G)	man's brother
žíila?	fPCf(G)	woman's sister
záana?	aPCb(G)	cross-sex sibling

Further specification of consanguineal relationship requires a descriptive phrase (**žíila-nu šiná?a** *my father's sister*) or a Spanish kinship term (**tio** *uncle*).

Sex and age of a kinsman can be specified by preposing one or another of three forms: **bíni?** *man*, **nigúla** *woman*, or **bí?i** *child*. The man or woman term is usually added to the appropriate sibling term to designate a sibling or cousin who is an adult as indicated by their having a spouse and children. Siblings or cousins who do not meet this requirement are termed child siblings as in **bí?i bŕča?** *child sibling of a man.*

The sex of a younger relative is indicated by combining **bí?i** with the man or woman term: **bí?i bíni? ši?sóa?** *my nonadult grandson*, or **bí?i nigúla keánu nigúla žíilanu šiná?a** *nonadult female child of my mother's sister.*

The term **dí?a ẓa** is used to designate a person as a consanguineal kinsman. It is applied to anyone whose consanguinity can be traced. In practice this is usually not remembered beyond second cousins.

The parent-in-law terms are based on grandparent and child terms and may be translated literally *grandparent of my child.* The child-in-law terms are built on **žóa?** *corn*, **líja?** *my home*, and **žá** *clothing.* The meaning of **ója?** is not known.

što? ží?ina?	SPm	father-in-law
to? ží?ina?	SPf	mother-in-law
žá ója?	CSm	son-in-law
žóa? líja?	CSf	daughter-in-law

The words for man and woman are possessed to designate spouses.

| bíni? | Sm | husband |
| nigúla | Sf | wife |

All other affinals are denoted by descriptive phrases or by Spanish terms.

YATZACHI EL BAJO ZAPOTEC KINSHIP TERMS

Inez Butler

Both the social organization and the system of kinship terminology of the Yatzachi el Bajo Zapotec lie between the Eskimo and the Hawaiian types as set forth by Murdock (1949). To summarize the main features of social organization: descent is bilateral, residence predominantly and preferably patrilocal with a minority of matrilocal residences, monogamy is the rule with few exceptions though there is a high frequency of frustrated marriages resulting in second marriages, the family is typically a patrilocal extended family, incest taboos extend bilaterally to second cousins, and there is evidence that the village community may have consisted of an endogamous deme in the recent past. At present, marriage within the village is still the rule for first marriages.

The basic consanguineal terminology includes terms for each of the members of the local extended family. The grandparent terms are derived from the parent terms by the use of **goⱡi** *old*. There are three sibling terms which are used reciprocally between males, between females, and between siblings of the opposite sex. The terms for child and grandchild do not distinguish sex though this may be done by the addition of descriptive words.

| şa | Pm | father |
| ẓnaʔ | Pf | mother |

329

ẓiʔinn	C	child
ṣa gołi	PPm	grandfather
ẓnaʔa gołi	PPf	grandmother
ẓesoa	CC	grandchild
bišiʔ	mPCm(G)	man's brother
biłi	fPCf(G)	woman's sister
zan	aPCb(G)	cross-sex sibling

Parents' siblings, their cousins, and their uncles and aunts are referred to by terms derived from parent terms. Either a personal name or **benniʔ** *person* are preposed as in **benniʔ ṣaʔ** for male collateral kinsmen of ascending generations and **benniʔ ẓnaʔ** for corresponding females. These terms are also extended to include the wives and husbands of all these relatives.

Children and grandchildren of siblings and cousins are designated by a similar derivative usage. If the relative is a child, either the name of the child or the word **biʔi** *child* precedes the term **ẓiʔinn**. If the relative is an adult, **benniʔ** may be used rather than **biʔi**. (**biʔi**, however, is never used for an uncle who is a child even though he may be younger than ego. Respect demands **benniʔ** or the personal name for relatives of ascending generations.) Husbands and wives of these relatives of descending generations are referred to by the same terms as their spouse.

All cousins use sibling terms. The optional addition of **blaʔa**, as in **bišiʔ blaʔa, zan blaʔa**, and **biłi blaʔa**, indicates that the relative is not a full sibling. He may be either a half sibling or a cousin. Further definition of the relationship requires a descriptive phrase. The terms **benniʔ** and **biʔi** are also optionally used with the sibling terms for older and younger relatives, respectively.

Stepparents and stepchildren use consanguineal terms with the addition of **-ziʔ**.

ṣaziʔ	stepfather
ẓnaʔaziʔ	stepmother
ẓiʔinnziʔ	stepchild

Affinal terminology has suffered under pressure from Spanish, particularly for relatives of ego's generation. Siblings of ego's spouse and spouses of those ego refers to by sibling terms are all referred to by the Yatzachi form of Spanish *cuñado*.

ẓtaobiʔin	SPm	father-in-law
taobiʔin	SPf	mother-in-law
ẓoʔož	CSm	son-in-law
ẓoʔoliž	CSf	daughter-in-law
koniad	PCS(V,G)	sibling-in-law
beʔen	Sm	husband
ẓoʔol	Sf	wife

beʔen *person* is only one of three terms used to refer to one's husband. **benniʔ** occurs with equal frequency, and a third term **ẓyogwaʔ** *my man* which is more rare (from **ẓyo** *man of*) is also heard. **ẓoʔoli** *wife* is the possessed form of **noʔoli** *woman*. It occurs with **liž** *house* in the term for *daughter-in-law*. The parent-in-law terms differ from each other by ẓ- which elsewhere in the language occurs as a possessive prefix. These last terms are also used between parents and parents-in-law.

Relationships established through the ritual act of water baptism involve five reference terms. Godmother and godchild terms are derived from consanguineal terms by adding **nis** *water*. The godfather term seems to be cognate for the term for father in other Zapotec languages. The co-parent terms are from Spanish *compadre* and *comadre*.

ṣoz	*godfather*
ẓnaʔa nis	*godmother*
ẓiʔinn nis	*godchild*
mpar	*co-father*
mal	*co-mother*

In general, the reference terms or personal names are used in addressing relatives. **nagwe** *mother*, however, occurs rather than **ẓnaʔ** in vocative usage, but this only rarely, since **mama** and **papa** (from Sp.) are more common for addressing parents. Terms for grandparents employ **gołi** *old* as in the reference terminology: **papa gołi**, **mama gołi**. One's child may also be addressed using these Spanish terms as in **papa daoʔ** *little man* and **mama daoʔ** *little woman*.

PROTO-ZAPOTEC KINSHIP TERMS

†María Teresa Miranda de Fernández

México, D.F, Octubre 16 de 1963

Muy estimado Sr. Merrifield:

Hasta ahora puedo contestar, aunque sea brevemente, a su carta de febrero 14, en parte porque su carta me llegó muchos meses después de enviada, su trabajo sobre parentesco llegó aún más tarde y por último, cuando tuve todo en mi poder, mi salud no me permitió ocuparme de ello hasta ahora. Espero que todavía le sirvan los datos que le mando.

Por causa de mi mala salud, hace más de un año que suspendí la reconstrucción del proto-Zapoteco, y aunque ésta quedó bastante adelantada, una nueva revisión quizá introdujera algunos pequeños cambios en las reconstrucciones. De todos modos, le envío las reconstrucciones de los términos de parentesco que logré hacer. Algunas las considero como algo inseguras por falta de datos de todos los ramos Zapotecos, es decir, los ramos que yo llamo del *Norte* (Atepec [A], Villa Alta [Yt] y Rincón—Talea para Ud.—[Yg]), del *Centro* (Istmo o Juchitán [I], Mitla [M] y del *Sur* (Cuixtla [Cx], Coatlán

334 POM Kinship

[Ct]). Estas reconstrucciones *no* serán incluidas en mi trabajo y por lo tanto son menos dignas de confianza que las otras.
No he reconstruido, ni reconstruiré por falta de datos, el tono.
Para que entienda mis reconstrucciones le daré la siguiente clave:

- en medio de formas indica división morfémica.
' apóstrofe antes de consonante indica que la vocal que la sigue es acentuada.
V signo de vocal indica que no hay datos suficientes para mostrar la calidad de la vocal, pero que es seguro que existió una vocal. Datos de otros idiomas en que no se pierde la vocal final no acentuada permitirán algún día conocer la calidad de la proto vocal.
L signo de ele (l) fortis en contraste con l para lenis.
R signo convencional para representar una consonante cuya calidad fonética no es posible precisar, pero que por tener reflejos de trinada uvular en Yt y Yg, he decidido representar como -R. La reconstruyo sólo en encliticos.

Los símbolos que tradicionalmente se usan para representar fonemas sonoros (b, d, ž, n, z, etc.) se emplean aquí para indicar fonemas reconstruidos lenis; los símbolos que tradicionalmente se emplean para los sonidos sordos (t, s, š, ɛ, č, etc.) los uso para los fortis. Cuando un símbolo fortis o lenis va subrayado, quiere decir, si es fortis, que la mayoría de los idiomas tienen reflejo fortis pero alguno lo tiene lenis; si es lenis, indica lo contrario, es decir, que casi todos los idiomas tienen reflejo lenis pero alguno lo tiene fortis.
El ʔ entre paréntesis quiere decir que está reconstruido a base de una sola rama porque en las otras no aparece su reflejo por tratarse de sílabas no acentuadas.
Casi siempre tengo reconstrucciones alternantes pero pongo después de cada una los idiomas en que está basada.

Reconstrucciones seguras

hermana **'bäLa (I, M, Cx, Ct, Yt), *'yila (A), *'žila (Yg).
hermana *b̲i'z̲aʔna(ʔ) (I, Cx, Ct), *bi'sanaʔ (M), *'zaʔna (A, Yt, Yg).
hermano **'be(ʔ)či? (I, A, Yt, Yg), *'weči? (Cx, Ct).
hijo *žiʔin̲i? (I, A, Yt, Cx, Ct, M, Yg).
madre *-'naʔa (I), *'nana (A, M), *s̲i-'naʔ (Yt, Yg, Cx, Ct).
padre, sacerdote *bi's̲o̲zV-RV (I, A, Yt, Cx, Ct, M, Yg).

Reconstrucciones más seguras

nieto, abuela *šiʔ-'sowa (Yg), *ži-'sowa (A, Yt), *'žosV (Cx, Ct).
cuñada *bi'žisV (Cx) fšit, (Ct) pšiɛ, (M) bižihs.
padre **'tad̲a (I, A, Cx, M, Yg), *'taʔta (Ct).

Hay algunas diferencias tonales entre sus notas y las mías y añado algunas formas que Ud. no tiene.

En (A) yo tengo žíʔnī, žīlá *hijo, hermana* añado b̲ēs̲ūd̲īā *sacerdote.*
En (Ct) tatʔ[1] *señor* pero šuz[13] *padre.*
En (Cx) añado **tad** *señor.*

En (I) añado **ta** *señor* y yo tengo **bìšòzè** *padre*.
En (Yg) añado **dad** *papá* y **bišúz** *sacerdote*.
En (Yt) añado **bṣ̌ōz** *sacerdote*.

Espero que le sean de alguna utilidad estos datos y que disculpe que haya tardado tanto en enviarlos.

Saludos cordiales de

(signed) *María Teresa Miranda*

P.D. La copia que me envió la remitiré a la oficina de Héroes.

YAITEPEC CHATINO KINSHIP TERMS
Kitty Pride

The Chatinos are located in the mountains of western Oaxaca, Mexico near the Pacific Ocean. These data were gathered in field trips to the town of Santiago Yaitepec under the auspices of the Summer Institute of Linguistics from December, 1959 to the present. The town of Yaitepec is central to a dialect of Chatino spoken by some 20,000 people (1950 census) which roughly corresponds geographically to the District of Juquila, Oaxaca. Informants include Benigno Velasco (23 years), Vicente (65 years), and Tema Francisco (c. 33 years), all of whom are monolingual speakers and natives of Yaitepec.

All terms cited in this paper are given in their first person singular possessed form. In addition to tone, first person is also characterized by nasalization of the ultimate vowel. Stems ending in **a** change to **ǫ** in the first person, and stems ending in **o** change to **ų**. Parent terms in addition require a special first person pronominal suffix -ʔǫ³ ~ -yǫʔ² which does not occur elsewhere in the language.

Seven terms form the basis of Yaitepec Chatino consanguineal kinship nomenclature. Elementary parent and child terms are followed by the attributives **kula³** *old* and **stę?³²** *my clothes* when specifying relatives of the second ascending and second descending generations, respectively. The custom of parents giving new clothes to their son's bride may account for the fact that the term for grandchild can be translated literally *my clothes-child*.

All siblings and collateral relatives are classed together under a single term to which attributive **ngula**^{32} *born* may be added to specify a sibling. Collateral relatives of parents' and grandparents' generation may be specified by words borrowed from Spanish: **tiyu**^{34} and **tiya**^{34}. Further definition of such a relationship requires a descriptive circumlocution such as **ta?a**^{23} **ngula**^{1} **stį**^{32}**yǫ?**^{3} *my father's sibling*.

stį^{1} **yǫ?**^{2}	*Pm*	*father*
y?ǫ^{1} **yǫ?**^{2}	*Pf*	*mother*
snyę?^{32}	*C*	*child*
stį^{2}**?ǫ**^{3} **kula**^{3}	*PPm*	*grandfather*
y?ǫ^{1}**?ǫ**^{3} **kula**^{3}	*PPf*	*grandmother*
snyę?^{32} **stę?**^{1}	*CC*	*grandchild*
ta?ǫ^{43}	*PC(0)*	*relative*

Consanguineal terms followed by the attributive **no?ǫ**^{3} *house* are used to specify relationships established through second marriages. Stepsiblings often do not live together in the same household, and are not considered related.

stį^{1} **no?ǫ**^{3}	*my stepfather*
y?ǫ^{1} **no?ǫ**^{3}	*my stepmother*
snyę?^{43} **no?ǫ**^{3}	*my stepchild*
ta?ǫ^{43} **no?ǫ**^{3}	*my half sibling*

If a child's mother dies, his maternal grandparents usually take the responsibility of his upbringing; but if his father dies, he usually stays with his mother who is very likely to return to her parents' home which also brings the child under the care of his maternal grandparents.

Parent- and child-in-law terms utilize consanguineal terms with postposed elements. Of these, all but daughter-in-law add **-la** which occurs as **-lǫ**^{43} ~ **-lyǫ**^{43} in the first person. This morpheme possibly could be identified with la^{3} *church*, but this is by no means certain. It is also a question whether it is part of the term **kulyǫ**^{43} *man's brother*, but if it is, the term as a whole functions as a single morpheme, and **ku-** is an inactive morph.

stilyǫ^{43}	*SPm(L)*	*father-in-law*
y?ǫ^{1}**lǫ**^{43}	*SPf(L)*	*mother-in-law*
snyę?^{3}**lǫ**^{43}	*CSm(L)*	*son-in-law*
snyę?^{3}**šę**^{43}	*CSf(L)*	*daughter-in-law*

kula^{3} *old* is added to parent-in-law terms to specify grandparents-in-law.

The daughter-in-law term occurs in an alternate form **šę**^{3} **?yǫ**^{21}, where **šę**^{3} is unpossessed and requires a pronoun **?yǫ**^{21} *my*. This is the only kinship term which occurs in this type of possessive phrase except the co-parent-in-law terms which are borrowed from Spanish.

The sibling-in-law terms are three in number and are used reciprocally between males, females, and persons of the opposite sex. They extend to include spouses of all persons referred to by ego as **ta?ǫ**^{43}, and to all persons referred to by ego's spouse as **ta?ǫ**^{43}.

kulyǫ⁴³	mPCSm(V,0)	man's brother-in-law
štyǫ⁴³	fPCSf(V,0)	woman's sister-in-law
hynǫ?⁴³	aPCSb(V,0)	cross-sex sibling-in-law

A single term refers to spouse of either sex, while sex of both alter and ego are distinguished by four terms for the parent-in-law of one's child.

kwilyo?ụ³	S	spouse
mba⁴³ ?yǫ²¹	mCSPm	co-father-in-law
mbare³⁴ ?yǫ²¹	fCSPm	co-father-in-law
mare³⁴ ?yǫ²¹	mCSPf	co-mother-in-law
mblyi²¹ ?yǫ²¹	fCSPf	co-mother-in-law

Christian usage has been superimposed on Chatino ritual practice so that the two have become fused. Baptism of infants and the ceremony where children are blessed by the bishop are the Chatino-Christian practices by which ritual relationships are established.

An infant may have two or three kinds of godparents, all of whom are of the same sex as the child. Spouses of these godparents are also referred to as godparents, but the relationship implied is nonfunctional. The terms used to specify these relationships involve consanguineal terms followed by **tya¹** *baptism*, **kitša³** *demon*, and **biya?²** *blessing*.

sti² tyǫ⁴³	my baptism godfather
y?ǫ¹ kitšǫ³²	my demon godmother
snye?³ biyǫ?⁴³	my blessing godchild
etc.	

Godparents are expected to give items of clothing to their godchild immediately after birth. The baptism and demon godparents together with the child and the priest are the main participants at the baptism. The baptism godparent holds the child while the priest drops a bit of salt on its tongue giving it a name. The demon godparent stands nearby with a lighted candle. The child's parents play no part in the ceremony or in choosing the name, but stand and watch from a distance, near the door of the church.

All children have baptism and demon godparents. In addition, the eldest child usually has a blessing godparent, whose responsibility it is to take the child to a special ceremony for a blessing by the bishop when he arrives in the village from Oaxaca. The child is eligible to participate in this ceremony at any time before the age of about ten years.

A person usually has just one *blessing* and one *baptism* godparent, but any grave emergency may stimulate the acquisition of further *demon* godparents, particularly if the individual is away from his home town and unable to contact his original *demon* godparent, or if the godparent has died. In the case of very serious illness, for example, a new *demon* godparent may be acquired and charged with the responsibility of praying for his godchild by lighting a candle regularly for him.

The co-parent-in-law terms of Spanish origin which are mentioned above as being used between parents and parents-in-law are also used between parents and godparents.

Vocative terminology embraces a larger community than the reference terminology extending beyond actual relatives to include all acquaintances. Respect is vocatively demonstrated towards all elderly people, the Mayor and town Council members and their wives regardless of age, godparents, co-parents, and parents-in-law. In conversation these individuals are addressed using the respectful pronominal suffix -wǫ³ *you*. Contemporaries and close relatives use the familiar form -nuʔwį³ *thee*.

ta³² šuʔ²	*grandfather*
nǫ³² šuʔ²	*grandmother*
ta³²	*father*
nǫ³²	*mother*
snyę̌ʔ³²	*my child*
ti³²	*boy*
nyy³²	*dear*
mba⁴³	*co-father*
mblyi²¹	*co-mother*
mbare³⁴	*co-father*
mare³⁴	*co-mother*
tše³²	*male companion*
tšoʔ³²	*female companion*
bi³	*friend (with respect)*

Grandparent, parent, and child terms are only used for lineal relatives. **ti³²** *boy* is used by parents or older siblings. There is no equivalent term for girls. **nyy³²** *dear* is used reciprocally between members of a household, and by an older relative to any younger relative.

The companion terms are typically used between contemporaries of the same sex whether or not they are related. They connote dissatisfaction with a person, if used with someone of a different generation than that of the speaker.

Friend is only an approximation of the meaning of **bi³** which is used between any two acquaintances regardless of their age or station.

Co-parents-in-law either by marriage, baptism, or blessing use the appropriate vocative terms which indicate their relationship to each other in initial greetings. Thereafter, however, in any ensuing conversation, the more general forms of address mentioned above are used.

There are no specific vocative terms in use between godparents and godchildren. Godchildren greet a godparent as *my blessing godfather*, etc., and the godparent will reply *my child*, or occasionally use the full relationship term.

CHAPTER 12
CHINANTECAN KINSHIP TERMS

This chapter reports Chinantec kinship terms.

AYOTZINTEPEC CHINANTEC KINSHIP TERMS

†*Evelyn L. Krotzer*

The following description applies to the system of kinship terminology used by the Chinantec-speaking inhabitants of San Juan Ayotzintepec as well as those of San Pedro Ozumacín. The system is extremely simple.

Lineal relatives (less siblings) are classed as of a senior or junior generation, distinguishing two degrees of generation distance in either direction by primary terms. Terms for second ascending and descending generations also may refer to lineals of more distant generations without adding modifiers.

tä³¹ kią̧n³	*Pm*	*father*
ma·¹ kią̧n³	*Pf*	*mother*
hǫn³	*C*	*child*
tä²giü·?¹ kią̧n³	*PPm(L)*	*grandfather*
ma²?ia·¹ kią̧n³	*PPf(L)*	*grandmother*
jon³²	*CC(L)*	*grandchild*

All terms are given with inflection for first person possessor, possession being indicated either by a possessive pronoun (**kią̧n³**) or by tonal inflection. There are suppletive stems for the third person forms of two terms: **hmi·²** *his father* and **čó·i¹** *his mother*.

343

The sex of a lineal consanguine is marked by the primary terms for relatives of ascending generations only; to specify the sex of a descending lineal, a modifier must be added to the primary terms: **hǫ·² mï³²** *daughter*, **hǫ·² ŋiǔn?²** *son*.

Siblings are classified together with collateral relatives, with two terms distinguishing the sex of relatives older than ego, and a single term for all siblings and collaterals younger than ego. The last term is used reciprocally between small children, ignoring seniority; but the three-term system and relative age distinctions are picked up in the vocabulary of the children as they grow up.

ŋió¹ kiąn³	ePCm(0)	elder male collateral
ní·¹ kiąn³	ePCf(0)	elder female collateral
ön?¹	yPC(0)	younger collateral

Two terms which literally mean *my man* and *my woman* serve as the terms for spouses. The son-in-law term is a primary term, but the daughter-in-law term means *my child's woman*. The two parent-in-law terms are built on the parent terms. A single term (from Spanish *cuñado*) classifies together the spouses of all siblings and collaterals as well as the siblings and collaterals of one's spouse.

ŋiü·?² kiąn³	Sm	husband
ẓa² mḗ³ kiąn³	Sf	wife
ẓó² hmin³	SPm	father-in-law
ma² čon³	SPf	mother-in-law
ŋo³¹ kiąn³	CSm	son-in-law
më¹ hǫn³¹	CSf	daughter-in-law
kǫ·²ŋia³ kiąn³	SPC(V,0)	collateral-in-law

The mother and father of a child's spouse are referred to as **go·²mo·¹ kiąn³** and **bon³²**, respectively.

An inflected form of **?ma** is postposed to parent and child terms to indicate a step-relationship.

hmi·² ?man²	PSm	my step-father
ma·¹ kiąn³ ?ma²	PSf	my step-mother
hǫ·² ?man²¹	SC	my step-child

An inflected form of the word for *water* is postposed to indicate a ritual relationship established through sponsorship in baptism.

ya¹ hman³	godfather
ča¹ hman³	godmother
hǫ·² hman³	godchild

COMALTEPEC CHINANTEC KINSHIP TERMS
Wanda Pace

The terms presented below represent the usage of Highland Chinantec speakers who reside in the village of Santiago Comaltepec, Ixtlán, Oaxaca. The principle informants were Virginia H. Martínez de Luna and Juan H. Martínez Hernández.

There are six terms for lineal consanguines and three for collaterals, siblings being classified with the latter. Sex of relative is distinguished for senior relatives, but not for peers or juniors. Two ascending and two descending generations are distinguished for lineals, but a two-way distinction is made for collaterals: relatives of ascending generations and relatives of nonascending generations. Terms for senior collaterals extend to include their spouses.

ŋyé?²e	Pm	*father*
sée¹e	Pf	*mother*
hǫo¹o	C	*child*
ti¹yü?¹³	PPm	*grandfather*
ni¹yúŋ?¹²	PPf	*grandmother*
gyée¹³e	CC	*grandchild*
?ę́¹²e	PPCm(1,-S)	*uncle*

nі̃¹²ї	PPCf(1,-S)	aunt
rú?²n	PC(1)	collateral

An alternate term for mother is **ni²¹ kié²e** *my mother*.

Affinals are divided into two groups: consanguineals' spouses vs. spouse's consanguineals. In the first group, children-in-law terms extend to include spouses of nonsenior collaterals.

ҙya¹ŋóo¹³	CSm(2)	consanguineal's husband
ҙya¹ma¹lóo¹³o	CSf(2)	consanguineal's wife

In the second group, a spouse's ascending lineals are distinguished by sex, and a third term (from Spanish *cuñado*) classifies all spouse's collaterals.

ҙya²¹ ŋyé?²e	SPm(L)	father-in-law
?yée¹³ mḯ¹sée¹e	SPf(L)	mother-in-law
ku¹ŋyaa²	SPC(0)	spouse's collateral

Terms for man and woman serve as spouse terms by adding a possessive pronoun.

ҙya¹ ñǚ?¹ kyé²e	Sm	husband
ҙya²¹ mḯ¹ kyé²e	Sf	wife

Two additional terms (from Spanish *compadre* and *comadre*) are used between the parents of spouses.

ka¹bóo¹³	CSPm	co-father
ka¹móo¹³	CSPf	co-mother

LALANA CHINANTEC KINSHIP TERMS
Calvin R. Rensch

The Lalana Chinantec language is spoken by some ten thousand individuals who reside in the extreme southeast portion of the Chinantec region of northeast Oaxaca, Mexico. The kinship terms cited here are all given in the form marked for first person singular. Inflection of kinship terms (as well as that of many other nouns) for person and number referent is accomplished by a complex system of vowel and tone alternations and suffixation.

The consanguineal system of terminology consists of ten primitive forms plus derivatives. Four terms are used to denote ascending-generation, lineal kinsmen of ego and spouse.

ñu?n²³	*Pm(S)*	*father*
še·n²³	*Pf(S)*	*mother*
yi²³u·?n²³²	*PPm(S)*	*grandfather*
ši²?ya·n²³	*PPf(S)*	*grandmother*

The grandparent terms also extend to the spouse of grandparent (stepgrandparent). In the case of a stepparent, a parent term is used, but the form **?mo³** may be postposed to

347

specify the surrogate relationship when desired. ?mo³ appears to be related morphologically to ?mó·² *death* in reference to the death of the biological parent.

The parent terms are used independently of one another, or they may be combined, especially in the first person plural form: šo·³ra² ñö?¹ra² *our parents*.

The child term is only occasionally made specific as to sex, and this has only been observed in third person forms. It also extends to the spouse of a child or to the child of a spouse (with postposed ?mo³ as for parent terms).

ha·n²³	C(S)	*child*
ho²³ñö·?³¹	Cm(S)	*son*
ho²³mɨ·³¹	Cf(S)	*daughter*

Siblings are distinguished from cousins, the term for the latter being a loan-word from Zapotec (Cf. Earl, this volume).

ha·n³²	PC	*sibling*
ẕa·n³¹na¹	PPCC	*cousin*

Siblings of parents and grandparents are denoted by two terms which distinguish sex of relative, though siblings of grandparents may be specified more exactly by postpositional addition of ha³?la·h²³ *great*.

The male term extends to spouses of collaterals as well as to collaterals of spouse, but a third term based upon it denotes corresponding female affines.

?e·n³²	PPCm(L,S)	*uncle*
tʌn²³	PPCf(L)	*consanguineal aunt*
ki²³?e·n³²	PPCSf(V,L)	*affinal aunt*

A final term of the consanguineal system classifies together the descendents of ego's children and the descendents of ego's siblings, as well as corresponding affinals.

ja·n³²	CC(2,S)	*grandchild*

As indicated above, certain affinals are classified terminologically with consanguineals. Thus, parents-in-law are referred to by parent terms, and reciprocally the child term is most frequently used in referring to the spouse of one's child. Two specific terms do exist, however, for children-in-law.

ẕo·h²³ kwɨ·n³²	CSm	*son-in-law*
ki²³ha·n²³	CSf	*daughter-in-law*

There are three terms for in-laws of ego's generation which take into consideration the sex of both ego and alter: one is used reciprocally between a male and his wife's brother, one is used between a female and her husband's sister, and one is used between siblings-in-law of the opposite sex.

tu³ñy?n²³	mSPCm(V)	*man's brother-in-law*
ki²³u·?n³²na²³	fSPCf(V)	*woman's sister-in-law*
lʌ?n³²	aSPCb(V)	*cross-sex sibling-in-law*

A spouse is usually referred to as the mother or father of one's children, but a wife may also be referred to as **mįh³ kyah²³** *woman at my house* or **mįh³ ra·n³ kye·n²³nạ²³** *my old woman*, and a husband through an indirect reference as **ʔñę·h²** *he* or **ʐo·h²³** *man*. Very rarely, a childless woman may refer to her husband by name.

Two terms based on consanguineal terms refer to the relationship between the parents of a man and the parents of the man's wife.

mį³hạ·n²³	*CSPm*	*co-father*
ši²hạ·n²³	*CSPf*	*co-mother*

These terms may be derived from the child term to which is preposed **mį³**, probably from **hmi·³** *his father*, or **ši²**, from **šo·h²** *his mother*. This relationship is also expressed between men by **ku³pa²**, the Chinantec rendering of Spanish *compadre*.

Relationships established through baptism are referred to by certain of the above consanguineal terms. Thus, a child refers to the man who sponsored him by the father term, and to the husband of a sponsor's daughter as a sibling-in-law. The co-parent terms used between parents of spouses are also employed between the parents and baptismal sponsors of a child.

The inflection may be removed from most of the terms of reference for vocative use, but one special term **nį·²³²** is the vocative term for *mother*.

OJITLAN CHINANTEC KINSHIP TERMS
Paul Smith

Three terms designate lineal kinsmen of one generation distance from ego, and three of two generations distance, distinguishing sex of kinsman only in ascending generations.

ñi?^{24}	*Pm*	*father*
se^{24}	*Pf*	*mother*
yi^2 ho^2	*C*	*child*
hmi^2?yi?^{24}	*PPm*	*grandfather*
si^1?ye^{24}	*PPf*	*grandmother*
yi^2 cye^{24}	*CC*	*grandchild*

The term for father has a suppletive form **hmi^2** which occurs in reference to third person.

Third generation lineals are designated by postposing **rï^{2}kwa^{24}** to grandkin terms.

All remaining consanguineal kinsmen—all collaterals including siblings—are classified by a single term.

ro?^{24}	*PC(0)*	*collateral*

351

Two terms denote parents of spouse, two denote spouses of children, and a single term denotes spouse of either sex.

co⁴ñi?²⁴	*SPm*	*father-in-law*
?ye³¹ mi³se²⁴	*SPf*	*mother-in-law*
yi²ŋo³¹	*CSm*	*son-in-law*
yi²lo²	*CSf*	*daughter-in-law*
hi¹kwo²⁴	*S*	*spouse*

PALANTLA CHINANTEC KINSHIP TERMS

William R. Merrifield

The Palantla Chinantec system of kinship terminology has been described elsewhere (Merrifield, 1959). The present statement merely reframes the data in the format of this volume and updates the phonemic transcription of the terms.

Two ascending and two descending generations of lineals are distinguished by primary terms. Parents and direct descendents are always distinguished from collateral relatives.

ti³ɲie?¹	Pm	father
mi³cie¹	Pf	mother
hǫw¹²	C	child
ʑiew¹	CC(S)	grandchild

Siblings and grandparents are merged with collateral kinsmen according to their age relative to ego. Three age classes exist for each ego. One term denotes all siblings or collaterals younger than ego. Two terms denote all siblings and collaterals older than ego, except that collaterals who are age peers of grandparents or older (the symbol e_2 is coined to designate this age class) are classified with grandparents. Thus, the generation parameter is completely ignored in the classification of collaterals. The grandparent terms also extend to include both the spouses of all consanguines referred to as grandparents and all to whom spouse refers by a grandparent term.

hị²giu?¹³	PPm(e≥0,S)	grandfather
ci³?io¹³	PPf(e≥0,S)	grandmother
ŋiu¹	ePCm(0)	elder brother
nïy¹	ePCf(0)	elder sister
ro?¹²	yPC(0)	younger sibling

Two special terms based on parent terms denote parents of spouse, and two simple terms denote spouses of children. Spouses of grandchildren are referred to by compounding these last terms with the grandchild terms.

ʐu²ŋie?¹	SPm	father-in-law
mï²cie¹	SPf	mother-in-law
ŋo¹³	CSm	son-in-law
lo¹³	CSf	daughter-in-law
ŋo¹³ ʐiew¹	CCSm	grandson-in-law
lo¹³ ʐiew¹	CCSf	granddaughter-in-law

The spouse of any collateral or a collateral of spouse (unless denoted by a grandparent term as mentioned above) is referred to by a Chinantec form of the Spanish term *cuñado*. A single term based on a phrase which means *to get married* is used between spouses.

| ku²ɲi¹³ kią¹ | SPC(V,0) | sibling-in-law |
| hị²guw¹ | S | spouse |

Only the *sibling-in-law* term requires a possessive pronoun, of which kyą¹ is the first person singular form. All the other terms are inalienably possessed and inflected for person by complex alternations of segments, tones, and stress. The term for father has a suppletive alternant for first plural or third person: tỉ³hmi².

Most terms of reference, as presented above, may also be used in direct address with first person plural inclusive inflection. A younger brother away from home will address a letter to ŋiu¹ hniaw³ *(Dear) our inclusive older brother*. He initiates the Lord's Prayer with hmi² jniaw³ *Our inclusive father*. There are, however, two special vocative terms for parents which are only infrequently heard in reference.

| tiá³ | Pm(vocative) | father |
| mai¹³ | Pf(vocative) | mother |

An alternate form of the grandfather term based on this vocative term for father serves as a respectful greeting to any elderly male in the community. There are two corresponding terms for females, depending upon whether they are past child-bearing years.

tỉ³giu?¹³		Sir
?io¹³		Madam (premenopause)
?io³		Madam (postmenopause)

QUIOTEPEC CHINANTEC KINSHIP TERMS

Frank E. Robbins
Richard Gardner

The Quiotepec system of kinship reference has undoubtedly undergone a good deal of change due to pressure from Spanish, but it is nevertheless useful for the comparative study of Chinantec systems in general. Quiotepec terms fall into two sets on the basis of patterns of possession. (See Robbins, 1968, for a fuller discussion of this subject.) Person of possessor is marked on consanguineal terms by tone inflection, whereas it is marked by a possessive pronoun with affinal terms. The parent-in-law terms, which are apparent exceptions to this rule, are built on consanguineal terms. The first person possessive pronoun **tyiá·**[13] *my* is cited with examples.

Elementary terms distinguish lineal kinsmen of two ascending and two descending generations, distinguishing their sex in all but the second descending generation.

ñű?³ü	Pm	*father*
sá³a	Pf	*mother*
ha³ñű?³ü	Cm(third)	*son*
ha³mí³ï	Cf(third)	*daughter*
yű?¹³ü	PPm	*grandfather*
sï³?yiá³a	PPf	*grandmother*
tyiá·³a	CC	*grandchild*

355

All forms are presented with first person inflection except the words for son and daughter for which third person forms are cited. These kinship terms are only used in the third person in Quiotepec. For other persons, the possessed form of the noun meaning *baby* is used. It does not, by itself, distinguish the sex of kinsman.

yṳ·² tyiá·¹³   *my baby*

Kinship terms inflected for various persons display, for the most part, minor differences of tone and stress. The term for father, however, is suppletive in the third person.

hmi·²ì   *father (third)*

Collateral kinsmen are classified by three terms for *uncle*, *aunt*, and *sibling*. The sibling term usually denotes a consanguineal kinsman of ego's generation, but it is also used generically of any collateral consanguine. In the absence of nephew and niece terms, this term, used generically, is the only direct means of designating the relationship of collateral consanguineals of descending generations. Such relationships may be specified by means of circumlocutions of the type *my collateral relative's child*.

?ą̇·³ą	*PPCm(1)*	*uncle*
nï·³ï	*PPCf(1)*	*aunt*
rú?²¹na	*PC(0)*	*collateral*

The term for husband is, literally, *my male*, and that for wife *my female person*. The morpheme **cá²** *person* also appears as part of the daughter-in-law term. The parent-in-law terms, as mentioned above, are based on parent terms with a preposed element which indicates sex: **cá·²³** *male* and **?yiá·¹³** *female*. Compare the following phrases with **tu¹** *turkey*: **tu¹ cá·²³** *tom turkey* and **tu¹ ?yiá·¹³** *turkey hen*.

cá·²³ ñṳ́?³ü	*SPm*	*father-in-law*
?yiá·¹³ ṳ³sa¹³a	*SPf*	*mother-in-law*
ŋó·¹³ tyiá·¹³	*CSm*	*son-in-law*
cá² ṳ³ló·¹³ tyiá·¹³	*CSf*	*daughter-in-law*
ñü?¹ tyiá·¹³	*Sm*	*husband*
cá² mï̃² tyiá·¹³	*Sf*	*wife*

Whereas consanguineal terms extend to include relatives as far removed as a relatonship can be traced, affinal terms include a much smaller group of individuals: spouse, parent of spouse, spouse of child, spouse of collateral of ego's generation, and collateral of ego's generations's spouse. The term **ñá·²³** *collateral-in-law* which covers these last two categories is from Spanish *cuñado*. There is no term for other affinals, nor are other relative's of spouse or spouses of relatives considered to be kinsmen.

ñá²³ tyiá·¹³   *SPC(V,G)*   *collateral-in-law*

SOCHIAPAN CHINANTEC
KINSHIP TERMS
David Foris

The following terms were elicited from Florentino Ramírez Mariscal, native of San Pedro Sochiapan, Cuicatlán, Oaxaca. All forms are presented as they occur with postposed first-person personal pronoun **hná**[13].

Elementary terms distinguish lineal kinsmen of two ascending generations, distinguishing their sex, and two descending generations, merging sex.

ŋiu?³²	Pm	*father*
mí²Өia³²	Pf	*mother*
hǫ³²	C	*child*
ŋiú²de?³	PPm	*grandfather*
dí²?io³	PPf	*grandmother*
ciau³²	CC	*grandchild*

All other consanguineal kinsmen—siblings and all collaterals—are classed together by a single term, though specific terms may be used to specify elder or younger sibling.

rę?²	PC(0)	*collateral*
cá² má²hán³ rę?²	ePC	*elder sibling*
dá²hạu³²	yPC	*younger sibling*

Two parent-in-law terms are morphologically based on parent terms, but elementary terms refer to children-in-law.

ca³ɲiuʔ³²	*SPm*	*father-in-law*
mï³Ɵia³²	*SPf*	*mother-in-law*
ŋó³²	*CSm*	*son-in-law*
ló³²	*CSf*	*daughter-in-law*

A single term (from Spanish *cuñado*) classes together at least three generations of spouses of siblings and siblings of spouse.

kú²ɲia²¹	*SPC(V,0)*	*collateral-in-law*

Finally, a single term is used for spouse of either sex.

ɲï² uó³², ɲï² uǫ́³²	*S*	*spouse*

TEPETOTUTLA CHINANTEC
KINSHIP TERMS
David O. Westley

The following terms were elicited from Félix Osorio Martínez, native of Santa Cruz Tepetotutla, Oaxaca. All forms are presented as inflected for first person singular possession, and all but two occur followed directly by the personal pronoun **hniá²** *I, my*. The second term for child and the collateral-in-law term are alienable nouns for which possession is indicated by a following possessive pronoun, in this case **kyá³** *my*. Tone is here indicated by numbers: /¹/ high, /²/ mid, /³/ low, /²¹/ mid-high glide, /³²/ low-mid glide, and /³¹/ low-high glide. For further detail on phonology, see Westley (1971).

ŋe?³	*Pm*	*father*
cya³	*Pf*	*mother*
hǫ́³	*C(vocative)*	*child*
cyi?²	*C(L)*	*child*

A modified form of the child term occurs with forms marking sex to yield **ha¹ŋi?³¹** *son* and **ha¹mǐg²¹** *daughter*. The regular child term is used only vocatively; other cases are expressed by the possessed form of the nonkinship term meaning *child*: **cyi?² kyá³** *my child*. This form is used not only for one's own children, but in an extended sense for grandchildren as well.

359

Two grandparent terms extend to all collaterals of senior generations and corresponding affinals, both spouses of consanguineals and consanguineals of spouse.

i²gi?³¹	*PPm(2,S)*	*grandfather*
cyi¹?yo³¹	*PPf(2,S)*	*grandmother*

This classification of collateral kinsmen of the first ascending generation with grandparents is most likely a shift in referential range that is due to the loss of other terms for
these kinsmen. The shift has resulted in something of an oddity in that the grandparent
terms have a grandchild term as reciprocal when referring to a kinsman two generations
removed but a term for collateral kinsman as reciprocal when referring to a kinsman only
one generation removed. The term for collateral kinsman has as its primary reference
collateral consanguineal kinsmen of ego's own and first descending generation—this is
the only term to designate such kinsmen; but it also has a more general sense as well, in
which it indicates collateral kinsmen, consanguineal or affinal, of the first ascending
generation and of all descending generations. In this extended sense, its reference
overlaps the grandparent terms in the first ascending generation.

cyi?² ʐyo²¹	*CC(L,S)*	*grandchild*
rḭ?³	*PC(2,S)*	*collateral*

Unlike the kinship system in nearby Palantla, relative age is not a factor in the
classification of kinsmen in Tepetotutla. A collateral relative of the first ascending
generation, consanguineal or affinal, is classified as a grandparent even though younger
than ego.

Six terms classify remaining affinals, including spouse. The sex of parents-in-law and
children-in-law is distinguished, with terms for the former being based morphologically
on parent terms. The collateral-in-law term is a loan based on Spanish *cuñado*.

ʐi²ŋe?³	*SPm*	*father-in-law*
mi²cya³	*SPf*	*mother-in-law*
ŋo³¹	*CSm*	*son-in-law*
lo³¹	*CSf*	*daughter-in-law*
ko²ŋya³¹	*SPC(V,G)*	*collateral-in-law*
ʐi²i²gu³	*S*	*spouse*

USILA CHINANTEC KINSHIP TERMS
Leo E. Skinner

The principal conceptual dimensions which divide the kinship reference map in Usila Chinantec are lineality, seniority, and consanguinity. Lineal consanguineals are divided into two senior generations and two junior generations, with sex of kinsman marked only for seniors.

nei?³	*Pm*	*father*
sia³⁴	*Pf*	*mother*
a³hǫ³⁴	*C*	*child*
ni³dyei?³²	*PPm*	*grandfather*
si²?dyie³²	*PPf*	*grandmother*
a³tyie³⁴	*CC*	*grandchild*

The term for father has a suppletive form **hmai³** which occurs in reference to third person and first person plural.

Collateral consanguineals are classified together by a single term (to which a respect form may be preposed to designate a collateral of an ascending generation).

a³rǫu?³	*PC(1)*	*collateral*

Lineal affinals are divided into seniors and juniors, and by sex, terms for seniors being based morphologically upon parent terms.

a⁵nei?³	*SPm(L)*	*father-in-law*
a¹sia³⁴	*SPf(L)*	*mother-in-law*
a³ŋo³²	*CSm(L)*	*son-in-law*
a³lo⁴	*CSf(L)*	*daughter-in-law*

A single term (based on Spanish *cuñado*) classes together all collateral affinals (spouses of collaterals and collaterals of spouse) and a single term refers to spouse of either sex.

ku³ña²³ kią³⁴	*SPC(V,0)*	*collateral-in-law*
i³kue³⁴	*S*	*spouse*

YOLOX CHINANTEC (1730)
KINSHIP TERMS

The following terms have been taken from Nicolás de la Barreda's eighteenth century Doctrina Christiana en Lengua Chinanteca (Cline, 1960). Barreda's orthography is presented in parentheses, following an approximation of probable phonemic forms.

ŋiuʔ	(ñuh)	Pm	father
sia	(xa)	Pf	mother
hą	(jna)	C	child
zyuʔ	(nyuh)	PPm	grandfather
zia·	(nyaa)	PPf, CC(2)	grandmother
ʔią·a	(heaya)	PPC	senior collateral
ruʔn	(run)	PC(G)	collateral
ŋiu	(ñu)	Sm	husband
mï	(mui)	Sf	wife
ŋa·	(ngaa)	SPm	father-in-law
mïsia	(muixa)	SPf	mother-in-law

MISCELLANEOUS CHINANTEC
KINSHIP TERM FIELD NOTES
William R. Merrifield

The following terms have not been subjected to phonemic analysis, but represent only a single brief contact from each language area.

Chiltepec Chinantec

ŋiu?	*Pm*	father
Ɵia	*Pf*	mother
hǫ	*C*	child
ŋidạu	*PPm(1)*	grandfather
di?io	*PPf(1)*	grandmother
ciǫ	*CC*	grandchild
rụ?	*PC(0)*	collateral
caŋiu?	*SPm*	father-in-law
mïƟia	*SPf*	mother-in-law
ŋo	*CSm*	son-in-law
lo	*CSf*	daughter-in-law
kuŋia	*SPC(V,0)*	collateral-in-law
mihŋio	*CSPm*	co-father
dihǫ	*CSPf*	co-mother

Mayultianguis Chinantec

ŋiuʔ	Pm	*father*
Θia²¹	Pf	*mother*
hǫ¹²	C	*child*
ŋi¹dauʔ¹²	PPm	*grandfather*
ndi¹gyi³	PPf	*grandmother*
ŋi¹dauʔ¹² ta¹kwa²	PPPm	*great-grandfather*
ndi¹gyi³ ta¹kwa²	PPPf	*great-grandmother*
cie¹²	CC	*grandchild*
ruʔ²	PC(0)	*collateral*

Tlacoatzintepec Chinantec

niuʔ	Pm	*father*
Θią	Pf	*mother*
hǫ²¹	C	*child*
ʔi²dąuʔ¹	PPm	*grandfather*
ti²įǫ¹	PPf	*grandmother*
ʔi¹duʔ² kua¹	PPP	*great-grandparent*
cįǫ²	CC	*grandchild*
rų̨ʔ	PC(0)	*collateral*

Valle Nacional Chinantec

noiʔ	Pm	*father*
cia	Pf	*mother*
hǫa	C	*child*
hoŋiüʔ	Cm	*son*
homag	Cf	*daughter*
hmigiüʔ	PPm(1)	*grandfather*
ciʔie	PPf(1)	*grandmother*
ʐoi	CC	*grandchild*
nigiüʔ	PPCm(G)	*uncle*
ʔįąg	PPCf(G)	*aunt*
iuʔ¹³	PC(1)	*collateral*
ʐonoiʔ	SPm	*father-in-law*
mïcia	SPf	*mother-in-law*
ŋoa	CSm	*son-in-law*
mïhǫa	CSf	*daughter-in-law*

CHAPTER 13
OTHER OTOMANGUEAN
KINSHIP TERMS

This chapter reports Amuzgo, Huave,
and Tlapanec terms as well as an earlier analysis of Proto Chiapanec-
Mangue terms.

XOCHISTLAHUACA AMUZGO
KINSHIP TERMS

W. Cloyd Stewart

Six elementary terms form the basis of Amuzgo consanguineal nomenclature, distinguishing lineal and nonlineal kinsmen, senior and junior kinsmen, and sex of senior kinsmen.

Parent terms include a prefix **co¹-** which is related historically to the free form **c?ą²** and the bound form **cą-**, a generic marker which can mean *person, animal,* or *thing.* Alternate parent terms are **tá¹²** *my father* and **ną¹²** *my mother.* Grandparent terms are built on parent terms preposed to the adjective root **tkie²** *old.* Lineal descendants beyond the first generation may be specified by modifying the child term with **ka²ñthɔ́²** *next-generation.*

co¹tyą́¹	*Pm*	*father*
co¹ñtɔ́³	*Pf*	*mother*
hnta²¹	*C(L)*	*child*
co¹tyą́¹ cą¹tkie²	*PPm(L)*	*grandfather*
co¹ñtɔ́³ cą¹tkie²	*PPf(L)*	*grandmother*
hntá² ka²ñthɔ́²	*CC(L)*	*grandchild*

Three sibling terms extend bilaterally to all collaterals as far as can practically be traced. No records are kept, and in actual practice such relationships are remembered or not, largely on the basis of social proximity.

369

šiɔ²¹	ePCm(0)	elder brother
šhɔ²¹	ePCf(0)	elder sister
tyhɔ́¹²	yPC(0)	younger sibling

There is a set of prefixes used with the nouns of Amuzgo, including the kinship terms, to indicate the sex of and degrees of respect toward the referent: tíʔ- is used between men, ñé² is used by a woman of a man, tyó³- is used of men by either sex, and stâ²- and nóʔ³- are used of women by either sex. These prefixes always occur with a kinship term as the head noun of a Head-Modifier phrase, but they are usually left off when the term is followed by a Possessor, especially if the phrase is long or the sex of the referent has already been specified. Descriptive phrases may more accurately define family relationships.

tíʔ²šiɔ²¹ hntá² co¹ñtɔ́³ *my elder brother, child of my mother (male speaker)*
tíʔ²šiɔ²¹ hntá² tíʔ²šiɔ²¹ šió² co¹ñtɔ́³ *my elder brother, child of my elder brother (who is) my mother's elder brother (male speaker)*
tíʔ²tyhɔ́¹² hntá² nǫ̃³šhɔ²¹ *my younger brother, child of my elder sister (male speaker)*
tíʔ²tyhɔ́¹² tyhe³² co¹ñtɔ́³ *my younger brother, younger brother of my mother (male speaker)*
tíʔ²šiɔ²¹ hntá² nǫ́³šhɔ²¹ *my elder brother, child of my elder sister (male speaker)*

Even these phrases leave a certain amount of ambiguity since none of the basic terms used in them are strictly denotative in the Murdock sense (1949:99).

Half siblings refer to each other by sibling terminology. The relationship is more carefully defined by a phrase which names the common parent.

tíʔ²šiɔ¹² hntá² co¹ñtɔ́³ kwi²čę́² cʔą́² *my elder brother, child of my mother with someone else (male speaker)*

Stepparents and stepchildren use parent and child terms modified by **tʔmą́³** *large.*

co¹tyá̧¹ tʔmą³	PSm	stepfather
hntá² tʔmą́³	SC	stepchild

As in the consanguineal terminology, six terms make up the inventory of affinal terms.

Those who marry into ego's family are distinguished from relatives of ego's spouse, the former presumably being of more social importance to him if we can judge by the fact that they are denoted by two terms that distinguish sex as opposed to just one term for relatives of spouse. All three terms can be modified in the same manner as consanguineal terms, however, to indicate sex of referent and speaker.

šę³	SP(0)	spouse's consanguineal
lko²	CSm(0)	consanguineal's husband
n¹nca²	CSf(0)	consanguineal's wife

The terms for spouse are seldom used in everyday speech. Phrases such as *mother of my children*, *the one who grinds for me to eat*, *the one I live with*, *the old woman at my house* are more commonly heard.

sʔá³	Sm	*husband*
skú³	Sf	*wife*

A co-parent-in-law term is used between the consanguineal relatives of a man and those of his wife.

ñtɔ³² tkiá́²	CSP(0)	*co-affinal*

Exogamy is the rule within the consanguineal group.

Compadre and *comadre* relationships are established through sponsorship of one's child in baptism and marriage, of one's religious picture for a blessing, or of a sick person in one's household for healing. The person who sponsors a religious picture for a blessing takes it to the priest and returning it brings with him musicians, a cantor, and a procession of people. The one who seeks healing carries a piece of clothing from the sick person, along with a candle, before one of the saints in the church, or before the most important village cross.

A person sponsored for baptism, marriage, or healing refers to his sponsor as **co¹tyá̧ʔ¹²** **cʔɔ̧²** *my godfather*, and **co¹ñtɔ̧³ cʔɔ̧²** *my godmother*; and is in turn referred to as **hntá̧ʔ²** **cʔɔ̧²** *my godchild*. The term **cʔɔ̧²** differs from the word for *heart* only by tone and is probably etymologically related to it.

The terms used reciprocally by sponsors with the persons who make the original contract with them to sponsor their relative or religious picture are from Spanish.

co¹mpá¹²		*my compadre*
co¹ma²rä́³		*my comadre*

The Vocative Terminology

When two persons greet one another they use the formula **šmá̧²ñtú̧ʔ²** followed by one of several terms which denotes primarily distinctions of sex, relative age, and affection.

tá́¹, tyéʔ³, tá¹²	*very old man*
ná̧¹²	*very old woman*
šiɔ²¹	*older man*
šhɔ²¹	*older woman*
ré¹²	*man's male peer*
šú¹	*woman's female peer*
ško¹	*male peer*
lei¹	*female peer*
tyhɔ́¹²	*younger person*
ʔnta¹	*very young person*

The three parent terms (**tyéʔ³** is very similar to the third person form of father: **co¹tyé²**) show formal respect and are used to address older persons. Courtesy is shown by the use of sibling terminology when greeting a relative or acquaintance. These sibling terms which are optionally preceded by sex-distinguishing elements as have been described above under reference terminology, always have such preposed forms when used in direct address.

The terms ré¹² and šu¹² are more reserved than ško¹ and lei¹ which are affectionate. A man must be very careful in his use of lei¹ to a woman of his own age for this reason.

Besides being used to greet a very young person, ʔnta¹ *baby* is also used affectionately to an adult by very old people.

HUAVE KINSHIP TERMS
Milton Warkentin

A detailed analysis of Huave kinship has been made by Diebold (1966) who finds coexisting systems within the same community which correlate with patterns of co-residence. Both of the systems he describes involve a small number of elementary terms which combine in descriptive phrases to denote the full range of kinsmen. The difference between the two systems lies in the range of denotation of the elementary terms. In one system (variant B here), elementary terms denote only lineal kinsmen and siblings. In the other system (variant C here), the denotation of the same elementary terms is extended along generation lines to those collaterals living within the same residential unit. Diebold also reports how five of the consanguineal terms are used in direct address.

Our data differ somewhat from Diebold's but we do not present them as necessarily being in contradiction to his findings. He has presented two ways Huaves use kinship terms. Though we do not know how our data fit in with his, we believe they also reflect Huave usage. The terms are presented with Diebold's two variants marked as B and C, and our data marked as A. Vocative usage as presented by Diebold is also listed, marked as V.

In variant A, parent terms are strictly denotative, while the child term extends to all direct descendants. Grandparent terms extend to all direct ancestors as well as all collaterals who are peers of the direct ancestors as defined by relative age. Thus, an uncle very much older (e^2) than ego is referred to as grandfather.

	A	B	C	V	
téàt	*Pm*	*Pm*	*Pm(G,-S)*	*Pm(1)*	*father*
mȋm	*Pf*	*Pf*	*Pf(G,-S)*	*Pf(1)*	*mother*
kwál	*C(L)*	*C*	*C(G)*	*C(1)*	*child*
šéèč	*PPm(e²0)*	*PPm*	*PPm(G)*		*grandfather*
nčéy	*PPf(e²0)*	*PPf*	*PPf(G)*		*grandmother*

The remaining collaterals are classified as older than ego (but not old enough to be classified as a grandparent) or as younger than ego.

	A	B	C	V	
kóh	*ePC(0)*	*ePC*	*ePC(G)*	*ePC(G)*	*elder sibling*
čȋg	*yPC(0)*	*yPC*	*yPC(G)*	*yPC(G)*	*younger sibling*

There are two reciprocal terms for lineal ancestors of spouse and spouses of lineal descendants: a son-in-law term used reciprocally between him and his parents-in-law, and a daughter-in-law term used reciprocally between her and her parents-in-law. A loan from Spanish classifies together all collaterals of spouse and all spouses of collaterals, and two terms refer to spouse. A final term refers to the parent of a child's spouse.

	A	B	C	
òkwáác	*mSP(L,R)*	*mSP(R)*	*mSP(R)*	*parent/son-in-law*
ápîw	*fSP(L,R)*	*fSP(R)*	*fSP(R)*	*parent/daughter-in-law*
kùñádà	*PCS(V,0)*	*PCS(V)*	*PCS(V,G)*	*sibling-in-law*
nóh	*Sm*	*Sm*	*Sm*	*husband*
ntáh	*Sf*	*Sf*	*Sf*	*wife*
hȋy	*CSP*	*CSP*	*CSP*	*co-parent*

MALINALTEPEC TLAPANEC KINSHIP TERMS

Mark L. Weathers

Malinaltepec kinship data were first obtained for this paper from Antonio Cristino Carrasco, then 17 years old, a native of Xochiatenco, Malinaltepec, Guerrero, Mexico. Additional data were later collected from older speakers of other villages of the municipality. Although some terms have special uses in their uninflected form, a possessed form is more natural. In this paper, the quality of the final vowel of each term, the tone of that vowel, and the final glottal represent inflection for first person singular possessor.

The system involves alternative terms at several points as well as overlapping extension of terms. The most common parent terms are of the nana/tata variety, but alternate terms are used as well, especially by older speakers. A single term for child fails to distinguish sex, but modifiers can be added to do so, if desired.

táté?, ānù?	Pm	*father*
náné?, rūdú?	Pf	*mother*
à?dé?	C	*child*

Unpossessed forms **tátà** and **nánà** are used as pronouns or as titles *sir* and *madam*, respectively, in addition to their use in reference to parents (when possessed).

There is also variation in terms for grandkinsmen and collateral kinsmen not of ego's generation. The following usage is attributed by some to be an innovation of the younger generation, but a survey to verify the distribution of the system has not been taken: terms for senior collateral kinsmen occur with parent terms to specify grandparents, while a specially modified form of the child term designates junior collaterals.

tátà šì?yú?	PPm(L,S)	grandfather
nánà šíyù?	PPf(L,S)	grandmother
à?dá šíyĭ?	CC(L,S)	grandchild
šì?yú?	PPCm(1,S)	uncle
šíyù?	PPCf(1,S)	aunt
drîšè?	PCC(1,S)	junior collateral

This last term, for junior collateral, appears to be a possessed and contracted form of à?dá ríšã *patio child* (which never actually occurs in this full, uncontracted form), the reference presumably being to a child of the extended family as opposed to a true child (à?dá gũ?wá, lit. *house child*) or an illegitimate child (à?dá šáná, lit. *forest child*).

Other speakers, purportedly of the older generation, show another pattern for senior kinsmen which incorporates two additional terms for senior collaterals and employs the senior collateral terms of the other system in reference to kinsmen beyond the first ascending generation, as follows:

šì?yú?	PPm(1,S)	grandfather
šíyù?	PPf(1,S)	grandmother
àmú?	PPCm(G,S)	uncle
nìyú?	PPCf(G,S)	aunt

The form ígò? may be further postposed to grandparent and grandchild terms to designate lineal kinsmen more than two generations removed from ego's generation.

Four sibling terms, designating true siblings who share at least one parent with ego, distinguish both sex of ego and sex of alter.

jíyò?	mPCm	man's brother
díyè?	fPCm	woman's brother
jwî?gú?	fPCf	woman's sister
jágwî?	mPCf	man's sister

Two other sibling terms fail to indicate sex of either ego or alter, but indicate their relative age. They extend to all kinsmen of ego's generation and to all corresponding affinals.

jáhù?	ePC(G,S)	elder sibling
gè?té?	yPC(G,S)	younger sibling

Cousins may be specifically designated by a contraction of the junior collateral terms (different from the contraction presented above) followed by gàhmè? *with me*, viz. à?dá ršàhmù? (lit. *my junior collateral with me*).

There are two terms for parents of spouse, two for spouse of child, and two for spouse—each pair distinguishing sex of alter. The child-in-law terms extend to the spouses of ego's kinsmen of his generation.

hmégwì?	*SPm*	*father-in-law*
jàgwì?	*SPf*	*mother-in-law*
nìgwį́?	*CSm(G2)*	*son-in-law*
gù?gwį́?	*CSf(G2)*	*daughter-in-law*
àhmbé?	*Sm*	*husband*
à?gwì?	*Sf*	*wife*

The spouse terms are possessed forms of words that otherwise have reference to male or female: **āhmbā** *male*, **à?gò** *female*.

The child-in-law terms may also be modified by the grandchild modifier to designate spouses of grandchildren, thus providing an assymetry in the system in regard to reciprocals. (Remember that the grandparent terms extend directly to grandparents of spouse where symmetry would expect modified parent-in-law terms for these kinsmen).

nìgų́ šíyį̀?	*CCSm(L)*	*grandson-in-law*
gù?gų́ šíyį̀?	*CCSf(L)*	*granddaughter-in-law*

Another descriptive phrase matching **à?dá ršàhmò?** *my cousin* designates siblings of spouse. It is built on the child term and the father-in law term.

à?dá mègwì?	*SPC*	*sibling-in-law*

Both the descriptive terms, as well as the child-in-law terms in their extended sense referring to spouses of ego's kinsmen of his generation, designate individuals who may alternatively be referred to by the older and younger collateral terms. Subsequent study should seek to determine the factors in determining how to appropriately choose between these competing sets of terms.

Four final terms designate the parents of a child's spouse and the spouse of a spouse's sibling.

mbáli?	*CSPm*	*co-father*
máli?	*CSPf*	*co-mother*
nīgwáhmù?	*SPCSm*	*co-brother-in-law*
gū?gwáhmù?	*SPCSf*	*co-sister-in-law*

TLACOAPA TLAPANEC KINSHIP TERMS

H. V. Lemley

Tlacoapa Tlapanec kinship terms are presented as inflected for first person singular possessor, the pronominal suffix having a variety of phonemic realizations but in general involving a back vowel followed by a glottal. In some contexts it also involved a palatal element which precedes the back vowel.

A detailed presentation of morphophonemic rules will not be attempted here, but one point is worthy of noting for purposes of comparison; namely, that a velar consonant is replaced by a corresponding alveolar consonant when the grammar places it in a position immediately preceding y. Thus, in rough form, the rule: **k → t** and **g → d** in the context —**y**.

The uninflected form of **ni³dyy̨?¹** *my son-in-law* is thus (with perhaps a change of tone) **ni³gy̨¹**. Needless to say, all sequences **gy** do not come from **d + y**. The uninflected form of **a?³dyo?¹** *my child* is **a?³da¹**.

Lineal kinsmen are strictly distinguished from collateral as are lineal consanguines and lineal affinals. Collaterals are merged with affinals except in ego's generation where the maximum differentiation occurs in classifying kinsmen.

Although the child term does not itself distinguish sex, the forms **ja¹ma¹** *boy* and **ja?¹gu¹** *girl* may be postposed to it for this purpose. The modifier which designates an offspring to be of the second descending generation is apparently the grandmother term.

a²nu?³	Pm	*father*
ru³du?¹	Pf	*mother*
a?³dyo?¹	C	*child*
ši?³ñu?¹	PPm	*grandfather*
ši¹ñu?¹	PPf	*grandmother*
a?³da¹ ši¹ñu?²yo?³	CC	*grandchild*

Grandparent terms may be modified to indicate lineals beyond the second ascending generation.

ši?³ñu¹ a²ga?²yo?³	PPPm	*great-grandfather*
ši¹ñu² a²ga?²yo?³	PPPf	*great-grandmother*

The term **ska³ho³** *undeveloped ear of corn* is suffixed to parent and child terms to specify a step-relationship, and **sa²ku³** *prayer* is so suffixed to indicate a ritual kinship established through Christian baptism.

There are two sets of sibling terms. The first distinguishes sex of both ego and alter by four terms; the second distinguishes relative age of ego and alter by two terms.

ji²³yu?³	mPCm	*man's brother*
dya?¹²yo?³	fPCm	*woman's brother*
jwe?³¹gu?¹	fPCf	*woman's sister*
ja¹dyu?¹	mPCf	*man's sister*
gi?³ñu?²	ePC	*elder sibling*
gi?³tyo?³	yPC	*younger sibling*

There are two terms for senior collateral kinsmen, distinguishing their sex, and one for junior collateral kinsmen. They extend to all collaterals not of ego's generation and to corresponding affinals. The junior collateral term for nephews and nieces is based on the child term, but the meaning of the modifier is unknown [but see Weathers, this volume].

a³mu?²	PPCm(1,S)	*uncle*
ni³ñu?¹	PPCf(1,S)	*aunt*
a?³da¹ ri¹šyo?¹	PCC(1,S)	*junior collateral*

The cousin term is built on the nephew/niece term with an additional modifier which also occurs in co-sibling-in-law terms. Its meaning is *with me*, in the sense of sharing some characteristic. Cousins are *nephews with me* while co-siblings-in-law are *in-laws with me* of the same family.

a?³da¹ ri¹ša¹ ga³hmu?³	PPCC(G)	*cousin*

Affinal terms designate parents-in-law, children-in-law, and spouses, all by sex.

hme¹³dyu?³	SPm	*father-in-law*
ja³dyu?³	SPf	*mother-in-law*
ni³dyu?¹	CSm	*son-in-law*
gu?³dyu?¹	CSf	*daughter-in-law*

| a³hmba?²³yo?³ | Sm | husband |
| a?³dyu?³ | Sf | wife |

All these terms (except *Sm*) have a partially similar form in the second syllable (with **g** → **dy** as mentioned above) which suggests they are morphemically compound. A phrase with literal translation *my father-in-law's child* designates *sibling of spouse*.

| a?³da¹ me³dyu?³ | SPC | spouse's sibling |

Co-sibling-in-law terms also make reference to the mutual relationships with a father-in-law by use of **ga³hmu?³** *with me* and child-in-law terms.

| ni³gy¹ ga³hmu?³ | SPCSm | co-brother-in-law |
| gu?³gy¹ ga³hmu?³ | SPCSf | co-sister-in-law |

PROTO CHIAPANEC-MANGUE
KINSHIP TERMS

Detailed kinship materials are not available for this family of Otomanguean languages, but the following terms and possibly-related words from Chiapanec (Ch), Proto Chiapanec (PCh), and Proto Chiapanec-Mangue (PCM) have been taken from Fernández de Miranda and Weitlaner (1961), with a few adjustments by the present author.

PCM 34. *ngu-tá?	Pm	father
PCM 221. *pu-yu-wa(?)	Pm	father
PCM 221. *nu-wa	m	man, male
PCM 158. *hwe, *nu-hwe	m	man, male
PCM 158. *mbu-hwe, *nu-hwi	Sm	husband
PCM 179. *ngu-má?, *ngi-má?	Pf	mother
PCM 197. *mba-hwi, *nu-hmi	Sf	wife
PCM 159. *na-hwí	f	woman, female
PCM 37. *na-tu-me, *na-ru-me	C	child
PCM 206. *mba-ña	C	child
PCh 87. *na-ču-ndi		small
PCM 182. *ña-mu		small
PCM 188. *na-mu-mu		seed
PCM 110. *ma-ngu, *ma-mba	PC(G)	sibling
Ch 181. *ni-mà-hi		family
PCM 277. *aka		big

383

BIBLIOGRAPHY

The following references are divided into two sections, Otomanguean Studies and General Background. The Otomanguean Studies are listed according to language family with a section at the end for general Otomanguean works.

1. Otomanguean Studies

Amuzgo

Bauernschmidt, Amy. 1965. Amuzgo Syllable Dynamics, Language 41:471-83.
Longacre, Robert E. 1966a. On Linguistic Affinities of Amuzgo. International Journal of American Linguistics 32:46-49.
_____. 1966b. The Linguistic Affinities of Amuzgo. A. Pompa y Pompa (ed), Summa Anthropologica: en Homenaje a Roberto J. Weitlaner. Mexico: Instituto Nacional de Antropología e Historia. Pp. 541-60.

Chiapanec-Mangue

Fernández de Miranda, María Teresa, and Roberto J. Weitlander. 1961. Sobre algunas relaciones de la familia mangue. AL 3:7:1-99.

Hamp, Eric. P. 1962. Toward the Refinement of Chiapanec-Mangue Comparative Phonology. Proceedings of the International Congress of Americanists 35:387-402.

Olmsted, David L. 1961. Lexicostatistics as "proof" of Genetic Relationship: The Case for "Macro-Manguean". AL 3:6:9-14.

Chinantecan

Barreda, Nicolás de la. 1730. Doctrina Cristiana en lengua chinanteca. Republished in Cline 1960, this document contains important, though limited, data from Yolox of the early eighteeth Century.

Cline, Howard F. 1960. Doctrina Christiana en chinanteca. Papeles de la chinantla 2, serie científica 6. México: Museo Nacional de Antropología.

Foris, David. 1973. Sochiapan Chinantec Syllable Structure. International Journal of American Linguistics 39:232-235.

Gardner, Richard and Wm. R. Merrifield. (To appear). Quiotepec Chinantec Tone. C. R. Rensch (ed), Chinantec Studies I, Summer Institute of Linguistics Publications in Linguistics and Related Fields.

Merrifield, William R. 1959. Chinantec Kinship in Palantla, Oaxaca, Mexico. American Anthropologist 61:875-81.

_____. 1963. Palantla Chinantec Syllable Types. Anthropological Linguistics 5:5:1-6.

_____. 1966. Linguistic Clues for the Reconstruction of Chinantec Prehistory. A. Pompa y Pompa (ed), Summa Anthropologica: en Homenaje a Roberto J. Weitlaner. Mexico: Instituto Nacional de Antropología e Historia. Pp. 579-96.

Mugele, Robert L. 1976. Lalana Chinantec y-: Why?. Workpapers of the Summer Institute of Linguistics (University of North Dakota) 20:1-38.

Pace, Wanda, Judi Lynn Anderson, and Wm. R. Merrifield. (To appear). Comaltepec Chinantec Tone. C. R. Rensch (ed), Chinantec Studies I, Summer Institute of Linguistics Publications in Linguistics and Related Fields.

Rensch, Calvin and Carolyn Rensch. 1966. The Lalana Chinantec Syllable. A Pompa y Pompa (ed), Summa Anthropologica: en Homenaje a Roberto J. Weitlaner. Mexico: Instituto Nacional de Antropología e Historia, Pp. 455-63.

Rensch, Calvin R. 1968. Proto-Chinantec Phonology. Papeles de la chinantla 6, serie científica 10. México: Museo Nacional de Antropología.

Robbins, Frank. 1961. Quiotepec Chinantec Syllable Patterning. International Journal of American Linguistics 27:237-50.

Skinner, Leo E. 1962. Usila Chinantec Syllable Structure. International Journal of American Linguistics 28:251-55.

Smith, Paul and Dorothy Smith. Chinantec Phonemes with Special Reference to the Tonal System. Unpublished manuscript.

Weitlaner, Roberto J. and Paul Smith. 1962. Detalles de la fonología del idioma proto-chinanteco: un informe preliminar. Revista Mexicana de Estudios Antropológicos 18:117-23.

Westley, David O. 1971. The Tepetotutla Chinantec Stressed Syllable. International Journal of American Linguistics 37:160-63.

Huave

Diebold A. Richard, Jr. 1966. The Reflection of Co-residence in Mareño Kinship Terminology. Ethnology 5:37-79.

Warkentin, Milton and Clara Warkentin. 1952. Vocabulario Huave. Mexico: Instituto Lingüístico de Verano.

Mixtecan

Arana Osnaya, Evangelina. 1957a. Relaciones internas del tronco mixteco. M.A. thesis, Escuela Nacional de Antropología e Historia. México.

———. 1957b. Divergencias internas del mixteco y del macromixteca. Semana lingüística del Consejo de Lenguas Indígenas.

———. 1960. Relaciones internas del mixteco-trique. Mexico: Instituto Nacional de Antropología e Historia.

Bradley, C. Henry. 1965. The Proto-Mixteco Kinship System. Workpapers of the Summer Institute of Linguistics (University of North Dakota) 9:18-39.

———. 1970. A Linguistic Sketch of Jicaltepec Mixtec. Norman, Oklahoma: Summer Institute of Linguistics (University of Oklahoma).

Bright, William. 1958. Review of Longacre 1957. Language 34:164-67.

Dahlgren de Jordan, Barbro. 1954. La mixteca: su cultura e historia prehispánicas. México: Imprenta Universitaria.

Daly, John P. 1977. A Problem in Tone Analysis. W. R. Merrifield (ed), Studies in Otomanguean Phonology. Dallas: Summer Institute of Linguistics (University of Texas, Arlington). Pp. 3-20.

———. 1978. Notes on Diuxi Mixtec Tone. Work Papers of the Summer Institute of Linguistics (University of North Dakota) 22:98-113.

Fernández de Miranda, María Teresa. 1958. Review of Longacre 1957. American Anthropologist 60:983.

Holland, William R. 1959. Dialect Variations of the Mixtec and Cuicatec Areas of Oaxaca, Mexico. Anthropological Linguistics 1:8:25-31.

Hollenbach, Barbara E. 1973. El parentesco entre los triques de Copála, Oaxaca. América Indígena 33:1:167-86.

Longacre, Robert E. 1952. Five Phonemic Pitch Levels in Trique. Acta Linguistica Academiae Scientarum Hungaricae 7:62-81.

———. 1955. Rejoinder to Hamp's Componential Restatement of Syllable Structure in Trique. International Journal of American Linguistics 21:189-94.

———. 1957. Proto-Mixtecan. Bloomington: Indiana University Research Center in Anthropology, Folklore, and Linguistics.

———. 1959. Trique Tone Morphemics. Anthropological Linguistics 1:4:5-42.

———. 1961. Swadesh's Macro-Mixtecan Hypothesis. International Journal of American Linguistics 27:9-29.

Mak, Cornelia. 1950. A Unique Tone Perturbation in Mixteco. International Journal of American Linguistics 16:82-86.

———. 1953. A Comparison of Two Tonemic Systems. International Journal of American Linguistics 19:85-100.

——— and Robert E. Longacre. 1960. Proto-Mixtec Phonology International Journal of American Linguistics 26:23-40.

Needham, Doris and Marjorie Davis. 1946. Cuicateco Phonology. International Journal of American Linguistics 12:139-46.

North, Joanne and Jäna Shields. 1977. Silacayoapan Mixtec Phonology. Wm. R. Merrifield (ed), Studies in Otomanguean Phonology. Dallas: Summer Institute of Linguistics (University of Texas, Arlington). Pp. 21-33.

Overholt, Edward. 1961. The Tonemic System of Guerrero Mixteco. Benjamin F. Elson and Juan Comas (eds), A William Cameron Townsend en el Vigesimoquinto Aniversario del Instituto Lingüístico de Verano. Pp. 597-626.

Pankratz, Leo and Eunice V. Pike. 1967. Phonology and Morphotonemics of Ayutla Mixtec. International Journal of American Linguistics 33:287-99.

Reyes, Fray Antonio de los. 1593. Arte en la lengua mixteca. Mexico (Reprinted in 1890, Paris, Charencey).

Otopamean

Andrews, Henrietta. 1949. Phonemes and Morphophonemes of Temoayan Otomí. International Journal of American Linguistics 15:213-22.

Bartholomew, Doris A. 1959. The Structure of Proto-Otomi-Pame. M.A. Thesis, University of Pennsylvania.

_____. 1960. Some Revisions of Proto-Otomí Consonants. International Journal of American Linguistics 26:317-29.

_____. 1965. The Reconstruction of Otopamean (Mexico). Ph.D. Dissertation, University of Chicago.

_____. 1975. Some Morphophonemic Rules in Mazahua. International Journal of American Linguistics 41:293-305.

Blight, Richard C. and Eunice V. Pike. 1976. The Phonology of Tenango Otomí International Journal of American Linguistics 42:51-57.

Driver, Harold E. and Moisés Romero Casillo. 1963. Kinship Terminology and Behavior. In Driver and Driver, Ethnography and Acculturation of the Chichimeca-Jonaz of Northeast Mexico. Indiana University Research Center in Anthropology, Folklore, and Linguistics 26:157-69. (=International Journal of American Linguistics 29, Number 2, Part II).

Ecker, Lawrence. 1930. Los términos de parentesco en otomí, tarasco y maya. (Includes appendix listing Otomí terms from an anonymous ms. bearing the date 30 January 1640.) Ms. 57 pp.

Gibson, Lorna R. 1954. El sistema de parentesco pame. Yan 2:77-82.

_____. 1956. Pame (Otomí) Phonemics and Morphophonemics. International Journal of American Linguistics 22:242-65.

Hasler, Juan A. 1961. Reconstrucciones matlatzinca-ocuiltecas. Anales 13:269-78. Mexico: Instituto Nacional de Antropología e Historia.

Jenkins, Joyce. 1958. Morphological Phoneme Sequences in Eastern Otomí. Phonetica 2:1-11. Abstract: Bright, International Journal of American Linguistics 30:296. 1964.

Manrique Castañeda, Leonardo. 1958. Sobre la clasificación del otomí-pame. Proceedings of the International Congress of Americanists 33:551-59.

Newman, Stanley and Weitlaner, Roberto J. 1950a. Central Otomian I: Proto-Otomi Reconstructions. International Journal of American Linguistics 16:1-19.

_____. 1950b. Central Otomian II: Primitive Central Otomian Reconstructions. International Journal of American Linguistics 16:73-81.

Spotts, Hazel. 1953. Vowel Harmony and Consonant Sequences in Mazahua. International Journal of American Linguistics 19:253-58.

Wallis, Ethel E. 1968. The Word and the Phonological Hierarchy of Mezquital Otomí. Language 44:76-90.

Popolocan

Cowan, Florence. 1947. Linguistic and Ethnological Aspects of Mazatec Kinship. Southwestern Journal of Anthropology 3:247-56.

Fernández de Miranda, María Teresa. 1951. Reconstrucción del protopopoloca. Revista Mexicana de estudios antropológicos 12:61-93.

_____. 1956. Glotocronología de la familia popoloca. Serie Científica 4. México: Museo Nacional de Antropología.

_____. 1961. Diccionario Ixcateco. México: Instituto Nacional de Antropología e Historia.

Gudschinsky, Sarah C. 1953. Proto-Mazatec. Memoria del congreso científico mexicano 12:171-74.

_____. 1955. Lexico-statistical Skewing from Dialect Borrowing. International Journal of American Linguistics 21:138-49.

_____. 1958. Mazatec Dialect History: A Study in Miniature. Language 34:469-81.

_____. 1959. Proto-Popolocan: A Comparative Study of Popolocan and Mixtecan. Indiana University Research Center, Memoir 15. (=International Journal of American Linguistics 25:2)

Hamp, Eric. P. 1958. Protopopoloca Internal Relationships. International Journal of American Linguistics 24:150-53.

_____. 1960. Chocho-Popoloca Innovations. International Journal of American Linguistics 26:62.

Hoppe, Walter A. and Roberto J. Weitlaner. 1969. The Chocho. Robert Wanchope (ed), Handbook of Middle American Indians 7:506-15. Austin: University of Texas Press.

Jamieson, Allen R. 1977a. Chiquihuitlan Mazatec Phonology. Wm. R. Merrifield (ed), Studies in Otomanguean Phonology. Dallas: Summer Institute of Linguistics (University of Texas, Arlington). Pp 93-105.

_____. 1977b. Chiquihuitlan Mazatec Tone. Wm. R. Merrifield (ed), Studies in Otomanguean Phonology. Dallas: Summer Institute of Linguistics (University of Texas, Arlington). Pp 107-135.

Kalstrom, Marjorie R. and Eunice V. Pike. 1968. Stress in the Phonological System of Eastern Popoloca. Phonetics 18:16-30.

Kirk, Paul L. 1962. Jalapa Mazatec Kinship Terms of Address. University of Washington Master's thesis.

_____. 1966. Social vs. Consanguineal Distance as Reflected by Mazatec Kinship Terminology. A. Pompa y Pompa (ed), Summa Anthropologica: en Homenaje a Roberto J. Weitlaner. Mexico: Instituto Nacional de Antropología E Historia. Pp. 471-80.

_____. 1966. Proto-Mazatec Phonology. Ph.D. dissertation, University of Washington.

Pierson, Esther. 1953. Phonemic Statement of Popoloca. Lingua 2:426-29.

Pike, Kenneth L. and Eunice V. Pike. 1947. Immediate Constituents of Mazateco Syllables. International Journal of American Linguistics 13:78-91.

Schram, Judith L. and Eunice V. Pike. 1978. Vowel Fusion in Mazatec of Jalapa de Diaz. International Journal of American Linguistics 44:257-61.

Stark, Sharon and Polly Machin. 1977. Stress and Tone in Tlacoyalco Popoloca. Wm. R. Merrifield (ed), Studies in Otomanguean Phonology. Dallas: Summer Institute of Linguistics (University of Texas, Arlington) Pp. 69-92.

Tlapanecan

Rensch, Calvin R. 1977. Classification of the Otomanguean Languages and the Position of Tlapanec. In Two Studies in Middle American Comparative Linguistics. Summer Institute of Linguistics Publication in Linguistics 55:53-108.
Weathers, Mark. 1976. Tlapanec 1975. International Journal of American Linguistics 42:-367-71.

Zapotecan

Briggs, Elinor. 1961. Mitla Zapotec Grammar. Mexico: Instituto Lingüístico de Verano and Centro de Investigaciones Antropológicas de México.
Córdova, Fray Juan de. 1578. Vocabulario en lingua zapoteca. Republished in 1942 as: Vocabulario castellano-zapateco (edición facsimilar), introducción y notas de Wigberto Jiménez Moreno (=Biblioteca Lingüística Mexicana I). México: Instituto Nacional de Antropología e Historia.
Earl, Robert. 1968. Rincón Zapotec Clauses. International Journal of American Linguistics 34:269-74.
Fernández de Miranda, María Teresa. 1963. Personal communication based on her unpublished reconstruction of Proto-Zapotec phonology.
Leal, Mary. 1950. Patterns of Tone Substitution in Zapotec Morphology. International Journal of American Linguistics 16:132-36.
Lyman, Larry and Rosemary Lyman. 1977. Choapan Zapotec Phonology. Wm. R. Merrifield (ed), Studies in Otomanguean Phonology. Dallas: Summer Institute of Linguistics (University of Texas, Arlington). Pp. 137-61.
MacLaury, Robert E. 1970. Ayoquesco Zapotec: Ethnography, Phonology and Lexicon. Unpublished M.A. Thesis, University of the Americas.
McKaughan, Howard. 1954. Chatino Formulas and Phonemes. International Journal of American Linguistics 20:23-27.
Nader, Laura. 1967. [Lists of Zapotec kinship terms] in: A.K. Romney, Kinship and Family. Manning Nash (ed), Handbook of Middle American Indians 6:235-6. Austin: University of Texas Press.
Nellis, Jane Goodner. 1947. Sierra Zapotec Forms of Address. International Journal of American Linguistics 13:231-32.
Olson, Donald. 1963. Spanish Loan Words in Pame. International Journal of American Linguistics 29:230-38.
Parsons, Elsie Clews. 1936. Mitla: Town of the Souls. Chicago: University of Chicago Press.
Pickett, Velma B. 1951. Nonphonemic Stress: A Problem in Stress Placement in Isthmus Zapotec. Word 7:60-65.
_____ et al. 1965. Vocabulario zapoteco del istmo (2nd edition). Serie de vocabularios indígenas Mariano Silva y Aceves 3. México: Instituto Lingüístico de Verano.
_____ and Virginia Embrey. 1974. Zapoteco del Istmo: Juchitán, Oaxaca. México: Instituto de Investigación Social del Estado de Oaxaca.
Pride, Leslie. 1963. Chatino Tonal Structure. Anthropological Linguistics 5:2:19-28.

_____ and Kitty Pride. 1970. Vocabulario chatino de tataltepec: castellano-chatino, chatino-castellano. México: Instituto Lingüístico de Verano.

Robinson, Dow F. 1963. Field Notes on Coatlán Zapotec. Hartford: Hartford Seminary Foundation.

Ruegsegger, Manis and Jane Ruegsegger. 1955. Vocabulario zapoteco del dialecto de Miahuatlán del estado de Oaxaca. México: Instituto Lingüístico de Verano.

Speck, Charles H. 1978. Texmelucan Zapotec Suprasegmental Phonology. Work Papers of Summer Institute of Linguistics of University of North Dakota 22:1-28.

Swadesh, Morris. 1947. The Phonemic Structure of Proto-Zapotec. International Journal of American Linguistics 13:220-30.

Upson, B. W. and Robert E. Longacre. 1965. Proto-Chatino Phonology. International Journal of American Linguistics 31:312-22.

Whitecotton, Joseph W. 1977. The Zapotecs: Princes, Priests, and Peasants. Norman: University of Oklahoma Press.

General Otomanguean

Casasa García, Glorinella Patricia. 1976. Analysis componential y formal de los sistemas de parentesco de la familia lingüística otomangue and reconstrucción del sistema de parentesco proto-otomangue. México: Universidad Iberoamericana.

Diebold, A. Richard, Jr. 1960. Determining the Centers of Dispersal of Language Groups. International Journal of American Linguistics 26:1-10.

Fernández de Miranda, María Teresa. 1959. Review of Gudschinsky 1959. American Anthropologist 61:1142-43.

_____, Morris Swadesh and Roberto J. Weitlaner. 1959. Some Findings on Oaxaca Language Classification and Culture Terms. International Journal of American Linguistics 25:54-58.

Hamp, Eric P. et al. 1963. On Aboriginal Languages of Latin America. Current Anthropology 4:317-19.

Harvey, Herbert R. 1963. Términos de parentesco en el otomangue. Publication 13, Instituto Nacional de Antropología e Historia. Mexico.

_____. 1964. Cultural Continuity in Central Mexico: A Case for Otomanguean. Proceedings of the International Congress of Americanists 35:525-32.

Longacre, Robert E. 1960. Review of Swadesh 1959. Language 36:397-410.

_____. 1962. Amplification of Gudschinsky's Proto-Popolocan-Mixtecan. International Journal of American Linguistics 28:227-42.

_____. 1964. Progress in Otomanguean Reconstruction. Horace G. Lunt (ed), Proceedings of the Ninth International Congress of Linguistics, 1016-25. The Hague: Mouton.

_____. 1967. Systematic Comparison and Reconstruction. Robert Wauchope (ed), Handbook of Middle American Indians 5:117-59. Austin: University of Texas Press.

_____. 1968. Comparative Reconstruction of Indigenous Languages. Thomas A. Sebeok (ed), Current Trends in Linguistics 4:320-60. The Hague: Mouton.

_____ and René Millon. 1961. Proto-Mixtecan and Proto-Amuzgo-Mixtecan Vocabularies. Anthropological Linguistics 3:4:1-44.

Rensch, Calvin R. 1973. Otomanguean Isoglosses. Thomas A. Sebeok (ed), Current Trends in Linguistics 11:295-316. The Hague: Mouton.

_____. 1976. Comparative Otomanguean Phonology. Language Science Monograph 14. Bloomington: Indiana University.

———. 1978. Typological and Genetic Consideration in the Classification of the Otomanguean Languages. Actes du XLIIe Congrès International des Américanistes 4:623-33.

Swadesh, Morris. 1959. Mapas de clasificación lingüística de México y las Américas. Cuadernos del Instituto de Historia, serie antropológica 8. México.

———. 1960. The Oto-Manguean Hypothesis and Macro-Mixtecan. International Journal of American Linguistics 26:79-lll.

———. 1962. Afinidades de las lenguas amerindias. Proceedings of the International Congress of Americanists 34:729-38.

———. 1964. Interim Notes on Oaxacan Phonology. Southwestern Journal of Anthropology 20:168-89.

Weitlaner, Roberto J. 1941. Los pueblos no nahuas de la historia tolteca y el group lingüístico Macro-Otomangue. Revista Mexicana de Estudios Antropológicos 5:249-69.

2. General Background

Aberle, David F. 1953. The Kinship System of the Kalmuk Mongols. University of New Mexico Publication in Anthropology 8.

———. 1967. A Scale of Alternate Generation Terminology. Southwestern Journal of Anthropology 23:261-76.

Atkins, John R. 1974. On the Fundamental Consanguineal Numbers and Their Structural Basis. American Ethnologist 1:1-31.

Barnes, J.A. 1971. Three Styles in the Study of Kinship. Berkeley: University of California Press.

Berlin, Brent, D.E. Breedlove and P. Raven. 1968. Covert Categories and Folk Taxonomies. American Anthropologist 70:290-99.

Bock, R. 1968. Some Generative Rules for American Kinship Terminology. Anthropological Linguistics 10:1-6.

Bright, J.O. and William Bright. 1965. Semantic Structures in Northwestern California and the Sapir-Whorf Hypothesis. Hammel (ed), Formal Semantic Analysis. American Anthropologist (special publication) 67:5, Part II. Pp. 249-58.

Bright, William and J. Minnick. 1966. Reduction Rules in Fox Kinship. Southwestern Journal of Anthropology 22:381-88.

Brockway, Earl. 1969. Términos de parentesco del náhuatl (dialecto del norte de Pueblo). Anales 7:123-25. México: Instituto Nacional de Antropología e Historia.

Buchler, I.R. 1964. Measuring the Development of Kinship Terminologies: Scalogram and Transformational Accounts of Crow-type Systems. American Anthropologist 66:765-88.

———. 1966. On Physical and Social Kinship. Anthropological Quarterly 39:17-25.

——— and Henry A. Selby. 1968. Kinship and Social Organization. New York: Macmillan.

Burling, Robbin. 1964. Cognition and Componential Analysis: God's Truth or Hocus-pocus? American Anthropologist 66:20-28.

———. 1965. Burmese Kinship Terminology. Hammel (ed), Formal Semantic Analysis. American Anthropologist (special publication) 67:5, Part II Pp. 106-17.

———. 1969. Linguistics and Ethnographic Description. American Anthropologist 71:817-27.

———. 1970. American Kinship Terms Once More. Southwestern Journal of Anthropology 26:15-24.

Condominas, George. 1960. The Mnong Gar of Central Vietnam. Murdock (ed), Social Structure in Southeast Asia. Viking Fund Publications in Anthropology 29. Chicago: Quadrangle Books. Pp. 15-23.

Delbrück, B. 1889. Die Indogermanische Verwandtschaftsnamen: Ein Beitrag zur vergleichenden Altertumskunds. Abhandlungen der sächsischen Akademie der Wissenschaften 11:381.

Dyen, Isidore and David F. Aberle. 1974. Lexical Reconstruction: The case of the Proto-Athapaskan Kinship System. London; Cambridge University Press.

Eggan, Fred. 1937. Historical Changes in the Choctaw Kinship System. American Anthropologist 39:34-52.

_____. 1950. Social Organization of the Western Pueblos. Chicago: University of Chicago Press.

_____. 1955a. Social Anthropology of the North American Tribes (revised edition). Chicago: University of Chicago Press.

_____. 1955b. Social Anthropology: Methods and Results. In Eggan 1955a, Pp. 485-554.

Elkins, Richard E. 1968. Three Models of Western Bukidnon Manobo Kinship. Ethnology 7:171-89.

Fields, Harriet and Wm. R. Merrifield. 1976. Parentesco mayoruna (pano). Comunidades y culturas peruanas 9. Pucallpa: Instituto Lingüístico de Verano. 37 pp.

_____. 1980. Mayoruna (Panoan) Kinship. Ethnology 19: 1-28.

Fischer, J.L. 1960. Genealogical Space. Oceania 30:181-87.

Fox, Robin. 1967. Kinship and Marriage. Baltimore: Penguin Books.

Fried, Jacob. 1969. The Tarahumara. Vogt, Evan Z. (ed), Ethnology, Part 2. Handbook of Middle American Indians 8:846-70. Austin: University of Texas Press.

Gates, H. Phelps. 1971. The Kinship Terminology of Homeric Greek. Indiana University Publications in Anthropology and Linguistics 27 (=International Journal of American Linguistics 37:4, Part 2).

Goodenough, Ward H. 1956. Componential Analysis and the Study of Meaning. Language 32:195-216.

_____. 1961. Review of Murdock 1960a. American Anthropologist 63:1341-47.

_____. 1964a. Explorations in Cultural Anthropology. New York: McGraw-Hill.

_____. 1964b. Componential Analysis of Könkäma Lapp Kinship Terminology. In Goodenough 1964a:221-38.

Goodenough, Ward H. 1965. Yankee Kinship Terminology: A Problem in Componential Analysis. A. Hammel (ed), Formal Semantic Analysis. American Anthropologist (special publication) 67:5, Part II. Pp. 269-87.

_____. 1967. Componential Analysis. Science 156:1203-09.

_____. 1968. Componential Analysis. International Encyclopedia of the Social Sciences 3:186-92. New York: Macmillan and Free Press.

_____. 1970. Description and Comparison in Cultural Anthropology. New York: McGraw-Hill.

Graburn, Nelson, 1971. Readings in Kinship and Social Structure. New York: Harper and Row.

Grimes, Joseph E. and Barbara E. Grimes. 1962. Semantic Distinctions in Huichol (Uto-Aztecan) Kinship. American Anthropologist 64:104-14.

Hammel, A. 1965. Formal Semantic Analysis. American Anthropologist (Special publication) 67:5, Part II.

Hockett, Charles F. 1964. The Proto-Central-Algonquian Kinship System. In Goodenough 1964a:239-57.

Hoijer, Harry. 1956. Athapaskan Kinship Systems. American Anthropologist 58:308-33.

Hoogshagen, Searle and Wm. R. Merrifield. 1961. Coatlán Mixe Kinship. Southwestern Journal of Anthropology 17:219-25.

Hopkins, N.A. 1969. A Formal Account of Chalchihuitán Tzotzil Kinship Terminology. Ethnology 8:85-102.

Hymes, Dell H. and Harold E. Driver. 1958. Concerning the Proto-Athapaskan Kinship System. American Anthropologist 60:152-55.

Kay, Paul. 1965. A Generalization of the Cross/Parallel Distinction. American Anthropologist 67:30-43.

_____. 1966. Comment on Colby's Ethnographic Semantics. Current Anthropology 7:20-23. Reprinted in Tyler 1969.

_____. 1967. On the Multiplicity of Cross/Parallel Distinctions. American Anthropologist 69:83-85.

_____. 1968. Correctional Notes on Cross/Parallel. American Anthropologist 70:106-7.

_____. 1970. Theoretical Implications of Ethnographic Semantics. Current Directions in Anthropology. American Anthropological Association Bulletin 3:3, Part 2.

_____. 1975a. The Generative Analysis of Kinship Semantics: Reanalysis of the Seneca Data. Foundations of Language 13:201-14.

_____. 1975b. Constants and Variables in English Kinship Semantics. Language Behavior Research Laboratory Working Paper 45. Berkeley.

Keesing, Roger. 1968. Step-kin, In-laws, and Ethnoscience. Ethnology 7:59-70.

Kroeber, A.L. 1909. Classificatory Systems of Relationship. Journal of the Royal Anthropological Institute 39:77-84.

_____. 1917. California Kinship Systems. University of California Publications in American Archaeology and Ethnology 12:339-96.

_____. 1937. Athapaskan Kin Term Systems. American Anthropologist 39:602-8.

Lamb, Sidney M. 1964. The Sememic Approach to Structural Semantics. Romney and D'Andrade (eds), Transcultural Studies in Cognition. American Anthropologist (special publication) 66:3, Part II, Pp. 57-78.

_____. 1965. Kinship Terminology and Linguistic Structure. A. Hammel (ed), Formal Semantic Analysis. American Anthropologist (special publication) 67:5, Part II. Pp. 37-64.

Law, Howard W. 1961. A Reconstructed Proto-Culture Derived from some Yuman Vocabularies. Anthropological Linguistics 3:4:45-57.

Lévi-Strauss, Claude. 1965. The Future of Kinship Studies. Proceedings of the Royal Anthropological Institute. Pp. 13-22.

_____. 1969. The Elementary Structures of Kinship. London: Eyre and Spottiswoode.

Lounsbury, Floyd G. 1956. A Semantic Analysis of Pawnee Kinship Usage. Language 32:158-94.

_____. 1964a. A Formal Account of the Crow- and Omaha-type Kinship Terminologies, Goodenough (ed), Explorations in Cultural Anthropology. New York: McGraw-Hill. Pp. 351-93.

_____. 1964b. The Structural Analysis of Kinship Semantics. H.G. Lunt (ed), Proceedings of the Ninth International Congress of Linguists. The Hague: Mouton. Pp. 1073-93.

_____. 1965. Another View of the Trobriand Kinship Categories. A. Hammel (ed), Formal Semantic Analysis. American Anthropologist (special publication) 67:5, Part II. Pp. 142-85.

Matthews, G.H. 1959. Proto-Siouan Kinship Terminology. American Anthropologist 61:252-78.

McQuown, N. 1955. The Indigenous Languages of Latin America. American Anthropologist 57:501-70.

Merrifield, William R. 1963a. Sierra Popoluca Kinship. American Anthropologist 65:660-61.

_____. 1974. Meso-American Indian Cultures. Encyclopaedia Brittanica 11:954-56.

_____. 1980. On the Formal Analysis of Kinship Terminologies. A. Makkai and V.B. Makkai (eds), Essays in Honor of Charles F. Hockett. Hamburg, N.Y.: The Press at Twin Willows.

Morgan, Lewis H. 1871. Systems of Cosanguinity and Affinity of the Human Family. Smithsonian Contributions to Knowledge 17. Washington

_____. 1877. Ancient Society. Chicago: C.H. Kerr.

Murdock, George P. 1949. Social Structure. New York: Macmillan.

_____. 1960a. Social Structure in Southeast Asia. Viking Fund Publications in Anthropology 29. Chicago: Quadrangle Books.

_____. 1960b. Cognatic Forms of Social Organization. Murdock (ed), Social Structure in Southeast Asia. Viking Fund Publications in Anthropology 29. Chicago: Quadrangle Books. Pp. 1-14.

_____. 1968. Patterns of Sibling Terminology. Ethnology 7:1-24.

_____. 1970. Kin Term Patterns and their Distribution. Ethnology 9:165-207.

_____. 1971. Cross-sex Patterns of Kin Behavior. Ethnology 10:359-68.

Nerlove, Sara and A. Kimball Romney. 1967. Sibling Terminology and Cross-Sex Behavior. American Anthropologist 69:179-87.

Pehrson, Robert N. 1957. The Bilateral Network of Social Relations in Könkämä Lapp District. Indiana University Research Center in Anthropology, Folklore and Linguistics. Bloomington: Indiana University.

Pospisil, Leopold. 1960. The Kaupauku Papuans and their Kinship Organization. Oceania 30:188-205.

Reining, Priscilla. 1972. Kinship Studies in the Morgan Centennial Year. Washington: The Anthropological Society of Washington.

Romney, A. Kimball. 1965. Kalmuk Mongol and the Classification of Lineal Kinship Terminologies. A. Hammel (ed), Formal Semantic Analysis. American Anthropologist (special publication) 67:5, Part II. Pp. 127-41.

_____. 1967. Kinship and Family. Robert Wauchope (ed), Handbook of Middle American Indians. Austin: University of Texas. Pp. 207-37.

_____ and Roy G. D'Andrade. 1964a. Transcultural Studies in Cognition. American Anthropologist (special publication) 66:3, Part II.

_____. 1964b. Cognitive Aspects of English Kin Terms. Romney and D'Andrade (eds), Transcultural Studies in Cognition. American Anthropologist (special publication) 66:3, Part II. Pp. 146-70.

Sahlins, Marshall D. 1962. Moala: Culture and Nature on a Fijian Island. Ann Arbor: University of Michigan Press.

Sapir, Edward. 1916. Time Perspective in Aboriginal American Culture: A Study in Method. Reprinted in David G. Mandelbaum (ed), Language, Culture, and Personality. Berkeley: University of California Press.

Scheffler, Harold W. 1967. On Scaling Kinship Terminologies. Southwestern Journal of Anthropology 23:159-75.

_____. 1972. Baniata Kinship Terminology: The case for Extensions. Southwestern Journal of Anthropology 28:350-81.

_____. 1972b. Dravidian-Iroquois: The Melanesian Evidence. Jayawardena and L. Hiatt (eds), Anthropology in Oceania: Essays for H.I. Hogbin. Sydney: Angus Robertson Ltd.

_____. 1972c. Systems of Kin Classifications: A Structural Typology. Reining (ed), Kinship Studies in the Morgan Centenniel Year. Washington: The Anthropological Society of Washington. Pp. 113-33.

_____. 1972d. Kinship Semantics. Annual Review of Anthropology 309-28.

_____ and Floyd G. Lounsbury. 1971. A Study in Structural Semantics: The Sirionó Kinship System. Englewood Cliffs: Prentice-Hall.

Schneider, David M. 1968. American Kinship. Englewood Cliffs: Prentice-Hall.

_____. 1972. What is Kinship all About? Reining (ed), Kinship Studies in the Morgan Centennial Year. Washington: The Anthropological Society of Washington. Pp. 32-63.

Shimkin, D.B. 1941. The Uto-Aztecan System of Kinship Terminology. American Anthropologist 43:223-245.

Simpson, Lesley Byrd. 1961. Many Mexicos. Berkeley: University of California Press.

Spier, Leslie. 1925. The Distribution of Kinship Systems in North America. University of Washington Publications in Anthropology 1:69-88.

Steward, Julian. 1955. Theory of Culture Change. Urbana: The University of Illinois Press.

Tyler, Stephen A. 1966. Whose Kinship Reckoning? Comments on Buchler. American Anthropologist 68:513-16.

_____. 1969a. The Myth of P: Epistemology and Formal Analysis. American Anthropologist 71:71-78.

_____. 1969b. Cognitive Anthropology. New York: Holt Rinehart and Winston.

Wallace, A.F.C. 1965. The Problem of the Psychological Validity of Componential Analysis. Hammel (ed), Formal Semantic Analysis. American Anthropologist (special publication) 67:5, Part II. Pp. 229-48.

_____ and John Atkins. 1960. The Meaning of Kinship Terms. American Anthropologist 62:58-80.

Waterhouse, Viola and Wm. R. Merrifield. 1968. Coastal Chontal of Oaxaca Kinship. Ethnology 7:190-95.

Weitlaner, Roberto J. and Searle Hoogshagen. 1960. Grados de edad en Oaxaca, Revista Mexicana de Estudios Antropológicos 16:183-209.

White, Charles B. 1957. A Comparison of Theories on Southern Athapaskan Kinship Systems. American Anthropologist 59:434-48.

_____. 1958. Rejoinder to Hymes and Driver. American Anthropologist 60:155-6.

Wordick, Frank J.F. 1970. A Generative-Extensionist Analysis of the Proto-Indo-European Kinship System. Ann Arbor: University Microfilms.

SIL MUSEUM OF ANTHROPOLOGY PUBLICATIONS

1. SARAYACU QUICHUA POTTERY by Patricia Kelley and Carolyn Orr, 1976. (Also available in Spanish as CERAMICA QUICHUA DE SARAYACU.). . . . . $ 3.00

2. A LOOK AT LATIN AMERICAN LIFESTYLES by Marvin Mayers, 1976 $ 6.45

3. COGNITIVE STUDIES OF SOUTHERN MESOAMERICA by Helen Neuenswander and Dean Arnold, Eds., 1977. (Also available in Spanish as ESTUDIOS COGNITIVOS DEL SUR DE MESOAMERICA.) $10.95

4. THE DRAMA OF LIFE: GUAMBIANO LIFE CYCLE CUSTOMS by Judith Branks and Juan Bautista Sánchez, 1978. . . . . $ 5.00

5. THE USARUFAS AND THEIR MUSIC by Vida Chenoweth, 1979 . . . . . $14.90

6. NOTES FROM INDOCHINA: ON ETHNIC MINORITY CULTURES by Marilyn Gregerson and Dorothy Thomas, Eds., 1980. . . . . $ 9.45

7. THE DENI OF WESTERN BRAZIL: A STUDY OF SOCIO-POLITICAL ORGANIZATION AND COMMUNITY DEVELOPMENT by Gordon Koop and Sherwood G. Lingenfelter, 1980. (Also available in Portuguese as OS DENI DO BRASIL OCIDENTAL—UM ESTUDIO DE ORGANIZAÇÃO SOCIO-POLITICA E DESENVOLVIMENTO COMUNITARIO.) . . . . $ 5.95

8. A LOOK AT FILIPINO LIFESTYLES by Marvin Mayers, 1980 . . . . . $ 8.45

9. NUEVO DESTINO: THE LIFE STORY OF A SHIPIBO BILINGUAL EDUCATOR by Lucille Eakin, 1980. . . . . $ 2.95

10. A MIXTEC LIME OVEN by Kenneth L. Pike, 1980 . . . . $ 1.25

11. PROTO OTOMANGUEAN KINSHIP by William R. Merrifield. (Also available in Spanish as PARENTESCO PROTO OTOMANGUE.)

These titles are available at

The SIL Museum of Anthroplogy
7500 W. Camp Wisdom Road
Dallas, TX 75236

Residents of Texas add 5% sales tax.